War, States, and Internatio

MW00826243

Who has the right to wage war? The answer to this question constitutes one of the most fundamental organizing principles of any international order. Under contemporary international humanitarian law, this right is essentially restricted to sovereign states. It has been conventionally assumed that this arrangement derives from the ideas of the late-sixteenth century jurist Alberico Gentili. Claire Vergerio argues that this story is a myth, invented in the late 1800s by a group of prominent international lawyers who crafted what would become the contemporary laws of war. These lawyers reinterpreted Gentili's writings on war after centuries of marginal interest, and this revival was deeply intertwined with a project of making the modern sovereign state the sole subject of international law. By uncovering the genesis and diffusion of this narrative, Vergerio calls for a profound reassessment of when and with what consequences war became the exclusive prerogative of sovereign states.

Claire Vergerio is Assistant Professor of International Relations in the Institute of Political Science, Leiden University, the Netherlands.

Cambridge Studies in
International Relations: 159

Cambridge Studies in International Relations is a joint initiative of Cambridge
University Press and the British International Studies Association (BISA).
The series aims to publish the best new scholarship in international studies,
irrespective of subject matter, methodological approach or theoretical
perspective. The series seeks to bring the latest theoretical work in International
Relations to bear on the most important problems and issues in global politics.

Series list continues after index

War, States, and International Order

Alberico Gentili and the Foundational Myth of the Laws of War

Claire Vergerio

Leiden University

CAMBRIDGE UNIVERSITY PRESS

CAMBRIDGE
UNIVERSITY PRESS

Shaftesbury Road, Cambridge CB2 8EA, United Kingdom

One Liberty Plaza, 20th Floor, New York, NY 10006, USA

477 Williamstown Road, Port Melbourne, VIC 3207, Australia

314–321, 3rd Floor, Plot 3, Splendor Forum, Jasola District Centre, New Delhi – 110025, India

103 Penang Road, #05–06/07, Visioncrest Commercial, Singapore 238467

Cambridge University Press is part of Cambridge University Press & Assessment, a department of the University of Cambridge.

We share the University's mission to contribute to society through the pursuit of education, learning and research at the highest international levels of excellence.

www.cambridge.org
Information on this title: www.cambridge.org/9781009107594

DOI: 10.1017/9781009105712

First published 2022
First paperback edition 2024

A catalogue record for this publication is available from the British Library

ISBN   978-1-009-09801-4   Hardback
ISBN   978-1-009-10759-4   Paperback

À mon grand-père

When the king asked him what he meant by infesting the sea, the pirate defiantly replied: "The same as you do when you infest the whole world; but because I do it with a little ship I am called a robber, and because you do it with a great fleet, you are an emperor."

– Augustine, City of God, IV.4, 147–48.

Contents

Acknowledgments

Nine years have passed since I began working on my doctoral dissertation, out of which this book eventually emerged, and I owe many thanks to those who chose to walk by my side as I trudged on. Some marched vigorously along for short but intense stretches; others have wandered with me for years. It is hard to do full justice to their support, but I will mention them at least in name here as a small token of gratitude.

To begin, a few practical acknowledgments are in order. First, I would like to thank John Haslam and the editors of the *Cambridge Studies in International Relations* for their encouragement and positivity, and for including my book in their series. I would also like to thank the three anonymous reviewers for their helpful feedback. Duncan Bell and Jennifer Welsh examined my doctoral dissertation and gave me plenty of food for thought when it came time to rework the manuscript into a book. Many thanks as well to Chloe Quinn, Amala Gobiram, and Simon Fletcher for assisting me with the final production process.

I am also grateful to the various institutions that financially supported my research. At Oxford University, I received funding from the Department of Politics and International Relations, Balliol College, the Jenkins Memorial Fund, and the Scatcherd European Scholarships. Later I had the opportunity to rework the manuscript thanks to a Global Fung Fellowship at Princeton University. Before this book came into being, I had published some elements of my research as separate articles and would like to thank the editors of *International Theory* and *The Journal of the History of International Law* for permitting me to incorporate them into the content of the book (Chapters 1 and 2, respectively). Looking back to the early days of this project at Oxford, my heartfelt thanks go to the dedicated archivists of the Weston and Codrington Libraries, in particular Gaye Morgan at All Souls College.

This project took me to many places, and each of them brought its share of felicitous encounters. At Princeton, I benefitted greatly from the feedback of the "Fungs": Jeremy Adelman, Nicole Bergman, Bastiaan Bouwman, Ayça Çubukçu, Onur Ulas Ince, Sophia Kalantzakos, and

Pascale Siegrist. Particular thanks go to Bastiaan for spontaneously organizing our remarkably productive writing workshop, a weekly exercise we eventually moved online and turned into a daily meet-up to stay motivated despite pandemic restrictions. Had it not been for these shared writing sessions, I would probably have taken at least another year to finish the manuscript. I would also like to thank Francesca Iurlaro, with whom I had many fruitful exchanges in New York during this period.

I spent six months during my doctoral work at the University of Helsinki's Erik Castrén Institute for International Law and Human Rights. From those formative days up north, I would like to thank Paolo Amorosa, Mónica García-Salmones Rovira, Manuel Jiménez-Fonseca, Jan Klabbers, Nana Klabbers, Martti Koskenniemi, Walter Rech, Sahib Singh, Pamela Slotte, and Nadia Tapia. I also went home to Paris for a few months at Sciences-Po's Centre d'Étude des Relations Internationales, where Samuel Faure, Guillaume Sauvé, and Swann Bommier were particularly welcoming companions.

As for my Oxford days, a full book of thank yous would be in order, so I hope those named will know it is merely due to the lack of space that I am not saying more. For their invaluable mentorship over the years: Kalypso Nicolaïdis, Karma Nabulsi, and, last but not least, Edward Keene. Although Eddie only supervised me over the final stages of the DPhil process, he has been the single strongest influence on my intellectual development over the years and, through the sharpness of his mind and the kindness of his heart, continues to exemplify what it means to be a good scholar. For their precious friendship and their vivacious minds: Puneet Dhaliwal, Alexandra Reza, Michael Sampson, Akram Salhab, Omar Shweiki, Leila Ulrich, and Daniel Brinkerhoff Young. For becoming my intellectual family, as well as cherished friends: Arthur Duhé, Eric Haney, Julia Costa López, and Tomas Wallenius. For becoming *des amies de coeur* and real pillars in my life: Marion Vannier, Maïa Pal, and in Leiden, Gisela Hirschmann. From my Oxford days and beyond, I would also like to thank Quentin Bruneau, who was my partner in crime throughout graduate school and without whom I would have never reached the end of the DPhil.

Beyond the academy, Sarah Aoun and Claire Vincent, my oldest friends, have provided endless encouragement over the years as I embarked on increasingly demanding academic expeditions. Claire is a talented graphic designer and is responsible for making the citation figure in Chapter 2 presentable.

My family has played a central supporting role in the realization of this project. I finished writing the manuscript in the serene home of

Gordon Cetkovski and Elizabeth Evans, who have welcomed me into their family with open arms. Audrey, Vincent, Timothée, and Oriane infallibly brought laughter and warmth to my holidays back home. Manon and Alex are precious to me beyond description, and to my parents, Pierre Vergerio and Geneviève Castelain, I owe more than I can say. My partner, James, has been my single greatest source of strength as I grappled with this book manuscript; I am immensely grateful for his patience, his gentleness, and the peace he brought to my tired mind.

In my final weeks of work on this project, my beloved grandfather fell ill and passed away. During our weekly Skype chats these past years, he asked me many questions about the book, keeping up on its progress and encouraging me forward at each step along the way. He will not see it in print, but I hope he knows, somewhere, that it is to my favorite *amateur d'histoire* that this book is now dedicated.

Introduction

When the sixteenth-century jurist Alberico Gentili was pulled back from the dead and celebrated with great fanfare amongst English and Italian international lawyers in the 1870s, not everyone was entirely on board with the festivities. Gustave Rolin-Jaequemyns, a prominent Belgian lawyer who had been at the forefront of the efforts to codify the laws of war and to professionalize the discipline of international law since the late 1860s, was skeptical. He expressed some strong reservations about the narrative his peers were weaving around the man who had once been a controversial character of his time, the Oxford-based Protestant who defended absolutist rule and Catholic Spain's interests in the midst of the Dutch Revolt. "We doubt," he cautioned, "that it is rigorously accurate to represent the wise lawyer of the Spanish embassy as a sort of inspired apostle of peace."[1] Palpably frowning between the lines, he further warned his colleagues about the risks of making Gentili a founding father for their own nineteenth-century endeavors: "[T]o drape a great jurist from three centuries ago into such ultra-modern garments is not a good example for the artist who will be in charge of his statue."[2] Rolin-Jaequemyns certainly had a point, but he turned out to be a lone voice of reason amidst what has been described as the *Gentilimania* of the 1870s.[3]

Alberico Gentili (1552–1608) was an Italian jurist who, persecuted for his Protestant faith, fled to England, where he had a flourishing career both as a professor of law at Oxford in the 1580s[4] and as a practicing lawyer in London in the 1590s and until his death in 1608.[5] To his admirers,

---

[1] Rolin-Jaequemyns, "Albéric Gentil," 142. ["Nous doutons… qu'il soit rigoureusement exact de représenter le savant avocat de l'ambassade d'Espagne comme une sorte d'apôtre inspiré de la paix."]

[2] Ibid. ["Revêtir un grand juriste d'il y a trois siècles d'un costume aussi ultra-moderne, n'est pas d'un bon exemple pour l'artiste qui sera chargé de sa statue."]

[3] I borrow this term from Luigi Lacchè in "Monuments of International Law. "

[4] He held the title of Regius Professor of Civil Law until his death but was mostly active as a scholar in the 1580s.

[5] I will provide a fuller biographical summary of Gentili at the start of Chapter 2.

he was a prescient hero of their own humanitarian efforts to formalize the regulation of warfare, and potentially the "true founder of international law," as opposed to the more well-known Grotius. Most importantly to them, Gentili – unlike Grotius – had established that war was a public matter, and thus the sole legal prerogative of sovereign states. Grotius had putatively remained "medieval" in his definition of war, including private wars in it as well, while Gentili's now famous definition from his *De iure belli* of 1598: *bellum est publicorum armorum iusta contentio*[6] – war is a just contest of *public* arms – had brought the regulation of warfare into modernity. This understanding of Gentili seemed to dovetail perfectly with the broader narrative that had emerged about the rise of the modern international states-system in the seventeenth century and particularly with the 1648 Peace of Westphalia. A seamless line could be drawn between, on the one hand, Gentili's 1598 definition of war and, on the other, the story of the emergence, exactly fifty years later, of a system of sovereign states concentrating authority in the hands of distinct territorial entities that acknowledged no higher authority and recognized each other as legal equals. According to this narrative, the allocation of the legal right to wage war only to sovereign states, penned by a humanitarianly minded Gentili and implemented in practice through the seventeenth century, became one of the core stabilizing factors of the new states-system in the aftermath of the cataclysmic wars of religion.

Today, this narrative holds a remarkable degree of traction, notwithstanding the thorough debunking of the so-called myth of Westphalia, the highly popular but misleading claim that the modern states-system emerged in 1648.[7] The ideas that war became "modern" once the right to wage it was restricted to sovereign states, that this restriction was put in place in order to limit the horrors of warfare, and that this development hinged in large part on the work of Gentili is a widely shared assumption amongst scholars of international relations and international law. It appears across diverse areas of scholarship broadly interested in analyzing war and international order in historical perspective, from the musings of the English School to the profoundly influential work of scholars investigating the decline of interstate warfare and the rise of "new" wars.[8] The new wars thesis, in particular, hinges on a description of the "old wars" as armed conflict between sovereign states, and though the chronology varies from one author to the next,

---

[6] Gentili, *De iure belli*, Book 1, Chapter 2, §18.
[7] See most notably Osiander, "Sovereignty, International Relations, and the Westphalian Myth"; Teschke, *The Myth of 1648*.
[8] See *infra* notes 10–12 for examples from these various areas.

scholars generally place the origins of this form of warfare in the seventeenth century as well.[9]

The emphasis on the specific importance of Gentili is striking across these diverse fields. One finds it spelled out just as much in the classic works on the history of international law,[10] in foundational texts on international relations,[11] and in contemporary writings on the "new wars" and the legal challenges of counterinsurgency.[12] Even in the latter, the links between Gentili and our modern way of conceptualizing and regulating war are – curiously, considering these works are hardly of a historical bent – drawn in an explicit manner. To cite but one example, in *The Rule of Law in War: International Law and United States Counterinsurgency Doctrine in the Iraq and Afghanistan Wars*, a contemporary, practice-oriented text, we are told that "the present epoch of LOAC [law of armed conflict] dates back to Albericus Gentili's 1598 *De Jure Belli*."[13]

This narrative is used widely because it is a seductively simple story about modernity, the rise of the state, and the taming of war in the international system. As a shared set of assumptions about the emergence of the modern world, it deeply influences the way both scholars and practitioners think about the changing role of war in international relations. With the emergence of the modern states-system still widely understood as a positive, stabilizing development in international relations, the restriction of the right to wage war to sovereign states has also been deemed to possess some intrinsic normative value, to be a sort of humanitarian principle. Specifically, scholars argue that the purpose

---

[9] These scholars sometimes revert to a much vaguer claim according to which the process of restricting the right to wage war to sovereign states began in the fifteenth century and reached completion in the late eighteenth century; see Münkler, *The New Wars*, 41; Kaldor, *New and Old Wars*, 15. When pressed for a more specific chronological anchor, however, it is the inevitable 1648 benchmark that comes up. For instance, Münkler explains that international law established the broad principle that only sovereign states could legally wage war in Europe from the "mid-seventeenth century," with the principle then gaining "general acceptance there for several centuries." Münkler, *The New Wars*, 63–64. For a similar statement, with an emphasis on 1648 specifically, see also Van Creveld, *Nuclear Proliferation and the Future of Conflict*, 126.

[10] Grewe, *The Epochs of International Law*, 211–14; Schmitt, *Nomos of the Earth*, 158–59.

[11] See, for instance, Bull, *The Anarchical Society*, 29. Bull considers Gentili as the only "early internationalist" to have come to terms with "the idea that is the foundation of later attempts to accept war between states as an institution of international society." Before him, others "do not do more than grope towards the modern doctrines that only public authorities are entitled to wage war, and that only states can be regarded as such authorities." See also, for instance, Knutsen, *A History of International Relations Theory*, 71–72.

[12] Münkler, *The New Wars*, 64.

[13] McLeod, *Rule of Law in War*, 36–37.

and effect of this restriction of the right to wage war was the promotion of order in the international system.[14]

This powerful narrative has long informed the development of the laws of war in practice: The idea that only sovereign states should have the legal right to wage war has been one of the foundational pillars of the laws of war since their codification in the late nineteenth century, and it remains central to our way of regulating armed conflicts to this day. Widening the ambit of this legal right to include nonstate actors, the story suggests, would essentially take us back to medieval forms of violence and perhaps risk the complete collapse of the international order. As Hedley Bull once put it, "[w]e are accustomed ... to contrast war between states with peace between states; but the historical alternative to war between states was more ubiquitous violence."[15]

The aim of this book is to challenge this story about modernity, states, and the taming of war by exposing how it was constructed and eventually popularized in the disciplines of International Relations and International Law. Its core argument is that the narrative about Gentili and the emergence of "modern war" is largely a myth. It was first elaborated in the late nineteenth century, when the modern sovereign state actually triumphed in international law, and then went on to be repeated, inflated, and enshrined through the works of twentieth-century scholars, notably those of Carl Schmitt. The book tells the story of the construction of this myth and shows the power it continues to hold over our collective imagination.

In doing so, its broader goal is to open the way for scholars to put forward alternative explanations and chronologies of the process through which the legal right to wage war became the exclusive prerogative of sovereign states. Based on the recent literature on the myth of Westphalia and the prominence of composite polities, hybrid private/public actors, and other entities that looked nothing like the "modern" territorial sovereign state throughout the early modern period,[16] the time seems ripe to revisit our old narrative. There is already an extensive debate about the monopolization of external violence by states in

---

[14] See, for instance, Luard, *War in International Society*; Holsti, *The State, War, and the State of War*; Bull, *The Anarchical Society*; Schmitt, *Nomos of the Earth*; Pejcinovic, *War in International Thought*; Bartelson, *War in International Society*.

[15] Bull, *The Anarchical Society*, 178–79.

[16] Historical IR scholars have now debunked the idea that the modern states-system emerged at the time of the Peace of Westphalia; see notably Osiander, "Sovereignty, International Relations, and the Westphalian Myth"; Teschke, *The Myth of 1648*; Osiander, *Before the State*; Nexon, *The Struggle for Power in Early Modern Europe*; Branch, *The Cartographic State*. Both in certain parts of Europe (e.g., the Holy

practice,[17] but much less has been written about the question of when states became the only entities legally allowed to wage war.[18] While sometimes conflated,[19] these are two empirically distinct questions, and reassessing the legal one could have important repercussions. One could, for instance, hypothesize that the restriction of this legal right to sovereign states happened not in the seventeenth century but around the late nineteenth century, when concepts such as demi- and semi-sovereignty came to be considered anomalies in international law,[20] and when Gentili was actually celebrated on the basis of his newly discovered prescience. This chronology would associate the restriction of the legal right to wage war not with a period of greater stability after the devastating early modern wars of religion, but with the dawn of what many consider the bloodiest century in human history, the period spanning high imperialism and the two world wars.

Putting forward these alternative histories could perhaps be done without a sense of what exactly might be wrong with our existing

Roman Empire) and in the extra-European world, sovereignty was understood to be divisible, meaning that entities not considered full sovereign states could possess certain prerogatives of sovereignty, including, presumably, the legal right to wage war. Benton, *A Search for Sovereignty*; Keene, *Beyond the Anarchical Society*; Nexon, *The Struggle for Power in Early Modern Europe*; Stern, *The Company-State*; Cavanagh, "A Company with Sovereignty and Subjects of Its Own?"; Phillips and Sharman, *International Order in Diversity*; Learoyd, "Configurations of Semi-Sovereignty in the Long-Nineteenth Century"; Sharman and Phillips, *Outsourcing Empire*.

[17] "External violence" in this debate refers to violence conducted by the state against both state and nonstate actors *outside* its geographical boundaries. Tilly, "War Making and State Making as Organized Crime"; Tilly, *Coercion, Capital, and European States, AD 990–1992*; Thomson, *Mercenaries, Pirates, and Sovereigns*; Newman, "The 'New Wars' Debate"; Percy, *Mercenaries*; Colás and Mabee, *Mercenaries, Pirates, Bandits and Empires*; Berdal, "The 'New Wars' Thesis Revisited"; Scheipers, *Unlawful Combatants*.

[18] The main exception remains Lesaffer, *Peace Treaties and International Law in European History*; Lesaffer, "Peace Treaties and the Formation of International Law." However, while Lesaffer examines the right to wage war through the more practical lens of peace treaties, he dismisses the remarkably important Holy Roman Empire as a mere exception, and he does not examine treaties between Europeans and non-Europeans, although Europeans at times signed even more treaties with non-Europeans than amongst themselves over the course of the early modern period. On the underestimated importance of the Holy Roman Empire, see Wilson, *Heart of Europe*. On the numerous treaties signed between Europeans and non-Europeans, see Alexandrowicz, *An Introduction to the History of the Law of Nations in the East Indies*; Alexandrowicz, *The European-African Confrontation*; Keene, "The Treaty-Making Revolution of the Nineteenth Century"; Alexandrowicz, *The Law of Nations in Global History*; Pitts, *Boundaries of the International*. Other recent works in IR on the historical relationship between war and international order have paid virtually no attention to the laws of war; see notably Pejcinovic, *War in International Society*; Phillips and Sharman, *International Order in Diversity*.

[19] Van Creveld, *The Transformation of War*, 41; Münkler, *The New Wars*, 64; Kaldor, *New and Old Wars*, 19.

[20] Learoyd, "Configurations of Semi-Sovereignty in the Long-Nineteenth Century."

narrative. Exposing its genesis, however, is a crucial step in the context of how the history of international law has long been conceptualized, researched, and taught. The very idea of what "the history of international law" consists of has been nebulous at best, and more often than not, scholars have reduced it to a history of ideas, or sometimes a history of doctrine. In recent years, there has been a strong call to instead tell this history as one of international legal practices.[21] To put the practice argument bluntly, we are likely to get a much better sense of how international law actually impacted international relations – or how interpolity law impacted interpolity relations, to put it in less anachronistic terms – if we examine the legal tools that were used on the ground in settling interpolity disputes rather than the meditations of a few canonized jurists. Of course, some of the famous jurists were practitioners as well – Grotius' employment by the Dutch East India Company is perhaps the most famous case in point – but even in those cases, it is often their more theoretical work we turn to, without much evidence that these theoretical considerations had a tangible impact on the ground. As such, the new emphasis on practice has made a powerful case for telling the history of international law either without the usual handful of famous treatises or by supplementing their analysis with extensive empirical evidence of concrete legal practices. This is a very important call, but it is currently undermined by the resilience of the old, canon-based stories we tell about the development of international law.

Indeed, it is clear that despite these recent injunctions, much of the field continues to tell the story of international law through the canonical writings of the usual suspects, sometimes with a few creative additions.[22] This is particularly striking within the specific area of the history of the laws of war, which continues to primarily navigate from Francisco de Vitoria and Pierino Belli – a somewhat lesser-known sixteenth-century jurist and soldier remembered for his 1563 treatise *De re militari et de bello* – to Gentili and Grotius through Pufendorf and Bynkershoek before delving into textbooks and conventions once we get to the nineteenth century.[23] Even more concerningly, while one could imagine a certain complementarity between the histories of international law that emerge through studies of practices and studies of

---

[21] See especially Benton and Ford, *Rage for Order*; Wallenius, "The Case for a History of Global Legal Practices."

[22] See, for instance, Kadelbach, Kleinlein, and Roth-Isigkeit, *System, Order, and International Law*.

[23] Neff, *War and the Law of Nations*; Bartelson, *War in International Thought*. For a recent exception and an insightful set of reflections on the matter, see Tischer, "Princes' Justifications of War in Early Modern Europe."

ideas, what is regularly the case is that these two types of narratives clash in the chronologies they put forward and the turning points they identify.[24] As a result, an area like the history of the laws of war that is still almost exclusively based on a history of ideas ends up being so adamantly committed to a particular historical narrative that it precludes the emergence of the alternative chronologies that could come out of more practice-based studies. To truly make space for a new history of the laws of war, it is thus necessary to begin showing the flimsy character of the pillar this old approach rests on.

This is not to say, of course, that ideas do not matter in the history of international law. There is an inevitable dialectic between ideas and practices, and this book is not intent on making some general directional argument one way or the other. What it does want to highlight, though, is the extent to which the ideas that matter in practice are not necessarily the ones we take for granted. Ideas need to be mediated by those intent on using them, and in that sense they sometimes come to have a much greater impact when reformulated – or downright remodeled – by comparatively unknown receivers than they do in their more famous original form.

In order to examine this phenomenon and the broader emergence of our narrative about Gentili and modern war, the book follows a two-step approach. First, it examines what Gentili intended to achieve in his own time with his famous 1598 treatise of the laws of war, *De iure belli* (*DIB*), and how his work was received then, delving into the world of the late sixteenth and early seventeenth centuries. It then homes in on Gentili's late nineteenth-century canonization and the subsequent path-dependent developments that led contemporary scholars to inherit the famous narrative about Gentili, modern war, and the emergence of the states-system. This two-part approach stems from a simple rationale: By having some sense of what the text was intended to achieve in its original context, we can have a much better grasp of the extent to which its meaning was distorted by its later readers, whether intentionally or unintentionally, for often the most compelling distortions are the ones that are unintentional and built on a kernel of truth. It also helps us move away from a mere acknowledgment that a distortion took place and try to grasp the form that this distortion took. The aim of this approach is to go beyond simply showing that a disciplinary canon is a retrospective construction and instead to shed light on the specific ways in which an author and his text were appropriated by his later readers, allowing for a

---

[24] See, for example, the case of the "Standard of Civilization" discussed in Wallenius, "The Case for a History of Global Legal Practices," 11–18.

more critical analysis of the development of disciplinary canons and of broader "traditions" of thought. It presupposes, not uncontroversially, that we can at least partly recover authorial intention, and that it can be used as a benchmark against which to compare later interpretations of the text. I discuss this more at length in Chapter 1, drawing on the insights of both Skinnerian contextualism and reception theory.

Based on this approach, the story at the heart of the book centers on the revival of Gentili and the emergence of the now ubiquitous story about modernity, the rise of the states-system, and the taming of war. Chapters 4, 5, and 6 are about the period from the 1870s onward. However, reading Alberico Gentili in his own context, the task of Chapters 2 and 3, provides some essential insights into what was at stake in his work back in the late sixteenth century, which was then erased during his nineteenth-century revival. At the forefront of Gentili's mind were debates about the locus of political authority and the legitimacy of rebellion. He came to occupy an extremely awkward position in England as one of its staunchest absolutist intellectuals in the late sixteenth century and, in the final years of his life, as a lawyer for the dreaded Spanish crown. As is often the case with famous thinkers,[25] he was hardly representative of the zeitgeist of the early modern period, let alone of the late sixteenth century. If anything, he was a controversial figure, both in his own lifetime and in the decades following his death. I contend that his famous treatise on the laws of war can in large part be read within the broader debate about the locus of political authority and through the prism of his contentious absolutist ideas. Within these debates, he advanced certain claims about the "public" character of war, before touching on the question of who could be deemed a "public" actor in relatively piecemeal fashion. Clearly, he did not imagine the world as one of the sovereign territorial states in the so-called Westphalian sense of the term.

After his death, Gentili nearly fell into the dustbin of history in light of his polemical writings, remaining a relatively minor figure – when he is mentioned at all – in the international law treatises of the next two and a half centuries.[26] Tellingly, the few lengthier entries about him, for instance in Pierre Bayle's famous *Dictionnaire* of 1697, mention his works on war and embassies in passing, and then focus on his controversial absolutist writings.[27] He remained occasionally cited as a secondary figure, sometimes being rather demeaningly presented as

---

[25] Keene, "International Intellectual History and International Relations," 344–45.
[26] Haggenmacher, "Grotius and Gentili," 134.
[27] Bayle, *Dictionnaire Historique et Critique*, Vol. 7, 66.

someone whose writings on war were "not useless to Grotius."[28] It is only with his revival in the 1870s that he came to be seen as one of the founders of international law, and more specifically of the modern laws of war. In order to understand why Gentili rose to fame and why his name became so deeply entwined with the story of the emergence of the "modern" concept of war, one thus needs to travel forward in time to the late nineteenth century and to understand the context in which his writings were reappraised. Most importantly, Gentili's revival in the 1870s took off in the midst of international law's transformation into a formal "science" and at a remarkable time for historical thinking, two crucial developments which I will briefly outline here.

The late nineteenth century was an era that saw history acquire an unprecedented amount of clout, becoming, in certain respects, the ultimate authority of the time, "the paradigmic form of knowledge to which all others aspired."[29] Following a spike of interest after the French Revolution and the professionalization efforts of the likes of Leopold von Ranke (1795–1886),[30] what had long been an "amateur activity,"[31] a branch of rhetoric practiced mostly by dabblers and dilettantes,[32] now became a formal academic discipline. From the 1830s and 1840s, universities, which until then had only taught classics, started putting history in the curriculum.[33] This new discipline's primary function was to be at the service of the state, providing genealogies for nation-states at a time when their centralization throughout Europe was often being met with resistance.[34] Suddenly, excavating the past was no longer an amateur hobby but rather an essential exercise for those interested in shaping the present. This new historical fervor was characterized by two more specific developments, both of which are essential to the story I am about to tell.

First, the nineteenth century marked the emergence of various linear narratives of progress. Whether these teleological metahistories were about the victory of liberal ideas, the imminent revolt of the working

---

[28] Ibid.
[29] Bann, *Romanticism and the Rise of History*, 3. This is not to say, of course, that history was not important prior to the nineteenth century. Simply, its importance reached an unprecedented intensity in the nineteenth century with the emergence of more linear and teleological narratives about the past. I will in fact also discuss the sixteenth-century "turn to history" in Chapter 2, drawing on the work of Donald Kelley, for example, "The Rise of Legal History in the Renaissance."
[30] Doran, "Choosing the Past," 4.
[31] White and Rogne, "The Aim of Interpretation Is to Create Perplexity in the Face of the Real," 72.
[32] Doran, "Choosing the Past," 3.
[33] White and Rogne, "The Aim of Interpretation Is to Create Perplexity in the Face of the Real," 72.
[34] Ibid. See also Lorenz and Berger, *Nationalizing the Past*.

class, or the inevitable triumph of the white race, they all sought to order the past as a logical sequence inexorably moving toward the achievement of a clear goal. This teleological thinking also became central to the telling of the history of international relations. It is this period that witnessed the emergence of the idea that the seventeenth century – and often specifically the 1648 Peace of Westphalia – had marked the emergence of the modern states-system, that is, an international system composed of formally equal sovereign states.[35]

Second, the nineteenth century also witnessed an unprecedented search for founding fathers and their corresponding genealogies. The period saw the ascent of the romantic idea of the genius and the canonization of various men (for they were almost invariably men) across disciplines, most notably within music and the arts. This view of history became most famously embodied by Thomas Carlyle's famous claim that "the history of the world is but the biography of great men."[36] The broader "great men theory" associated with him, according to which "great men" were the decisive factor in shaping the course of history owing to their unique genius, was embraced by the likes of Kierkegaard, Hegel, and Weber and would become a dominant form of historical writing until World War II. The two trends often converged: Along with this romantic conceptualization of the genius came the attempt to tie specific individuals to breakthroughs within teleological accounts of modernity. The most famous example is perhaps that of Leonardo da Vinci, who came to be understood as the universal genius par excellence, the "first modern man" who unleashed "the dawn of modern art."[37]

International law did not escape the zeitgeist and witnessed a strong shift toward historicization as well, unleashing a newfound enthusiasm for identifying founding fathers and telling stories of the inevitable rise and rise of modernity.[38] The seeds were planted in the closing years of the eighteenth century, when international lawyers began to "envisage their project in distinctively historical terms," writing the first historical accounts of international law as a discipline and inaugurating what

---

[35] Keene, *Beyond the Anarchical Society*, 19–29; Pitts, "International Relations and the Critical History of International Law," 286; Devetak, "Historiographical Foundations of Modern International Thought."

[36] Carlyle, *On Heroes, Hero-Worship, and The Heroic in History*, 34.

[37] Bullen, "Walter Pater's 'Renaissance' and Leonardo da Vinci's Reputation in the Nineteenth Century," 270.

[38] Naturally, this process was not entirely linear and some figures had already been at least partly canonized earlier. The most obvious case is that of Hugo Grotius, although the actual chronology of his canonization is now rather debated. For some time, Grotius was understood to have been canonized in the eighteenth century within the realm of moral philosophy, long before the broader rise of historicism in the

would eventually become the "almost compulsory practice of opening international law textbooks with a historical introduction."[39] This trend then deepened over the following decades and took off full-scale with the establishment of international law as an academic discipline in the late 1860s and 1870s, when this newfound historical consciousness acquired unprecedented traction within the shared historical imagination of international lawyers.[40] International law was becoming not only a science but also a science with a clear historical pedigree and a strong awareness of its ageless roots.

Developing this history in itself was a relatively indeterminate endeavor, considering the past can always be written in a myriad of different ways, and international law absorbed the aforementioned trends. First, it latched onto the increasingly popular narratives about the development of the modern world, and especially the myth of Westphalia. This particular myth eventually became absolutely central to both the disciplines of International Law and International Relations, which, before their divergence in the twentieth century,[41] were deeply intertwined in their attempt to become proper sciences. Both disciplines attempted to strengthen their scientific character by establishing sovereignty as their "foundational principle,"[42] with Westphalia as the rallying standard, the starting point of the presumably state-based system these sciences were meant to analyze.[43]

---

nineteenth century and his canonization within the history of the law of nations; see Hochstrasser, *Natural Law Theories in the Early Enlightenment*. Martine van Ittersum's ongoing work about the dispersal of Grotius' papers in the seventeenth century and their "rediscovery" in the late nineteenth, followed by a spectacular "Grotiusmania" in the Netherlands, adds nuance to this story and highlights the many, sometimes divergent routes canonization can take. I will return to this case in Chapter 4.

[39] Craven, "Invention of a Tradition," 364–65. Of course, as Craven notes (365), this "is not to say … that prior to this time, international lawyers were unaware of historical precedents or of the contribution made by earlier scholars." There simply was no such overarching story of historical continuity, or metanarrative of the development of the discipline in the sense elaborated in the nineteenth century.

[40] In the words of one scholar, one of the most defining features of nineteenth-century international legal thought became "the emergence of a consciousness of its own historical character." Ibid., 364.

[41] Koskenniemi, "Law, Teleology and International Relations."

[42] Pitts, "International Relations and the Critical History of International Law," 283.

[43] As one scholar puts it, in the second half of the nineteenth century, "both the professional study of History and of Law at the national level – and with them, of international law and the history of international law – were born in a way that was tied to the European national state-building project." As a result, both have "remained tangled in their development" with the Westphalian narrative, and, relatedly, with methodological nationalism. Rasilla del Moral, "The Shifting Origins of International Law," 424. On methodological nationalism and its pitfalls, see Chernilo, "The Critique of Methodological Nationalism."

Second, the discipline of International Law – and later on that of International Relations as well – came to imagine its past through "stylized histories populated by founding fathers and origin myths."[44] Indeed, despite the fact that the writings of "haloed jurists" were not necessarily the driving force behind the development of international law,[45] the late nineteenth century is the moment when international law's history became "penned as biographical accounts of European publicists,"[46] or to put it slightly more irreverently, as "a story of individual lawyers acting like so many chivalrous knights, defending the oppressed against the oppressors, peace against war, carrying the torch of civilization (from Greece and Rome) through dark ages to the present."[47] As in other contexts, the canonization of personal heroes was a particularly fruitful way to harness history's power as a reservoir for ideology.[48] The international lawyers of the period pieced together the history of their endeavor, relying on what Quentin Skinner has critically termed "the mythology of prolepsis,"[49] that is, the endless search for the "antecedents" or "origins" of ideas or practices. They turned international law into a science "not only through the renewal of methods, concepts, purposes but also ... through *the invention of traditions*, centered around precursors, founders and followers."[50] The history of international law therefore emerged not so much as a history of legal practices, as is being redeveloped today, but as a history of ideas, and only those of a handful of glorified European men. Through these two entwined trends, the late nineteenth century began to see the emergence of a history of international law that primarily consisted in pinning teleological stories of modernity onto some newly discovered founding fathers.

---

[44] Pitts, "International Relations and the Critical History of International Law," 282. This is not to say that all the literature on the history of international law produced in the twentieth century can be characterized as flawed in this particular way. However, a number of histories of this kind – including the ones put forward by Carl Schmitt and Wilhelm Grewe – have had a significant impact on our collective imaginary as scholars, not just within the subfield of the history of international law, but also within the broader discipline of IR. They are therefore worth examining closely and further deconstructing in order to reassess some of the assumptions we inherited from them. In the present case, what I am interested in calling into question is not international legal historiography as a whole (that would be very bold indeed) but simply a specific approach to the history of international law that has led a particular and rather dubious narrative about the monopolization of the right to wage war by states to become widely accepted both in the specialized literature and in more general texts.

[45] See notably Benton and Ford, *Rage for Order*.

[46] Singh, "Book Review," 977.

[47] Koskenniemi, *Gentle Civilizer*, 78.

[48] Sylvest, *British Liberal Internationalism, 1880–1930*, 148–94.

[49] Skinner, "Meaning and Understanding in the History of Ideas," 73.

[50] Lacchè, "Monuments of International Law," 147 (emphasis in original).

It is within this context that Gentili's contemporary fame can be understood. Yet rather than being a mere case study of an otherwise widespread trend, Gentili's revival in the late nineteenth century was unique in at least two respects. First, while Grotius' name had already been floating around for quite some time as a foundational figure in the field of international law, Gentili was the first early modern jurist to be pulled back from the dead and presented as Grotius' competitor for the title of "father of the modern law of nations."[51] The pantheon of the founders of international law would later be expanded to include numerous other figures, most notably through the efforts of James Brown Scott and Elihu Root in the early twentieth century,[52] which would inevitably relegate Gentili to a somewhat less grandiose position after having been presented as just one of two competitors for such a grand title. However, this story is about the period before the expansion of the pantheon; it is about the early European attempts to identify the founding fathers of modern international law, and specifically of the modern laws of war – for at the time, the laws of war emerged as a synecdoche for international law at large[53] – before the enterprise turned into a full-blown cottage industry on the other side of the Atlantic. It gave the discipline of international law its initial momentum in developing its canon, and, crucially, it put down some of the narrative pillars about international law, the rise of the modern concept of war, and the emergence of the modern states-system that would remain at the heart of the broader construction of the history of international law central to the discipline's identity.

Second, Gentili's revival was a remarkably high-profile, institutionalized endeavor. This suggests that the stakes of his canonization were high, or at least that they were perceived to be so. Gentili's revival was orchestrated from 1874 onward through a major international effort generally considered to have been spurred by Thomas Erskine Holland (1835–1926) in England. All the main figures involved were or would soon become members of the epoch-making Institut de droit international, founded in 1873 with the goal of turning international law into a true "science" and professionalizing the field accordingly. They created an International Committee for the revival of Gentili and his work, made up of three distinct subcommittees: an Italian one, an

---

[51] Phillipson, "Albericus Gentilis," 1911, 5.

[52] Amorosa, *Rewriting the History of the Law of Nations*. This later period notably witnessed the revival of Francisco de Vitoria.

[53] I will return to this phenomenon in Chapter 4. For a brief overview of the relationship between international law and the laws of war, see also Vergerio, "International Law and the Laws of War."

English one, and a Dutch one, each endowed with its share of eminent jurists and high-profile figures. An example amongst many, Pasquale Mancini (1817–1888), who was a remarkably important jurist at the time – "one of the most authoritative internationalists" enjoying "world renown"[54] – was the first president of the Institut and also the president of the Italian subcommittee for the revival of Gentili. At a time when the field of international law was being turned into the academic discipline we know today, many eyes were turned to the rediscovery of a long-dead Italian jurist and his musings on the laws of war.

These men's dedication to Gentili's momentous revival is noteworthy, and it leaves one wondering why Alberico Gentili and his *DIB* suddenly benefited from such considerable attention on the part of prominent scholars and jurists. Why did these international lawyers turn specifically to Gentili, what did they emphasize in his work in trying to construct the history of their own endeavor, what alternative canonizations did they consider, and what does it tell us about their own motives? These are some of the questions addressed at the core of this book. Fascinatingly, as we will see, their actual engagement with his work remained rather superficial,[55] but that did not prevent them from putting forward all sorts of questionably grandiose claims about the Italian jurist. In light of this, rather than simply describe the process of reception, I seek to account for the motives that underpinned the direction the revival took, placing the canonization process within its broader socio-political context as well. Crucially, the men behind Gentili's revival were all deeply involved in the political affairs of their day, most notably in the codification of the laws of war and in the construction of the legal architecture of empire. At the forefront of their minds was the participation of irregular combatants in the American Civil War and, even more importantly, in the Franco-Prussian War. How was war to be regulated when it did not simply involve the official military forces of two recognized sovereign states? Their answers would obviously be pregnant with implications in the context of European imperial expansion, which was about to reach its fullest expression around the globe.

The narrative these lawyers developed about the importance of Gentili's work, I argue, ultimately served as a legitimizing mechanism for their state-centric project at a time when the modern concept of the sovereign state actually came to triumph in international law. The tale they told based on Gentili's definition of war allowed them to establish a sense of continuity between, on the one hand, their own commitment

---

[54] Lacchè, "Monuments of International Law," 171.
[55] The substantive reception of Gentili's writings would have to wait until the 1980s.

to ensuring that the legal right to wage war would be restricted to polities recognized as sovereign states and their immediate military forces and, on the other, an early modern period depicted as the cradle of modernity and progress. Enshrining the sovereign state as the sole legitimate subject of international law at the cost of all other forms of political organization was a bold move at the time. Yet the narrative they put forward around Gentili allowed them to give their approach a certain pedigree in the case of war and to normalize it as the mere formalization of a principle that had been accepted for centuries. It created a valuable precedent. While there were still some nuances to their story, some areas of uncertainty or of skepticism – as the opening anecdote about Gustave Rolin-Jaequemyns suggests – these would gradually be erased by twentieth-century scholars who developed an ever simpler story about Gentili, statehood, and modern war.

There is perhaps no single work in which this is more striking than in Carl Schmitt's profoundly influential *The Nomos of the Earth*. In this book, he drew heavily on the narrative developed by late nineteenth-century lawyers and added his own enhancing twist to it. While, of course, Schmitt's *Nomos* does not represent international legal historiography as a whole, his unequivocal crowning of Gentili as the great founder of the legally regulated institution of modern interstate warfare would become particularly influential both in the discipline of International Relations and in the institutionalized academic subfield of the history of international law that emerged in the 1990s, notably through what long remained the seminal overview of the history of international law, Wilhelm Grewe's *The Epochs of International Law*.[56] Both Schmitt and Grewe wrote histories of international relations and international law that celebrated the territorial sovereign state as a great stabilizing force in modern history, and they established the limitation of the right to wage war to sovereign states as a great leap forward in steadying the international system. Schmitt depicts a Bodin-inspired Gentili as the greatest hero of this development, while Grewe picks up on this narrative also to make Gentili a pillar of the modern regulation of warfare. Both of them tell the history of international law primarily through a collection of great thinkers; both of them base their chronology on the twists and turns of intellectual history. Their accounts were picked up by scholars of the younger discipline of International Relations, and together they gave us the narrative about the emergence of the modern concept of war in the early modern period and about the broader relationship between war and international order that is now ubiquitous across both fields.

---

[56] On the influence of Schmitt on Grewe, see Koskenniemi, "The Epochs of International Law."

The story I tell, ultimately, is one about the power of historiography and citations: Footnotes carry us from one epoch to the next, leaping across contexts with little regard for historicity, not entirely unlike legal precedents. As such, this is also a story that takes anachronisms seriously without giving in to anachronism itself.[57] It traces the emergence of a questionable account of history that ultimately became highly influential, shedding light on the different layers of construction and the gradual simplification of the narrative. In exposing this process, this book seeks to replace a story of continuity with one of disjuncture, where the nineteenth century appears as a turning point rather than a mere step forward along an already well-established path.

This story of disjuncture dovetails with the existing works on the watershed that was the emergence of international law as a science in the late nineteenth century.[58] However, it takes this scholarship further by turning the spotlight on the creative and self-legitimizing construction of the discipline's historical past, particularly regarding the history of the laws of war. Since the regulation of warfare was at the very heart of the "scientization" of international law, it is not entirely surprising that late nineteenth-century international lawyers turned specifically to this history. Yet their account has gone mostly unchallenged; if anything, it has been further amplified and internalized. Uncovering the process through which they gave us our now well-established narrative about the emergence of the modern concept of war, both in terms of their motivations and in terms of the various shortcuts they took in their historical interpretations, allows for a much more critical engagement with the narrative we inherited. Ultimately, examining the canonization of specific figures is not simply an exercise in the study of reception processes. Those deemed "great thinkers" constitute the hooks onto which we hang our schematized stories about the past, providing access to some of the most central themes we find across the discipline of International Relations: the emergence of modernity, the role of the state, the function of violence in international society. In turn, these narratives supply the worldviews, theories, and arguments that form the invisible bedrock of contemporary policymaking. We ignore their murky foundations at our own risk.

---

[57] On the use of anachronisms in the history of international law, see the recent debate: Orford, "On International Legal Method"; Koskenniemi, "Vitoria and Us"; Fitzmaurice, "Context in the History of International Law"; Benton, "Beyond Anachronism."

[58] The seminal account of this shift remains Koskenniemi, *Gentle Civilizer*. For an update on this dynamic area of research, see Nuzzo and Vec, *Constructing International Law*.

Importantly, this is a book about the emergence of a specific narrative about Gentili, war, states, and modernity that has proved influential across the disciplines of International Relations and International Law to this day. It is not meant to provide a comprehensive intellectual history of Gentili's place in the general historiography of international law. The point, instead, is to show how Gentili was used in forging a specific narrative about how the regulation of the right to wage war evolved over time. Thus, the story I tell is one about silences and periods of oblivion paired with revivals and sudden citations. Rather than providing a superficial but exhaustive account of Gentili's appearance (or lack thereof) in international legal historiographies over time, I have focused on the bursts of attention he received and dug deep into how we can explain them and relate them to the importance now conventionally attached to Gentili within narratives about the regulation of war. This is at once a much more specific project – it is about the dominant narrative on the laws of war and not on international law in general – and a much broader one as well. It does not investigate Gentili's canonization primarily to contribute to the ongoing reconstruction of the history of the discipline of International Law in the late nineteenth and early twentieth centuries, but to destabilize taken-for-granted assumptions about the regulation of war in the modern international order.

There is a growing amount of literature today in International Relations and International Law about the profound challenge that the proliferation of nonstate actors in international politics poses to the international legal order. Nowhere is this more apparent than in the field of armed conflict. Under contemporary international humanitarian law,[59] the legal right to wage war is essentially the prerogative of states.[60] The reigning consensus is that since the presumed emergence of the international states-system in 1648, this has been – and continues to be – a pillar of the modern international order, an essential tool for stabilizing what would otherwise be a war of all against all.[61] This means that those fighting in the name of nonstate entities are not recognized as legal combatants and do not benefit from the rights afforded by that status under the Geneva

---

[59] On the shift from the language of the "laws of war" to the language of "international humanitarian law" and the substantive changes it involved in the weighing of humanitarian concerns against military necessity, see Alexander, "A Short History of International Humanitarian Law."

[60] An exception was added in 1977 through Additional Protocol I to the Geneva Conventions of 1949; I discuss it below.

[61] This idea appears in various forms in, for instance, Bull, *The Anarchical Society*; Schmitt, *Nomos of the Earth*; Bartelson, *War in International Thought*; Pejcinovic, *War in International Society*; Luard, *War in International Society*; Holsti, *The State, War, and the State of War*.

Conventions of 1949. Instead, they are deemed to be sheer criminals, destined not for war veteran status or a seat at the negotiation table but for prosecution and imprisonment. Yet, since the end of the Cold War, the interstate outlook of international humanitarian law has come to be considered a weakness as much as a strength. International humanitarian law has come under fire for being a mere relic from the bygone days of interstate warfare, a rulebook that simply does not suit an age where the participation of nonstate actors in armed conflict has become the rule rather than the exception.[62] This raises a host of questions about what it would mean to adapt the laws of war to the widespread participation of nonstate actors in conflict, and about the extent to which we should be radically rethinking our existing frameworks.

Currently, much of the focus in terms of nonstate participation in armed conflicts is on private military companies such as Aegis and insurgent groups such as ISIS and Boko Haram. These are actors that few scholars – myself included – would rush to defend or claim rights for.[63] Yet, for much of the twentieth century, the nonstate actors who suffered most heavily from the interstate outlook of the laws of war were national liberation movements. Since they did not fight on behalf of a recognized state, they were instantly criminalized by imperial powers who had the law on their side. The 1977 Additional Protocols to the Geneva Convention sought to remedy this problem by including, under the international armed conflicts covered in Protocol I, "armed conflicts in which peoples are fighting against colonial domination and alien occupation and against racist regimes in the exercise of their right of self-determination."[64] This was a remarkable development[65] – an exception to the emphasis on status and a return to one on cause – but it was established once the vast majority of anti-colonial conflicts had ended, and it was not ratified by states who still harbored powerful national

[62] See, for instance, Greenwood, "International Law and the 'War against Terrorism,'" 301; Schöndorf, "Extra-State Armed Conflicts," 2. Referring to 9/11, Greenwood states that "a challenge on this scale by a non-state actor to the one superpower calls for entirely new thinking about the nature of international law."

[63] Though for an exception regarding the former, see Fabre, "In Defence of Mercenarism." For a thought-provoking read regarding jihadists, see Li, *The Universal Enemy*. I thank Ayça Çubukçu for bringing the latter to my attention.

[64] Protocol Additional to the Geneva Conventions of August 12, 1949, and Relating to the Protection of Victims of International Armed Conflicts (Additional Protocol I) 1977, Article 1 (4).

[65] For a discussion of the developments leading up to the Protocols, see Alexander, "A Short History of International Humanitarian Law"; Bernstoff, "The Battle for the Recognition of Wars of National Liberation"; Whyte, "The 'Dangerous Concept of the Just War.'"

liberation movements within their borders. As such, qualifying the principle that the use of force should be the sole prerogative of established states has remained optional; in practice, the system has barely changed.

There are of course different reasons why one may be wary of amending this system more extensively. One is pragmatic: Reformers are often concerned that states that feel pressured to sign onto clauses that curtail their power or grant some of that power to other entities may decide to step out of the regulatory scheme entirely. The other, more deep-seated reason is of a more normative kind: There is still a widespread sense that restricting the right to wage war to sovereign states was done so as to preserve order in the international system, or in other words, that it has served a stabilizing, pacifying function.[66] The alternative to war between states would not be peace, but a more uncontrollable and pervasive form of violence. One can thus make a humanitarian argument on behalf of the status quo.

Yet what this book suggests is that this impulse to associate the restriction of the right to wage war exclusively to sovereign states with the stabilization of the international order rests on an erroneous historical narrative about modernity, the emergence of the states-system, and the taming of war. It may well be the case, as this book ultimately gestures toward, that the restriction of the right to wage war to sovereign states was followed not by a period of relative peace but, on the contrary, by a surge of violence in the international system. As we try to adapt the regulation of warfare to the challenges of the twenty-first century, this should give us pause for thought. To what extent are our judgments about how best to allocate the right to use force in international relations undermined by their shaky historical foundations? If we are trying to limit the excesses of warfare, or to stabilize the international system, can we assume that placing all power in the hands of established sovereign states is the best way to achieve our goal? The question of who has been legally allowed to use force in international relations and how this has been justified is of critical importance, for the regulation of violence forms one of the key pillars of any international order. As things stand, our current justification for giving this right only to recognized states appears to be based on a deeply flawed account of the past. This book does not seek to directly tackle the questions I have just raised, but by destabilizing our existing narrative about how the "modern" way of regulating war came about, it does hope to open the way for some novel answers to emerge.

---

[66] See *supra* note 61.

1 Context, Reception, and the Study of Great Thinkers in International Relations

This is a book about the power of citations. It is about texts that refract and redeploy and about famous thinkers that become events in and of themselves. Citations are remarkable in that they enable the author and her readers to leap across time; we move between historical contexts seamlessly, sometimes with close to no regard for historicity. Citing past texts allows us to tell stories that connect us to the past, that draw continuities between the world of those we cite and the world we inhabit, between the questions we ask and those they strove to answer. The extent to which these continuities are actually meaningful is an endless source of debate,[1] and determining whether this can be settled in absolute terms is far beyond the scope of this book. What matters for our present purposes is how, in the case of Gentili, the connection came to be understood as meaningful in the past, whether the analysis that was made of it can withhold the test of a more rigorous form of historical scrutiny today, and if not, what, then, explains the substance of the narrative we have inherited about him.

As the old saying goes, *Habent sua fata libelli*[2] – books have their own destinies. The numerous references to Gentili in contemporary works about the history of the laws of war and of the broader development of the states-system show us that the narrative we inherited about Gentili has had a real impact on the construction of collective imaginaries. Beyond assessing the narrative's accuracy, it is thus essential for us to appreciate what it allowed past scholars and practitioners to achieve. Why was Gentili nearly forgotten? Why was he revived with great fanfare over 200 years after his death? What interpretations of his work became most popular, and why?

---

[1] Within the field of the history of international law, see the ongoing debate between various leading scholars: Orford, *What Is the Place of Anachronism in International Legal Thinking*; Koskenniemi, "Vitoria and Us"; Fitzmaurice, "Context in the History of International Law"; Benton, "Beyond Anachronism."

[2] This is from the longer saying, "*Pro captu lectoris habent sua fata libelli,*" literally, "According to the capabilities of the reader, books have their destiny."

Some would argue that analyzing the later trajectory of Gentili's work regardless of his original intentions in writing it – what would fall into the category of "historical effects"[3] – should be our sole focus.[4] This chapter seeks to show that the recovery of authorial intention and the analysis of an author's reception can in fact be made to complement each other. The rest of the book then follows this logic, providing first a synchronic, contextualist examination of Gentili's *De iure belli* (*DIB*) before moving to a diachronic analysis of his uneven posterity, with a particular emphasis on the elements of his reception that gave us the popular narrative about Gentili and the emergence of modern war. But beyond the present study of Gentili's mythologization, this chapter also seeks to help develop a more systematic methodological basis for the study of "great thinkers" more broadly, particularly within the field of International Relations (IR).

International Relations has a long tradition of analyzing, celebrating, and appropriating the thought of those it considers great thinkers. For much of the history of the discipline, these figures have been considered sources of transhistorical wisdom: "Machiavelli is a theorist of necessity and reason of state ... Hobbes is the quintessential theorist of anarchy, Grotius of international legal order," while "Rousseau has a structural realist theory of war, Kant a progressive theory of the democratic peace and global confederation and so on."[5] They have also commonly been used as ornaments for relatively ahistorical theories, in order to give a sense of timelessness to the theory being elaborated.[6] Across the disciplinary spectrum, great thinkers thus have been – and continue to be – an important component of IR scholarship.

Intellectual history and IR, however, have had a rather tumultuous relationship. While much of IR was shifting toward more economics-based approaches in the 1960s and 1970s, the English School doubled down on the importance of diplomatic and intellectual history and maintained a connection with historians. This connection, though, was often precarious in light of the English School's tendency to develop its own idiosyncratic historical narratives. Yet English School scholars did

---

[3] For an in-depth discussion of Gadamer's concept of *Wirkungsgeschichte*, see Veith, *Gadamer and the Transmission of History*.

[4] Boucher, *Appropriating Hobbes*.

[5] Bain and Nardin, "International Relations and Intellectual History," 214. Bain and Nardin cite various classic texts that rely on great thinkers in this particular way, including Waltz, *Man, the State, and War*; Bull, *The Anarchical Society*; Doyle, *Ways of War and Peace*; and Wendt, *Social Theory of International Politics*.

[6] For a detailed discussion of the use of great thinkers in IR, see notably Vigneswaran and Quirk, "Past Masters and Modern Inventions," 115–222.

successfully maintain a space for historical inquiry in IR, one which has now developed into a much larger and more rigorous subfield with the discipline's "historiographical turn" in the early 2000s,[7] a move that signaled IR scholars' intent to "take both history and the history of political thought more seriously."[8] After a so-called fifty-years rift between IR and intellectual history,[9] the two fields have thus gone through a significant rapprochement over the past two decades. They now share a particular interest in the history of "international thought," that is, political and legal thought on the relation between states, empires, and other political entities,[10] an area that long remained a blind spot of the history of political thought (HPT), which had generally focused on the state and its internal politics.

With this renewed interest in intellectual history, IR scholars have moved beyond the selective and rather tendentious misreadings of various great thinkers by earlier IR theorists, and particularly those of the English School, whose efforts to delineate some transhistorical "Grotian," "Machiavellian," and "Kantian" traditions or "realist," "rationalist," and "revolutionist" approaches[11] inevitably led to "gross abuses" of the HPT.[12] There is now a much more careful, historicist engagement with famous texts, much of it stemming from the precepts of "Cambridge School" contextualism, to which I will return shortly.

Along with this move away from preemptively confining famous thinkers to Procrustean categories, IR scholars have come to reflect more critically on the history of the discipline, accounting for the contingent development of certain approaches and theories and bringing to light their respective normative underpinnings.[13] Broadly speaking, historically minded IR scholars have emphasized the value of revealing "the

---

[7] Bell, "International Relations."

[8] Ibid., 115.

[9] Armitage, "The Fifty Years Rift." For a detailed analysis of the changing relationship between IR, political theory, and international political theory, see Brown, "Political Thought, International Relations Theory and International Political Theory." See also Martin Wight's classic text, "Why Is There No International Theory?"

[10] See, most notably, Keene, *International Political Thought*; and Armitage, *Foundations of Modern International Thought*.

[11] Wight and Porter, *International Theory*.

[12] Bell, "International Relations," 123. The criticisms of this approach are numerous and wide ranging. For a broader critique, see Armitage, *Foundations of Modern International Thought*, parts II and III.

[13] Efforts to make explicit different theories' normative underpinnings include Reus-Smit and Snidal, *The Oxford Handbook of International Relations*. Critical works on the history of the discipline of International Relations include Schmidt, *The Political Discourse of Anarchy*; Guilhot, *The Invention of International Relations Theory*; Vitalis, *White World Order, Black Power Politics*.

contingency of prevailing conventions"[14] and thus of undermining the pervasive tendency in the discipline to elevate "relatively recent structures and orientations to the status of enduring historical essences."[15] More specifically, IR scholars working on the history of international thought have pointed to the way in which a more rigorous engagement with canonical and noncanonical texts enables us to rethink crucial topics in the discipline, including "the primacy of the state, the emergence of the 'states system,' the consequences of anarchy and the principles of a just international order,"[16] to name but a few important examples.[17] At the deepest level, this type of work allows us to challenge disciplinary myths by helping IR scholars "understand how the International Relations canon was constructed and for what purposes."[18]

At the intersection of these two developments, a growing number of works have now carefully analyzed the historical reception of certain "great thinkers" into IR, examining the processes through which their ideas became considered foundational.[19] To take just one example, we now know that the coronation of Thucydides as the father of realism was by no means inevitable.[20] It emerged out of a rather contingent series of moves and culminated "when a group of highly influential scholars in US academia, such as Robert Keohane, Kenneth Waltz, and Robert Gilpin, identified him as a paramount realist thinker in the late 1970s and 1980s."[21] These scholars did so because Thucydides served

---

[14] Vigneswaran and Quirk, "Past Masters and Modern Inventions," 109.

[15] Ibid., 110. The literature around the "myth of 1648" is a case in point. See especially Osiander, "Sovereignty, International Relations, and the Westphalian Myth"; Teschke, *The Myth of 1648*.

[16] Bain and Nardin, "International Relations and Intellectual History," 215.

[17] For further reflections on this, see the contributions to a recent forum on IR and intellectual history, especially Bain and Nardin, "International Relations and Intellectual History"; Devetak, "'The Battle Is All There Is'"; Brown, "Political Thought, International Relations Theory and International Political Theory"; Hall, "The History of International Thought and International Relations Theory."

[18] Bain and Nardin, "International Relations and Intellectual History," 213. For a longer discussion of the significance of this kind of inquiry, see Amorosa and Vergerio, "Historicizing the Canon in International Law and International Relations."

[19] Keene, *Beyond the Anarchical Society*; Keene, "Images of Grotius"; Williams, "The Hobbesian Theory of International Relations"; Reid, "Reappropriating Clausewitz"; Keene, "The Reception of Thucydides in the History of International Relations"; Boucher, *Appropriating Hobbes*; Molloy, *Kant's International Relations*; Guilhot, "The First Modern Realist." For a related but somewhat different approach, see Nabulsi, *Traditions of War*. A number of works also speak to the circulation of ideas across time, though charting the process of reception is not necessarily their primary focus; see, for instance, Bain, *Medieval Foundations of International Relations*; Bain, *Political Theology of International Order*.

[20] Keene, "The Reception of Thucydides in the History of International Relations."

[21] Keene, 356.

a crucial purpose for them: He "could be used to illustrate what they saw as a fundamental underlying continuity in international relations" – a vital point for scholars seeking to develop a general, transepochal theory of international relations – and more specifically, a story could be weaved around his name to support the claim that this continuity "was expressed through the persistence of power politics and the logic of the balance of power"[22] Ultimately, as Edward Keene puts it, "their reading of Thucydides's *History* was, in a sense, an especially juicy cherry to be picked,"[23] and they did so with a lasting impact in the discipline. Indeed, although a real cottage industry has developed since the 1990s around identifying realist misreadings of Thucydides,[24] these works seldom question the reliance on Thucydides in the first place and as such have exacerbated rather than undermined his prevalence in the discipline.[25] This is despite the fact that, as Keene suggests, "Thucydides needs not be our only contemporary,"[26] and perhaps even more critically, it says nothing about the need to perhaps consider whether Thucydides – or any other classical figure for that matter – should be our "contemporary" to begin with.

A stronger sensibility to these processes is of the essence in IR. Of course, this study of the reception of ideas pertaining to the international echoes a broader move within intellectual history toward the study of the circulation, transmission, and reception of texts, thinkers, and ideas across time and space.[27] Yet there is perhaps no intellectual field more in need of these insights than IR's reconstruction of past thinkers' ideas. International Relations scholars have had a tendency to substantially overestimate the impact that single thinkers can have on the form and conduct of international relations, seamlessly associating the thought of Grotius with the emergence of the modern states-system, to name but one of the most famous examples. Notwithstanding the delightful anecdote about the King of Sweden going to war with a copy of Grotius' *De iure belli ac pacis* under his saddle,[28] the actual impact of the famed author's text is often assumed away. The emerging

---

[22] Ibid., 360.
[23] Ibid.
[24] Keene, 359. Citing Welch, "Why International Relations Theorists Should Stop Reading Thucydides," 307.
[25] Graham Allison's wildly popular concept of "Thucydides's trap" is an obvious example of this continued prevalence.
[26] Keene, "The Reception of Thucydides in the History of International Relations," 367.
[27] See, for instance, Moyn and Sartori, *Global Intellectual History*.
[28] Ringmar, *Identity, Interest and Action*, 172. See also Grotius, *The Rights of War and Peace*, 69.

literature on the reception of canonical texts thus seems a particularly productive avenue for the discipline to turn to in order to track the actual impact of great thinkers.

Even more critically, IR scholars have historically – directly or indirectly – provided influential frames of reference for policymakers even though their readings of the past have often been wildly anachronistic.[29] Beyond the aforementioned case of Thucydides, we now know for instance that the English School built its "traditions" based on "a conflation of nineteenth century appropriations of seventeenth century thinkers, such as Grotius and Hobbes, with the ideas of those thinkers themselves."[30] There is thus much work to be done in terms of systematically untangling what these thinkers actually thought – to the extent that it is possible – from what later generations of historians, lawyers, and other practitioners claimed they did. Doing so is what can ultimately enable us to shed light on the actual provenance of our disciplinary narratives and evaluate their political and normative underpinnings.

Existing works open two particularly promising paths for methodologically rethinking the study of great thinkers in IR. The first entails taking stock of the more rigorous approach for studying these figures in their context available in the neighboring field of HPT. This is a now well-established roadmap. Since IR's historiographical *prise de conscience*, various efforts have been made to import the methodological insight of HPT into the discipline,[31] and especially the contextualism of the so-called Cambridge School.[32] The rest of the chapter draws explicitly on this move.

---

[29] Armitage, *Foundations of Modern International Thought*, 7.

[30] Hutchings et al., "Critical Exchange," 389. A different but similarly concerning claim is the argument that, because Hedley Bull studied Grotius through the works of Cornelius van Vollenhoven, Lassa Oppenheim, and Hersch Lauterpacht, who were all "instrumental in the development of the 'Grotian tradition' of international law in the twentieth century" and whom "Bull considered members of a wider 'Grotian tradition'," his understanding of "Grotius as an intellectual entity separable from the 'Grotian tradition' ... is in fact situated wholly within what he constitutes as the tradition itself." As a result, Jeffery rightly notes, it is therefore "not at all surprising that Bull is able to draw a set of 'remarkable' resemblances between the two sets of ideas." Jeffery, "Tradition as Invention," 79. See also Bain, "Grotius in International Relations Theory."

[31] See, especially, Bell, "Language, Legitimacy, and the Project of Critique"; Bell, "Political Theory and the Functions of Intellectual History."

[32] The label "Cambridge School" has often been criticized in light of the profound disagreements between its main figures, most notably Skinner and Pocock. I use it here, as historians of political thought often do, as a shorthand for a loosely coherent set of premises for how to study historical texts that does not preclude remaining well aware of the sharp differences between the scholars associated with this approach.

The second consists in developing an explicit method for examining the reception of these authors' ideas. This is an area where much work remains to be done. Currently, the discipline of IR simply does not provide a method for studying the reception of great thinkers. There appear to be two main reasons behind this lacuna. First, it is partly a corollary of the discipline's aforementioned misportrayal of great thinkers' ideas more broadly, and of its longstanding aversion to methodological reflection on this front. Second, and more importantly, it probably stems from the fact that historians of political thought in the Anglophone academy have themselves seldom explicitly theorized the methodologies required to study the reception of authors.[33] This is of course not to say that historians of political thought have not studied the reception of authors in practice; to cite but one example, in his main works, Quentin Skinner extensively studies the reception of ancient classics such as Aristotle,[34] Cicero,[35] or Quintilian,[36] as well as the reception of continental rhetorical works in Britain in the early modern period.[37] The point here is that while reception theory is a well-established subfield in literary studies,[38] in the not so distant field of the HPT, the method for studying the reception of famous texts and authors has hardly been theorized in any explicit way, leaving little for IR scholars interested in the reception of great thinkers to draw from. As one scholar puts it, "the practice of writing history and the practice of theorizing about it remain two quite distinct activities";[39] here I am explicitly concerned with the latter.[40]

With contextualism now being the most popular methodological starting point for historians of political thought, the most compelling attempts to develop a more systematic approach to the study of the reception of ideas have tried to merge contextualist insights with a concern for the afterlife of classic works and famous concepts. Two such

---

[33] Though one notable call to address this problem is Thompson, "Reception Theory and the Interpretation of Historical Meaning."

[34] Notably in Skinner, *The Foundations of Modern Political Thought*, Vol. 1.

[35] Ibid.

[36] Skinner, *Visions of Politics*, Vol. 1, 175–87; Vol. 2, 264–85; Vol. 3, 87–41.

[37] Skinner, *Forensic Shakespeare.*

[38] The study of reception is also well established amongst media historians. More broadly, scholars across the history of science, the history of scholarship, and media history are currently converging toward a shared field centered around the reception, transmission, and broader circulation of ideas known in the German-speaking world as *Wissensgeschichte.* Marchand, "Intellectual History Confronts the Longue Durée," 486.

[39] Thompson, "Reception Theory and the Interpretation of Historical Meaning," 257.

[40] For a related attempt by IR scholars to systematize the discipline's engagement with history, see MacKay and LaRoche, "The Conduct of History in International Relations."

attempts stand out. The first is the call to pair Cambridge School contextualism with the tenets of *Begriffsgeschichte*.[41] This approach entails "tracing the different meanings and usages of political concepts over time, tracing the shifts and rupture in their employment."[42] The focus on the history of concepts is presented as a potential remedy to the "temporal problem" of the Cambridge School approach,[43] that is, the overwhelming emphasis that scholars associated with the Cambridge School label (most notably Skinner and Pocock) are – perhaps wrongly – considered to place on the context of writing at the cost of the context of reception.

This approach shares much with a second proposal, which is what David Armitage has termed "history *in* ideas": a new history of ideas based on "a model of transtemporal history, proceeding via serial contextualism to create a history in ideas spanning centuries, even millennia."[44] Like historians working within the tradition of *Begriffsgeschichte*, Armitage puts forward a means for doing intellectual history over the *longue durée* through the study of specific concepts over time, such as the idea of civil war.[45] While Armitage's call for a shift toward "serial contextualism" is a particularly interesting development for the study of international political thought,[46] to which I will return, both of these proposed approaches are geared toward the study of the reception of specific concepts rather than of specific authors. Conversely, while there is a

---

[41] Bell, "Language, Legitimacy, and the Project of Critique," 334. For a similar call in HPT, see especially Palonen, *Politics and Conceptual Histories*; Richter, *The History of Political and Social Concepts*. See also Lehmann and Richter, *The Meaning of Historical Terms and Concepts*; Palonen, "Rhetorical and Temporal Perspectives on Conceptual Change." For a critique, see Bevir, "The Contextual Approach," 20.

[42] Bell, "Language, Legitimacy, and the Project of Critique," 333.

[43] Ibid.

[44] Armitage, "What's the Big Idea?," 494. There has been an explosion of works in *longue durée* intellectual history over the past decade. Other examples of studies of conceptual transformation (works sometimes called "neo-Lovejoyian," despite the significant differences) include Seigel, *The Idea of the Self*; McMahon, *Happiness* and *Divine Fury*; Daston and Galison *Objectivity*; Peter Garnsey *Thinking about Property*; Rosenfeld, *Common Sense*; Forst *Toleration in Conflict*; and Kloppenberg *Toward Democracy*. For more theoretical and historiographical reflections on the relationship between *longue durée* and intellectual history, see Straumann, "The Energy of Concepts"; Potts, *Ideas in Time*; Marchand, "Intellectual History Confronts the Longue Durée."

[45] Armitage, "What's the Big Idea?"; Armitage, *Civil Wars*. Another example would be the concept of "empire," as analyzed in Muldoon, *Empire and Order*. A particularly interesting corollary to this new approach to the diachronic history of concepts is the recent turn toward the role of translation in the diffusion of concepts. See notably the introduction to Burke and Richter, *Why Concepts Matter*; in IR, see Wigen, "Two-Level Language Games."

[46] Armitage, "What's the Big Idea?," 494.

growing number of studies that examine the reception of great thinkers in IR,[47] they do not theorize their methodological approach explicitly.

Therefore, what I seek to do in this chapter is to build on the existing methodological reflections put forward by historians in order to offer an alternative form of "serial contextualism," focused on the reception of an author rather than of a concept and anchored in that author's original context of writing. In doing so, I am also building on existing studies of actual reception processes in IR, history, and international law, but my aim is to give a more systematic account of how one might go about studying the reception of a famous author and what this type of inquiry can contribute.

The approach is based on a two-part method. The first part entails what may be termed a conventional contextualist analysis, based on a synchronic understanding of context. It is geared first and foremost toward attempting to recover the original intention that the author had in writing the relevant text, and particularly her intention in making one or more conceptual moves within that text. The second part takes stock of the recent shift in intellectual history toward a diachronic understanding of context and seeks to understand the impact of that author's move by tracing the reception of her text over time. In doing so, it parts with concept-based methods that stem from the history of ideas and draws on the precepts of what is broadly known as "reception theory," focused on analyzing the reception of a specific author. The serial contexts that are examined are therefore not those in which a concept appears, but those in which the author – or one of the author's most famous texts – is explicitly drawn on, reinterpreted, and reused. The book puts this methodological approach to work, examining Gentili's conceptual moves in his original context before analyzing the main receptions of Gentili's treatise on the laws of war.

In developing this approach, I will make the case that, rather than constitute two separate and potentially irreconcilable forms of methods, namely a classic contextualist analysis of an author's idea versus a diachronic study of the reception of the said author, these two paths can actually be combined in highly productive ways. There is nothing in the contextualism associated predominantly with Quentin Skinner that precludes the study of reception; on the contrary, contextualism does in fact provide some theoretical and conceptual resources for addressing the issue of reception. The main issue is that its adherents – whether in HPT or in IR – have not discussed them adequately or utilized them

---

[47] See *supra* note 19.

explicitly in their work. In this chapter, I therefore bring together some of the methodological insights of Skinnerian contextualism and of reception theory, developing an explicit method for the study of great thinkers in IR and beyond that aims to be eclectic while avoiding the pitfalls of indiscriminate association.

In the first part of the chapter, I begin by outlining the core insights of a conventionally contextualist approach, before highlighting both the possibility and the current limitations of contextualism when it comes to understanding the reception of a particular thinker's ideas. In the second part, I turn to reception theory and I argue that the latter can be effectively paired with a more conventional contextualist methodology in order to better evaluate the journey of an author's ideas over time. I ultimately put forward an approach for the study of great thinkers in IR that is both synchronic and diachronic, but that, unlike recent attempts to reinvent the history of ideas based on the return of the *longue durée*, is focused not on the reception of a particular concept but on that of a particular author. While this approach is relevant to the study of political thought in general, it is particularly potent within IR, where the tendency has been to think about great thinkers diachronically, if without articulating a specific methodology for doing so and resultantly falling into various traps. Using IR's reliance on Kant and Thucydides as brief examples to illustrate my claim, I show the extent to which a more systematic use of this approach would benefit the discipline's engagement with historical works. Importantly, this book does not take a stance on the question of whether or not IR scholars ought to draw any philosophical insights from classical texts without extensive concerns for historicity. The aim here is merely to take into account the very concrete consequences of the frequent anachronistic readings of texts and to consider these moments of rediscovery and reinterpretation in their own historical right, teasing out the stories they tell us about our constructions of the past.

1.1   Taking Context Seriously: Tracking the Aims of Innovating Ideologists

Considering the numerous critiques of IR's abuse of the HPT in the construction of its canon and its traditions,[48] the value of contextualist methodologies seems fairly self-explanatory. This avenue is particularly promising in light of the recent surge of interest in international

---

[48] Bell, "Language, Legitimacy, and the Project of Critique." More broadly, see Jahn, "Introduction."

political thought, both from IR scholars and from historians.[49] In its broad commitment to historicism, contextualism urges scholars not to consider great thinkers as taking part in perennial debates across time and space, nor to consider them as speaking a common language and providing insights into solving timeless problems, including those of our own period.[50] More specifically, contextualism emphasizes that texts must be "regarded as extremely complex historical objects, which were written with a purpose in mind" and thus as "a form of action."[51]

What exactly this entails in terms of conducting research has been the subject of fierce methodological battles. Skinner is of course the most famous of the Cambridge School contextualists, and his brand of contextualism, sometimes called "Skinnerian contextualism" or "Skinnerian linguistic contextualism,"[52] is often associated with the broader label. However, as Bell notes, "not all contextualists are Skinnerian."[53] In fact, Skinner himself seems to have evolved quite significantly over the course of his career and is now rather difficult to place in terms of his own commitment to his initial methodological claims as well as his evaluation of more recent alternatives, most notably postanalytical historicism.[54] Much of the problem here stems from the incredibly demanding character of Skinner's original methodological recommendations, which resulted from his stark philosophical stance and which even he struggled to accommodate in his own historical research.[55] Despite these unresolved tensions and debates, some broad principles for investigation can be drawn out. Indeed, these issues around Skinner's original philosophical position notwithstanding, contextualists virtually all agree with the general aim of Skinner's

---

[49] This body of works is to be distinguished from the "problem-solving" approach to international political thought discussed (and criticized) by Beate Jahn in "Introduction." In IR, see especially Keene, *International Political Thought*. In history, see, for instance, Tuck, *The Rights of War and Peace*; Armitage, *The Ideological Origins of the British Empire*.

[50] For the seminal critique of such approaches (most notably that of Leo Strauss), see Skinner, "Meaning and Understanding in the History of Ideas."

[51] Bell, "Language, Legitimacy, and the Project of Critique," 116.

[52] Sometimes also called conventionalism, particularly by Mark Bevir; see, for example, Bevir, "The Contextual Approach."

[53] Bell, "Political Theory and the Functions of Intellectual History," 153. Bell is thinking here of the other Cambridge School historians, particularly Pocock and Dunn. See his note 11.

[54] Bevir, "Contextualism." See also, for instance, Skodo, "Post-Analytic Philosophy of History." On Skinner's "genealogical turn" and its methodological implications, see Lane, "Doing Our Own Thinking for Ourselves."

[55] On the tension between Skinner's metatheoretical projects and his actual historical research, see Richter, *The History of Political and Social Concepts*, 135–36.

project, that is, "the historicisation of political thought and the attempt to locate texts within their original terms of reference."[56] Studying texts with no regard for the context in which they were written, they argue, is bound to lead to gross errors of interpretation.[57]

Outlining all the theoretical underpinnings of this broad contextualist project is beyond the scope of this book,[58] but it is important here to note a few essential aspects of a contextualist approach. While Skinner's early methodological writings were part of a general intellectual wave now known as "interpretivism" (written in dialogue with scholars such as Alasdair MacIntyre and Clifford Geertz) that made claims about society as a whole, and while Skinner would hardly have considered his early methodological writings to be solely aimed at instructing readers about how best to read old texts, Skinnerian contextualism is now associated first and foremost with the objective of recovering the intention of the author, and with the idea that the author's intention is necessarily suited to achieving a particular objective in a particular context. This entails acquiring a deep understanding of the socio-political context as well as – very importantly – the linguistic context of the author. There are some broad guidelines for achieving this understanding, mainly the study of "both minor and major texts that existed at the time of writing of the particular text under examination, in order to gain an understanding of the various political languages employed, and the links between them," and the attempt to relate them to "the general historical environment."[59] Furthermore, in reading the text of interest, it is essential to grasp both its locutionary and its illocutionary force. This distinction, drawn by Skinner, separates the mere lexical meaning of words (locutionary force) from what the author was actually doing in using them (illocutionary force). The two are deeply intertwined, and capturing the intention of the author ultimately depends on being able to distinguish them and truly grasp the illocutionary force of the text. In order to achieve this aim, Duncan Bell suggests that it is "highly advisable" to use "a dose of methodological pluralism"[60] rather than strictly follow Skinner's original methodological precepts, as suggested

---

[56] Bell, "Political Theory and the Functions of Intellectual History," 153.
[57] Skinner's seminal critique provides numerous examples of these errors. See Skinner, "Meaning and Understanding in the History of Ideas."
[58] For comprehensive theoretical accounts of contextualist methods in intellectual history, see Hunter, "The History of Theory"; Hunter, "The History of Philosophy and the Persona of the Philosopher," 200; Pocock, *Political Thought and History*; Skinner, *Visions of Politics*, Vol. 1.
[59] Bell, "Language, Legitimacy, and the Project of Critique," 332.
[60] Ibid. More broadly, see Dunn, *The History of Political Theory and Other Essays*.

by Skinner's own practice in *Liberty before Liberalism* and even more strikingly in his "Genealogy of the Modern State."[61]

Crucially, to the extent that one can recover authorial intention through a contextualist methodology,[62] the purpose of doing so is not mere antiquarianism. In Skinner's words, it enables one to speak to contemporary concerns by showing "how the concepts we still invoke were initially defined, what purposes they were intended to serve, what view of public power they were used to underpin."[63] Here, it is important to note that if Skinner has expressed a certain skepticism toward the history of concepts, and particularly the study of unit-ideas as advocated by Lovejoy, he does not reject the study of concepts altogether. In his own words, the argument is simply that "there can be no histories of concepts; there can only be histories of their uses in argument."[64] This caveat does not mean that it is impossible to write about concepts altogether; ultimately, Skinner himself finds it sufficiently manageable to write about concepts such as liberty or the state. Simply, he reminds us that "concepts must not be viewed simply as propositions with meanings attached to them; they must also be thought of as weapons (Heidegger's suggestion) or as tools (Wittgenstein's term)."[65] As a result, one can only understand a particular concept and the text in which the concept occurs if one knows "who is wielding the concept in question, and with what argumentative purposes in mind."[66]

Skinner provides some specific tools for analyzing the use of concepts under this specific angle, two of which are of particular importance for our purposes: the idea of an "innovating ideologist" and the related notion of what Skinner calls "evaluative-descriptive terms." The innovating ideologist seeks "to legitimate a new range of social actions which, in terms of the existing ways of applying the moral vocabulary prevailing in his society, are currently regarded as in some way untoward or illegitimate"[67] The innovating ideologist does so through speech acts centered

---

[61] Skinner, *Liberty before Liberalism*; Skinner, "A Genealogy of the Modern State (British Academy Lecture)."

[62] There is, of course, a broader debate within hermeneutics about whether it is at all possible, or even desirable, to recover authorial intention in the first place. I engage with this question in greater detail in an earlier version of this chapter published in article form as Vergerio, "Context, Reception, and the Study of Great Thinkers in International Relations."

[63] Skinner, *Liberty before Liberalism*, 110.

[64] Restated by Skinner in 1988, in "A Reply to My Critics," 283. For a critique of this position, see Freeden, *Ideologies and Political Theory*, 110–11.

[65] See Quentin Skinner's contribution in Collini, "What Is Intellectual History?"

[66] Ibid.

[67] Skinner, "Some Problems in the Analysis of Political Thought and Action," 112.

on "evaluative-descriptive terms," that is, words that are used both to describe and to either commend or condemn certain actions. These terms are of particular importance because, as Skinner puts it, "it is essentially by manipulating this set of terms that any society succeeds in establishing and altering its moral identity."[68] The innovating ideologist thus seeks to manipulate the meaning of concepts (and/or their application) with the aim of modifying political behavior. In my analysis of Gentili in his context, I identify the Italian jurist as an innovating ideologist and take the concept of the "enemy of mankind" to be an evaluative-descriptive term that Gentili sought to manipulate in his writings on war in order to redraw the boundaries of "public war" and defend an absolutist position.

The insights provided by a close analysis of innovating ideologists and of their use of evaluative-descriptive terms, and by a contextualist approach more broadly, present a real potential for critique in IR. This potential has been laid out in some detail by scholars such as Duncan Bell,[69] Beate Jahn,[70] Gerard Holden,[71] as well as Darshan Vigneswaran and Joel Quirk[72] and to some extent Richard Devetak,[73] and I will not restate their arguments here. Suffice it to say that this approach can shed significant light on the role of language in the constitution of political and social life, particularly in terms of how the vocabularies of a given time can both enhance and constrain political legitimacy, and how they can be consciously manipulated in attempts to impact political behavior. As Alasdair MacIntyre puts it, "since to possess a concept involves behaving or being able to behave in certain ways in certain circumstances, to alter concepts, whether by modifying existing concepts or by making new concepts available or by destroying old ones, is to alter behavior."[74]

There are, however, two broad types of limitations to this contextualist approach. First, as mentioned earlier, Skinner has not always been consistent in applying his own methodological precepts, and various critiques have been made of Skinner's original philosophical stance, most notably by Mark Bevir.[75] These are part of an ongoing debate on the modalities of textual interpretation, the details of which stem from

---

[68] Ibid.

[69] Especially in Bell, "Language, Legitimacy, and the Project of Critique"; Bell, "Political Theory and the Functions of Intellectual History."

[70] Especially in Jahn, "Introduction."

[71] Holden, "Who Contextualizes the Contextualizers."

[72] Vigneswaran and Quirk, "Past Masters and Modern Inventions."

[73] Devetak, "A Rival Enlightenment?" For a more skeptical view emphasizing the limits of contextualism in IR, see Hall, "The History of International Thought and International Relations Theory."

[74] MacIntyre, *A Short History of Ethics*, 2–3.

[75] For an introductory discussion, see Bevir, "The Contextual Approach."

disagreements about the philosophy of history that are beyond the scope of this book. Second, and more urgently for our purposes, Skinnerian contextualism currently presents some limitations when it comes to analyzing the reception of texts. Once they have been published, texts take on a life of their own – sometimes for centuries – which often leads them to be understood in novel ways and used for purposes that have little to do with the author's original intention so carefully unearthed by a Skinnerian approach. In other words, there is often an important divide between the context of writing and the context of reception.

Skinner has repeatedly come under fire for what is perceived as his overly restrictive understanding of context, focused almost exclusively on the immediate context of the author at hand, and for his resulting failure to address the reception, transmission, and translation of texts.[76] This is not so much inherent to Skinner's methodological approach, as merely the result of his deliberate prioritization of the recovery of authorial intention over other pursuits, a point which Skinner has made explicitly.[77] Though his methodological writings have focused predominantly on the question of how best to recover authorial intention, in his substantive works Skinner has in fact analyzed processes of reception and the multiplicity of contexts they call upon. In examining, for instance, the revival of Aristotle's *Politics* in the second half of the thirteenth century or in qualifying its impact through an emphasis on the weight of Roman moralists and historians (especially Cicero and Sallust) decades earlier,[78] Skinner makes it very clear that classical texts were participants in a range of different debates across time and space.

If anything, questions of reception and transtemporal transmission have long been staples of Cambridge School contextualism, both in Skinner's famous *Foundations of Modern Political Thought* and, even more conspicuously, in the works of another Cambridge historian, John Pocock, who gradually came to place "much more emphasis upon the historical significance of reception, reading, and the modes of interaction among author, text, and reader,"[79] and whose concerns for Kuhnian "paradigms" and competing "languages" speak directly to these issues.[80] As such, the claim here is not so much that the study of the reception of texts constitutes an addition to Cambridge School contextualism,

---

[76] For various critiques of Skinner's strict understanding of and emphasis on context, see notably McMahon and Moyn, *Rethinking Modern European Intellectual History*, particularly the essays by McMahon, Gordon, Müller, and Moyn.

[77] Skinner, "A Reply to My Critics," 271–73.

[78] See notably Skinner, *Visions of Politics*, Vol. 2, 10–38.

[79] Thompson, "Reception Theory and the Interpretation of Historical Meaning," 271.

[80] See notably Pocock, *Politics, Language and Time*.

but rather that it is an immanent possibility within this form of contextualism that has not been sufficiently theorized as a methodological
approach for studying great thinkers in IR and beyond.[81] In order to further develop and systematize this approach, I therefore turn to the tenets
of what broadly falls under the label of "reception theory."[82]

1.2 From Context to Contexts: The Diachronic Lives of Great Thinkers

First, it is worth noting that, within the study of international political thought, an important attempt has already been made to address
the perceived shortcomings of Skinner's brand of contextualism: David
Armitage's notion of a history *in* ideas, based on the notion of "serial
contextualism." Echoing the usual line of critique, Armitage argues
that since Skinner's famous 1969 piece,[83] intellectual historians who
identify as contextualists have "construed context synchronically and
punctually: that is, defined with a narrow chronology and implicitly
discontinuous with other contexts."[84] By contrast with this approach,
Armitage suggests "deploying the distinctive procedures of Anglo-
American intellectual history, but by doing so diachronically as well as
synchronically."[85] His method entails "the reconstruction of a sequence
of distinct contexts in which identifiable agents strategically deployed
existing languages to effect definable goals such as legitimation and
delegitimation, persuasion and dissuasion, consensus-building and radical innovation."[86] As I have noted, in practice, this approach is actually
hardly different from what historians associated with the Cambridge
School label – including Skinner – have done in their own work. And
indeed, Armitage concedes that Cambridge historians have pursued
this approach to a certain extent, pointing to Pocock's *Machiavellian
Moment*,[87] Tuck's *Rights of War and Peace*,[88] and Skinner's "Genealogy

---

[81] The fact that, in a certain sense (and depending on how one defines a "text"), historians
who focus on authorial intent ("intentionalists" such as Skinner) and historians inspired
by reception theory undertake compatible tasks that simply seek to unpack different
aspects of given texts is briefly discussed by Bevir, *The Logic of the History of Ideas*, 58.

[82] Importantly, reception theory is itself a broad form of "contextualism." The so-called
Cambridge School contextualism is merely the dominant strand of contextualism
amongst historians of political philosophy; see Bevir, "The Contextual Approach," 11.

[83] Skinner, "Meaning and Understanding in the History of Ideas."

[84] Armitage, "What's the Big Idea?" 498.

[85] Ibid., 497.

[86] Ibid., 498.

[87] Pocock, *The Machiavellian Moment*.

[88] Tuck, *The Rights of War and Peace*.

of the Modern State."[89] Ultimately, he seems to suggest that what is revolutionary in his approach is not the practice of studying series of contexts, but the fact of explicitly theorizing context in diachronic terms.[90]

Generally speaking, the renewed focus on *longue durée* intellectual history is a promising move for IR scholars who share with intellectual historians an interest in international political thought. Constructing diachronic histories of "big ideas," that is, "central concepts in our political, ethical and scientific vocabularies,"[91] based on serial contextualism is certainly a fruitful enterprise, if also a tremendously challenging one in light of the knowledge of each context required for a rigorous application of this method. This book, however, is concerned with the impact that a specific author can have as such, in light of the reception of his texts, rather than with the broader impact he may have once a concept he has contributed to shaping travels and is applied by others, with the author's name receding into the background. As a result, this book also takes stock of the potential of diachronic histories, but it does so from an altogether different angle. Concept-based diachronic approaches, whether those like Melvin Richter's stemming explicitly from *Begriffsgeschichte* or those like Armitage's that seek the "reinvention" of the history of ideas altogether (hence the "history *in* ideas"), do not provide an explicit methodology for the study of how a specific author – rather than a specific idea – travels. In order to outline such an approach, it is necessary to turn to reception theory and examine the value of combining its insights with those of contextualism in the study of great thinkers in IR and beyond.

Though it initially struggled to travel from its German bases to the Anglophone academy,[92] reception theory has now been used extensively across numerous fields,[93] but it has not had much success in IR despite the existence of a handful of works that directly examine the reception of certain great thinkers.[94] These few forays have emerged in the context of the aforementioned turn toward the study of international political thought, but they remain the exception in a field that continues to acclaim and appropriate original texts without examining how these

---

[89] Skinner, "A Genealogy of the Modern State (British Academy Lecture)."
[90] Armitage, "What's the Big Idea?" 499.
[91] Ibid., 497.
[92] For the original texts, see mainly Jauss, *Literaturgeschichte als Provokation*; Grimm, *Rezeptionsgeschichte*; Iser, *Der Akt des Lesens*. For a discussion of the lukewarm reaction to reception theory in the United States, see Holub, "Trends in Literary Theory."
[93] For a brief survey of the history of reception theory, see Burke, "The History and Theory of Reception." For a general introduction to reception theory, see Holub, *Reception Theory*.
[94] See *supra* note 19.

texts came to form part of the disciplinary canon in the first place. The neighboring field of HPT has a longer and more sustained tradition of engaging with these questions in practice, but as Armitage argues, it has not explicitly theorized how to study context in diachronic terms either. The extensive literature on the reception of classical thinkers in the medieval and the early modern period[95] – with Aristotle and Tacitus being two of the most famous cases – is an obvious testament to this substantive engagement, while the literature on the reception of late medieval and early modern thinkers in the nineteenth and twentieth centuries, though noticeably slimmer, is another promising avenue of research in the discipline.[96] In another closely related though much younger field – the history of international law – some work has notably emerged on the revival of Vitoria by James Brown Scott in the early twentieth century,[97] with Anne Orford making an explicit call for the wider study of the reception of great thinkers in international law, a call that is now being answered.[98]

Examining the reception of great thinkers is an obvious – if, in IR, insufficiently exploited – means of assessing the actual impact of their ideas by evaluating the way their concepts were used, reused, and misused in their intellectual afterlife. While IR scholars can draw some insights from the way the reception of various authors has been analyzed in HPT, it is essential to develop a clearer, explicit method for doing so systematically. In what follows, I thus draw two core insights from reception theory that allow for a more rigorous study of the reception of particular authors and then highlight two crucial payoffs of applying these methodological precepts.

---

[95] Ancient historians and classicists who focus on the legacy of classical antiquity in the later history of political thought include Peter Garnsey, Fergus Millar, Wilfried Nippel, Paul Rahe, Elizabeth Rawson, and Jennifer Tolbert Roberts, cited in Straumann, *Crisis and Constitutionalism*, 13. The broader reception of classical and biblical authors is an increasingly popular area of research with its own outlet, the *Classical Receptions Journal*.

[96] See, for instance, Burke, *The Fortunes of the Courtier*; Botting and Zlioba, "Religion and Women's Rights."

[97] Orford, "On International Legal Method"; Orford, *What Is the Place of Anachronism in International Legal Thinking.*

[98] See, especially, Amorosa, *Rewriting the History of the Law of Nations*, which notably provides a more in-depth investigation of the revival of Vitoria by James Brown Scott. For earlier studies of this kind, see especially the work of Elisabetta Fiocchi Malaspina on the reception of Vattel's *Le droit des gens* in the nineteenth century: Fiocchi Malaspina, "Emer de Vattel's 'Le droit des gens'"; Fiocchi Malaspina, "Le droit des gens di Emer de Vattel." Fiocchi also provides some broader, fascinating insights into processes of appropriation and reproduction of the doctrines of international law during the nineteenth century; see Fiocchi Malaspina and Keller-Kemmerer, "International Law and Translation in the 19th Century."

First, recipients are not passive followers, and what is received or inherited is not necessarily what was given or handed over.[99] In other words, those who "receive" the texts of great thinkers have a considerable amount of agency, and they may alter the text in significant ways, whether they directly add elements to it or simply reinterpret it for their own purposes.[100] Aquinas' famous formulation is often cited on this point: *Quidquid recipitur, ad modum recipientis recipitur*: whatever is received is received according to the manner of the receiver.[101] It is thus much more useful to think of the process of reception as one of translation rather than transmission. This is a crucial point in thinking about the impact of a specific author's ideas, but as Peter Burke remarks, "[a]lthough the famous epigram attributed to Karl Marx, 'I am not a Marxist,' has been circulating for a long time, the implications for intellectual history of the distance between founders and followers have rarely been made explicit."[102] A particularly useful tool for further conceptualizing these differences is the concern with the "horizon of expectations" (*Erwartungshorizont*), found notably in the works of the aforementioned Hans-Georg Gadamer and his student Wolfgang Iser. The underlying idea here is that different readers will approach a specific text with different expectations – including different questions and concerns associated with their own environment – and that this will shape the way they understand the text in various respects. The results can be conceptualized through terms such as "appropriation" (Ricoeur) or "re-employment" (Certeau), or as a form of intellectual "*bricolage*" (Lévi-Strauss) that turns consumption into a form of production in itself.[103]

Second, and relatedly, this emphasis on active/creative rather than passive/faithful reception suggests that in order to understand the importance of an author's text, we must examine it not just in its original context but in the various contexts in which it came to play an important role. In other words, it is crucial to examine not just the "reception" of a text, but its multiple receptions, across different groups, countries, and epochs. Through this process, one may conceptualize the multiple embodiments of the same author, used for different purposes under

---

[99] Burke, "The History and Theory of Reception," 22.

[100] On this phenomenon in the context of international law, see notably Wallenius, "The Case for a History of Global Legal Practices."

[101] Aquinas 2015, 1a, q. 75, a. 5; 3a, q.5, cited in Burke, "The History and Theory of Reception," 29.

[102] Burke, "The History and Theory of Reception," 23. Burke mentions Schwartz, "Some Polarities in Confucian Thought," as an important exception.

[103] Ricœur, "Appropriations"; Certeau, *L'invention du quotidien*, cited in Burke, "The History and Theory of Reception," 25.

different circumstances – or, for example, under the same circumstances but for different political purposes. For instance, Kinch Hoekstra speaks of "multiple Thucydides" in the early modern period and highlights the gap between Alberico Gentili's Thucydides and Thomas Hobbes' Thucydides.[104] The impact of a particular text can thus become kaleidoscopic, refracted through the many contexts in which it is creatively put to use. In analyzing this process, two related avenues of investigation seem particularly fruitful. On the one hand, one should compare the original reception of the text, the impact the author had in her original context, with later receptions, which may have altered the author's reputation quite drastically.[105] On the other hand, one should pay particular attention to the impact the text will have when it is seized on by influential individuals who actually have the means of giving the text a renewed importance and of redefining what is in fact important about it.

Applying these two methodological tenets opens the way for a number of productive intellectual moves, two of which stand out as especially fruitful payoffs. First, studying an author not just in her original context but through her different receptions over time is a methodological approach that answers David Armitage's call for a return to *longue durée* intellectual history, though in a different way from his own application of it.[106] It is an approach that is deeply committed to examining the author and her work diachronically, sacrificing some of the depth of traditional contextualist investigations for the breadth of transepochal comparisons. This seems a particularly useful approach within IR, a discipline in which scholars almost invariably analyze great thinkers diachronically despite lacking an explicit methodology for how to do so adequately. Of course, the point of a diachronic approach based on reception theory is not to study authors in a decontextualized manner, applying their categories and concepts indiscriminately across time and space, but rather to pay close attention to the various contexts in which they were explicitly received, potentially stretching the story of their impact over continents and centuries. As such, it distances itself from the English School's concept of traditions[107] as well as from the broader

[104] Hoekstra, "A Source of War"; Hoekstra, "Hobbes's Thucydides."

[105] This is the approach taken in Lee and Morley, *A Handbook of the Reception of Thucydides*, for instance. The *Handbook* juxtaposes a chapter on Thucydides' ancient reputation with one on his reception in the Renaissance.

[106] Armitage and Guldi, "The Return of the Longue Durée"; Guldi and Armitage, *The History Manifesto*. For a brief discussion of the study of receptions as an example of *longue durée* intellectual history, see Straumann, *Crisis and Constitutionalism*, 20.

[107] For an early discussion of these traditions, see Dunne, "Mythology or Methodology?" For a more recent analysis, see Keene, "Three Traditions of International Theory."

practice of diachronically examining the history of a concept through a long collection of great thinkers.[108]

Second, reception theory provides a particularly useful set of tools for analyzing the construction of intellectual canons.[109] The importance of "canons" and "traditions" has not escaped IR scholars,[110] and indeed, Bell points out that while Skinner is right to be suspicious of "claims about easily delineated transhistorical ideational bodies," we must also "recognize the vital role of *perceived* traditions," that is, "the relationship theorists sustain with those they consider to be their intellectual progenitors."[111] As Freeden explains, "[i]nasmuch as people come to attach importance to reified traditions, however erroneously conceived the latter are, they become factors in the formation of human thought and in the explanation of human behavior."[112] Perceived traditions can of course be based on various elements, including concepts, as in the case of liberalism,[113] or authors, as in the case of a "Grotian tradition" of international law and political thought.[114] With respect to the latter, an approach that focuses first and foremost on the reception of the

[108] For instance, this is a particularly popular approach in the field of just war theory with regard to the study of the "just war tradition"; see notably O'Driscoll and Brunstetter, *Just War Thinkers*.

[109] Thompson, "Reception Theory and the Interpretation of Historical Meaning," 249.

[110] Though some have been explicitly critical of any attempt to construct them, such as Brian Schmidt, who sees these traditions as developed either for polemical purposes or as a way to legitimize contemporary ideas; see Schmidt, *The Political Discourse of Anarchy*, 24. For a more sympathetic approach, see Nabulsi, *Traditions of War*, 66–79; Nabulsi and Hazareesingh, "Using Archival Sources to Theorize about Politics."

[111] Bell, "Language, Legitimacy, and the Project of Critique," 333. For a similar emphasis on the importance of "invented traditions" in IR, see also Jeffery, "Tradition as Invention."

[112] Freeden, *Ideologies and Political Theory*, 110. This echoes Hobsbawm's concern with "invented traditions," the study of which "throws a considerable light on the human relation to the past … For all invented traditions, so far as possible, use history as a legitimator of action and cement of group cohesion." Hobsbawm and Ranger, *The Invention of Tradition*, 12. Importantly, these approaches differ from Mark Bevir's own concept of tradition as explained in Bevir, "On Tradition." Bevir is also concerned with traditions and their legitimating power, but he has a different understanding of what a tradition consists in. For him, "[a]n account of a tradition must identify a set of connected beliefs and habits that intentionally or unintentionally passed from generation to generation at some time in the past" (Bevir, "On Tradition," 46), which is a separate endeavor from the study of retrospectively established "traditions" that often rest on imaginary links between otherwise separate individuals and pursuits. More broadly, see Bevir, *The Logic of the History of Ideas*. On the value of using his understanding of "tradition" in IR, see Hall and Bevir, "Traditions of British International Thought."

[113] Bell, "What Is Liberalism?"

[114] Lauterpacht, "The Grotian Tradition in International Law"; Bull, "The Grotian Conception of International Society"; Kingsbury, "A Grotian Tradition of Theory and Practice"; Jeffery, *Hugo Grotius in International Thought*; Van Ittersum, "Hugo Grotius." See also Nabulsi, *Traditions of War*.

author's text(s) appears essential and fulfills a distinct purpose from one focused on the transformation of concepts. As such, for author-based traditions, it becomes essential to track the complex story of the reception of the author, particularly as, in the case of a discipline such as IR, the interpretation of an author will have been shaped and reshaped many times before entering the field. Ultimately, the novel interpretation put forward by the receivers "may have shaped core concepts in the discipline," in which case "a historical recovery of their roots is one way of opening up these concepts for critical reflection."[115]

If one wishes to understand the emergence, evolution, modification, and reproduction of a canon and ultimately the development of perceived traditions or legacies based on particular authors, it thus becomes imperative to examine the context(s) of an author's reception, closely examining the shifting representation(s) of that author over time and space. The attribution of "greatness" to a thinker, her enshrinement into a disciplinary canon, is an active, conscious process. Forgotten thinkers are unearthed and branded as great by those who want to claim them for their own camp, while the rightful legacy of an established "great thinker" can be a source of extensive debate.[116] Inventing a tradition linking one's ideas to those of a long-dead, respected, famous mind is one of the many ways in which one can defend something by giving it "the sanction of perpetuity."[117] As a result, once an author is placed in the category of "great thinkers," her name comes to bear a certain weight, to provide a certain degree of legitimacy to those who invoke her as their forerunner. Since reception theory is explicitly geared toward understanding the factors that "shape" the reception of a text,[118] it is thus particularly relevant for shedding light on the dynamics behind the canonization of an author. It is notably attuned to the role of political agendas in shaping reception,[119] a factor that is likely to be found at play in the construction of disciplinary canons.

---

[115] Jahn, "Introduction," 13.
[116] For example, on the role of Hobbes as the presumed founder of liberal political theory, and the emergence of this conception of his legacy in the twentieth century, see Farneti, *Il canone moderno*. See also Vaughan, "The Decline of Sovereignty in the Liberal Tradition." For a critique of IR's perilous caricature of Hobbes, see Malcolm, "Hobbes' Theory of International Relations." On the similarly divergent receptions of Rousseau, see Lifschitz, *Engaging with Rousseau*.
[117] Hobsbawm and Ranger, *The Invention of Tradition*, 2.
[118] Burke, "The History and Theory of Reception," 32.
[119] Consider, for instance, the various receptions of Erasmus, notably in Spain and Italy. Silavana Seidel Menchi emphasizes the fact that Erasmus' Italian readers had their own agenda, which included disguising their Protestant beliefs and legitimating a political attack on the papacy; see Menchi, *Erasmo in Italia, 1520–1580*, cited in

Ultimately, while the claim here is that we must distinguish between a study of the reception of ideas based on concepts and one based on authors, it may be said that in the case of the canonization of an author, the author itself becomes, in some way, a form of concept. Invoking the author in question becomes a means to refer to a set of ideas, to a particular understanding of what abstract and contested terms such as "power politics," "sovereignty," or "liberalism" might mean. In the broadest sense, Bell reminds us that "[t]raditions are usually constructed around a canon of renowned thinkers, which serves simultaneously as a reservoir of arguments, an index of historical continuity, and a powerful source of intellectual authority."[120] But more specifically, an author's name can become associated with a precise position, providing a shorthand for what may otherwise necessitate extensive – and possibly contestable – elaboration. When one invokes, for instance, Thucydides, Hobbes, or Kant within a tradition, the reference is often not so much to the individuals, with their idiosyncratic lives and the specific aims they had in writing their canonized treatises, but rather to the intellectual statement they provide within a debate, to the positions that are automatically associated with their person. Their name entails a set of arguments (or many different sets, if one takes into account the different interpretations of a single author), a collection of assumptions and their associated ramifications, in a way that is not dissimilar to the role played by a concept such as "absolute sovereignty" or "liberalism." In using great thinkers as such, the receivers of the text come to "decontextualize" the author they are engaging with in order to make her fit their own context and aspirations while nonetheless claiming her historic heritage. In this sense, the emphasis in this chapter on the distinction between the study of authors and the study of concepts is made primarily to highlight a shift in terms of the object of study and therefore of the chosen methodology, keeping in mind that a more diligent study of authors and of their reception may in fact underline the

---

Burke, "The History and Theory of Reception," 26–27. Another example is the case of Locke, whose diverse receptions come to light in Mark Goldie's fascinating anthology *The Reception of Locke's Politics*. On the diverging receptions of Locke in the nineteenth and the twentieth centuries and the ultimate establishment of his "liberal" credentials, see Bell, "What Is Liberalism?" For a fascinating case beyond the history of political thought, see notably Martial Poirson, *Ombres de Molière*, on the reception of Molière in France from the seventeenth century onward, the evolution of which was dictated by political events from the necessity to reclaim Molière for the French republican tradition in the late eighteenth century to the desire to challenge the supremacy of an overbearing Britain and its equally imposing Shakespeare in the nineteenth century.

[120] Bell, "What Is Liberalism?" 686.

extent to which authors can become concepts, fulfilling similar discursive functions and sharing the same purposes as heuristic devices.

1.3   A Combined Approach

While it is common to read studies of authors in their original context, and possible to find a number of works that examine the subsequent reception of their ideas, contributions that combine the two have remained the exception. In this final section, I wish to conclude by emphasizing the methodological potential of an approach to the study of great thinkers that combines a synchronic analysis based on the methodological insights of Skinnerian contextualism with a diachronic analysis drawing on the tenets of reception theory.

An emphasis on the reception of a great thinker's ideas may seem at first as a complementary but separate project from the examination of the author's ideas in their initial context, and particularly from a close analysis of the author's original intentions. Indeed, reception theory long ignored the question of authorial intention or "authorial intended meaning" altogether, preferring to focus on the issue of "received meaning,"[121] and historians of political thought traditionally kept reception theory at bay just as cultural and intellectual historians were engaging with it at length. Yet two main arguments can be made for a unified approach that relies on these two avenues of inquiry at once in the study of great thinkers. First, and in the most obvious sense, any project that seeks to understand both the emergence and the impact of a particular author's idea will find this methodological approach greatly relevant. In IR, a discipline that has historically paid significant attention to the thought of a few great authors, emphasizing the continued importance of specific concepts within their thought (whether it be Hobbes on sovereignty or Kant on perpetual peace, to name but the most famous ones), developing an approach that encompasses both a rigorous understanding of the author's context and an analytical commitment to the *longue durée* would seem a valuable endeavor.

The call for such an approach is reinforced by the fact that the discipline of IR has sometimes erred in its appreciation of authors' ideas specifically because it remained abysmally unaware of the process of reception. If greater efforts have been made to tease out the normative assumptions of each theoretical approach,[122] surely the fact that IR

---

[121] For a detailed discussion, see Thompson, "Reception Theory and the Interpretation of Historical Meaning," 257–65.

[122] Reus-Smit and Snidal, *The Oxford Handbook of International Relations*.

textbooks continue to propagate a history of the modern states-system and of its presumed intellectual architects constructed by nineteenth-century counter-revolutionary historians[123] should be an immediate source of concern. If the study of IR's "great thinkers" continues to be an important part of the discipline, particularly in light of the turn to international political thought,[124] this untangling exercise can form the basis for a more rigorous approach both to the nature of their thought and to the impact they had through their actual reception over time.

Second, and more specifically, there is a rather straightforward case to be made for the continued methodological relevance of a more traditional, synchronic analysis of an author as a highly insightful component of the study of an author's reception. Naturally, reception studies encourage scholars "not to limit themselves to the reconstructions of major thinkers, but to ask a much wider range of questions about recontextualizations, responses, uses, and so on,"[125] pointing to "the illusion of perfect communication" and, in that process, "undermining the importance of the intentions of writers."[126] However, the intention of the author remains an important component of reception for a simple reason: It constitutes a benchmark against which one can measure the extent to which the text has been reinterpreted by the receivers. Burke emphasizes that in studying reception one must "look for what is 'lost in translation', or what is distorted," reminding us of Cervantes' famous observations that reading a text in translation is "like viewing Flemish tapestries from the wrong side."[127] In other words, he explains, one has to measure the "degrees of distance from the original."[128] It is not clear, however, how one might be able to achieve this without some understanding of what the text was originally intended to achieve.

In other words, and to push Cervantes' metaphor a step further, is it only by viewing both sides of the tapestry that one can appreciate the contrast between the two images. If we only view the "wrong side," we

---

[123] Keene, *Beyond the Anarchical Society*, 13–14. For a more detailed analysis, see Devetak, "Historiographical Foundations of Modern International Thought." Noting Armitage's remark that "the pivotal moments in the formation of modern international thought were often points of retrospective reconstruction," Devetak shows the extent to which historians played a role in the depiction of the modern world as a "world of states."

[124] Though for a call to locate "international political thought" beyond a canon of "great thinkers," see especially Keene, "International Intellectual History and International Relations." For a related call to examine the thought of practitioners, see Rothschild, "Arcs of Ideas," 220.

[125] Burke, "The History and Theory of Reception," 32.

[126] Ibid., 28.

[127] Ibid., 32.

[128] Ibid., 35.

may well be aware that it is indeed "wrong" to some extent and that the actual image is bound to differ in some way, but we remain within the realm of speculative abstraction; the actual image may be slightly different, or it could be entirely unrecognizable – we will never know. To the extent that one is interested in analyzing the construction of traditions and unveiling the scaffolding of intellectual canons, having a concrete understanding of what the gap between the original and its derivatives entails becomes essential. In fact, an awareness of the original is much more critical within this context than is suggested by Cervantes' example. If, in the example of the tapestry, the original and its flip side are literally co-constitutive of each other, this is clearly not the case when we speak of the reception of texts. Indeed, the reinterpretations can depart from the original to remarkable extents, as some receivers may use the text with few concerns for the dead author's original intentions.[129] One particular instantiation of this point is the fact that certain parts of an author's text can be heavily emphasized[130] while others are entirely ignored or even concealed.[131] As Bevir puts it, speaking of traditions more broadly, "because people want to improve their heritage by making it more coherent, more accurate, and more relevant to contemporary issues, they often do respond selectively to it; they accept some parts of it, modify others, and reject others."[132] In this context, authorial intention truly has an essential role to play in the study of an author's reception, and a commitment to the *longue durée* can thus be paired with a more traditional contextualist investigation.

There are, of course, certain limitations to this approach, or at least certain challenges that should be flagged. First of all, in studying the

---

[129] Though a notable point is that other receivers will read the text through their own understanding of the author's original intention. According to one approach ("reader-response criticism," broadly speaking), what the author actually intended is in this case ultimately a moot point; it does not matter, and it cannot be recovered. Mark Bevir, in *The Logic of the History of Ideas*, has put forward a compelling attempt to bring together the insights of intentionalism with those of reader-response criticism, emphasizing that the meaning of a text stems from the meaning it was given by individuals, whether these are the author herself or her later readers.

[130] For instance, in the case of Locke, Bell explains that "[w]hereas parliamentary constitutionalism was central to the British appropriation of Locke (via the retrojection of the Whigs), it was religious toleration (via the retrojection of key elements of Puritanism) that did much of the ideological labour in the United States." Bell, "What Is Liberalism?" 701.

[131] One notable example is the dismissal of Grotius' arguments for the legitimate character of divisible sovereignty; see Keene, *Beyond the Anarchical Society*, 40–59. This particular move in the reception of Grotius' writings in IR had a significant impact on the discipline, as it restricted the available set of conceptual tools in a way that largely undermined the study of empires.

[132] Bevir, "On Tradition," 39. More broadly, see Bevir, *The Logic of the History of Ideas*.

reception of an author, one must address the various silences that can occur around the author's work. This can be the case when, as I have suggested, certain ideas or elements of the text appear to be central to the original work but disappear during the reception process. Under such circumstances, one is left to carefully speculate as to what might explain the surprising omission. Even more strikingly, one must consider the fact that over the course of an author's afterlife, there will be periods during which her work may recede into the background or be ignored entirely. This can occur for various reasons, including mere neglect, a controversial reputation, or a falling out of favor of certain types of argument. In light of this, a serial contextualism based on an author rather than on a concept may well be episodic, with important chronological gaps between the different receptions. There is thus an important difference between the *longue durée* entailed by an author-based serial contextualism and that entailed by a concept-based one, as concepts are more likely to appear under different iterations in the work of various writers. When studying an author and her reception, a *longue durée* approach is just as much about continuity as it is about discontinuity; the expansive chronological coverage allows one to analyze the moments during which an author's popularity surged and to trace the construction of a seemingly continuous tradition of thought around that author's name, but also to shine a light on the various moments during which the author was not in fact considered particularly remarkable. The latter, of course, is a way to problematize the existing stories of continuity and to highlight the contingency of the established canon.

1.4   Conclusion

Though a growing number of scholars have now examined the reception of certain "great thinkers" in IR, there has been little explicit methodological reflection as to what these types of studies entail. The purpose of this chapter has been to dissect the different elements involved, drawing on reception theory to highlight the most significant methodological insights to keep in mind if one is to examine processes of reception rigorously and systematically.

Bringing together various methodological insights from HPT, intellectual history more broadly, and literary studies, I have made a case for the importance of first examining an author in her initial context in order to acquire a benchmark against which the characteristics of the reception process can be measured. This is in contrast to current approaches to intellectual history that focus either on analyzing an author's thought within her original context, or on examining the reception of the author at various points in time, without explicitly link-ing the two. The dual contextualization I propose may be applied to a single work, by analyzing it closely both in the author's original con-text and in the various contexts of the author's reception. Alternatively, a study seeking to focus more heavily on the reception process may establish this benchmark by drawing on the more classically contextual (i.e., "Cambridge School," broadly speaking) secondary literature to acquire a sufficient sense of what the author's original intentions were, if these are already relatively well established. It is worth noting that while processes of reception have received quite a bit of attention in the case of the rediscovery of classical authors between the Middle Ages and the early modern period, the same cannot be said for the reception of early modern authors in the nineteenth and twentieth centuries. The proposed methodological approach will thus be particularly relevant for future studies that seek to account for these understudied, more recent processes – which are of course particularly relevant to the discipline of IR – and its precepts can be applied to authors beyond the specific field of international political thought.[133]

While the growing number of works examining the reception of various great thinkers in IR is a very encouraging development, these processes of reception still remain an under-researched area in the discipline, and this comes with some significant costs. Systematically applying the present method in IR will allow for a better understand-ing of what great thinkers actually intended to express in their original context, and of the type of interests that shaped their legacies and gave us our contemporary interpretations of their works in the discipline. This is important for three reasons. First, as I have sought to highlight through various examples about the treatment of early modern authors in IR (Grotius, Hobbes, Thucydides), the histories of these authors' receptions into the discipline underline the extent to which our domi-nant understandings of their works were produced by later individuals with agendas of their own. As long as we simply accept these narratives, we are condemned to remain bound to these past agendas and to have little understanding of what insights these "great thinkers" can pre-sumably provide us with.

Second, and more importantly still, the approach I put forward pro-vides the tools for investigating the processes of instrumentalization – or even mere unintentional misreading – of famous texts by both scholars

---

[133] One example is the recent work on the emergence of a field of scholarship around Adam Smith; see Tribe, *The Economy of the Word*, 139–70; Liu, "Rethinking the "Chicago Smith" Problem."

and practitioners and to assess the impact of this phenomenon on international relations. As I have discussed, great thinkers are often rediscovered or celebrated anew at opportune moments, when they can be put to various broadly political uses. The glorification of their ideas and the novel forms under which these authors are celebrated in their new contexts often result from a conflation of contingent elements, be they of a personal, institutional, social, or more traditionally political kind. In providing an explicit method for studying these processes, the proposed approach offers a rigorous roadmap for assessing how ideas actually come to have an impact in practice, when they are for instance used as legitimating devices for various political projects.

Third, and relatedly, this approach calls for those interested in "great thinkers" in IR to perhaps turn a more significant part of their attention to the makers of greatness: the intermediaries who select various authors for canonization and seek to use them in particular ways and for particular purposes. Whether as scholars or as practitioners, they might not be particularly well known, but in their choices of whom to glorify, they can indeed have a significant impact both on disciplinary developments and – if they are lawyers or diplomats for instance – on the conduct of international relations. When great thinkers are used as weapons to defend particular projects or ideologies over others, the agency lies with those who wield their name, and the intellectual force of a Hobbes or a Grotius comes to be heavily mediated through the minds of those who claim these authors' legacy for themselves.

This brings us back to Alberico Gentili and his place in contemporary narratives about the emergence of modern war. Like the other famous figures I mentioned, Gentili's ideas came to us via the minds of various intermediaries, men who lived in other epochs, who had concerns of their own, and who, through their own priorities and idiosyncrasies, came to shape the Italian jurist's posthumous journey. Applying the methodological precepts put forward in this chapter, the rest of the book first examines Gentili's intentions in reshaping the definition of war within his own context before proceeding to a diachronic analysis of his reception across centuries. In doing so, I provide a critical account of the contemporary narratives about Gentili and modern war, unearthing their nineteenth- and twentieth-century origins and shedding light on what their rendition of history ultimately obscured.

Part I

Gentili's *De iure belli* in Its Original Context

2   Alberico Gentili's *De iure belli*
Between Bodin and the Reason of State Tradition

Recent years have witnessed a renewed interest in Gentili's writings – particularly his works on war[1] – leading to a surge in debates over how to interpret the sixteenth-century Italian émigré's ideas. Ever since Richard Tuck identified Gentili with a humanist tradition deeply opposed to the ideas of the scholastics in *The Rights of War and Peace*, Gentili's writings on the laws of war, and especially his masterpiece on the subject, *De iure belli* (*DIB*), have been scrutinized in order to determine where exactly Gentili stood amidst the conflicting ideologies and modes of thinking of his time. In addition, various claims have been put forward to explain the specificity of *DIB*, both in the specialized literature on early modern legal debates and within broader histories of international law and of the laws of war. This new surge of interest comes amidst a long tradition of treating Gentili's *DIB* as a pivotal text in the history of international law, notably for its "secular" underpinnings and for its "modern" conception of the laws of war.[2]

The purpose of this chapter is to clarify some of these disagreements by closely examining Gentili's use of sources in *DIB*. More specifically, through this focus on sources, the chapter seeks to resituate Gentili's *DIB* beyond the immediate legal debates that have conventionally

---

[1] The most notable contributions include Kingsbury and Straumann, *The Roman Foundations of the Law of Nations* and two new translations of his works on war: Gentili, *The Wars of the Romans* and Gentili, *Il diritto di guerra (de iure belli libri III, 1598)*.

[2] This is particularly obvious in the main reference works on the history of international law (Grewe, *The Epochs of International Law*; Schmitt, *The Nomos of the Earth*; Nussbaum, *A Concise History of the Law of Nations*). Gentili's modernity in his approach to the law of war, particularly when compared with Grotius, has also been emphasized in the more specialized literature, including by Haggenmacher, who notes that *DIB* "often seems closer, if not to the 1899/1907 Hague Rules of Land Warfare, at least to the spirit of eighteenth-century warfare as reflected by authors like Moser or Vattel, than is the Grotian system, however elaborate, coherent, and profound it may be," though he does point to the inherent anachronism involved in this type of assessment. Haggenmacher, "Grotius and Gentili: A Reassessment of Thomas E. Holland's Inaugural Lecture," 168 and 173.

framed its analysis, and to place the text within the broader political thought of the period. Gentili's text, the chapter claims, is particularly noteworthy in its attempt to straddle the legal and political debates of its epoch, looking beyond legal sources and turning to various contemporary political writers in what was quite a remarkable move at the time. His attempt to bridge what has been identified within international political thought as the two broad "languages" of the period – the legal and the political – is an aspect of his work that has not been sufficiently examined, despite its potential for shedding new light on the dynamics that underpinned the development of international law at the time.[3]

This is not to say, of course, that no attention has been paid to the more political aspects of *DIB*, and to its affinity, as a legal text, with certain strands of political thought. Much of the current debate about whether *DIB* – and Gentili more broadly – should be placed within the humanist category, can in a way be understood as a disagreement over Gentili's political leanings. Yet humanism was only one facet of the political thought of the period, and its age-old premises were being increasingly overshadowed by the rise of new modes of political thinking – particularly the concept of *raison d'état* – that eventually came to characterize the emerging era. This chapter pays closer attention to the latter, emphasizing *DIB*'s surprising and generally underappreciated affinities with these ideas.[4] It builds upon existing works that highlight Bodin's momentous influence on Gentili and expands this analysis by taking stock of Gentili's equally striking reliance on writers from the emerging reason of state tradition, thus articulating Gentili's use of Bodin through his broader engagement with the burgeoning

---

[3] In presupposing a distinction between the two, I am speaking exclusively here of the debates concerning inter-sovereign relations. At the inter-sovereign level, the initial separation between, on the one hand, a "political" language centered around the concepts of "reason of state" and the "balance of power," and, on the other hand, the "legal or jurisprudential" language centered on old notions of "natural law" and "law of nations" now repackaged to conceptualize the "rights" of sovereigns and people has been outlined particularly sharply by Keene; see Keene, *International Political Thought*, 98–133. The broader claim about the existence of different "languages" of early modern international political thought is drawn from Pagden; see Pagden, *The Languages of Political Theory in Early-Modern Europe*. A convincing case can be made for why the boundaries between these areas was much more porous at the domestic level; see, for instance, Kelly, *A Short History of Western Legal Theory*, xvi. For a fascinating attempt to overcome the divide between studies of political thought and studies of international legal thought, see Warren, "Hobbes's Thucydides and the Colonial Law of Nations."

[4] It is worth noting that in his seminal work on Grotius and his forerunners, Haggenmacher mentions Bodin and his influence only briefly, he cites Machiavelli just once (to note a "curious coincidence" between his thinking and that of Grotius regarding what the sovereign is entitled to do with his or her state, n. 898), and he never mentions Guicciardini. Haggenmacher, *Grotius et la doctrine de la guerre juste*.

intellectual currents of his time. In doing so, the chapter pushes back against the "(standard) argument" that "international law arose with modern statehood as a position and a craft that was opposed to the *raison d'état.*"[5] If Gentili's famous treatise on the law of war is by any means an indicator of how international law initially developed, *raison d'état* certainly needs to be placed back at the heart of how we study the history of international law.

Having set out the context within which Gentili's use of sources can be interpreted, I outline the most striking influences on his text and explain why these are key to understanding what was particular about the Italian jurist's famous treatise on the laws of war at the time. Ultimately, I argue that one of the most important reasons why Gentili's *DIB* stood out was that it was the work of an absolutist who tried to base a theory of the laws of war on what was at the time a groundbreaking and controversial conception of political authority. In doing so, Gentili's primary concern was to reconcile Bodin's concept of "sovereignty,"[6] the teaching of the reason of state writers, and his

---

[5] Koskenniemi, "International Law and raison d'état," 303.

[6] I use the terms "sovereigns" and "sovereignty" throughout Part I to talk about the debates around political authority in which Gentili was involved. These are the terms that are found in the 1933 English translation of *DIB*, and that are commonly used to discuss Gentili's writings. However, Gentili did not use the word "sovereignty" himself. Shortly before him, in *Les six livres de la république* (1576), Bodin had explicitly used and – famously – sought to define the term "*souveraineté*" in French. In the Latin version of his text, which is the version Gentili cites, Bodin used the term "*maiestas*" (the most direct translation of which is "majesty"). Gentili, for his part, refers to "princes" and to "principality" [*principatus*] where the English translation reads "sovereigns" or "sovereignty." Discussing Gentili's ideas around "sovereignty" can easily give a false sense that what "sovereignty" meant at the time was entirely straightforward. In fact, it was a major source of debate, and claims to the contrary have long been the source of much confusion (as we will see, it is precisely these types of claims that led to the establishment of an anachronistic narrative about Gentili's "modernity" in the nineteenth century). In general, there are a number of problems associated with using the term "sovereignty" to speak of the political world prior to the nineteenth century; for various reflections on this, see Costa Lopez et al., "In the Beginning There Was No Word (for It)."

As Julia Costa Lopez helpfully explains, we assume today that sovereignty means supremacy over a territory. But this touches only a part of the issue: In order to understand how the contemporary imagination of a "sovereign" works, it is crucial also to understand that the word designates membership of a category of political actors. Thus we think of actors as "sovereign," and other actors as "not sovereign"; we think of sovereign actors as relating to each other on terms of juridical (if not material) equality, and – in many important respects – of sovereign actors as occupying a superior hierarchical position to nonsovereign actors. Costa Lopez shows that this idea of a fundamental categorical difference between sovereigns and nonsovereigns – of, in Costa Lopez's phrase, "the sovereign system" – had not yet emerged in the late medieval period, even though the concept of "supremacy over a territory" was clearly in

own commitment to ensuring law would continue to matter in regulating external relations between sovereign polities. Gentili's absolutism, that is, his commitment to a radical understanding of political authority that granted almost unlimited powers to the established ruler, has of course been a hotly debated matter, not least because Gentili's stance evolved over the course of his career, and because branding him an absolutist was a very convenient way for Catholic critics to undermine the Protestant jurist's work when it was forcefully revived in the nineteenth century.[7] *DIB*, in particular, is not as stark in its absolutist claims as some of Gentili's later writings, nor as systematically coherent in its positions, thus leaving some room for debate. I address these points explicitly in the second part of the chapter.

To this purpose, I first outline some elements of clarification for how we may understand Gentili's work and particularly his *DIB*, providing a brief biographical sketch of the Italian jurist and highlighting some of the major debates concerning his writings. Second, I point to the well-established influence of Bodin on Gentili, particularly in terms of his absolutist conception of sovereignty, but conclude that while Gentili fully embraced Bodin's absolutist position, he had to look elsewhere in order to adapt Bodin's ideas to relations between early modern sovereigns. Third, I examine the reason of state writers to which Gentili turned in attempting to develop a framework for inter-sovereign relations. Fourth and finally, I argue that the main challenge Gentili faced was adapting the ideas of these writers, who saw little use for law in facilitating and stabilizing external relations between early modern sovereigns, to his commitment to placing law at the center of this endeavor. In other words, Gentili took what was then the fairly counterintuitive

---

place at the time. The late medieval concept of *merum imperium* is a case in point. A ruler could hold *merum imperium* – defined at the time as "supreme authority" (*suprema potestas*) over a territory – and still be considered hierarchically inferior to other rulers (500–01). By the time we get to Bodin – and shortly thereafter, to Gentili – the political imagination of the "sovereign system" is still in the making, and much of the European continent is continuing to operate based on jurisdictional arrangements much more fluid than the sovereign/not sovereign binary. The present chapter thus seeks to put forward some elements of analysis regarding Gentili's approach to the laws of war in the context of his participation in debates about political authority, but to fully do justice to the issue, one would need to delve deeper into his use of concepts such as *principatus* within the linguistic context of his time.

[7] See, for instance, Rolin-Jaequemyns, "Quelques mots sur les hommages projetés à la mémoire de Grotius et d'Albéric Gentil, et sur les dernières publications y relatives," 694. In fact, it is worth noting that the term "absolutism" itself only emerged as an abstract notion in the nineteenth century; Gentili's contemporaries would thus not have described his positioning as such. Throughout this chapter, I follow the scholarly convention of using the term "absolutism" in the context of the sixteenth century as an analytical category, rather than an anachronistically applied historical one.

step of trying to incorporate the increasingly popular concepts of *raison d'état* and balance of power into a legal framework for inter-sovereign relations.

Before I begin, a bibliographical note: *De iure belli libri tres* was first published in 1598, as a revised and expanded version of Gentili's earlier lectures *De iure belli commentationes tres* (1588/89). A few reeditions then appeared, in 1604, 1612, 1770, and in 1877 during the nineteenth-century revival of Gentili's work. Finally, in 1933 the treatise was reedited in what is now the most commonly used edition, which contains both a photographic reproduction of the 1612 edition and an English translation of the original Latin. In the analysis that follows, I have referred to this 1933 edition, which allows one to consult the 1612 text in parallel with its English translation. Importantly, the marginalia in the 1933 English translation mirror exactly those of the 1612 Latin original, and the marginalia of the 1612 version are identical to those of the original 1598 edition.[8]

2.1 Reading Gentili's *De iure belli*: Some Elements of Clarification

While Gentili's life is not as widely known as that of Grotius, it was also a rather adventurous journey. Unlike Grotius, Gentili did not pull off anything quite as spectacular as escaping from prison hidden in a chest of books. Yet he was born a Protestant in Catholic Italy, had to flee alongside his family, and eventually ended up in England, where his background in Roman and civil law – rather than English common law – made him an unusual intellectual creature. There he became a prominent figure as Regius Professor at Oxford University, the first non-English person to be granted this prestigious position. The full details of his biography are available elsewhere,[9] but I will briefly outline the main elements of his life and works here before delving into some of the disagreements about how to interpret his writings.

Gentili was born in 1552 in a noble family in San Ginesio, a small but lively town in what is now Italy's province of Macerata in the Marche region. The eldest of seven children, he attended the University of

---

[8] I have verified this by comparing the 1612 photographic reproduction to John Selden's copy of the 1598 original, which is available at the Bodleian Library under the filing number 8°G.6.Jur.Seld. On the often underestimated evolution of marginalia in posthumous editions of canonical treaties, see Wallenius, "The Case for a History of Global Legal Practices."

[9] The most up-to-date account, which I have drawn on for this summary, is Vadi, *War and Peace*, 41–90.

Perugia, which had its own school of jurisprudence – a bastion of the Italian style of studying law, the *mos italicus*, to which I will return – and was a reputable place of learning, attracting students from all over Europe. Gentili received his doctoral degree in civil law (*in iure caesareo*) in 1572 and went on to become a judge (*praetor*) in Ascoli before taking up advocacy work back in San Ginesio, where he revised part of the municipal statute between 1574 and 1578.

During those early years, San Ginesio, and the Gentili family in particular, were strongly affected by the Inquisition. San Ginesio was reputed to be a haven for Protestants (*asylum lutheranorum*), and in 1567, Gentili's father and uncle were arrested. They remained in jail for three years, were subjected to lengthy interrogations, and were released only upon formally renouncing their faith and reconciling with the Church. Upon returning to San Ginesio, however, Gentili's father continued to maintain his Protestant faith, and it soon became unsustainable for him to remain in the Papal States. Taking his two most gifted sons – Alberico and Scipione – with him, he fled. They first went north to Padua, and then, in the autumn of 1579, they reached Laibach (Ljubljana), the capital of the Duchy of Carniola under Habsburg rule. This is where Matteo settled down, eventually becoming the chief physician of the duchy. Meanwhile, the Inquisition excommunicated all three of them, confiscating their belongings and requiring the erasure of their records in San Ginesio (*damnatio memoriae*).

Alberico and Scipione continued their journey in search of places more suitable for their careers; Alberico eventually made his way to England, parting with Scipione who remained in continental Europe and became one of the leading jurists of his time, his fame in fact probably supplanting Alberico's.[10] After a first few challenging months in London in 1580, Alberico became part of a small network of Italian Protestants and was introduced to Giovanni Battista Castiglione (1516–1598), the Italian tutor of Queen Elizabeth I, via letters of reference from his father. Castiglione in turn introduced Gentili to a number of influential figures, including Robert Dudley (1532–1588), Earl of Leicester, Chancellor of the University of Oxford, great patron of letters, and favorite of Elizabeth I from her accession until his death. Leicester became Gentili's mentor, facilitating his admission to Oxford in 1581 and his promotion to the Regius Chair of Civil Law in 1587 in spite of a strong opposition from a group of Puritans in Oxford led

---

[10] Pallant, "Scipione Gentili," 91. Pope Clemens VIII even offered him a chair in Rome, an honor Scipione declined since he would have had to abjure and feared that the Inquisition would take action against him nonetheless. Vadi, *War and Peace*, 69.

by the theologian John Rainolds. Gentili would then hold the position until his death in 1608.

While at Oxford, Gentili published about thirty works on a broad range of topics. Importantly, his work shifted gradually from dry, theoretical, and mostly domestic concerns toward broader practical matters of foreign policy, with his social network bringing him closer to centers of power that were keen to consult him on pressing politico-legal issues. Three of these works are particularly well known: *De legationibus* (1585, On Embassies), *De iure belli* (1598, On the Law of War), and *Hispanicae advocationis* or the *Hispanica advocatio* (1613, a posthumous compilation of the legal writings he produced as an advocate for Spain).[11] Importantly, in terms of the contexts in which these different works were produced, Gentili moved to London in 1590 to dedicate an increasing proportion of his time to his legal practice, having delegated his lectures in Oxford to a deputy. Ten years later, in 1600, he was admitted to Gray's Inn, which was at the time the most prominent professional law association in England.

While Gentili retained the Regius Chair until his death, his time in England can thus be divided roughly into a scholarly stretch at Oxford until 1590 and a more practice-oriented period after that date. As such, *De legationibus* was written in his scholarly period, while the *Hispanica advocatio* squarely reflects his work as a practicing lawyer. His single most famous text, *De iure belli*, is an interesting hybrid. The text started off as three "commentaries" on the laws of war, which were essentially published versions of three lectures he had given in Oxford over the course of 1588 and 1589, shortly after the defeat of the Spanish Armada. These lectures sought to clarify some of the legal issues at the heart of the Anglo-Spanish War (1585–1604) that had yet to be properly addressed. It was then over the following decade, while practicing law in London, that Gentili extensively revised these lectures and brought them together as a single volume, *DIB*.

I will be returning to the substance of both *DIB* and the *Hispanica advocatio* in some detail later. *De legationibus*, for its part, is an expanded version of the advice he gave on the Mendoza case upon being consulted by the government in 1584. Don Bernardino de Mendoza (1540–1604), Ambassador of the King of Spain to the Queen of England, had been discovered to be part of a conspiracy to assassinate the Queen, and the government was unsure as to what legal action would be most

---

[11] The formal title of the edited papers is *Hispanicae advocationis libri duo*, but in the literature it is more common to refer to it in the singular as the *Hispanica advocatio* (often *Hispanica Advocatio*) or, occasionally, the *Advocatio hispanica*.

appropriate against him. Execution was the most likely punishment on the table, and the Privy Council's preferred option. Instead, Gentili recommended his expulsion from the country, and it is his advice the government followed. The treaty is now remembered as an important contribution to the development of diplomatic law, including the concept of diplomatic immunity.

For all the celebrations of Gentili as a great founder of international law, there is a certain amount of confusion and mystery that shrouds his work. Often his positions across his different publications seem inconsistent, making it difficult to understand where he stood and how exactly his different writings relate to each other. Three main reasons for this confusion stand out: first, as my brief biographical sketch conveys, while Gentili spent his first Oxonian decade (1581–1590) teaching and writing the treatises that established him as a leading jurist of his day,[12] the later part of his career (1590–1608) was more fully dedicated to practice and, consequently, he wrote numerous opinions that depended primarily on his clients' interests and thus often contradicted each other. Second, Gentili evolved significantly during his career, from a staunch anti-humanist Bartolist following his training in Perugia to what Randall Lesaffer has termed a "moderate humanist" over the course of his time in England, embracing "a *via media* between Bartolism and humanism."[13] Third, and relatedly, the term "humanism" has come to encompass a number of meanings, and in the longstanding debate over whether or not Gentili was indeed a humanist, it is not always clear whether the humanism in question is of a civic, rhetorical, or legal kind. In this section, I will thus outline four crucial elements for situating the work of Gentili – specifically his *DIB* – and navigating this somewhat muddled contextual landscape.

First of all, Gentili wrote at a time of nothing short of a methodological revolution in international law and history,[14] pitting the traditional ideas of Bartolists (the "*mos italicus*") against the sensational innovations

---

[12] In the words of K. R. Simmonds, "there can be little doubt that at his death in 1608 much of his reputation as a scholar and publicist rested upon the work of his earlier career in Oxford." Simmonds, "The Gentili Manuscripts," 546.

[13] Lesaffer, "Alberico Gentili's ius post bellum and Early Modern Peace Treaties," 216; Simmonds, "The Gentili Manuscripts," 546–49. For a brief overviews of this point, see Wijffels, "From Perugia to Oxford," 59–61. For longer analyses, see Minnucci, *Alberico Gentili tra mos italicus e mos gallicus*; Minnucci, "Per una rilettura del metodo gentiliano."

[14] Franklin, *Jean Bodin and the Sixteenth-Century Revolution in the Methodology of Law and History*.

of the initially Toulouse-based legal humanists (the *"mos gallicus"*),[15] and his position within that debate evolved significantly throughout his career. The debate was essentially one over how best to understand, interpret, and use Roman law, the vast majority of which was compiled in what became known as the *Corpus iuris civilis*. Throughout the Middle Ages, the assumption of the Bartolists *(mos italicus)* had been that the *Corpus iuris* was a perfect system of jurisprudence, and the resulting approach had been to focus on exegesis of the Roman law and to creatively adapt Roman concepts to the medieval world. The scholastic method, on which this was based, entailed virtually pure logical analysis with very little historical perspective. The French legal humanists *(mos gallicus)* started out seeking to improve Roman jurisprudence by restoring its original meaning, which sometimes had been lost through misinterpretation, erroneous translations, or copying errors. Their initial endeavor, however, developed into a full-blown critique of Roman law when they realized that their attempt to discover the unifying logical underpinnings of the *Corpus iuris* was bound to fail because these were in fact, they concluded, nonexistent. Roman law, they explained, was riddled with inconsistencies and logical incoherence, and, perhaps even more importantly, it was based on concepts that were developed in the particular historical context of Rome and that were sometimes completely at odds with the realities of their own world.

As a result, these legal humanists advocated taking a much more critical stance toward Roman law and particularly toward the writings of great medieval authorities on the matter (such as Bartolus and Baldus), as well as looking beyond Roman law to create a better system of jurisprudence. This led to a renewed focus on domestic legal custom, but even more importantly, it led to a crucial turn toward the use of "universal history" in the reconstruction of a juristic science.[16] In other words, legal humanists – and particularly Jean Bodin on this specific matter – hoped to remedy the deficiencies in the Roman legal system by turning to universal history. Bodin puts it most clearly himself in *République*: the sole way to build a truly universal juristic science, he explained, was to compare "all the laws of all, or the most famous,

---

[15] Though as Haggenmacher notes, the relationship of the *mos gallicus* to the *mos italicus* should be characterized as an effort to broaden and transform rather than as a move toward clear rupture and a complete rejection of tradition. In his writings on war, Alciatus, one of the most famous proponents of the *mos gallicus*, is clearly indebted to both the humanists and the Bartolists. Haggenmacher, *Grotius et la doctrine de la guerre juste*, 47–48.

[16] Franklin, *Jean Bodin and the Sixteenth-Century Revolution in the Methodology of Law and History*.

states, and to select the best variety."[17] The legal humanists thus turned their attention away from the medieval commentators and toward a vast web of sources, with a particular emphasis on the work of historians.

Gentili was trained at Perugia as a Bartolist of the purest kind, and when he first arrived in Oxford, his first publication was a famous attack on legal humanism, *De iuris interpretibus* (1582), which categorically condemned the arguments of the great three – Budaeus, Alciatus, Zasius – and their followers.[18] In the following two years, he published another attack on legal humanism: his polemical collection of letters and lectures entitled *Lectionum et epistolarum quae ad ius civile pertinent* (1583–84).[19] However, by the time he wrote the first draft of *DIB* for his 1588/89 lectures on the laws of war, he had gradually moved away from this complete rejection of the *mos gallicus* and, while he remained faithful to his Bartolist training, he clearly embraced many of the tropes of legal humanism, most notably in his use of sources.[20] Indeed, in addition to citing the *Corpus iuris civilis* and the numerous commentaries on it – particularly those of Baldus – Gentili relies extensively on classical philosophers and rhetoricians (especially Cicero), classical historians (especially Livy), classical poets (especially Virgil),[21] and contemporary historians (such as Paolo Giovio and Paolo Emilio). More tellingly still, he cites Alciatus, one of the foremost legal humanists, whom he calls a "great jurist,"[22] 231 times in *DIB*, second only to the main Bartolist authority, Baldus, whom he cites 315 times, and the *Corpus iuris* itself, which he cites 465 times.[23] Furthermore, while Gentili does regularly cite the Bible (with an overwhelming preference for the Old Testament), it is, with 193 citations, an important source but by no means as central as in the works of his more traditional

---

[17] Bodin, *On Sovereignty*, xvi.

[18] For a summary and analysis of *De iuris interpretibus,* see Binns, *Intellectual Culture in Elizabethan and Jacobean England*, 338–46.

[19] Gentili, *lectionum & epistolarum quæ ad ius civile pertinent.*

[20] A helpful summary of the different ways in which the influence of humanism can be felt in Gentili's work can be found in Lesaffer, "Alberico Gentili's ius post bellum and Early Modern Peace Treaties," 218. This shift toward combining traditional and modern layers of legal expertise should be understood as part of the broader effort by lawyers to maintain their position at the heart of the political decision-making process; see Wijffels, "Antiqui et recentiores."

[21] For a detailed discussion of Gentili's reliance on poetry, see Warren, "Gentili, the Poets, and the Laws of War."

[22] Ibid., 149. Gentili also calls him "the wise Alciati" (Gentili, *De iure belli*, Book I, §17.).

[23] There is also clear evidence that over his time at Oxford he became friends with Hugo Donellus and François Hotman (both dedicated supporters of Cujas), the latter of whom he cites twenty-five times. In fact, Gentili cites Cujas himself thirty times in *DIB*. On the presence of evidence in the Bodleian manuscripts of Gentili's friendship with Donellus and Hotman, see Simmonds, "The Gentili Manuscripts," 548.

predecessors. Similarly, he only cites Church Fathers (Tertullian, St. Ambrose, St. Jerome, St. Bernard) between twenty and thirty times each, a rather low ratio compared with the wealth of other sources that are cited more frequently. Thus, while Gentili ultimately never fully adopted the skepticism of the *mos gallicus* toward the *Corpus iuris civilis* and its medieval interpreters, the influence of legal humanism can be felt strongly in *DIB* and clearly had a significant impact on the way Gentili developed his positions. As such, the Gentili of the late 1580s and the 1590s is best understood as a "moderate humanist" in the legal sense, with one foot still squarely within the Bartolist tradition and the other increasingly anchored within the *mos gallicus* and the challenges raised by legal humanism.

Second, while a number of scholars have questioned the idea of a definite cleavage between Gentili and the School of Salamanca (particularly Vitoria),[24] it is also far from clear that Gentili's main interlocutors in *DIB* are in fact the theologians. The now conventional emphasis on the humanist/scholastic distinction presupposes that if, as Richard Tuck and Diego Panizza argue, Gentili was indeed a humanist, his main opponents and interlocutors were the theologians of the Second Scholastic, and particularly those of the School of Salamanca.[25] However, the diversity within forms of humanism suggests that different debates may have been at stake, and that Gentili's "humanist" affinities did not necessarily make engaging the Salamancans his primary interest. In terms of citations, Gentili only cites Covarruvius[26] (or Covarrubias, 1539–1613) twenty-two times, Vitoria seven times, and Soto (1494–1560) four times (there is no mention of Molina, 1535–1600). By contrast, he cites political

---

[24] In the words of Blane and Kingsbury, "[a]ll three were Christian believers who were engaged in theological debates; Vitoria was a professional theologian influenced by jurists; Gentili and Grotius were theologically-informed jurists." Blane and Kingsbury, "Punishment and the ius post bellum," 246–47. For an insightful account of the similarities between Gentili and the Salamancans on the subject of the treatment of the Ottomans, see Malcolm, "Alberico Gentili and the Ottomans." More broadly, Lesaffer and Pagden question Tuck's classic divide between humanists (which in Tuck's account, supported by Diego Panizza, include Gentili) and scholastics, with Padgen arguing that "the more one examines the humanist/scholastic or humanist/theologian distinction, the more fuzzy it becomes." Pagden, "Gentili, Vitoria, and the Fabrication of a 'Natural Law of Nations'," 345. See also Lesaffer, "The Classical Law of Nations (1500–1800)," 424–30.

[25] Tuck, *The Rights of War and Peace*; Panizza, "Alberico Gentili's De Iure Belli: The Humanist Foundations of a Project of International Order"; Panizza, "Political Theory and Jurisprudence in Gentili's De Iure Belli: The Great Debate between 'Theological' and 'Humanist' Perspectives from Vitoria to Grotius."

[26] Covarrubias was a canon lawyer rather than a theologian, but he was deeply influenced by the School of Salamanca.

writers – who had little interest in arguing with the theologians – such as the Italian historian and statesman Francesco Guicciardini (1483–1540) and the French jurist and political philosopher Jean Bodin sixty-three and thirty-nine times respectively. In fact, the influence of Bodin on Gentili and the considerable weight Gentili gave to Bodin and his arguments in *DIB* are well documented,[27] and I will return to this important point later in the chapter. For now, this mainly hints toward the fact that Gentili's main motivation in writing *DIB* may not have been to undermine the arguments of the theologians – who were nonetheless his political rivals – as much as to address the ideas of the French *politiques* and the Italian *ragion di stato* writers, who were stirring up considerable debates at the time.

As this discussion suggests, the methodological debates that surrounded Gentili make his use of citations deeply revealing. Summing up and expanding on this analysis, Figure 2.1 gives an overview of the main sources cited by Gentili in DIB, dividing them into broad categories based on their nature. It is worth noting that unlike Grotius, Gentili does not appear to follow a systematic pattern in citing different sources. For instance, while Grotius tends to cite religious authorities on each point, before moving on to nonreligious ones – surely an effective way to satisfy different audiences – Gentili's citations simply seem to follow the trajectory of his argument, with what he considers the most relevant authors cited in support of particular points, regardless of their affiliation. Ultimately, although this quantitative collection of data presents certain limits in terms of establishing how Gentili actually engaged with the different sources he invokes, Figure 2.1 provides an overview of Gentili's universe of citations and constitutes a first set of insights for assessing the impact of various types of sources on Gentili's thought in *DIB*. I provide a more in-depth analysis of his use of certain key sources, particularly Bodin and Guicciardini, later in the chapter.[28]

What becomes clear from Figure 2.1 and Table 2.1 is that in addition to the sources one would expect to find in the writings of a civil lawyer of this period, educated within the Bartolist tradition and influenced by both rhetorical and legal humanists – namely, the *Corpus iuris* and various commentaries on it from both legal traditions (Baldus,

---

[27] Quaglioni, "The Italian 'Readers' of Bodin"; Quaglioni, "Pour une histoire du droit de guerre au début de l'âge moderne"; Schröder, "Vitoria, Gentili, Bodin"; Wijffels, "From Perugia to Oxford."

[28] This type of two-tier quantitative/qualitative approach is not entirely uncommon; see, for example, Haggenmacher, "Grotius and Gentili," 146–47.

Gentili's main sources

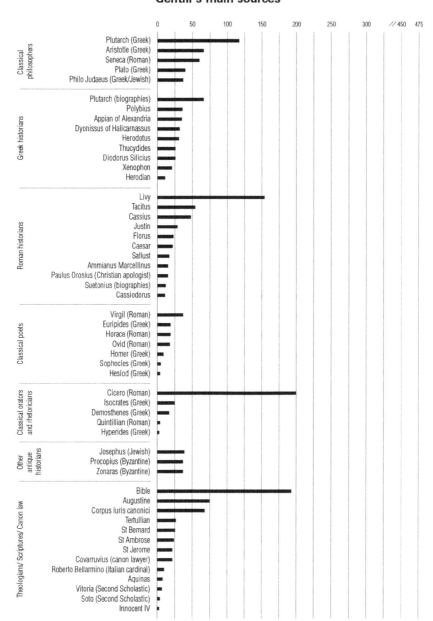

Figure 2.1 Gentili's main sources, by type

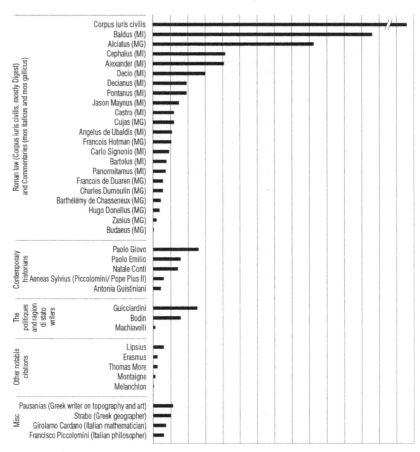

Figure 2.1 *(cont.)*

Alciatus, etc.), scriptural sources (Bible, Church Fathers, canon law, theologians), classical philosophers and rhetoricians (Cicero, Plutarch, Aristotle, etc.) – one key aspect of Gentili's universe of citations stands out as particularly unusual. This is his considerable reliance on historians from all ages, and most notably – an uncommon feat at the time amongst jurists – on contemporary historians. Indeed, Gentili relies significantly on classical historians (Livy, Plutarch's biographies, Tacitus, Cassius, etc.) and on other antique historians, especially Jewish and Byzantine ones (Josephus, Procopius, Zonaras), but also on a range of modern historians, particularly historians of Italy, most importantly Paolo Giovo, Francesco Guicciardini, and Paolo Emilio. Additionally, Bodin, who had died just two years before the publication of *DIB*, is one

Table 2.1 *Gentili's main sources, by overall citation ranking*

Rank	Source	Number of citations
1	Corpus iuris civilis	465
2	Baldus	315
3	Alciatus	231
4	Cicero	200
5	Bible	193
6	Livy	154
7	Plutarch	117
8	Cephalus	104
9	Alexander	102
10	Augustine	75
11	Decio	75
12	Corpus iuris canonici	68
13	Aristotle	66
14	Plutarch (biographies)	66
15	Paolo Giovo	65
16	Guicciardini	63
17	Seneca	60
18	Tacitus	54
19	Cassius	48
20	Decianus	48
21	Pontanus	48
22	Plato	40
23	Josephus	39
24	Paolo Emilio	39
25	Bodin	39
26	Philo Judaeus	37
27	Virgil	37
28	Procopius	37
29	Zonaras	37
30	Jason Maynus	37

of Gentili's contemporaries who gets the most citations, and as I will explain at greater length in Section 2.2, he is in fact discussed extensively throughout the text and has been established as a major influence on *DIB* through an analysis of Gentili's manuscripts. Moreover, in light of the present discussion on the use of different types of sources, it is worth mentioning that there is indeed a close connection between Gentili's methodological turn to history and his heavy reliance on his French contemporary, a point to which I will return later.

Third, although *DIB* was published in full in 1598, the fact that Gentili wrote most of its content at the end of his scholarly period suggests that the positions he defends within *DIB* stem from a genuine attempt at developing a coherent legal approach rather than the sort of interest-based positions found in works such as the *Hispanica advocatio*, the collection of opinions he wrote while controversially defending the Spanish Crown in the final part of his career. His other main work on war, *De armis romanis* (*DAR*), although the second part was only published in 1599 (after his scholarly period), was also written around the same time, with the first part published in 1590 and the full draft ready by 1593. While the interpretation of this second work, and particularly its relationship to *DIB*, is notoriously arduous, it is clear that Gentili spent a significant amount of his scholarly period reflecting on the laws of war from an academic standpoint, prior to dedicating himself to practice and writing on some of these matters (particularly piracy and privateering) as an advocate in admiralty courts. One should thus appreciate the qualitative difference between what Gentili was attempting to do in writing *DIB* (and *DAR*) and in later defending what have been pointed out as contradictory positions within the context of his career as a lawyer. Importantly, this does not, however, mean that one should discount all of Gentili's later writings as unreliable or written for exclusively instrumental purposes. Gentili did still write some pieces as a scholar rather than as a practitioner (such as his *Regales disputationes tres* of 1605), and his work as a lawyer still offers important insights into his thinking. The main point is that while his arguments as an advocate on, most notably, piracy and privateering sometimes contradict each other (depending on who his client is) and are sometimes at odds with his earlier claims in *DIB*, these inconsistencies are not necessarily surprising and should be understood in the context of his dual professional identity.

Finally, one of the most important characteristics of Gentili to keep in mind in analyzing *DIB* is that he was a Roman law expert, or what the English called a "Civilian." This feature followed from his training in Italy and was further accentuated when he took up the position of Regius Professor of Civil Law at the University of Oxford in 1587. "International"[29] jurists were logically Roman law experts, as Roman law provided numerous rules for dealing with international or proto-international issues within the Roman Empire, whereas common law was based on the assumption that it applied solely within a domestic context, there being no higher authorities than the domestic ones. Yet being a civilian in a common law country was a rather peculiar situation,

---

[29] Throughout the chapter, I use the term "international" as a shorthand to speak of the realm pertaining to relations between independent sovereign polities. At the time, these relations were obviously "inter-sovereign" rather than "international" in the modern sense, and Gentili had no concept of "the international" per se.

and in fact the Regius Chair had only been founded in the 1540s, along with a similar one at Cambridge. In a common law system, Roman law experts were only relevant within two specific types of courts that applied Roman-based civil law, namely ecclesiastical courts and admiralty courts. The latter in particular were a very important space for jurists such as Gentili, as they dealt directly with international issues, particularly with issues of prize and booty at the heart of which stood perennial questions about how to distinguish pirates from privateers. For all other matters, the common law ruled, and there was a deep cleavage between common lawyers and their civilian rivals, who were indeed deeply unpopular. In fact, sometime in the late fifteenth or early sixteenth century, civil lawyers had come to form a separate society of their own, called the Doctors' Commons or College of Civilians, where its members could live, work, consult the library, and follow proceedings of the civil law courts. Gentili thus held a peculiar position as Oxford's Regius Professor of Civil Law, and his work could easily have generated suspicion from his contemporaries working within the common law tradition, as we will see later with regard to his support of James I. Importantly, it may also go some way in explaining why Gentili's work lost much of its clout after his death only to be properly revived two and a half centuries later.

Ultimately, Gentili's near-veneration of Roman law was uncommon even for a civilian. His great admiration for Rome led him not only to give pride of place to Roman law in DIB, but in fact to equate Roman law with the *ius gentium*, and to construct the latter as the content of natural law itself.[30] For Gentili, Roman law constituted the content of both the *ius gentium* and the *ius naturale*, making the *ius gentium* not only universal but also immutable. Roman law, in the eyes of Gentili, constituted the finest and final achievement of mankind and provided an eternal legal framework for all. This position was notably different from that of the Romans themselves (and from that of his later rival, Grotius).[31] Indeed, the Romans considered the *ius gentium* to be the law regulating the relationships between Romans and non-Romans; they did not construe it as a universal law in the same way as the early modern jurists did, and especially not as Gentili did. In addition to being a Roman law expert, Gentili was thus quite unusual in his conception of Roman law, and it is essential to keep in mind the centrality Gentili gave it in his system of law in order to understand the particularity of *DIB*. Most importantly, Roman law generally presupposes an emperor, a supreme authority whose doings

---

[30] Pagden, "Gentili, Vitoria, and the Fabrication of a 'Natural Law of Nations'."

[31] Though it would later be taken up by Giambattista Vico with his concept of the "natural law of nations."

nobody can judge.[32] This underpinned what is perhaps Gentili's most crucial characteristic, to which I next turn: his absolutism.

2.2   Conceptualizing Sovereignty: The Influence of Bodin

Gentili expressed his strikingly strong absolutism most famously in 1605, in the first disputation of his *Regales disputationes tres*, entitled *De potestate regis absoluta* and dedicated to the new Stuart King, James I. In fact, Gentili's three disputations of 1605 have sometimes been called "the most absolutistic piece of writing that appeared in England in the early seventeenth century,"[33] and Gentili himself "the theoretical founder of absolutism in England."[34] Gentili's absolutism made him stand out as a jurist (particularly in England) and is, I will argue, a fundamental element to understand the specificity of his approach to the laws of war. Gentili's absolutism stemmed from a combination of his admiration of Roman law with the profound influence that Bodin's theory of sovereignty had on him. Yet Bodin's theory raised as many problems for Gentili as it provided solutions, and Gentili had to search elsewhere to address these issues. In this section, I give an overview of the importance of Bodin's ideas for Gentili before turning, in the final section of the chapter, to the writers he drew from in constructing a system of laws geared toward the interaction of independent sovereign polities.

While the French Bodin was not an absolutist from the start,[35] as is apparent in his *Methodus* of 1566 (which Gentili does not cite in *DIB*), by the time he wrote the *Six livres de la République* in 1576

---

[32] Although it is worth noting that the Roman tradition also had a republican phase, and that medieval glossators and commentators had managed to interpret Roman law as to justify a complex web of overlapping sovereignties that was far removed from any sort of absolutist system.

[33] Levack, "Law and Ideology," 229. Though for a more ambiguous interpretation, see Sharp, "Alberico Gentili's Obscure Resurrection as a Royalist in 1644."

[34] Levack, *The Civil Lawyers in England, 1603–1641*, 98. In making this argument, Levack is following Gesina Van der Molen, *Alberico Gentili and the Development of International Law*, 227–30.

[35] Jean Bodin was a French jurist who wrote in the context of a tentatively constitutionalist France, operating based on a notion of limited supremacy. Two of his major works (the third being the later *De la démonomanie des sorciers*, which addresses a different set of questions), the *Methodus* of 1566 and the *République* of 1576, are conventionally seen as marking a remarkable shift in his thinking, with the *République* shedding the constitutionalist orientation of the *Methodus* and systematically developing a theory of royal absolutism. This shift is commonly associated with the St. Bartholomew Day Massacre of 1572, which dramatically polarized French opinion and led Bodin, frightened by the rise of a revolutionary movement based on theories of legitimate resistance, to develop his unprecedented positions.

("*République*"), he had – almost unintentionally – come to adopt the absolutist position he would remain famous for.[36] That being said, it is well established that what Gentili took away from Bodin's work was an uncompromising embrace of the staunchest absolutism. His position – and the influence of Bodin on this point – is at its clearest in his aforementioned 1605 tract on the *Absolute Power of the King* (*De potestate regis absoluta*), in which Gentili defends the absolutist theory that the Stuart King James I – who was likely to have been influenced by Bodin himself[37] – had put forward in 1598, shortly before his accession to the throne (1603), in *The Trew Law of Free Monarchies*.[38] In order to support his position, Gentili cites Bodin even more frequently than Baldus (or Bartolus) as the most relevant authority on the matter of sovereignty,[39] and he combines Bodin's novel theory[40] with the Roman law principles of *Princeps legibus solutus est* ("the sovereign is not bound by the laws") and *Quod Principi placuit, legis habet vigorem* ("what pleases the prince has the strength of law").[41] Gentili makes his reliance on Roman law explicit: "The civil law says that the *princeps* is unbound by the laws and that law is whatever pleases the *princeps*. This law is not foreign, but Roman: It is indeed the most excellent [*praestantissima*] among the laws of men."[42] Importantly, Gentili argued that these Roman law principles were directly applicable to the situation in England, and specifically, in an influential move within the English context, "that 'absolute' authority was not an exclusively Roman notion, restricted only to those

[36] Franklin, *Jean Bodin and the Rise of Absolutist Theory*, 102. Although there is now an ongoing debate about the extent to which Bodin actually had an absolutist conception of sovereignty at all, even in the *République*. For a brief overview of the literature, see Lee, *Popular Sovereignty in Early Modern Constitutional Thought*, 161, n. 12. Lee himself is quite radical in his approach and considers that Franklin erred in his interpretation, confusing popular sovereignty with popular resistance, and he seeks to "dismantle the interpretive orthodoxy that Bodin was fundamentally hostile to popular sovereignty." On the contrary, Lee claims, "Bodin deserves to be properly recognized as perhaps the most important systematic early modern theorist of popular sovereignty" and a profound influence on Locke, Rousseau, and Sieyès (Lee, *Popular Sovereignty in Early Modern Constitutional Thought*, 163.) See also his forthcoming work, *The Right of Sovereignty*.

[37] Quaglioni, "The Italian 'Readers' of Bodin," 373.

[38] Koskenniemi, "International Law and raison d'état," 303. On Gentili's defense of absolutist principles, see also Wijffels, "Assolutismo politico e diritto di resistenza."

[39] Schröder, "Vitoria, Gentili, Bodin," 170.

[40] Obviously, Bodin's theory did not materialize out of thin air. The French writer drew heavily on various preexisting arguments for his conception of sovereignty, and notably on canonist thought. I will discuss canonist ideas in greater detail in the following chapter.

[41] Koskenniemi, "International Law and raison d'état," 303.

[42] Gentili, *Regales disputationes tres*, 9. Translation from Lee, *Popular Sovereignty in Early Modern Constitutional Thought*, 278.

nations recognizing the civil law, but a universal one to be found in all independent states, including even in England."[43]

As I have noted earlier based on Figure 2.1 and Table 2.1, the influence of Bodin is also very deeply felt in *DIB*. While it is true that Bodin is not necessarily at the very top of the citation chart, he stands out for being extensively discussed in the text itself whenever he is mentioned. As Diego Quaglioni, drawing heavily on the earlier work of Alain Wijffels,[44] explains, "the references to the *République* form the framework of Gentili's *DIB*, from the first to the last page of the long treatise" and "Gentili draws on Bodin's masterpiece not only for his absolutistic scheme of supreme power, but also for many arguments and formulae already proposed by the French jurist."[45] Bodin's doctrine, Quaglioni continues, "seems to be the first and major source of Gentili's *DIB*."[46] This may be somewhat of an overstatement; indeed, in addition to the fact that there are numerous authors cited many more times than Bodin in *DIB*, Peter Schröder reminds us that given the abundance of sources cited by Gentili, and his reliance – shared by his contemporaries, particularly the humanists – on a complex "web of authors," it is somewhat risky to single out one author as the leading authority in the context of *DIB*, including Bodin himself on the discussion of sovereignty.[47] That being said, and while Gentili does not always agree with Bodin when he cites him, the extent to which sections of *DIB* read as direct discussions of Bodin's arguments is indeed striking.

Quaglioni provides numerous examples of Gentili's discussion of Bodin in the text of *De iure belli*, along with a helpful analysis of what argument Gentili is making in each case, whether he is in agreement with Bodin or demarcating himself from him. I will not repeat this discussion here, but to give an idea of the breadth of topics on which Gentili cites Bodin – either approvingly or disapprovingly as a springboard for his own argument – these include the relationship with exiles, war in the defense of religion, the theory of self-preservation, preventive self-defense, defensive treaties, sureties given to enemies, hostages,

43   Lee, *Popular Sovereignty in Early Modern Constitutional Thought*, 278–79. Straumann, "The Corpus iuris as a Source of Law between Sovereigns in Alberico Gentili's Thought."
44   Wijffels, "From Perugia to Oxford."
45   Quaglioni, "The Italian 'Readers' of Bodin," 376. See also Quaglioni, "Pour une histoire du droit de guerre au début de l'âge moderne," 38. "Le Bodin de la *République* est le point de départ et la principale référence de la doctrine gentilienne."
46   Quaglioni, "The Italian 'Readers' of Bodin," 378.
47   Schröder, "Vitoria, Gentili, Bodin: Sovereignty and the Law of Nations," 170.

expenses, damages from war, and slavery.[48] In other words, through-out *DIB*, Gentili is extensively engaging with Bodin (*République*, over-whelmingly). He is not merely citing him in passing as a source of support or acknowledging him equally fleetingly as the exponent of a conflicting view, but actively dissecting Bodin's arguments and build-ing up his own vis-à-vis those of the famous French jurist.

In addition, Bodin is cited at key moments in *DIB* – including within the first two pages of Gentili's treatise – which does support the idea that Gentili was drawing on Bodin in framing his arguments. And indeed, Alain Wijffels notes that Gentili's manuscripts, held in the Bodleian's D'Orville collection, make clear that he read the *République* cover to cover while he was carrying out the preparatory work for *DIB*.[49] Gentili's twenty pages of annotations on the *République* closely follow the order of the six books, and the most often encountered annotation in the margins – the capital letter "B" – is believed to stand for "*bellum*" and thus to indicate the passages used in *DIB*.[50] Thus it is clear at the very least that Gentili had read the *République* very attentively, and that he profoundly admired Bodin's work, even if on certain points, such as the question of slavery, he occasionally did find Bodin "exceedingly silly."[51] All in all, what comes across from Gentili's engagement with Bodin in *DIB* is, on the one hand, a constant back and forth between agreeing and disagreeing with Bodin on various specific issues, and, on the other hand, a broad acceptance of Bodin's wider principles, both in substance and in method.

There are two core elements of Bodin's *République* that appear to have had a particularly important impact on the way Gentili framed his theory of the laws of war. First, Gentili draws heavily on Bodin in his method, praising his critique of modern commentators who seek to derive military law from Roman law alone. More specifically, Gentili "appreciated Bodin's attempt to put in order and, so to speak, system-atize the late-medieval tradition of *ius gentium* into a new comparative legal-historical doctrine."[52] Like Bodin, Gentili was quite sympathetic to the criticisms of conventional approaches to Roman law waged by the French legal humanists, and he drew extensively from Bodin's methodology in developing his legal framework in *DIB*. While unlike

---

[48] An in-depth discussion of some of these examples can be found in Quaglioni, "The Italian 'Readers' of Bodin," 376–82.

[49] Wijffels, "From Perugia to Oxford," 68–69. I was also able to access the manuscripts and follow Wijffels' analysis based on the original documents.

[50] Ibid., 69.

[51] Gentili, *De iure belli*, Book I, Chapter 9, §541.

[52] Quaglioni, "The Italian 'Readers' of Bodin," 383.

Bodin, Gentili saw Roman law as timeless and thus directly applicable to all the problems of his day,[53] he stepped away from the Bartolists' traditional uncritical and unconditional reliance on medieval authorities to analyze the *Corpus iuris* and drew instead on an extensive web of sources, notably giving pride of place to historians – both modern and classical – in his analysis. Bodin himself had broken off from the conventional *mos gallicus* and drawn extensively from both the legal humanists and the Bartolists in his attempt to elaborate a new legal system, an eclectic approach that must have appealed to Gentili. Gentili's discussion of Bodin on this point – which, as we shall see, also includes a critical dimension – appears at the very start of *DIB*, in the fourth paragraph of the first chapter, and clearly serves an important framing function for the work as a whole.

Second, Gentili quite clearly appears to be striving for a way to reconcile Bodin's absolutist conception of sovereignty with traditional understandings of the just war. As Quaglioni puts it, Gentili "did not ignore the ambiguity of Bodin's concept of just war, the difficulty of finding in it a clear definition, and especially the problem of adapting it to Bodin's concept of supreme power (*summa potestas*)."[54] It is true that Bodin had in fact written "a complex elaboration on the concept of just war and more generally of an international law doctrine for it"[55] in *République*, Book VI, Chapters 5 and 6. However, it is not clear whether or not Gentili was actually aware of it, as he only cites the Latin text in *DIB* and therefore may never have read the French edition which Bodin expanded between 1576 and 1583.[56] In any case, it is obvious from Book I, Chapter 3, entitled "War Is Waged by Sovereigns," that Gentili's considerations on war were driven by the question of how to reconcile supreme authority with ideas about the just war, and one detects in his work a palpable sense of urgency fostered by the intractable wars that were decimating Europe at the time.

Although he does not explicitly cite Bodin in the chapter, the fact that he is indebted to the Frenchman for his conceptualization of sovereignty is hard to miss, and it is unsurprising to note how heavily – and this time, explicitly – Gentili came to rely on Bodin's ideas in his seminal defense of absolutism, *De potestate regis absoluta*, a few years later. Bodin defined sovereignty according to the four following principles: It had to be supreme

---

[53] This is particularly striking when Gentili defends the application of Roman law to constitutional issues of his day, as discussed in Straumann, "The Corpus iuris as a Source of Law Between Sovereigns in Alberico Gentili's Thought," 106–08.

[54] Ibid. See also Quaglioni, "Il 'Machiavellismo' di Jean Bodin ('République', V, 5–6)."

[55] Quaglioni, "The Italian 'Readers' of Bodin," 383.

[56] Ibid.

(no superior except for God), absolute (the sovereign cannot be tried, unless he explicitly consents to it), indivisible (it is metaphorically held in only one set of hands, such as the King or Parliament – but not both), and perpetual (it cannot be changing hands).[57] The sovereign had a specific set of prerogatives held by him alone, most importantly the right to make laws, the "one attribute above all others," which "included the privilege of declaring war and concluding peace, as well as the right of selecting the highest magistrates in the state."[58] Echoing these ideas very closely, Gentili begins the chapter by stating that sovereigns are "supreme," that they "acknowledge no judge or superior," and, importantly, that "they alone merit the title of public, while all others are inferior and are rated as private individuals."[59] "The sovereign," he continues, "has no earthly judge, for one over whom another holds a superior position is not a sovereign."[60] The central idea of the chapter, that only sovereigns can make war, also closely follows Bodin's ideas, particularly as private wars and mixed wars (public/private) were still a dominant feature of the age. Gentili repeats and expands on the latter theme in Book I, Chapter 10 ("On the Compacts of Leaders"), emphasizing that sovereigns "alone can make agreements binding on the state," that the sovereign "alone can make war, therefore he alone can end it," and "just so it is said that only the sovereign can give a safe-conduct, since he alone can suspend sentence and give immunity from the consequences of a crime."[61]

There are, it is important to note, a few elements in the *DIB* that seem less aligned with Bodin's ideas. This raises two interrelated questions: First, how should these elements be understood within Gentili's broader framework? In other words, why might these passages be included in light of their apparent incompatibility with the rest of Gentili's approach? Second, may this suggest that five years before the publication of the incontestably absolutist and Bodinian *Regales disputationes tres*, Gentili was in fact, and despite relying on Bodin very extensively, not yet an absolutist? As I have mentioned, the debate over the extent of Gentili's absolutism has been tainted by political motives, with Gentili's opponents pointing to his absolutist leanings as a way to undermine his broader reputation, particularly during his revival in the late nineteenth century when the accounts of his "greatness" as an international

---

[57] This definition of *maiestas* or *summum imperium* can be found in Bodin, *Les six livres de la république*, Book V, vi. For a brief analysis, see Bourke and Skinner, *Popular Sovereignty in Historical Perspective*, 2.

[58] Bourke and Skinner, *Popular Sovereignty in Historical Perspective*, 3.

[59] Gentili, *De iure belli*, Book I, Chapter 3, §23.

[60] Ibid.

[61] Gentili, *De iure belli*, Book I, Chapter 10, §288.

jurist were systematically elaborated. Since it is now well established that Gentili made his absolutism eminently clear in the *Regales disputationes tres*, I will address the main elements in DIB that may suggest he held a different position a few years earlier and argue that these should be understood primarily as exceptions made in light of the surrounding political context and of Gentili's personal obligations.

First, it is true that, as Van der Molen notes, on certain points, Gentili's absolutism is not as stark in DIB as it is in the *Regales disputationes tres*.[62] The debate on the right of the people to take up arms against a tyrant was an important theme during the religious wars, and Gentili's position noticeably evolved on this point over the course of his career. In the *Regales disputationes tres*, he suggested the absolute illegitimacy of armed resistance even against a tyrant. In DIB, however, he allowed some form of resistance, notably by foreign rulers against a tyrant, an unsurprising exception to which I will return in Chapter 3. In general, however, the caveats to sovereign authority that Gentili introduces are hardly incompatible with an absolutist position, as the latter was emphatically not supportive of tyrannical sovereigns. For example, Gentili puts forward certain limitations to absolute sovereign power within very specific cases, notably in his discussion of the rather extreme situation where a sovereign would alienate his subjects (i.e., make them subjects of another sovereign) or abandon them altogether.[63] While this does suggest some limitation to sovereign power, Gentili makes it very clear that these limitations are minimal and mainly intended to avoid tyranny: "Imagine that the emperor has the freest possible power; yet it is not for purposes of tyranny, but of administration."[64] The distinction between an all-powerful king and a tyrant

---

[62] Van der Molen, *Alberico Gentili and the Development of International Law*, 227–30, n. 27.

[63] Gentili, *De iure belli*, Book I, Chapter 23, §185. "It is true," Gentili explains, "that the people conferred all sovereignty and power, but they did so in order that they might be governed like men, not sold like cattle" (Book III, Chapter 15, §609). He cites Alciatus approvingly, concurring that "[t]he theologians are mistaken and the jurists flatter, when they maintain that everything is allowed to princes and that they have supreme and unrestricted power" (Ibid.).

[64] Ibid., Book III, Chapter 15, §610. Similarly, when Van der Molen cites passages from Book I, Chapter 23, "Of the Overthrow of Kingdoms," in which Gentili talks about the mutual dependence between princes and subjects and the obligation princes have to rule justly, this is again within a discussion about what subjects can do if their sovereign abandons them altogether. Gentili focuses much of his discussion throughout the chapter on the context of Rome and the division of the empire: "[O]ur jurists say, and reason clearly testifies, that subjects deprived of the aid of their prince, as the Roman were by the removal of the emperor to Constantinople, and harassed by the arms of foes, as the Romans then were by the Lombards, may take refuge with another sovereign and adopt him as their own" (Book I, Chapter 23, §185). Ultimately, the fact that Gentili gives some power to subjects within these extreme cases can hardly be seen to undermine his broader absolutist positions.

was actually quite common, including in Bodin's writings, and Bodin himself considered tyrannicide permissible (something which Van der Molen tellingly finds "strange").[65] And in fact, while Van der Molen highlights the existence of restrictions to the rights of the sovereign found in *DIB* "in spite of no fewer than thirty-five references to Bodin's 'De Republica,'" it is worth noting that Bodin himself introduced a number of such restrictions in his magnum opus.[66]

Second, at the end of his crucial chapter, "War Is Waged by Sovereigns," Gentili does raise some difficult questions and introduces some additional caveats in his conceptualization of sovereignty, this time with direct references to his geopolitical environment. Most notably, he makes some pragmatic concessions regarding the status of "states such as Venice," which he considers to "have the same power as any supreme sovereign."[67] However, this is not entirely surprising, as Bodin's definition of sovereignty raised some extremely difficult questions for the established order in most countries, including France, which had long had a mixed constitution, and most importantly for the Holy Roman Empire. Following the publication of the *République*, there was an almost panic-stricken debate amongst German jurists about how to reconcile Bodin's ideas with the realities of the feudal empire, which would last for over thirty years.[68] Gentili, who by definition had to engage with the existence of different forms of polities on the international stage in devising his system of laws, was left in a similarly uncomfortable position by Bodin's arguments, and to some extent he tried to make some space for a slightly looser definition of sovereignty in the context of the right to wage war.[69]

Gentili can thus be understood as already having been an absolutist in DIB, with his reliance on Bodin further deepening in the following years. However, in light of Gentili's difficulty in adapting some of Bodin's ideas to the geopolitical configurations of his time, it is clear that there were some limits to how far Gentili could rely on the *République* to develop his arguments for *DIB*, particularly in the sense that *DIB* was specifically geared toward regulating relations *between* sovereigns. Bodin's "great concern, like that of the whole group of '*politique*' jurists, was civil war and the good and unity of France."[70] The *politiques* saw

---

[65] Van der Molen, *Alberico Gentili and the Development of International Law*, 227.

[66] Franklin, *Jean Bodin and the Rise of Absolutist Theory*, 70–92.

[67] Gentili, *De iure belli*, Chapter 3, §34.

[68] Franklin, "Sovereignty and the Mixed Constitution," 309–23.

[69] A final inconsistency can be found in his chapter entitled "Defending the Subjects of Another Against Their Sovereigns," which I will explore more at length in Chapter 3.

[70] Koskenniemi, "International Law and raison d'état," 308.

the preservation and broader well-being of the French polity as their utmost priority, and the *République* is an attempt to restore order in the French kingdom and to reestablish the institutional bases of French rule at the height of the French civil and religious wars. As a result, these thinkers "had little to say about any law applicable in France's external relations beyond what was said by Bodin about there being absolutely no real universal empire and that only a kind of *ius fetiale* [the Roman set of rules under which treaties were to be handled] regulated the relations between sovereigns," a framework which merely provided "a limited right of enforcement in cases of outrages against natural law."[71] Yet these external relations were precisely what Gentili was concerned with. In fact, Bodin's chapter in the *République* on the ancient *ius fetiale* (and on treaties and peace)[72] is "one of the most extensively annotated chapters in Gentili's manuscript notes, and, correspondingly, one of the most frequently quoted chapter from Bodin's book in Gentili's *DIB*."[73] In other words, Bodin's ideas were of great appeal to Gentili, who attempted to draw on as much of Bodin's work as he could in light of his own interests, but there were clearly some areas that were central to Gentili's endeavor which Bodin had not covered sufficiently.

Most importantly, Bodin's ideas on sovereignty had significant implications for inter-sovereign relations and raised one particularly delicate issue. His all-important concept of the Commonwealth (*République*), the entity to which his concept of indivisible and absolute sovereignty was to apply, was the central element of his plan for restoring order. Within each Commonwealth, a single sovereign authority would have the power to arbitrate disputes and establish final rules, thus providing a way out of otherwise intractable confessional strife. At a time when constitutional arrangements had been the norm in France, with the King expected to respect the rules of consent and work with institutions such as the General Estates and the *Parlement* of Paris, Bodin's defense of indivisible and absolute sovereignty was a bold conceptual move, bolder than even he ever seemed to realize.[74] Bodin's concept of the Commonwealth stood as a powerful tool for reestablishing order and stability within France and other similar kingdoms. However, it raised a problem at a higher level. If each Commonwealth was characterized by indivisible sovereignty, and if each prince was thus the highest authority deciding upon all matters of the land, then how

---

[71] Ibid.
[72] Bodin, *Les six livres de la république*, Book V, vi.
[73] Wijffels, "From Perugia to Oxford," 70.
[74] Franklin, *Jean Bodin and the Rise of Absolutist Theory*.

would one settle disagreements amongst Commonwealths? This was a critical question at a time when, following the Reformation and the collapse of the religiously united Latin West, various polities had all of a sudden achieved external sovereignty,[75] and as with the question of how to define sovereignty within the Holy Roman Empire, Bodin appears to have launched a seminal debate which he himself was not necessarily interested in. The issue of settling disagreements amongst Commonwealths is the main *problématique* underpinning *DIB*, and Gentili found little by means of an answer in Bodin's work.

In sum, while Bodin and the *politiques* were concerned with how best to ensure order in France, Gentili was attempting to cope with the consequences of Bodin's conceptual move for the inter-polity plane, and to develop a standalone set of rules[76] for managing the conflicts that would inevitably arise between independent and absolutely sovereign polities.[77] Thus, Bodin cannot have been Gentili's sole (or even main) source of inspiration for his considerations on inter-sovereign relations. For this, he turned to reason of state writers who, by contrast with Bodin, had written extensively about what we would now call "the international."

2.3 Thinking the International: The Influence of the *ragion di stato* Tradition

The most famous treatise on *raison d'état*, Giovanni Botero's *Della ragion di stato*, was published just three years (1586) before Gentili's lectures on the laws of war, and Gentili was clearly influenced by this

---

[75] Lesaffer, "Alberico Gentili's ius post bellum and Early Modern Peace Treaties," 216. More broadly, see Lesaffer, "The Classical Law of Nations (1500–1800)," 408–22.

[76] Gentili's *DIB* was part of a broader move toward the emancipation of the laws of war from the law at large and the gradual emergence of the *ius belli* as a new discipline. By the second half of the sixteenth century, "the genre of self-standing treatises [on the laws of war] imposed its own rules," which meant that authors could "isolate the relevant texts from the glossators, commentators, and humanist jurists on the laws of war and military discipline from the rest," leaving out "direct references to rules of private law from the Justinian and canon collections and the glosses thereon." This is clear in the works of the two most famous sixteenth-century jurists of war (prior to *DIB*) – Pierino Belli (1505–1575) and Balthazar Ayala (1548–1584), both Roman law specialists and military judges – who took important steps in that direction. Gentili, however, took another important step in also emancipating his treatise on the laws of war from nonlegal considerations of the rules of military discipline. Haggenmacher, "Il diritto della guerra et della pace di Alberico Gentili," 36–37; Lesaffer, "Alberico Gentili's ius post bellum and Early Modern Peace Treaties," 216.

[77] In fact, one of the main interpretations of the puzzling *De armis romanis* is that it is an attempt to justify the application of the *Corpus iuris* to inter-sovereign relations. Straumann, "The Corpus iuris as a Source of Law Between Sovereigns in Alberico Gentili's Thought," 120–21. This interpretation is supported by Pagden, "Gentili, Vitoria, and the Fabrication of a 'Natural Law of Nations'," 340–41.

intellectual *courant*, particularly in *DIB*. Indeed, one of the most striking influences on Gentili in *DIB* is Guicciardini, whom he cites no less
than sixty-three times, nearly twice as many times as Bodin (although
the latter tends to be discussed more directly in the text). This extensive
reliance on the Florentine author denotes Gentili's admiration, indirectly, for Machiavellian policies. The fact that Gentili relies much less
on Machiavelli (1469–1527) – whom he does cite but only on three
occasions and referring neither to *The Prince* nor to the *Discorsi* – may
well be a result of the stigma that was associated with Guicciardini's
friend and would be in line with the attitude adopted by later reason of
state writers. As Burke explains, one of the primary problems for these
writers was that while they strongly disliked Machiavelli – he was seen
as the master of the devil's reason of state – they could not do without
his ideas.[78] Guicciardini, who put forth a set of considerations similar to
those of his Florentine friend, was a much more palatable authority to
cite. Similarly, in DIB Gentili makes over fifty citations of the Roman
historian Tacitus, whose revival was deeply intertwined with the development of the *ragion di stato* literature, and who is sometimes said to
have been a direct cover for references to Machiavelli.[79] Another possible explanation is that while Machiavelli was nearly obsessed with the
Romans, Guicciardini drew much more on the contemporary world,
particularly Florentine history, something which must have appealed
greatly to Gentili, whom as we have seen relied on contemporary historians to an uncommon degree. In any case, beyond these mere numbers
in terms of citation, it is quite obvious that Gentili thought of the *ragion
di stato* writers – and particularly of Guicciardini – very highly. In fact,
Gentili explicitly writes that Guicciardini is "not merely a great historian and a political philosopher, but a great jurist as well."[80]

It is true that Gentili only cites Guicciardini's *Storia d'Italia* (History
of Italy); there is no mention of his *Ricordi politici e civili*, his collection of maxims on political, social, and religious topics. However, it is
clear that Gentili draws heavily on Guicciardini's work for its matter-
of-fact understanding of politics so central to the reason of state tradition, more so than as a source of purely illustrative historical anecdotes.
For instance, he cites him to support the claim that sovereigns often
cloak their dishonesty in religion;[81] to explain the rejection of Luther's

---

[78] Burke, "Tacitism, Scepticism, and Reason of State," 483.
[79] Toffanin, *Machiavelli e il "tacitismo,"* 12.
[80] Gentili, *De iure belli*, Book II, Chapter 8, §167. Gentili reiterates this, calling him "the
famous historian and eminent jurist." Ibid., Book III, Chapter II, §483.
[81] Ibid., Book I, Chapter 9, §63.

doctrines (they are "unfavourable to the power of princes");[82] to praise the policies of Lorenzo de Medici, "that wise man, friend of peace, and father of peace" who ensured "that the balance of power should be maintained amongst the princes of Italy";[83] to suggest that princes will only come to the rescue of oppressed people if they are "led by a desire for personal gain";[84] to point out – rather irreverently – that it is "characteristic of pontiffs not to keep their promises" and that it is "an established custom for the Church, regardless of contracts, promises, or receipt of favours, to renounce its obligations and even directly to oppose what the prelates had solemnly agreed upon";[85] and the list goes on. On at least one occasion, a remark Gentili makes based on Guicciardini's historical writings sounds very much like one of the latter's maxims: "[I]t is a grave error to consider what ought to be done, not what a man will do who has the power to act."[86] In fact, when he elaborates on this point and explains that "every pledge is capable of being broken," he cites Tacitus approvingly, claiming that "the statement of Tacitus is always true, that enduring faith never exists between victors and vanquished."[87] What is more, Gentili seems to disagree explicitly with Guicciardini on just one occasion, on the question of whether kings should "fight in single combat for the dominion to which both sides laid claim,"[88] a rather minor detail in light of the extent to which Gentili draws on Guicciardini otherwise.

What, then, were the main insights of this reason of state tradition so extensively drawn on by Gentili? The remainder of this section lays out the core features of the reason of state literature, outlining the context in which it emerged, the basic tenets of the new strand of thought it ushered in, and the sources it turned to – particularly Tacitus, another key influence on Gentili's *DIB*. Most importantly, the reason of state writers developed a set of principles that could be applied not just domestically, but also – and explicitly – to relations between sovereigns. As I have briefly indicated earlier, there is no doubt that, for his part, Gentili was deeply concerned by the regulation of inter-sovereign relations and the specific problem of how to resolve conflicts between sovereigns, whom he saw as recognizing no superiors by definition.[89] During his eventual

---

[82] Ibid., Book I, Chapter 10, §43.
[83] Ibid., Book I, Chapter 14, §105.
[84] Ibid., Book I, Chapter 15, §115.
[85] Ibid., Book III, Chapter 19, §403.
[86] Ibid., Book III, Chapter 13, §584.
[87] Ibid.
[88] Ibid., Book III, Chapter 15, §607.
[89] Ibid., Book I, Chapter 2, §18.

revival, he would in fact come to be celebrated for his advocacy of international arbitration, which he portrayed as an alternative to war, "the arbitrament of Mars."[90] It is thus not entirely surprising that in light of the limitations of Bodin's rather inward-looking text, Gentili turned to those writers who seemed most explicitly interested in addressing the issues raised by inter-sovereign relations.

At its core, the rise of reason of state thinking marked a transition from the Renaissance concept of politics as "the art of ruling a republic according to justice and reason" (paraphrasing Brunetto Latini's famous definition of 1266) to a new understanding of politics as the means of preserving a "state," or in other words, politics as the knowledge of the means of preserving domination over a people (paraphrasing Botero's equally famous formulation of 1586).[91] The Renaissance concept of politics, sometimes also couched as the art of good government, had flourished in the age of Civic Humanism; its principles were rooted in traditions of political virtue, civil law, and Aristotelianism,[92] and the model it sought to follow was that of the Roman republic, as described by Cicero and Livy. Machiavelli and Guicciardini, although they were both symptomatic of a transitional epoch and in many ways remained anchored in the tradition of politics as the art of the republic, took some important steps in a different direction, which Guicciardini would, in the 1520s, first term "reason of state." Their key contribution was to carve out a new space of morality, one that applied distinctly to the prince's task of *mantenere lo stato* – that is, "maintaining the state" as in *his* state, his "estate," or his "standing"/"status," rather than "the state" as a separate, abstract political entity[93] – and which could entail using certain means that would otherwise have been condemned as immoral.

Two elements are particularly important here. First, they argued that the prince should readily use force when in the interest of his "state"; second, they placed prudence – rather than justice – as the heart of their system of princely virtues. In other words, although much of their approach was still grounded in the Florentine republican tradition,

---

[90] Ibid., Book I, Chapter 3, §32.
[91] Viroli, *From Politics to Reason of State*, 2–3.
[92] Ibid., 2.
[93] The meaning of Machiavelli's use of "lo stato" has generated much discussion, and much confusion as well. The extent to which Machiavelli's use of "stato" departed from the idea of personal patrimony and toward a more impersonal understanding of the state is still debated. The most famous engagement with the question is still Skinner, *Visions of Politics*, Vol 2. For a recent overview of the continuing disagreements about his work and the "modern" character of his ideas, see Johnston, Urbinati, and Vergara, *Machiavelli on Liberty and Conflict*.

they put forward a revolutionary analysis of what should count as virtuous behavior for a prince, discarding the traditional approach based on personal virtue. They made, in modern terms, "a virtue of necessity," and they broke down the classical divide between violence and virtue, arguing – most famously in the case of Machiavelli – that because of the circumstances of reality, it was sometimes necessary to act in beastly ways, like the fox and the lion (turning Cicero's classic quote on its head, that "[w]hile wrong may be done, then, in either of two ways, that is, by force or by fraud, both are bestial: fraud seems to belong to the cunning fox, force to the lion; both are wholly unworthy of man ..."[94]). Ultimately, these writers were advocates of pragmatic compromises and the use of sometimes ruthless methods to ensure the well-being of the "state"; as explained by Guicciardini, "one simply could not govern a state according to conscience."[95]

In developing these ideas, Machiavelli, Guicciardini, and their contemporaries were responding to the challenges of their time. After years of flourishing republican government, Florence was torn between its republican antecedents and the rule of the Medici, changing governments four times between 1494 and 1530. In light of the atmosphere of considerable political instability – and not unlike the French *politiques* a few decades later – these writers became increasingly concerned with how to avoid, above all, the collapse of their polity. In his quest for answers, Guicciardini, in particular, turned not to Livy and Cicero, who had written during the heydays of the Roman republic, but to Tacitus, whose *Annals*, most importantly, pertained to the unstable transitionary period between the republic and the empire in the aftermath of Caesar's assassination in 44 BCE. Guicciardini's turn to this other classical historian was central to his ideology and eventually became widely popularized by Justus Lipsius, whose inauguration lecture at the university of Jena is "one of the most dynamic applications of Tacitus to politics in the Renaissance."[96] Although this particular lecture was not published until 1607, Lipsius (who is cited thirteen times in DIB) generally became the greatest Tacitus scholar and advocate of the crucial contemporary relevance of his work – seeing Livy's writings as "sweet nothingness" in comparison[97] – and inspired an entire generation of thinkers to investigate Tacitus' writings. Lipsius' new edition of Tacitus' works in 1574 became the first of a very long series of

---

[94] Cicero, *De officiis*, I, 41.
[95] Guicciardini, *Dialogue on the Government of Florence*, 159.
[96] Schellhase, *Tacitus in Renaissance Political Thought*, 118.
[97] Ibid.

reeditions, a testimony to an explosion of interest in the thought of the Roman historian. The key turning point, however, was again with Bodin, who criticized Machiavelli, More, Patrizi, and others for not having drawn sufficiently on Tacitus, and who, in his case for monarchy as the most excellent form of government, argued that Tacitus was "the most useful ancient historian for illustrating the principles upon which monarchies operate."[98] His reevaluation of Tacitus as the go-to historian for political instruction on how to run a monarchical government was "enlarged and refined by others" and this process was key to the eventual development of the reason of state tradition of the late sixteenth and seventeenth centuries.[99] Thus, although much can be written about the differences between these individuals and their respective works, the names of Tacitus, Machiavelli, and Guicciardini became intertwined and perceived as the ideological basis of the "reason of state" movement.

The practices put forth by Machiavelli were hugely controversial, and he and Tacitus – now couched as a classical precursor to the Florentine writer – came to be seen as advocates of a "bad" reason of state, irreconcilable with Christian principles. This was made especially clear from the late sixteenth century in the work of Botero and his contemporaries, and the distinction between "good" and "bad" reason of state became a classical trope of early seventeenth-century thinking.[100] The challenge, ultimately, for writers such as Botero was to reconcile the insights of Machiavelli – which were extremely perceptive and uncontestably valuable – with a more palatable normative framework. As Comparato explains, "behind the façade of deference and virtue which [late sixteenth-century] writers presented, contemporary politics continued to reflect Guicciardini's maxim that 'one cannot keep a state according to conscience.'"[101] Crucially, in their attempt to respond to the unstable political atmosphere of their time, political thinkers continued to draw extensively on the analyses of historians such as Tacitus; not only did history provide princes with the

---

[98] Ibid., 111.

[99] Ibid.

[100] This distinction between good and bad reason of state gradually lost traction in the seventeenth century, most notably through the seminal work of Henri Duc de Rohan, *De l'intérêt des princes et des états de la chrétienté* (1638). See Christian Lazzeri's 1995 introduction to Rohan's treatise. Henri Duc de Rohan, *De l'intérêt des princes et des états de la chrétienté* (1638), edited by Christian Lazzeri (Paris: Presses Universitaires de France, 1995).

[101] Comparato and Quaglioni, "From Machiavellism to the End of the Seventeenth Century," 78.

"experience" so central to the exercise of prudence,[102] but the work of historians, stripped of illusions, appeared far more useful than the preaching of moralists.[103] One of their key concerns in searching these historical texts for advice was how to navigate what had become an explosive network of external relations between sovereigns. Lipsius had famously compared the Duke of Alba to Tiberius, the Roman emperor described as a notorious tyrant by Tacitus, and indeed, the conflict between Spain, England, and the Low Countries was squarely on the mind of both legal and political thinkers at the time.

Raison d'état writers thus had a keen interest in the question of how best to conduct external affairs, a fact that did not escape Gentili in his own attempt to grapple with the issue of inter-sovereign matters. This shared interest was not surprising in light of the developments of the period: As the theoretical foundations of absolutism and reason of state in internal affairs became "sufficiently comprehensive to provide ready-made justifications for the many measures ... believed to be required by political necessity,"[104] foreign policy became an even more pressing topic. This is not to say that full internal sovereignty was achieved before or faster than external sovereignty. If anything, the process went the other way around, with sovereigns suddenly achieving external sovereignty after the collapse of the unity of the Latin West, while internally, struggles for power continued well into the eighteenth and even the nineteenth century.[105] The point here is that in terms of legal rules, the basis for how a polity would operate internally under an absolute sovereign was fairly clear, while by contrast, foreign policy "was subject to no generally recognized principles, legal or moral,"[106] and thus required the development of some clear guidance for sovereigns.

In the broadest sense, *raison d'état* writers "held it self-evident that the same principles and techniques that would ensure the strength of the prince's rule inside his realm would also be applicable in his external relations."[107] Prudence, necessity, and the prince's interests were systematically at the heart of their recommendations. This meant that, for instance, they considered the use of frauds and ruses to be perfectly acceptable in the conduct of external relations, although they did try

---

[102] Ibid., 82.
[103] Ibid., 79.
[104] Church, "The Decline of the French Jurists as Political Theorists, 1660–1789," 37–38.
[105] Lesaffer, "The Classical Law of Nations (1500–1800)," 419.
[106] Church, "The Decline of the French Jurists as Political Theorists, 1660–1789," 37–38.
[107] Koskenniemi, "International Law and raison d'état," 308.

to establish some rules of decency in the use of such stratagems in an effort to demarcate themselves from the notoriously more permissive Machiavelli. It was possible, Justus Lipsius argued, for virtue to remain intact if prudence was mixed with trickery with a good end. Lipsius then developed this Procrustean doctrine in greater detail; he distinguished between light, medium, and great ruses and fraud, of which he only allowed the first two. Light ruses and frauds, generally to be blamed on the victim rather than the author, "did not depart seriously from virtue and included deceit and dissimulation"; medium ruses and frauds, which included "the corruption of another ruler's emissaries and agents, the sending of spies abroad, and the spreading of information," were "mid-way between virtue and open vice"; and finally, great ruses and frauds, such as "the willful breaking of treaties and other sworn agreements, and injustice contrary to the highest legal and moral principles," were considered to break "entirely with virtue and law, resulting in perfidy and injustice."[108]

Gentili could find plenty to draw on from reading these writers who, unlike Bodin, directly addressed the realm of inter-sovereign relations. However, while the limits they posited involved a certain respect for legal agreements, notably treaties, as a whole, reason of state writers had little consideration for the role of the law of nations in regulating relations between sovereigns. Their language was not that of law, but that of political necessity, interests, and, especially from the 1590s, balance of power.[109] In fact, the growing influence of their ideas in the seventeenth century – the development of what may be called "baroque statecraft" – went hand in hand with the demise of lawyers as influential figures in the conduct of politics, and particularly the conduct of external relations.[110] For a jurist like Gentili, this was bound to raise some issues. While he did deeply admire the reason of state tradition, one decisive factor made him stand out from this group: Unlike them, he saw law as a crucial ingredient for external relations.[111] In the final

---

[108] Church, *Richelieu and Reason of State*, 60–62.

[109] Tuck, *Philosophy and Government, 1572–1651*, 96.

[110] The French case is particularly illustrative here. While the writings of someone like Bodin could be of tremendous importance for matters of government in the late sixteenth century, jurists increasingly stepped away from matters of public law in the seventeenth century. On the decline of the importance of jurists with the rise of *raison d'état* thinking through Richelieu and Louis XIV in the French case, see Church, *Richelieu and Reason of State*; Church, "The Decline of the French Jurists as Political Theorists, 1660–1789." On the specific chasm between *raison d'état* and international law, see Church, *Richelieu and Reason of State*, 39.

[111] Koskenniemi, "International Law and raison d'état," 308.

section, I will thus argue that *DIB* can be understood as a text that tries to adapt not only Bodinian absolutism but also – and crucially – the insights of the reason of state writers to a system of laws for regulating interactions between independent sovereigns.

2.4   Between Law and Politics

In attempting to bridge the *ius gentium* and the reason of state tradition, Gentili was part of a long trend of trying to link political and legal thought together. In practice, lawyers had often been prominent figures in government, particularly in the critical context of Renaissance Italy.[112] In other words, they were deeply involved in statecraft, and their professional work as lawyers often overlapped quite extensively with their careers as government officials. More broadly, prior to the development of the *ragion di stato* literature, the rule of law culture had been essential in "the political governance of the late-medieval Italian polities where the law scholars and consultants of the *mos italicus* had thrived."[113] The result of this close overlap between law and politics was a significant effort on the part of lawyers to engage with questions of politics, and they did so specifically by turning to history. Although this turn to history would become most apparent – and most systematic – in the works of Baudouin and Bodin in the second half of the sixteenth century,[114] this interdisciplinary engagement had a long pedigree, with Bartolus being one of the first legal thinkers to write not simply as a lawyer but also as a historian.

As mentioned earlier, Bodin's work marked a turning point in that Bodin tried to base his construction of a new system of law on universal history. Bodin's turn to history was very much in line with what Machiavelli had attempted earlier in the century (and indeed, Bodin praises Machiavelli's method on this front in the *Methodus*), and this overlap is connected to these thinkers' focus on the prince as the sovereign. Since the focus, both for Machiavelli in *The Prince* and for Bodin in his advocacy of absolutism, was on the person of the supreme sovereign, they found it essential to unearth the history of former princes and assess the actions they had taken. As suggested earlier, history was, after all, a treasure trove of "experience" that would help

---

[112] Martines, *Lawyers and Statecraft in Renaissance Florence*.
[113] Wijffels, "From Perugia to Oxford," 78. See also Ibid., 63.
[114] See, generally, Franklin, *Jean Bodin and the Sixteenth-Century Revolution in the Methodology of Law and History*. On the specific role of François Baudouin in attempting to reconcile law and history, see also Kelley, *Foundations of Modern Historical Scholarship*, 116–48.

princes (and their advisors) determine how best to act prudently.[115] Yet, while Bodin and Machiavelli have often been juxtaposed as founders of a modern discipline of political science,[116] Bodin's emphasis on legal thought meant that in terms of method the two writers were "literally worlds apart."[117] Bodin, by virtue of his training and intellectual affinities, "worked in a much richer – and more inhibiting – context of legal, historical, and philosophical erudition" than Machiavelli, and he was "unable to separate politics from its legal and social environment."[118] In this respect, Kelley points to the insightful remark of one of "Bodin's most perceptive commentators," Moireau-Reibel: "[T]he *Republic* is the work not so much of a great politique as of a great legist, the work of a successor not of Machiavelli but of Beaumanoir and Bartolus."[119] In other words, what jurists such as Bodin and his followers were doing was distinct from the reason of state writers in that they considered law to be at the center of their intellectual endeavor and placed it in direct dialogue with politics and history.

Gentili, deeply influenced as he was by Bodin, was very much a follower of this approach, and notwithstanding his admiration for the reason of state writers, he made a sustained effort to assert the authority of the *ius gentium*. This attempt to reconcile the two approaches, particularly once combined with the initial tensions raised by the application of Bodinian absolutism to a *ius gentium* framework, put Gentili in a difficult position. On the one hand, he was a key advocate of absolutism, and in justifying his position, he had made much of the medieval distinction between the ordinary and extraordinary powers of the prince in a domestic context, thus limiting the constraints imposed on the prince by public law to the realm of ordinary power.[120] In other words, in the domestic context Gentili had tried to free the sovereign from the constraints of the law by expanding the scope of the prince's

---

[115] Comparato and Quaglioni, "From Machiavellism to the End of the Seventeenth Century," 82.

[116] It is worth mentioning that Bodin had rather mixed opinions about Machiavelli. While he praised him for his methodological innovations, particularly in the *Methodus*, he depicted his ideas about the prince as devilish in the *République*.

[117] Kelley, *Foundations of Modern Historical Scholarship*, 146.

[118] Ibid., 145.

[119] Ibid.

[120] Wijffels, "From Perugia to Oxford," 64. The ordinary/extraordinary power distinction was theological in origin and was used to describe the nature of God's power; it was then used to describe papal power and then regal power. Bodin himself appears to have inherited it from canon lawyers; see Pennington, *The Prince and the Law, 1200–1600*; Giesey, "Medieval Jurisprudence in Bodin's Concept of Sovereignty." On the extent to which Bodin then departed from these medieval ideas to forge his own original position, see Engster, "Jean Bodin, Scepticism and Absolute Sovereignty."

extraordinary powers and thus the primacy of the prince's discretion over the rule of law. In practice, sovereigns were indeed gradually shifting toward more absolutist forms of rule, and what had been "extraordinary" powers in the Middle Ages were now increasingly becoming part of the "ordinary" category. On the other hand, the autonomy of the *ius gentium* which Gentili was seeking to establish in *DIB*[121] risked being strongly undermined by the rise of supreme sovereigns acting as the sole legitimate actors internationally and actively pursuing the interest of their polity according to the principles of reason of state.[122] It was thus essential for Gentili to find a way to maintain the early modern sovereign within the late medieval Italian culture of accepting the constraints of the law. Gentili thus turned to a variety of sources – from those of his Perugian heritage to the work of Bodin – in order to try and adjust to early modern sovereignty the *ius gentium* as conceived in the *mos italicus* that had been so central to the government of late medieval Italian polities.[123]

As I have suggested earlier, by the time he wrote *DIB*, Gentili was not exactly a staunch follower of the *mos italicus* anymore and he may well have been following Bodin in cherry-picking what he found most useful in both the Bartolist and the legal humanist traditions in his construction of a new legal framework.[124] Bodin's work, in addition to the justification it provided of absolutism as discussed in Section 2.2, was indeed crucially important to Gentili on two further counts. First, his systematic approach had been hailed – in Protestant countries, but also in Catholic ones despite the condemnation of his books by Roman Catholics – "as a new model of scholarly teaching of public law."[125] Indeed, Bodin's "hyper-rationalizing tendencies"[126] had led him to approach the law in a way that would prove enormously influential for later jurists interested in systematizing the *ius gentium*. Second, his extensive considerations on sovereignty, his rigorous attempt to clarify what this concept meant in precise legal terms, and more broadly, his attempt to fuse the language

---

[121] Wijffels, "From Perugia to Oxford," 77.
[122] On the tensions inherent to Gentili's position, see also Suin, "Principi supremi e societas hominum."
[123] Wijffels, "From Perugia to Oxford," 77–78.
[124] On Bodin's turn to practice, his admiration for the Bartolism on which the practice of law relied, his move away from (or rather beyond) legal humanism, and his attempt to combine the best of both the *mos gallicus* and the *mos italicus* and overcome their respective (as well as overlapping) limitations, see Kelley, "The Development and Context of Bodin's Method."
[125] Quaglioni, "The Italian 'Readers' of Bodin," 372.
[126] Kelley, "The Development and Context of Bodin's Method," 144.

of power and interests with the language of rights and authority,[127] provided an essential resource for Gentili in trying to adapt the insights of *ragion di stato* to his legal framework.

The specific challenge Gentili faced, however, was to reconcile the *ius gentium* both with reason of state thinking and with his ringing endorsement of absolutism. It is with respect to the latter that Gentili and the theologians can be seen as explicitly political rivals, as the theologians' natural law theories grew out of their anti-Machiavellian stance and became the basis for their broader anti-absolutism.[128] Indeed, they rejected "not only autocratic forms of government but absolute monarchy altogether," leading to a lengthy controversy over what exactly natural and divine law "meant, enjoined, allowed, and restricted."[129] Gentili's challenge on this point, then, was to find a way to reconcile natural law theories with his absolutist position, a rather difficult (if not seemingly contradictory) endeavor.[130] Ultimately, Gentili's *DIB* is thus peculiar in that it tries to bring together the implications of Bodin's writings – both on absolutism and on the use of universal history as a way to ground a new approach to law – and the remarkably insightful but also deeply challenging ideas of the *raison d'état* writers about relationships amongst independent polities into a framework for the laws of war still anchored in the language of natural law.

2.5   Conclusion

The purpose of Gentili's magnum opus on the laws of war, *DIB*, has been a recurring source of disagreements, particularly within the recent wave of scholarship on the Italian jurist's work. In this chapter, I have sought to assess the broad features of *DIB* through an analysis of Gentili's use of sources, which indeed reveals a considerable amount of information about the type of arguments Gentili was seeking to make (and those he was leaving aside).

---

[127] Franklin, *Jean Bodin and the Rise of Absolutist Theory.*
[128] Oestreich, *Neostoicism and the Early Modern State*, 259.
[129] Ibid.
[130] As Alain Wijffels emphasizes, it seems a priori difficult to incorporate absolutism into a legal theory (generally speaking), as "absolutism's defining feature is to be a political system where the ruler is ultimately not bound by human law." In addition, Gentili's understanding of the concept of sovereignty was at odds with the realities of Italy that had inspired the Italian late medieval doctrines he was now relying upon. Indeed, in addition to the important constraints placed by law on public authorities in that context, these doctrines "took into account the – to some degree – concurrent political authorities of the Emperor, of the pope, and of a regional ruler or city-state." Wijffels, "From Perugia to Oxford," 63–64.

The chapter began, after a short biographical overview, by situating Gentili as a "moderate humanist" in the legal sense, that is, a Bartolist strongly influenced by legal humanism, relying almost as heavily on Baldus as on Alciatus along with their respective predecessors and followers. I outlined the crucial methodological implications of this particular positioning in the debates of the time, most notably Gentili's affinity with a more historical approach to legal analysis. I also explained the significance of Gentili's situation as a Roman law expert within the common law tradition and outlined the specificity of Gentili's rather unusual position on the status of Roman law.

I then turned to two particularly noteworthy influences on Gentili's *DIB*: Bodin and the reason of state writers. I first focused on Bodin and showed the striking way in which Gentili drew on the French writer in *DIB*, both in substance, with Gentili's commitment to absolutism, and in method, with Gentili's embrace of Bodin's deeply influential turn to comparative history. I ended this section by outlining the limits of Bodin's writings for Gentili's endeavor, particularly Bodin's domestic focus, and I highlighted the need for Gentili to turn to other writers who had thought more explicitly about the relations between independent polities. The following part of the chapter thus focused on the reason of state writers, particularly Guicciardini, upon whom Gentili also draws heavily. I explained the specificity of this particular tradition of thought at the time and its significance for Gentili's attempt to develop a legal framework for regulating inter-sovereign relations, but I also noted the challenge posed by the reason of state writers in their quasi-dismissal of law as a central component of inter-polity relations. Fourth and finally, I brought together these different elements and shed light on the tension between Gentili's embrace of absolutism and of reason of state ideas on the one hand, and his attempt to devise a legal framework for inter-sovereign relations on the other.

This focus on sources ultimately allows us to reevaluate the extent to which Gentili, in writing his famous *DIB*, was influenced by the tenets of what is sometimes termed baroque statecraft. In doing so it highlights the need to break down the division between the history of political thought and the history of international legal thought. It is often assumed that early modern thinkers, who gave us so many of the distinctions our contemporary world is based on – sovereignty, the state, territorial boundaries, reason of state, the balance of power – were split between those who thought about domestic political matters and those who thought explicitly about international ones, including international law. A handful of short pieces have now emerged that seek to go beyond this divide, notably within the (re)turn to early modern international legal thought.[131] My own analysis of Gentili's *DIB*, which seeks to move the debate away from the traditional focus on Gentili's disagreements with the theologians who wrote about the law of nations and to focus instead on the extent to which Gentili was engaging with Bodin and with the reason of state writers, points in a similar direction. It highlights the need to reassess the overlap between the different problems these early modern thinkers were confronted with, and to investigate the possible connections between their thought on sovereignty and matters internal to polities on the one hand, and on the *ius gentium*, conflicts between sovereigns, and relations with the new world on the other.[132] The turn in history and IR toward the history of international political thought provides an ideal framework to explore these links and move beyond the somewhat presentist domestic/international divide that has at times encouraged an overly siloed approach to early modern political and international legal thought.

Returning to the case of Gentili, the Italian jurist presents us with an unusual configuration of influences and concerns. While absolutism and reason of state would of course flourish in the seventeenth century, the importance of these ideas for an England-based jurist of the late sixteenth century explicitly addressing inter-sovereign relations is remarkable. The relationship between natural law, reason of state, and absolutism would come to take various forms, particularly as different conceptions of the relationship between law and the emerging state were fleshed out. Gentili's *DIB* constitutes a fascinating early attempt at juggling these ideas and reconciling them within the context of the tense inter-sovereign relations of the period. In Chapter 3, I examine Gentili's attempt to resolve the tensions he faced in elaborating his approach to the laws of war.

---

[131] For instance, a particularly intriguing piece suggests that Hobbes' translation of Thucydides, published as *Eight Bookes of the Peloponesian Warres*, should be understood not as a move within the debate about absolutism and domestic sovereignty, but as one within debates about the law of nations and about the place of law in the colonial world. See Warren, "Hobbes's Thucydides and the Colonial Law of Nations." More broadly, see notably the chapters on Niccolò Machiavelli and Jean Bodin in Kadelbach, Kleinlein, and Roth-Isigkeit, *System, Order, and International Law*.
[132] I briefly develop this idea in Vergerio, "Alberico Gentili's De iure belli."

3   Grounding an Absolutist Approach
to the Laws of War

Having embraced absolutism and the logic of *raison d'état*, Gentili's greatest challenge was to give supreme sovereign rulers an incentive to abide
by a set of laws in resolving conflicts amongst themselves. While Gentili
is often celebrated for having made a prescient case for third party arbitration,[1] he also accepted that war would at times be inevitable. In order
to curb the ongoing carnage of the Wars of Religion, jurists of the period
thought it necessary to, first, develop a set of rules that would limit the
extent of the devastation, and, second, encourage sovereigns to actually
follow these rules. While Gentili's work on the first point is well known, the
framework he developed for the second has rarely been addressed. This is
puzzling, because his work on this second point cries out for explication.
Given Gentili's positions on absolutism and the value of the reason of state
tradition, it is hard to see what resources he had available for encouraging sovereigns to play by the rules. In this chapter, I argue that Gentili
squared the circle through a dichotomy at the heart of his legal framework: the distinction between violence carried out by a "public" entity
and all other forms of violence. In Gentili's framework, those carrying out
the latter would immediately be discredited as "pirates" or "enemies of
mankind." The key, of course, was what Gentili meant by "public."

Gentili's unprecedented reliance on the concept of the enemy of mankind is particularly noteworthy given the central role it plays in contemporary scholarship. In the field of international law, David Luban, for
instance, has explicitly drawn on the old concept of the *hostis humani
generis* in order to ground the more recent concept of crimes against
humanity in historical tradition.[2] From a more critical perspective,

---

[1] Gentili, *De iure belli*, Book I, Chapter 3, §25.
[2] Luban's definition of the concept of a "crime against humanity" relies directly and
explicitly on the concept of the pirate as *hostis humani generis*: "Crimes against humanity are simultaneously offenses against humankind and injuries to humanness. They
are so universally odious that they make the criminal *hostis humani generis* – an enemy
of all humankind, like the pirate on the high seas under traditional international law."
Luban, "A Theory of Crimes against Humanity," 90.

Gerry Simpson argues that "[p]irates were ... international law's original enemies of humankind" and that "piracy is a founding metaphor for a whole sub-discipline of public international law: international criminal law or the law of war crimes." In short, "[p]iracy is international law's foundational *bête noire*."[3] In IR, Martin Wight has characterized the idea of piracy as international society's foundational other. "Since the sixteenth century," Wight claims, "international society has been so organised that no individuals except sovereign princes can be members of it, and these only in their representative capacity."[4] "All other individuals," Wight continues, "have had to be subjects or citizens of sovereign States. By a famous paradox of international law, the only persons emancipated from this necessity are pirates, by virtue of being *hostis humani generis*."[5] How are we to understand Gentili's reliance on this famous figure in his treatise on the laws of war?

This chapter proceeds in four parts. First, I summarize the specific set of rules Gentili developed for the conduct of war in *DIB* and place them in their immediate intellectual context. These rules have earned Gentili the title of "founding father" of the "classical" laws of war.[6] Indeed, much of the general literature on the history of international law credits Gentili's *DIB* with heralding a shift from the "medieval" to the "modern" conception of war.[7] This chapter provides a critical lens through which to evaluate these claims. In particular, I argue that it is within *DIB*'s immediate context that Gentili's central dichotomy between public violence and violence carried out by enemies of mankind is best understood.

Second, I argue that in order to "sell" his legal system to sovereigns – to give them an incentive to follow these rules – Gentili established a sharp binary between the honorable few who could play the game of war and those who were excluded from it. In this system, disagreeing sovereigns ought to respect each other as legitimate enemies, while their true hatred ought to be kept for the common enemies of all mankind.

---

[3] Simpson, "Enemies of Mankind," 87.
[4] Wight, "Why Is There No International Theory?" 18.
[5] Ibid.
[6] Grewe, *The Epochs of International Law*, 209–14. Grewe describes Gentili as "one of the most important founding fathers of a purely secular law of nations and, in particular, of the classical laws of war" (214). More specifically, he argues that Gentili was "the earliest theoretician to define and formulate" the style of war "reflected in the classic laws of war as they were codified in the Hague Conventions of 1899 and 1907" (211), i.e., what Grewe himself refers to as "non-discriminatory war," a concept to which I return in Chapter 6.
[7] As we will see in Chapter 6, this is nowhere more apparent than in Carl Schmitt's influential *Nomos of the Earth*.

In other words, if Gentili's framework calls for sovereigns to accept some constraints on their behavior, it makes doing so appealing by reinforcing their power through that very framework. I briefly outline Gentili's sharp distinction between legitimate and illegitimate fighters, and I examine what he allowed legitimate belligerents to do against those who took up arms illegally.

Third, I address the key question that Gentili had to answer in elaborating this framework: Who exactly qualifies as a sovereign? As we will see, this question was highly relevant within Gentili's political context: At the time he wrote, debates were raging about the nature of sovereignty and the corresponding status of various polities. Crucially, within Gentili's strict binary framework, those who cannot claim to be sovereigns – or to be fighting on behalf of one – become enemies of mankind when they take up arms.

Finally, I consider how Gentili was perceived in the period immediately following his death up until his rediscovery in the nineteenth century. Which features of his work were most commonly remembered? Was he perceived as a great figure of the history of the law of nations? To what extent were his absolutist leanings discussed? I examine how his work was interpreted both by his peers (who would have taken part in similar debates) and by later readers (who knew him through the eyes of those peers rather than through those of contemporary scholars).

Throughout the chapter I refer extensively to the text of *DIB*.[8] *De iure belli* is divided into three parts, which correspond to the contemporary

---

[8] As I mentioned in Chapter 2, Gentili did write another important text on war, *De armis romanis* (*DAR*). In this text, Gentili first presents thirteen chapters accusing the Romans of unjust warfare and then writes a chapter-by-chapter rebuttal of these accusations, thus presenting both sides of the debate (a classic trope of Renaissance classroom humanism). The interpretation of *DAR* has been a continuing source of dispute, particularly as regards its relationship to *DIB*. Since the main question it raises pertains to determining whether Gentili was a humanist or not, and since I have already addressed this debate in Chapter 2, and *DIB* is the text that is considered Gentili's masterpiece and his crucial contribution to the laws of war, I will focus exclusively on the latter in the present discussion. On the relationship between *DIB* and *DAR*, see Panizza, "Alberico Gentili's De Armis Romanis; Lupher," "The De armis romanis and the Exemplum of Roman Imperialism." Panizza argues that *DAR* was written in direct support of *DIB* (there is a "fundamental continuity between the two works"), and that Gentili is clearly siding with the defender of Roman imperialism (the speaker in Book II), making *DAR* a statement of Gentili's staunch (civic) humanism. Lupher, who translated *DAR* into English, is less sure about this interpretation, noting that, for instance, Gentili depicts the accuser of Book I in a way that sounds exactly like himself. Lupher, furthermore, finds the link between *DAR* and *DIB* much more tenuous: "While there is some point in labelling the treatise on the Roman wars a 'satellite' treatise to the more ambitious and systematic treatise on the laws of war, it seems likely that it was 'attracted' into that work's 'orbit,' not carefully designed to service as 'a legitimating topos' that elaborates and justifies the grand system of *DIB*." 99–100.

way of compartmentalizing the laws of war. Using modern terminology: Book I pertains to the *ius ad bellum* (questions of justice in declaring war), Book II to the *ius in bello* (questions of justice within war), and Book III the *ius post bellum* (questions of justice in the aftermath of war). Book I also contains some introductory chapters on international law and on the nature of war.

3.1   Gentili's Unusual Framework

As we saw in Chapter 2, for most of the sixteenth and the seventeenth centuries, the European continent was torn apart by devastating wars driven in part by religious disagreements.[9] What is usually understood is that the conflicts proved so destructive in part because most parties relied on the medieval notion of "just war." According to this conception, the "just" character of a war depended on the *iusta causa*, the justness of the cause promoted by the belligerent.[10] The "just" belligerent was a morally legitimate attacker, while the opponent was a criminal. As Francisco de Vitoria put it, "a prince who fights a just war becomes a judge of the enemy."[11] Under these circumstances, war was a punitive endeavor: There were few limits on the actions a "just" belligerent was allowed to take in order to defeat the criminal enemy.[12]

These rules began to be rethought, giving rise to a new set of writings on the laws of war. The most famous is Hugo Grotius' (1583–1645) *De iure belli ac pacis* (1625), but earlier key landmarks included Belli's (1502–1575) *De re militari et de bello* (1563), Balthazar de Ayala's (1548–1584) *De iure et officiis bellicis et disciplina militari* (1584), and Gentili's *DIB* of 1598. Belli's 1563 text was one of the most comprehensive treatments of military law and of the rules of war that had been written up to that time, and it had a significant influence on Ayala and Gentili in their efforts to systematize the laws of war. Along with these

---

9 While it used to be common to speak simply of devastating "wars of religion" ending with the Peace of Westphalia in 1648, it is important to remember that religion was only one of the many overlapping motives that drove these wars and that a number of conflicts continued after 1648. For a brief discussion of these points, see Osiander, "Sovereignty, International Relations, and the Westphalian Myth."

10 For a succinct overview of the concept of war and the laws of war in the Middle Ages, see Neff, *War and the Law of Nations*, 7–82. For a more detailed account, see Keen, *The Laws of War in the Late Middle Ages*.

11 Vitoria, *Political Writings*, 283.

12 This is not to say that the medieval notion of just war had no influence on the later development of the laws of war. On the contrary, feudal war did comprehend a number of rules – notably the rules of chivalry – which would eventually become one of the most important sources of the *jus belli*.

texts specifically on the laws of war, numerous other writers – from the theologians of the Second Scholastic to the French legal humanists – wrote about war and its laws. In this vibrant context, Gentili's writings are widely considered to have been of central importance to the development of the modern institutions of both diplomacy and war,[13] to have brought about the secularization of the law of nations, and to have marked the defining turn toward a "modern" conception of war. In this regard, Gentili is seen as having redefined what war meant within international society and what role the laws of war ought to play in ensuring the smooth operation of this necessary institution.

Evaluating these claims requires careful attention to Gentili's intellectual context. As we saw in Chapter 2, while Bodin had sought to do away with religious disputes as a factor undermining order at the domestic level, Gentili tried to extend this attempt to the inter-sovereign realm. The relationship between sovereign polities was bound to be a difficult issue, as "the very nature of their sovereignty and their claim to it undermined the possibility of adopting the solution Bodin had offered for pacifying the conflicting parties within France"[14] – namely, having all parties rely on a higher, single authority to resolve disputes. It is unsurprising, then, that Gentili put such a strong emphasis on the importance of arbitration between sovereigns.[15] As he put it, "differences among sovereigns ... must be decided by the law of nations."[16] Gentili was also conscious, however, that conflicts between sovereigns could not always be solved politically, and that sometimes war between sovereigns could therefore not be avoided. He thus took some steps toward developing a framework for war, one that would take into account the inevitability of differences arising between sovereigns and that would turn war into a formal means for solving these differences should all other methods fail. In this regard, the literature credits Gentili with making two major contributions: the claim that war must be public, and the claim that all legitimate belligerents must be placed

---

[13] On the importance of Gentili's writings, and particularly *De legationibus* (on embassies), for the development of the modern institution of diplomacy, and of international society more broadly, see, for example, Mattingly, *Renaissance Diplomacy*, Part IV; Kingsbury, "Confronting Difference"; Bull, *The Anarchical Society*, 30.

[14] Schröder, "Vitoria, Gentili, Bodin," 177.

[15] Gentili, *De iure belli*, Book I, Chapter 3, §25. For an analysis, see Van der Molen, *Alberico Gentili and the Development of International Law*, 116–17. Interestingly, there is actually no equivalent discussion of this issue in the first edition of Grotius' *De iure belli ac pacis*, but Grotius then seems "subsequently to have appreciated the importance of this element of Gentili's thought, and added a section on arbitration to later editions." Kingsbury, "Confronting Difference," 720.

[16] Gentili, *De iure belli*, Book I, Chapter 3, §25.

on equal legal footing. I will discuss these claims in turn, but first it is important to explain one further element of Gentili's intellectual context: his relationship to canon law, theology, and the just war tradition.

Like other early modern thinkers, Gentili was enormously influenced by medieval ideas about law, war, and political authority;[17] these stemmed from both Roman law and canon law, which were studied together and are generally – though perhaps inaccurately – referred to as the *ius commune*.[18] The continuities between these ideas and the arguments about the right to wage war presented in the works of jurists such as Gentili and Grotius are well known and have been examined at length elsewhere.[19] Indeed, these jurists often relied on medieval scholars explicitly in their work. As we saw in Chapter 2, Baldus de Ubaldis, one of the most famous figures of medieval Roman law, is the second most cited source in Gentili's *DIB* after the *Corpus iuris civilis* itself. Gentili also drew heavily from Thomas Aquinas and the broader Dominican tradition. These are important continuities, and I do not seek to erase them. Specific elements of discontinuity, however, help us to better understand the intervention Gentili was making at the time.

Gentili's ideas were also profoundly intertwined with theology, despite his reputation as a great secularizer of international law. Much of the confusion on this point – generated in large part, as we will see, by Gentili's late nineteenth-century revivers and later on by Carl Schmitt – stems from what we mean by secularization. As Domingo and Minnucci put it, "Gentili's secularization is theistic and firmly based on Christian principles and ideals,"[20] a statement that might seem oxymoronic to contemporary readers. Gentili did take important steps toward disentangling the law of nations from theology – some of which I will explain later – but there was nonetheless no question for him that the laws of God ruled supreme over human law, nor that natural law was divine law and therefore above civil law.[21] The puzzle only arises from our widespread but problematic periodization of a religious

---

[17] For an excellent overview of medieval debates over the nature of political authority, see Lopez, "Political Authority in International Relations."

[18] For a brief introduction to the impact of medieval thought on early modern international law, and notably on the idea of just and unjust wars, see Canning, "The Medieval Roman and Canon Law Origins of International Law." Canning notes the anachronistic character of the term *ius commune*, which has been used since the mid-twentieth century to refer to a medieval legal system, even though the medieval *ius commune* was merely a form of legal order, not a modern system of law.

[19] Haggenmacher, *Grotius et la doctrine de la guerre juste*.

[20] Domingo and Minnucci, "Alberico Gentili and the Secularization of the Law of Nations," 112.

[21] Ibid.

"medieval" and a secular "modern." In the early modern period, processes of "secularization," so to speak, entailed not the disappearance of the religious or the sacred but rather a focus on temporal rather than eternal matters.[22] I will return to this problem of periodization – predominantly a nineteenth-century inheritance – in Chapter 6. For now, suffice it to say that Gentili was a deeply religious man who, as an intellectual and a jurist, drew heavily on canon law and theological writings about just war from his medieval precursors; should a single label be assigned to his approach, he can most accurately be placed within the Protestant natural law tradition.[23] As part of this heritage, Gentili notably conflated the *ius gentium* and the *ius naturale* and considered them to be an expression of divine will, a fact that underlines the importance of speaking of some degree of "secularization" – if at all – with great contextual precision.

I return now to the two critical claims that underpin Gentili's framework. First, Gentili is (somewhat questionably)[24] considered to have been the first jurist of his time to argue that war "on both sides must be public and official and there must be sovereigns on both sides to direct the war."[25] Gentili defines war as *Bellum est publicorum armorum iusta contentio*:[26] war is a just contest of public arms (sometimes mistranslated as "war is a just and public contest of arms"). As we will see in Part II of the book, this definition is largely responsible for the idea of Gentili's "modernity." At the time Gentili wrote, his definition seemed to exclude a number of forms of violence that had previously been included – and would continue to be included by someone as important as Grotius – such as private wars (between private actors) and, more importantly, "mixed wars" (between a public and a private actor).

Private warfare, or feud, had been on the decline for some time already; it had been banned in France in 1367, in 1495 in the Holy Roman Empire, and the practice slowly declined, with the last traditional feud organized in 1567.[27] The case of mixed wars, however, was much more complex, as it involved a public actor. Gentili undermined the status not only of private warfare but also of mixed wars by

---

[22] For an excellent overview of this issue, see Bain, *Political Theology of International Order*, 58–81.

[23] On this tradition, see Brett, *Changes of State*.

[24] In fact, his contemporary Balthazar de Ayala made a similar claim a few years earlier – I return to this point later in this section.

[25] Gentili, *De iure belli*, Book I, Chapter 3, §23.

[26] Ibid., Book 1, Chapter 2, §18.

[27] Black, *European Warfare, 1494–1660*, 22.

imposing a requirement that both sides be public entities for a conflict to be legally considered a war. For Gentili, the violence carried out by the nonpublic belligerent must instead be considered an act of *brigandage*. Gentili's reasoning is simple: Only a war between sovereigns can be lawful because war is only justified by the absence of a jurisdiction capable of ruling upon a dispute and imposing its judgment. War is thus waged out of necessity, because only the "arbitrament of Mars" can settle a dispute between two sovereigns with no higher jurisdiction.[28]

The second central claim of Gentili's framework has to do with equal footing. Since war was to be a mechanism for arbitrating disputes among those who recognize no superior, Gentili put forward a set of rules, based on the idea of war as a form of duel between sovereigns.[29] The cornerstone of this approach was to place all legitimate (i.e., public) belligerents on equal legal footing in order to ensure mutual respect and reciprocity. And in turn, this move was made possible by what is perhaps Gentili's single most famous contribution, the claim that war can be just – not merely subjectively but also objectively – on both sides.[30] From this position, it followed that the laws of war had to apply equally to both sides and that belligerents' rights in war regarding matters such as prisoners and booty would be applied irrespective of the justness of their cause. This position is credited as a watershed moment in the general literature on international law, war, and international relations more broadly, as well as in some of the specialized literature on the Italian jurist.[31] According to Diego Panizza, for instance, Gentili's position meant that he "came to subvert the whole structure of the medieval doctrine, founded as it was on the basic assumption that the adversary's injustice, or *iniuria*, makes a war just and on the consequent assertion that one side must be in the wrong."[32]

In order to support these claims, Gentili cites a rather obscure figure, the jurist Raphael Fulgosius (1367–1427),[33] whom he refers to

---

[28] Gentili, *De iure belli*, Book I, Chapter 3, §32.

[29] Ibid., Book I, Chapter 2, §18.

[30] Gentili dedicates an entire chapter to this argument, "Chapter 6: That War May Be Waged Justly by Both Sides" (Gentili, Book I, Chapter 6.)

[31] See, for instance, Nussbaum, *A Concise History of the Law of Nations*, 97; Brownlie, *International Law and the Use of Force by States*, 12; Grewe, *The Epochs of International Law*, 211; Tuck, *The Rights of War and Peace*, 31–34.

[32] Panizza, "Political Theory and Jurisprudence in Gentili's De Iure Belli," 17.

[33] Fulgosius, "Just War Reduced to Public War." On Fulgosius' influence, see Haggenmacher, *Grotius et la doctrine de la guerre juste*, 201–09. As Haggenmacher explains, Fulgosius was completely out of line with Bartolist orthodoxy when he

only three times in the entire text of *DIB*.[34] As one might expect, though, Gentili was part of a longer development toward this "bilateral"[35] conception of war, and his radical break with his predecessors needs to be somewhat relativized. It is true that Gentili was quite peculiar in adopting a fully relativistic position with respect to the just cause question within the context of a debate about whether war could be just on both sides. Yet this was just one of the many different positions at the time that challenged the traditional "just cause" approach. Three groups are particularly worth mentioning here: the theologians of the School of Salamanca (most importantly Francisco de Vitoria), the French legal humanists, and the reason of state writers. All three groups made moves that undermined the just cause approach, and Gentili was very much embedded within these debates in developing his own position.

First, the theologians of the School of Salamanca (or "Second Scholastic"), who were profoundly indebted to the teachings of Augustine and Thomas Aquinas, had critically engaged the traditional theological perspective on war, which conceived of war as a unilateral act of justice.[36] While as with virtually all "schools," there was quite a bit of variation in the views of Soto, Cano, Molina, Suárez, and the like, the Salamancans were all pupils and followers of Francisco de Vitoria, who had made some decisive advances on previous theologians. I will draw examples primarily from the latter's work in order to illustrate their thought in very broad lines.

The original Thomist doctrine of war had three components: just authority, just cause, and purity of heart (or "right intention");[37]

---

wrote, and, with his Roman-style advocacy of a purely procedural understanding of bilateral war, "demeura longtemps le témoin incompris d'une conception apparemment révolue." Haggenmacher, *Grotius et la doctrine de la guerre juste*, 287.

[34] Gentili, *De iure belli*, Book I, Chapter 6, §48 (in text only); Book I, Chapter 22, §174; Book III, Chapter 23, §695.

[35] I borrow the term "bilateral" in this context from Haggenmacher.

[36] Though contrary to some interpretations, this was not equivalent to viewing war as a punishment imposed on a wrongdoer. Justice in this tradition could involve notions of correction, restoration, and restitution rather than mere punishment.

[37] "In order for a war to be just, three things are necessary. First, the authority of the sovereign by whose command the war is to be waged ... Secondly, a just cause is required, namely that those who are attacked, should be attacked because they deserve it on account of some fault ... Thirdly, it is necessary that the belligerents should have a rightful intention, so that they intend the advancement of good, or the avoidance of evil." Thomas Aquinas, *Summa Theologiae*, II, Q.40, art. 1. The concept of "right intention" is discussed at length by James Turner Johnson; see especially his *Just War Tradition and the Restraint of War* and *Ideology, Reason, and the Limitation of War*.

importantly, these criteria already did not discriminate between religions.[38] Vitoria made a decisive move in establishing that the only just cause (other than cases of legitimate self-defense) was a response to a previous "injury" [*inuria*], namely a violation of the law, thus heavily circumscribing Aquinas' original approach.[39] This shift from a fairly broadly defined "just cause" to a narrow focus on "injury" was applied to Aquinas' third requirement of "purity of heart" as well. In effect, this requirement would now be limited to a mere effort at honesty in the assessment that a serious enough injury had indeed taken place,[40] as well as a commitment to responding proportionally to the injury (thus excluding a war of revenge or war based on a fake cause). Vitoria had thus bracketed the requirements of "just cause" and "purity of heart" into a question of whether there had been an "injury" and whether the attacking party had identified such an injury in good faith.

Vitoria could not accept that war could be just on both sides, but he was willing to concede that in many conflicts, both sides would invoke the existence of an injury. Broadly speaking, he, along with his followers, put forward two ways of addressing this issue. First, they distinguished the prince and his advisors (those "invited to be heard in the public or royal council"[41]) on the one hand and common soldiers on the other. Since the latter were not entitled to question the judgment of their superiors, for them the war would have to be regarded as "just."[42] For common soldiers at least, a certain degree of justice could thus exist on both sides of a conflict. As for the prince and his advisors, Vitoria considered that a prince could also be cleared from injustice if he went to war mistakenly convinced of the existence of an injury (what Vitoria famously refers to

---

[38] And similarly, one could not wage war simply on the basis of religious difference. Vitoria reiterates this forcefully in *On the Law of War*, at the start of his discussion of "[w]hat are the permissible reasons and causes of just war." "First," he states, "difference of religion cannot be a cause for war." Vitoria, *Political Writings*, 302.

[39] Haggenmacher, *Grotius et la doctrine de la guerre juste*, 171. Vitoria states: "The sole and only just cause for waging war is when harm has been inflicted." Vitoria, *Political Writings*, 303.

[40] For indeed, Vitoria reminds us that "not every or any injury gives sufficient ground for waging war." Vitoria, *Political Writings*, 304.

[41] Ibid., 308.

[42] "[L]esser subjects who are not invited to be heard in the councils of the prince nor in public council are not required to examine the causes of war, but may lawfully go to war trusting the judgment of their superior." Ibid. It was crucial for the theologians to avoid turning matters of conscience into public law because they feared it would encourage disobedience and rebellion.

as "invincible ignorance" or "invincible error").[43] More broadly, since no one was entitled to question a prince's judgment as to the justice of war anyway, this question was effectively relegated to the realm of conscience: It was, in other words, ultimately a question between the prince and God. These considerations did not amount to the stronger claim that war could objectively be just on both sides, but in practice they paralleled a bilateral approach to war.

A second group to challenge traditional "just cause" accounts included French humanist jurists such as Alciatus and Budaeus. During the same period as the Salamancans, they had begun to emphasize the distinction between "formal justice," that is, justice as legality, and the notion of a just cause. Budaeus had contributed some important philological reflections, pointing out that for Roman lawyers *iustum* often referred to justice of a formal or procedural kind rather than a material or substantive one.[44] Alciatus, more importantly, had taken stock of Fulgosius' writings and developed an approach that placed both sides on equal footing. However, whereas Fulgosius had faithfully followed the Roman approach and established that both sides were to be equal by virtue of their nature as sovereigns obeying no higher authority, Alciatus reintroduces considerations about the material justice of each side's cause. Instead of embracing Fulgosius' purely formalistic approach, Alciatus bases the equality of belligerents on the difficulty of determining which side is in fact acting justly. It is not clear exactly where this uncertainty comes from: from each party's subjective understanding of their cause (coming close to the "invincible ignorance" approach put forth by the theologians), or rather from the fact that certain situations are simply too complex to allow a clear-cut conclusion. In any case, if one side's cause does indeed turn out to be unjust, the belligerent – regardless of their sovereign status – goes back from being a *hostis* to a *latrunculus*, from an enemy to a brigand. Alciatus had thus moved fairly close to a bilateral conception of war, based on a formalistic understanding of the equality of belligerents, while maintaining a "just cause" aspect to his reasoning.[45]

A third significant group to challenge the just cause approach were reason of state writers. In this regard, Machiavelli is often cited for claiming "that war is just which is necessary," with the implication that any prince may decide on the occasion for war.[46] What this quotation

[43] Ibid., 313. For a detailed discussion, see Haggenmacher, *Grotius et la doctrine de la guerre juste*, 209–21.

[44] Haggenmacher, *Grotius et la doctrine de la guerre juste*, 299.

[45] Ibid., 204–05.

[46] See, for instance, Brownlie, *International Law and the Use of Force by States*, 11.

means in context is not so clear,[47] and in any case, Machiavelli certainly did not think a capricious prince could simply do anything he wanted. Nevertheless, his approach to the justice of war did pose a profound challenge to the just war tradition; as we saw in Chapter 2, it postulated a completely different moral scheme. What was "just" was merely what was in the advantage of the prince in maintaining his *stato*, that is, his "estate" or "status," and the prince would be the one deciding what exactly this entailed. As a result, Machiavelli deemed expansion to be a perfectly legitimate cause of war. A prince could certainly do wrong by pursuing policies that were not in the interest of his *stato*, but this had little to do with any traditional just war considerations. Importantly, though, Machiavelli and his later followers, most notably Guicciardini (1482–1540) and Botero (1540–1617), would all consider the judgment of the prince on what was "necessary" to be without any legitimate challengers, particularly not foreign sovereigns.

Gentili seems to have been influenced by all three of these groups. As we saw in Chapter 2, he cites legal humanists and the reason of state writers quite frequently, and within the context of this particular debate, he also refers to the Salamancans. The most relevant chapter is Book I, Chapter 6, entitled "That War May Be Waged Justly by Both Sides." Within the first paragraph, Gentili claims that in arguing that war can be just on both sides, he is following Fulgosius, who has already been followed by Alciatus "in more than one place."[48] He adds to this "the proviso that there may be reasonable doubt as to the justice of the cause" and agrees with "other jurists and our theologians" that both sides may think they have a just cause due to "justifiable ignorance,"[49] this time citing Vitoria, Soto, and Covarrubias. Then, going back to Alciatus, he remarks that "[i]t is the nature of wars for both sides to maintain that they are supporting a just cause."[50] Importantly, Gentili does not seem to grasp the important difference between Fulgosius' approach and Alciatus' on the question of whether having a just cause matters. What if one side's cause is clearly unjust? Does he, like Fulgosius, dismiss it as irrelevant for the equal application of the law to

---

[47] In the original passage, which is in Machiavelli's chapter entitled "An Exhortation to Liberate Italy from the Barbarians," Machiavelli actually appears to be saying that this particular war – the liberation of Italy – is legitimate because it is a last resort: "The justice of the cause is conspicuous; for that war is just which is necessary, and those arms are sacred from which we derive our only hope." Machiavelli, *The Prince*, Chapter 26. The original phrase is from Livy (iustum est bellum, Samnites, quibus necessarium: Livy, Histories, IX.1.10).

[48] Gentili, *De iure belli*, Book I, Chapter 6, §48.

[49] Ibid.

[50] Ibid., Book, I, Chapter 6, §49.

both sides, or does he, like Alciatus, see it as taking us back to a unilateral form of war?

A few paragraphs later, Gentili comes to the crux of his argument and resolves this problem in a rather dubious manner. He begins by stating: "Of all our laws, however, that one seems to me the clearest which grants the rights of war to both contestants, makes what is taken on each side the property of the captors, and regards the prisoners of both parties as slaves."[51] Going against Fulgosius on this point is "pleasurable madness ... as was demonstrated by Alciati, who also insists on that equality among enemies of which we made note before."[52] It may be the case that war is "just on one side, but on the other ... still more just"[53] (a rather original bit of analysis based on Piccolomini's writings on virtue), and more importantly "it may sometimes happen ... that injustice is clearly evident on one of the two sides."[54] The latter, however, does not really matter, "for laws are not based upon rare instance and adapted to them; that is to say, on events which are rare in their own class, and which take place only occasionally, contrary to the general nature of the case."[55] Gentili thus wiggles out of the cleavage between Fulgosius and Alciatus and concludes that "this ought not to affect the general principle, and prevent the laws of war from applying to both parties."[56] As Gentili erects bilaterality as his general principle, the approach according to which a belligerent's rights depend on the justness of their cause seems virtually abandoned.

And yet, some may claim that Gentili must have thought that having a just cause mattered, since the majority of Book I (Chapters 8–20) is devoted to the discussion of what constitutes an appropriate cause for making war.[57] Indeed, Gentili does seem to suggest at one point that while sovereigns do not need a "just cause" to go to war, they still have to present a "plausible" claim.[58] He forcefully reiterates this point in Chapter 8, "Of the Causes of War," concluding that "therefore there

---

[51] Ibid., Book I, Chapter 6, §51.
[52] Ibid.
[53] Ibid.
[54] Ibid., Book I, Chapter 6, §52.
[55] Ibid.
[56] Ibid. In fact, Gentili contradicts himself on this point earlier in the chapter, when he states that "we say that if it is evident that one party is contending without any adequate reason, that party is surely practicing brigandage and not waging war." Ibid., Book I, Chapter 6, §49. This confusion, which is not entirely surprising considering Gentili is relying at once on Fulgosius, Alciatus, and the theologians, suggests that this was indeed a very thorny issue for him and that he very much struggled to resolve it properly.
[57] In this respect, Gentili's discussion, while rather unsystematic, was innovative in his extensive reliance on historic examples, both ancient and contemporary.
[58] Ibid., Book I, Chapter 6, §50.

should be grounds for war, and they should not be trivial."[59] In the ensuing discussion, he famously dismisses the traditional religious causes,[60] but he allows for various other ones,[61] including the need to enforce one's right to navigate freely (a crucial issue at the time).[62] In this lengthy discussion of acceptable and nonacceptable causes, Gentili's focus seems to echo the usual concerns of theologians.

There is, however, a catch in Gentili's presentation of the just and unjust causes of war, or the sort of claims that can constitute a plausible ground for resorting to war. Gentili does not provide a way for determining whether a claim is, in fact, "plausible." Crucially, he notes – in a remark that echoes the hard-headed pragmatism of the reason of state literature, although he does not cite any particular authority for it – that "princes always allege some plausible reason for beginning their wars; although frequently they have no reason at all."[63] Gentili's attempt to solve this problem takes him further down the relativist path. In short, Gentili considers that since equal sovereigns have no jurisdiction over each other – they do not recognize a superior – no one can assess the legitimacy of a prince's claim or cause prior to the armed conflict. In doing so, Gentili extended his concept of war as a duel to the aspect concerning the "cognition" of the law,[64] thus perplexingly rendering his own discussion of the just causes of war all but moot. The question of what constitutes a just cause becomes irrelevant if no one is entitled to adjudicate a prince's claim to justice.

The outcome of this somewhat muddled discussion of just cause leads Gentili to rely – like Fulgosius and to a lesser extent Alciatus – on another criterion for establishing the "just" character of a war: the "public" character of the conflict. The all-important concept of his approach is not the *iusta causa* but the *iustus hostis* – the "just" or "lawful" enemy. According to Gentili's approach – although he never says it in so many words – belligerents who have "proper authority," that is, established sovereigns, are by definition conferred the status of *iustus hostis*, regardless of their cause for war: "*hostis* is a person with whom war is waged and who is the equal of his opponent."[65] On the one hand, this claim implies the full equality of the belligerent powers. On the

---

[59] Ibid., Book I, Chapter 8, §55.
[60] With the exception of war against atheists (more on this later). Ibid., Book I, Chapter 9, §65.
[61] For an analysis of Gentili's arguments about the appropriate causes for making war, see Van der Molen, *Alberico Gentili and the Development of International Law*, 121–29.
[62] Gentili, *De iure belli*, Book I, Chapter 19.
[63] Ibid., Book I, Chapter 7, §54.
[64] Panizza, "Political Theory and Jurisprudence in Gentili's De Iure Belli," 18.
[65] Gentili, *De iure belli*, Book I, Chapter 2, §18.

other hand, this claim entails that a sovereign could lawfully declare war under any pretext, a position that seemed to echo the controversial *raison d'état* thinking a little too closely for many of Gentili's contemporaries.[66] This was a fairly bold position to advance, but it was not entirely new.

Balthazar de Ayala, who died just a few years before Gentili published his first, shorter version of *DIB* (1588/89), is generally seen as Gentili's most important predecessor. (In some respects, Gentili's writings were less definitive than Ayala's on some key points, but he has nonetheless been repeatedly identified as the figure who took the clearest step in the direction of a modern law of war.) Indeed, Ayala had already formulated some of Gentili's most notable positions in his *De iure et officiis bellicis et disciplina militari* (1584).

First, within the "secularization of international law narrative," Ayala is commonly portrayed as having been the first to begin formulating a juridical approach to the laws of war "which had nothing to do with the arguments of moral theology."[67] As we have seen, this is an overstatement at best. Second, and more importantly for our purposes, Ayala formulated an approach to the laws of war that had also made the public character of the belligerents its cornerstone. Ayala, just like Gentili, was influenced by the work of Pierrino Belli and attempted to systematize the laws of war in a context of devastating violence.[68] In doing so, he was also strongly influenced by Fulgosius, and in fact Ayala's approach is the only one that truly embraced Fulgosius' radical vision.[69] Crucially, Ayala was also profoundly influenced by Bodin,[70] and he relied extensively on his concepts in *De iure et officiis bellicis et disciplina militari*, particularly Bodin's understanding of sovereignty. Combining Fulgosius' formal approach to the justice of war with Bodin's groundbreaking conception of sovereignty, Ayala put forth a new framework for the laws of war with far-reaching consequences.

More than anyone since Fulgosius, Ayala embraced the idea of the "just" character of war being dependent not on the belligerent having a "just cause" but on the war being declared and waged according

---

[66] Gentili would come under fire from Grotius for this position, as well as, later on, from Rousseau and Kant. Grotius made it clear that he was under no circumstances prepared to accept the concept of war as a duel on the basis that only victory will decide the legitimacy of the cause; Rousseau and Kant made similar criticisms and emphasized that Grotius had also failed to resolve this problem. For a brief overview of these critiques, see Schröder, "Vitoria, Gentili, Bodin," 185.

[67] Grewe, *The Epochs of International Law*, 208.

[68] Van der Molen, *Alberico Gentili and the Development of International Law*, 85.

[69] Haggenmacher, *Grotius et la doctrine de la guerre juste*, 298.

[70] For Bodin's influence on Ayala, see Ibid., 300.

to certain formal principles.[71] A war is "just," in Ayala's sense, if it is waged according to a specific set of rules, regardless of the "cause" at hand. In other words, a war may be considered "just" even when it is not founded on a just cause [*de acquitate causae*].[72] More specifically – and crucially for Ayala's doctrine – the "justness" or "legality" of the war depends on it being "declared and undertaken under the authority [*auctoritas*] of a sovereign prince" [*summus princeps*].[73] There is no other source of "justice" for the war. In marked contrast to his predecessors, Ayala's bilateral application of the laws of war does not stem from the possibility of flawed judgment in assessing the just character of each side's cause. On this particular point, Ayala explicitly differs from Gentili: The fact that the cause of war is clearly unjust on one side is not dismissed as irrelevant to the general principle merely because it is rare. For Ayala, the justness of each side's cause is simply and purely irrelevant. This implies that any war conducted by a belligerent with proper authority is just [*iustus*], in the sense that no other authority can render a judgment upon its decision to resort to arms. Ultimately, the conclusion is the same as the one Gentili would later reach: Ayala concedes the legal status of *hostis* (*iustus hostis*) – "just enemy" – to both belligerents in the war, putting them on equal legal footing.[74]

In light of these continuities, it is thus rather puzzling that Gentili does not cite Ayala at all in *DIB*, a fact that seems to have escaped scholarly attention thus far. One hypothesis is that Gentili simply did not know Ayala's work at the time, even though he would come to cite him a few years later, in the *Hispanica advocatio*.[75] However, in light of its significance during the period, and since Ayala was Gentili's main intellectual rival within the specific area of the law of war,[76] this seems rather unlikely.

---

[71] See generally Ayala, *De jure et officiis bellicis et disciplina militari libri tres*, Book I, Chapter II.

[72] Ayala, *De jure et officiis bellicis et disciplina militari libri tres*, Book I, Chapter II, §33–34. For a more detailed discussion of Ayala's position on this point, see Haggenmacher, *Grotius et la doctrine de la guerre juste*, 298–300.

[73] Ibid., Book I, Chapter II, §7.

[74] Based on these contributions, some scholars have sought to reemphasize the importance of Ayala's work for the development of the laws of war and of international law more broadly. See especially Peralta, *Baltasar de Ayala y el derecho de la guerra*.

[75] Ayala's name appears both in the margins and in the text of the *Hispanica advocatio*, including in Gentili's original manuscript of 1605 (available at the Bodleian, MS. D'Orville number 608). It is hard to know when exactly Gentili first encountered the Spaniard's work – the collection of his personal papers held at the Bodleian does not seem to provide any clear indications on this front.

[76] Grotius would in fact cite them both as his most important predecessors in the Prolegomena of his *De iure belli ac pacis*.

A more plausible hypothesis is that within the greatest European conflict of the time – the revolt of the Protestant Dutch Provinces, supported by Protestant England, against their Roman Catholic Spanish ruler (1566/68–1648) – Ayala and Gentili stood on opposite sides of the battlefield. Gentili, a Protestant, had fled religious persecution in his native Italy and made Protestant England his home. Ayala, meanwhile, was a loyal subject of the Spanish king, a zealous Roman Catholic, and an intellectual spokesman for the Spanish legal position condemning the Dutch rebellion of the time.[77] In addition to his personal background, Gentili later dedicated his first main work, *De legationibus* (1585), to his friend and benefactor Sir Philip Sidney, who died the following year at the Battle of Zutphen, fighting for the Protestant cause against the Spanish.[78] When Gentili returned to England to take up the Regius Professorship at Oxford in 1587, he did so upon request by Queen Elizabeth herself, who since 1585 had made her country's support of the Dutch official. More tellingly still, when in 1605 he accepted, with the explicit approval of King James I, a position as counsel to the Spanish delegation to England – a decision that "provoked a great deal of public criticism"[79] and that "has been regarded by later commentators as one of the most surprising actions of his career"[80] – he felt compelled to pen a lengthy justification of himself a few months later.[81] This suggests the pushback Gentili might have elicited by associating himself with the Spanish crown. In *DIB*, it was perhaps just simpler not to cite his controversial Spanish rival at all.

Still, the overlap between their positions is striking. Gentili was adopting an approach very similar to that of the man who had sought

---

[77] Haggenmacher, *Grotius et la doctrine de la guerre juste*, 138; Van der Molen, *Alberico Gentili and the Development of International Law*, 84.

[78] Gentili, *De legationibus libri tres*.

[79] Simmonds, "The Gentili Manuscripts," 536.

[80] Ibid., 539.

[81] The unpublished piece, entitled *Responsio ad eos qui nobis vilio vertunt quod stamus pro Hispanis*, is available in the Bodleian's D'Orville manuscripts collection and has conveniently been typed up and reproduced as an annex to Simmonds, "The Gentili Manuscripts." As Simmonds explains, "there is no evidence in his published works to explain this enigma, but this manuscript opinion helps us to understand Gentili's purpose and attitude." England and Spain were on neutral terms by that point, and Gentili's conclusion, in the words of Simmonds, was the following: "[T]he Spanish commission was offered to him freely and without his seeking it and he intends to be a most diligent advocate in the cases entrusted to him, so long as peace is maintained between England and Spain." In other words, "Gentili took his stand on the duty of an advocate to give his services, wherever sought, according to the traditions of his profession." Simmonds sympathetically notes that this "gives to the modern reader a courageous and convincing defence of his position" but he also acknowledges that "it can hardly have won over his adversaries." Ibid., 540.

to establish the legitimacy of crushing the most well-known rebellion of the time simply in the name of sovereign authority. For Ayala, saying that the war had to be public on both sides meant it could be waged exclusively by princes, and he justified the Spanish use of force against the Netherlands based on their rebellion against their legitimate ruler rather than because of their defection from the true faith. More broadly, Ayala's approach had dramatic consequences for those deemed not to be sovereigns, which he explicitly discussed. The rules of war he laid out applied only to those who possessed the formal criterion of authority; in cases where one of the parties did not fulfill the criteria, the violence could not be called a war at all.[82] Ayala, as one might guess, makes this particularly clear in the case of rebels: "Now, rebels ought not to be classed as enemies, the two being quite distinct, and so it is more correct to term the armed contention with rebel subjects execution of the legal process, or prosecution, and not war."[83] Consequently, rebels were to be treated like robbers and pirates; they were not protected by the laws of war and they could be killed as enemies, enslaved as prisoners, their property could be confiscated as booty, and contractual engagements with them did not need to be observed.[84] In other words, they were to be treated not as enemies in a conflict, but as mere criminals, against whom all the means of war – and more – could be unleashed.

3.2   Incentivizing Sovereigns to Follow the Law

Armed with this intellectual and political context, we are better prepared to evaluate claims about Gentili's significance. *DIB* certainly denotes an effort to tame the sort of violence he was witnessing around Europe. In addition, he provided an in-depth examination of which means could be applied against an adversary in war and which were too cruel to be allowed; he expressed a fairly tolerant attitude toward barbarians;[85] and he denounced the practice of waging war on people simply because of their religion.[86] As a result, scholars have repeatedly

---

[82] Ayala, *De jure et officiis bellicis et disciplina militari libri tres*, Book I, Chapter 2, §14.

[83] Ibid.

[84] Ibid., Book I, Chapter 2, §14–15.

[85] Kingsbury, "Confronting Difference," 722.

[86] Gentili dedicates a whole chapter to "Whether It Is Just to Wage War for the Sake of Religion" and makes his disapproval very clear: "Now if religion is of such a nature that it ought to be forced upon no one against his will, and if a propaganda which exacts faith by blows is called a strange and unheard-of thing, it follows that force in connection with religion is unjust." Gentili, *De iure belli*, Book I, Chapter 9, §60. He also refers to a rule "forbidding one to injure or press with the yoke those whom we can accuse of nothing more serious than that they are of a different race from our own." Ibid., Book III, Chapter 9, §333.

stressed the progressive character of Gentili's thinking on the laws of war. We are told that his approach "was based on the idea of containing the horror of war and promoting chivalrous means of conducting war between the armed forces of belligerents," and that his theory of war constitutes "a first step towards the non-discriminatory concept of war which dominated the classical period of the law of nations."[87] More broadly, Gentili is characterized as the "exponent of a progressive law of nations,"[88] whose work paved the way for the development of a new, modern concept of war, based on a secular, formalized, and humanized approach to war that would form the basis of the classical laws of war.

Yet, as I concluded at the end of Chapter 2, in devising his approach to the laws of war, Gentili had gotten himself in a rather awkward position. On the one hand, he considered sovereigns to recognize no superior and showed a certain admiration for the reason of state tradition that held the prince's interest as its guiding principle. On the other hand, he was trying to encourage all sovereigns to respect an established legal order in settling their armed disputes. Gentili needed something to "bind" sovereigns, to give them an incentive to cooperate with each other in the absence of any higher authorities. That something else, I will argue, was the rather elusive and threatening figure of the "enemy of mankind," embodied first and foremost by the figure of the *latro* – the pirate/brigand[89] – but also, as I will explain later, quite a range of other important groups. Panizza has suggested that Gentili's legal framework is tied to the "new/ancient notion of a 'natural society of mankind.'"[90] This is plausible, but I focus here on the flip side of this

---

[87] Grewe, *The Epochs of International Law*, 214.

[88] Alexandrowicz, "Introduction," viii; Nézard, "Albericus Gentilis," 38.

[89] *Latro* (plural *latrones*) is generally translated as brigand (as well as robber or thief) or pirate. Gentili uses *latro* as an umbrella term, but he also at times refers specifically to the pirate (*pirata/piratae*). The figure of the pirate has been relied on very often throughout the modern period because it has allowed jurists to claim the existence of a certain continuity with the ancient practice of considering pirates to be enemies of all. The extent to which this continuity actually exists is, however, greatly debated today. What appears from the current debate on the subject is that ancient attitudes toward piracy were hardly clear-cut (see especially Heller-Roazen, *The Enemy of All*, chapter 3) and that the famous term *hostis humani generis* (enemy of mankind) emerged centuries later. On the debated origins of the term, see Nussbaum, *A Concise History of the Law of Nations*, 314 n. 73; Rubin and Boczek, "Private and Public History," 31; Gould, "Cicero's Ghost;" Edelstein, "Hostis Humani Generis"; Tai, "Marking Water."

[90] Panizza, "Political Theory and Jurisprudence in Gentili's De Iure Belli," 43. The notion of a "natural society of mankind" is, however, not to be confused with the eighteenth-century concept of "Humanität" and any subsequent notion of "human rights," as in Meron, "Common Rights of Mankind in Gentili, Grotius and Suarez." This notion was ancient in the sense that Gentili was referring to the Stoic notion of the "natural society of mankind," but new in that he was moving away from rationales centered on the Christian community. On the naturalization of international society in the early modern period, see Roshchin, "(Un) Natural and Contractual International Society."

coin, namely Gentili's reliance on a constitutive "other" against whom all have an incentive to unite and rally.

As Daniel Heller-Roazen has remarked, "[i]t has less often been observed that the very thinkers who conceived the doctrine of war as a formal duel between equal parties also elaborated a detailed theory of an antagonist too iniquitous to deserve the title of proper opponent."[91] Arthur Nussbaum does rightly note this in the case of Ayala,[92] but this critical lens has rarely been applied to the work of Gentili. Yet, in attempting to give sovereigns an incentive to abide by his framework, he too carved out a legal space in which cruel acts and unrestrained violence by sovereigns could be considered entirely legitimate. In simple terms, at a time when different groups were using force and claiming to do so legitimately, Gentili drew a very clear line between those who were indeed entitled to do so and those who were not. This was certainly appealing for those who found themselves on the correct side of the divide. But before I dive into the question of who ended up falling into which category, let me outline the purpose of Gentili's reliance on the "enemy of mankind" concept – something which he did not pioneer, strictly speaking, but which he certainly used more forcefully than any of his predecessors, giving the figure a foundational role in his approach to the laws of war.

I wish to build here on the scattered remarks that have been made by scholars regarding the "other side" of Gentili's writings on the laws of war.[93] In essence, Gentili placed the figure of the enemy of mankind [*hostis humani generis*] at the heart of his approach to the laws of war by relying on a concrete figure: the *latro* (pirate/brigand). Gentili's approach, naturally, was not entirely new. Prior to him, the idea that certain individuals or groups required a particular legal

---

[91] Heller-Roazen, *The Enemy of All*, 115.

[92] Nussbaum, *A Concise History of the Law of Nations*, 92.

[93] As far as I am aware, the only scholar who has written a full piece on this aspect of Gentili's work is Ileana Porras, who did not publish her piece but kindly agreed to share it with me. The piece is entitled "Atheists, Cannibals, Rebels and Pirates: Cementing the Bonds of Human Society in Gentili's *De iure belli.*" Peter Schröder includes similar claims in a more general piece entitled "Vitoria, Gentili, and Bodin: Sovereignty and the Law of Nations." He also touches on some of these points in his analysis of Carl Schmitt's engagement with the works of Bodin, Hobbes, and Gentili in Schröder, "Carl Schmitt's Appropriation of the Early Modern European Tradition of Political Thought on the State and Interstate Relations." The four other scholars who have written about the enemy of mankind in Gentili's *De iure belli* are Harry Gould, Daniel Heller-Roazen, Walter Rech, and Alfred Rubin. See Gould, "Cicero's Ghost," 30–32; Heller-Roazen, *The Enemy of All*, 105–09; Rech, *Enemies of Mankind*, 54–65; Rubin, *The Law of Piracy*, 28–29. For some brief but insightful reflections on pirates, barbarians, and shepherds in Gentili's work, see also Iurlaro, "Pirati, barbari e pastori."

status already had some traction. I therefore begin by outlining the type of arguments that were made prior to Gentili, particularly in the works of those generally considered to be his most direct and most influential predecessors: Belli, Bodin, and Ayala. I then turn to the work of Gentili himself, and I examine the leap that he took in his own approach. What is striking in Gentili's approach to the laws of war is his enormous emphasis on the distinction between legitimate and illegitimate belligerents, which he considered foundational to his framework.[94]

In *De re militari et de bello* (1563), Pierino Belli had argued that since all were at war with brigands/pirates (*latrones*), one did not have to abide by the rule of making a declaration of war before starting hostilities. He also explicitly stated that "it should be permissible for anyone to attack them ... even persons in private life may assault such outlaws – and to the point of killing them."[95] These considerations were nothing more than side notes in Belli's work, however. Much more importantly, these ideas feature prominently in the work of Bodin. The French jurist defines his famous concept of the *République* precisely by opposition to "bands of thieves and pirates."[96] Furthermore, Bodin actually uses these figures to clarify his concept of the enemy:

Quand ie dy [dis] ennemi, j'entens qui a denoncé, ou bien auquel on a denoncé la guerre autrement de parole ou de faict, quant aux autres, ils sont estimés voleurs ou pirates, avec lesquels le droit des gens ne doit avoir aucun lieu.[97]

---

[94] Rech, *Enemies of Mankind*, 55; Schröder, "Vitoria, Gentili, Bodin."

[95] Belli, *De Re Militari Et Bello Tractatus*, Part II, Title XI.

[96] "République est un droit gouvernement de plusieurs ménages, et de ce qui eut est commun, avec puissance souveraine ... Nous avons dit en premier lieu, droit gouvernement, pour la différence qu'il y a entre les Républiques, & les troupes de voleurs & pirates, avec lesquels on ne doit avoir part, ni commerce, ni alliance: comme il a esté en toute République bien ordonner, quand il a esté question de donner la foy, traiter la paix, denoncer la guerre ... & decider les differences entre les Princes & Seigneurs souverains." [A Commonwealth may be defined as the rightly ordered government of a number of families, and of those things which are their common concern, by a sovereign power ... We say in the first place right ordering to distinguish a commonwealth from a band of thieves or pirates. With them one should have neither intercourse, commerce, nor alliance. Care has always been taken in well-ordered commonwealths not to include robber-chiefs and their followers in any agreements in which honour is pledged, peace treated, war declared ... or the disputes of princes and sovereign lords submitted to arbitration.] Bodin, *Les six livres de la république*, 1; translation from Bodin, *Six Books of the Commonwealth*.

[97] Bodin, *Les six livres de la république*, 76. ["When I say enemy, I mean the one who has declared war, or to whom war has been declared either in words or in facts, as for the others, they are considered thieves or pirates, to whom the law of nations cannot apply."]

Bodin was of course concerned primarily with the French domestic situation, and he does not develop this position in greater detail. Nonetheless, his ideas were key in terms of both understanding sovereigns as equals in the context of war and considering others as outlaws. Applying the label of "thieves" or "pirates" to a group of fighters, following Bodin's approach, could mean stripping them of the protection of the law altogether.[98]

Ayala is the one who first took stock of Bodin's seminal opposition and developed it within the juridical realm. Crucially, in light of his personal stakes in the Spanish attempt to crush the Dutch Revolt, Ayala added "rebels" alongside Bodin's initial figure of the thieves/pirates in his category of those who could not legitimately wage a war. As I have suggested earlier, Ayala argued that rebels and pirates/brigands, although armed fighters, did not fall under the category of enemies, and that the action taken against them would therefore constitute not war but the mere "execution of legal process, or prosecution."[99] In addition to losing all the regular rights afforded to belligerents, this meant that they could legitimately be attacked using all the lawful means of battle, and with greater intensity than against public opponents, "for the rebel and the robber merit severer reprobation than an enemy who is carrying on a regular and just war and their condition ought not to be better than his."[100] As Nussbaum notes, in these cases the controversial Ayala presented the possibility of using "even tenets of extreme cruelty or perversion in a cool and logically disciplined manner."[101] Though this has almost entirely escaped scholarly attention, Gentili would develop these ideas into a much more elaborate position.

The opening chapters of Gentili's *DIB* make it clear that his approach to the laws of war gives considerable weight to the distinction between legal and illegal belligerents. Scholars generally tend to focus on the first three chapters of Book I: "International Law as Applied to War" (Chapter 1), "The Definition of War" (Chapter 2), and "War Is Waged by Sovereigns" (Chapter 3) – or more accurately, war is waged by princes [*Principes bellum gerunt*] – in which one finds the famous "*bellum est publicorum armorum iusta contentio*" [war is a just contest of public arms]. Yet if Gentili's definition of war as a public form of violence is

---

[98] Schröder, "Vitoria, Gentili, Bodin," 178.

[99] Ayala, *De Jure et Officiis Bellicis et Disciplina Militari Libri Tres*, Book I, Chapter 2, §14.

[100] Ibid., Book I, Chapter 2, §15. For a brief analysis of this position, see Gould, "Cicero's Ghost," 31.

[101] Nussbaum, *A Concise History of the Law of Nations*, 92.

underpinned by a clear statement of who may wage it – *principes* – it also relies on an equally clear statement of those who may not. Hence, Chapter 4 is entitled "Brigands Do Not Wage War" [*latrones bellum non gerunt*], and it explicitly sets out a category for illegitimate fighters who may be killed mercilessly by those who do have the right to use force.

In Chapter 4, Gentili does not use the famous term "*hostis humani generis*." He does, however, state that "*piratae omnium mortalium hostes sunt communes*," literally "pirates are the common enemy of all mankind," and the text that precedes and follows this statement leaves no doubt as to Gentili's indirect reliance on the "*hostis humani generis*" phrase, which was by now widely attributed to Cicero.[102] It seems that for a period, the exact legal category that was being created fluctuated between the *hostis omnium* [enemy of all], the *hostis humani generis*, and the *latro* (appearing in translation and sometimes in Gentili's own work as a pirate, a bandit, a brigand, or a thief). The specific figure of the pirate, however, would consistently appear as the go-to example in Gentili's concept of the enemy of mankind.[103] Importantly, while the figure of the pirate had generally enjoyed a rather sulfurous reputation, Gentili was "the first writer of lasting eminence to convert the confusions of the time to legal principle, to argue that the label 'pirate' carries with it the meaning of outlawry and that what 'pirates' do is forbidden by [the *ius gentium*]."[104] In other words, it is Gentili who first harnessed the powerful image of the pirate in order to frame his approach to the laws of war. Enemies of mankind, with

---

[102] Gentili, *De iure belli*, Book I, Chapter 4, §§35–36.

[103] On the use of the figure of the pirate as a way to claim continuity with ancient practices, see *supra* note 91. The figure of the pirate may also have acquired particular importance in Gentili's writing in light of the political conflicts of his time. Indeed, in the early modern period, Gentili and Grotius were "the two key writers elaborating new approaches to the law of the sea," and they were both responding to the maritime conflicts of their time, particularly those of the first decade of the seventeenth century; see Benton, *A Search for Sovereignty*, 124. Very importantly, the central role played by maritime violence in the Dutch Revolt, particularly through the Beggars of the Sea (Van der Molen, *Alberico Gentili and the Development of International Law*, 169) and the "pervasive practices of privateering and piracy" that accompanied the conflict with Spain, had a tremendous influence on the two jurists; see Benton, *A Search for Sovereignty*, 122. It is thus unsurprising to note that the development of the laws of war and of the laws of the sea were deeply intertwined and, consequently, that "the outlines of Gentili's approach to the law of the sea are readily apparent in his writings on the law of war." Benton, *A Search for Sovereignty*, 125. This helps further explain why, in addition to the historical lineage it allowed him to invoke, Gentili's ideas about the right of war focussed so heavily on the figure of the pirate.

[104] Rubin, *The Law of Piracy*, 28.

the pirate as the standard example, would be the ones systematically excluded from the ambit of this new legal framework.[105]

There are three steps within Gentili's approach to the laws of war in this regard. The first is to establish that those not entitled to wage war cannot be protected by the laws of war. The second is to establish what those who are, by contrast, entitled to wage war may do against them. I discuss these claims below. The third step – and the most critical, which I reserve for Section 3.3 – is to determine who falls into which category. The interesting twist is that since those who are allowed to wage war may only call it so when the violence is waged against another *iustus hostis*, the violence they wage against illegitimate belligerents falls into another category altogether, equivalent to Ayala's "execution of legal process, or prosecution." I analyze these three steps in turn, focusing on the three most relevant chapters in *DIB*, namely Chapter 4 of Book I on "Brigands Do Not Wage War," the closing chapter of Book I, Chapter 25, on "An Honourable Cause for Waging War," and Chapter 23 of Book III, "On Ratification, Private Citizens, Pirates, Exiles, and Adherents," as well as a few other scattered passages where Gentili further develops some of his ideas.

The first step is made eminently clear in Gentili's prose. He opens his chapter on "Brigands Do Not Wage War" with the following statement: "A state of war cannot exist with pirates and robbers" [*cum piratis & latrunculis bellum non est*], and he gives two reasons for this, and specifically for "why such men do not come under the law of war."[106] First,

---

[105] Gentili had already hinted in that direction in *De legationibus* (1585), though without developing it as much as in *DIB*. In a way reminiscent of his immediate predecessors, he states that pirates and brigands cannot receive the protection of the law in a chapter entitled "The Right of Embassy Does Not Hold in the Case of Brigands." The section reads: "Neither brigands nor pirates are entitled to the privileges of the *ius gentium*, since they themselves have utterly spurned all intercourse with their fellowmen and, so far as in them lies, endeavor to drag back the world to the savagery of primitive times. In that age, as you know, men passed their lives in the manner of wild beasts, and each one carried off what fortune offered to him as prey, trained to use his strength in accordance with his own impulses and to live for himself alone. In those days, as Thucydides observes, to be a robber was an honor rather than a disgrace." Gentili, *De legationibus libri tres*, Book II, Chapter VIII, §86. Gentili also hints toward his early distaste for rebels in *De legationibus*, dedicating a whole chapter to the question of "have rebels the right of embassy," and explaining that "[r]ebels, that is persons who secede from those under whose authority they are, should not dare to send any embassies to those against whom they have revolted. An example of quite recent date is furnished by the Spanish king's action towards the Belgian ambassadors." He concludes the chapter rather forcefully by stating: "Subject peoples ... cannot acquire [the right of embassy] by revolt, because rights are not acquired by offenses." Ibid., Book II, Chapter 8, §§83–85.

[106] Gentili, *De iure belli*, Book I, Chapter 4, §35.

he argues that these individuals have not, through their misconduct, emancipated themselves from the jurisdiction of their superior (meaning there is a higher authority above them and they therefore have no reason to resort to arms); second, he claims that "[the law of war] is derived from the law of nations, and malefactors do not enjoy the privileges of a law to which they are foes."[107] On this second point, Gentili asks most emphatically: "How can the law, which is nothing but an agreement and a compact, extend to those who have withdrawn from the agreement and broken the treaty of the human race."[108] Gentili then builds on Sassoferato's misreading of Cicero and asserts that "[p]irates are the common enemies of all mankind and therefore Cicero says that the laws of war cannot apply to them."[109] Further on, he reiterates that "with pirates and brigands, who violate all laws, no laws remain in force."[110]

The second step is also quite clear from the text, and it is fair to say that in practical terms, Gentili's approach had "far-reaching moral and juridical consequences" for those who could be deemed illegal belligerents, which were "immediately felt in concrete political terms."[111] Gentili imagined "an unrestricted right"[112] to punish these individuals in all senses of the term. Essentially, Gentili argued that it was necessary to unleash violence against these inferior opponents, but that in doing so, the legitimate belligerents did not have to respect any of the laws of war. Gentili gave a number of concrete examples of what this entailed, naturally citing the classic Ciceronian assertion that "one need not keep one's word to them, even if it has been given on oath,"[113] but also establishing some much more extreme rules. For instance, Gentili argues that "the righteous craft that is employed against brigands is of a different kind from that which is used against the enemy," making it lawful to use normally prohibited stratagems against brigands.[114] Similarly, it was "lawful, even under the conditions of peace as of the truce, to be hostile to pirates, and everywhere to shatter the lair of pirates,"[115] and no treaty would be violated by the slaying of pirates,

---

[107] Ibid.
[108] Ibid.
[109] Ibid.
[110] Ibid., Book I, Chapter 4, §38.
[111] Schröder, "Vitoria, Gentili, Bodin," 176.
[112] Benton, *A Search for Sovereignty*, 136.
[113] Gentili, *De iure belli*, Book I, Chapter 4, §35.
[114] Ibid., Book II, Chapter 3, §232. And indeed, Gentili reminds us repeatedly that against the likes of pirates, brigands, runaway slaves, and rebels no laws remain in force (Ibid., Book I, Chapter 4, §§35, 36, 38).
[115] Ibid., Book III, Chapter 23, §698.

as "once justly said to the Scotch by the English."[116] Going even further, Gentili appears to disagree with Solyman, King of the Turks, who "thought it unjust that the Venetians pursued pirates even to the port of Dyrrhachium and then fired on the citizens with artillery because they protected the pirates, and even laid waste their lands."[117] "But enough of this also," he tells us, and indeed, a few lines earlier, he explained that if the Scots relied on pirates, they became violators of the law as well.[118]

Gentili then dedicates the entire closing chapter of Book I to these "violators of the law of nature and of common law" and "monsters of lewdness"[119] and the sort of violence that may legitimately be waged against then. The chapter, entitled "An Honourable Cause for Waging War," is on the legitimacy of waging a war "which is undertaken for no private reason of our own, but for the common interest and on behalf of others." He then clarifies what he means, with a rather pressing tone: "Look you, if men clearly sin against the laws of nature and of mankind, I believe that any one whatsoever may check such men by force of arms."[120] Against the latter, all is permitted, and no jurisdiction is necessary to justify a punitive war.[121] They must merely be annihilated, through an exterminatory form of violence, in order to enforce some basic standards of justice at the level of mankind.[122] It is worth noting that Gentili uses an erroneous example from the ancient world to do away with the question of prior injury, arguing that the Romans "justly took up arms against the Illyrians, Balearans, and Cilicians, even though those people had touched nothing belonging to the Romans, to their allies, or to anyone connected with them; for they had violated the common law of nations."[123] The Romans were in fact acting based upon prior injuries,[124] but Gentili's mistakes about Roman beliefs and practices became starting points and commonplaces for jurists and scholars after him (and up to this day).

---

[116] Ibid., Book III, Chapter 23, §697. See also Ibid., Book II, Chapter 3, §232.

[117] Ibid., Book III, Chapter 23, §698.

[118] Ibid., Book III, Chapter 23, §697.

[119] Ibid., Book I, Chapter 25, §201.

[120] Ibid., Book I, Chapter 25, §198.

[121] Grotius would come to make a strikingly similar argument to Gentili, albeit "characteristically without acknowledgment." Panizza, "Political Theory and Jurisprudence in Gentili's De Iure Belli," 43.

[122] Gentili, *De iure belli*, Book I, Chapter 25. Gentili talks about "the generally recognized kinship of all men with their fellows." Ibid., Book I, Chapter 16, §120.

[123] Ibid., Book I, Chapter 25, §202.

[124] Gould, "Cicero's Ghost," 31.

Interestingly, Gentili seems to suggest in a passing comment that individuals can wage war against pirates and the like, whether they are sovereign or not: "Therefore since we may also be injured as individuals by those violators of nature, war will be made against them by individuals."[125] As Pagden notes, this is strange, as "it would seem to contradict his definition of war as a 'public contest' and his insistence that 'war on both sides must be public and official, and there must be sovereigns on both sides to direct the war.'"[126] However, Pagden explains that Gentili clearly does not – contra Grotius and later Hobbes – "allow to every person in the state of nature the right to punish."[127] Instead, "[f]or Gentili, a violation of the law of nature (and thus the *ius gentium*) would seem to transform warfare, which between civil beings would have been a resolution of differences following an initial attempt at a solution through dialogue, into a struggle for survival."[128] This thus seems to be one of Gentili's muddled positions, rather than a statement undermining the broader thrust of his approach.

Ultimately, it is quite clear that if Gentili is indeed trying to create some sort of "community of mankind" upon which to ground his legal framework, and within which sovereigns might see themselves as having a stake, he is doing so through the construction of a constitutive other. In his analysis of Gentili's attempt to sketch a "common law of mankind,"[129] Panizza indeed notes that what is striking in Gentili's theorization of the "honourable" offensive war is that "the moral principles common to all men, beyond religious and cultural diversity, which Gentili indicates expressly in that chapter, are sparsely mentioned."[130] Gentili thus sketches out these principles and the community of men they underpin not by positively asserting what these principles are, but by negatively pointing to those who violate them as the ultimate enemy. It is this dichotomous inside/outside vision that ultimately leads Gentili to lay out two radically different modes of belligerent engagement, with only one of them centered on the equal enemy, the *iustus hostis*, and deemed to deserve the legal status of "war." In the next section, I address the central question raised by Gentili's binary system: Who is it that can claim to have the proper *auctoritas*?

[125] Gentili, *De iure belli*, Book I, Chapter 25, 202.
[126] Pagden, "Gentili, Vitoria, and the Fabrication of a 'Natural Law of Nations'," 357.
[127] Ibid.
[128] Ibid.
[129] Panizza, "Political Theory and Jurisprudence in Gentili's *De Iure Belli*," 43. For a broader analysis of Gentili's argument on the legitimacy of waging war on behalf of human society, see Tuck, *The Rights of War and Peace*, 34–47.
[130] Panizza, "Political Theory and Jurisprudence in Gentili's *De Iure Belli*," 43.

3.3   The Question of Public Authority

Having established that the laws of war do not apply to those who may not wage it, and what may be done to those who resort to arms illegitimately, Gentili then makes a number of statements regarding who actually falls into that category. In settling the question of who should be considered a "public" actor possessing the "proper authority" to wage war, Gentili is not exactly at his clearest. Although he has been seen as approaching "the modern notion that only public authorities are entitled to wage war and that only states can be considered such authorities,"[131] thus sketching "a distinctly modern outline of interstate relations as an anarchical society,"[132] this is definitely a stretch. As Benedict Kingsbury notes, Gentili unsurprisingly "does not have a very precise concept of state – he discusses many different types of political entities without much distinction," and in addition, "the whole concept of sovereignty is not clearly developed, and the sovereignty of rulers and the people is not systematically separated from the sovereignty of the state as a legal entity, although Gentili does see this as an issue."[133] To more accurately contextualize his argument, I will look closely at the text of *DIB*, building on a handful of existing remarks from the literature and taking stock of Gentili's absolutist leanings.

While the figures of the pirate and the robber are Gentili's starting point in establishing his category of enemies of mankind – or more simply, illegitimate belligerents – he then proceeds to expand this category and to establish some further criteria in a rather unexpected way. What makes Gentili's argument surprising, especially within narratives that emphasize the progressive character of his work, is that outlaws are not limited to "those robbing others in absolute defiance of the notions of law, customs, and property."[134] In particular, Gentili applies the category of the outlaw or enemy of mankind not only to pirates and brigands, but also to Indians, whom he considers to be "cannibals," to atheists, to the Turks, and to one further, crucial category to which I will return in a moment: that of the rebel.[135] Atheists, for instance, are "living rather like beasts than men" and "such men, being the foes of all mankind, as pirates are, ought to be assailed in war and forced to adapt

---

[131] Knutsen, *A History of International Relations Theory*, 71.

[132] Ibid., 72.

[133] Kingsbury, "Confronting Difference," 714–15.

[134] Schröder, "Vitoria, Gentili, Bodin," 179.

[135] My attention was initially brought to these specific categories by Ileana Porras' unpublished manuscript, "Atheists, Cannibals, Rebels and Pirates: Cementing the Bonds of Human Society in Gentili's De iure belli." Her points are echoed by Schröder, who also discusses the case of the Turks; see Schröder, "Vitoria, Gentili, Bodin." For a wider contextualization of Gentili's position on this point, see Malcolm, *Useful Enemies*.

to the usages of humanity."[136] Similarly, Indians should be treated as enemies of mankind because they "practiced abominable lewdness even with beasts, and ... ate human flesh."[137] The Turks, in their case, are deemed too untrustworthy to be considered equal enemies.[138] In this discussion, Gentili is thus already seen to be oscillating between considerations of having the right *auctoritas* and the more substantive idea that some groups fall outside the protection of the laws of war because they violate the common law of mankind.[139]

Apart from these somewhat ad hoc remarks, and more importantly for our purposes, Gentili spends a considerable amount of energy excluding certain well-organized groups of fighters from the right to wage war. On this point, Gentili explicitly distances himself from all the sources he cites, seemingly spearheading a new approach. Gentili argues against all of his predecessors who sought to rehabilitate certain pirates on the ground that they could successfully challenge the Romans: Cicero is "in error," "[s]o too Augustine," and "[t]hus even Alciati is misled."[140] He develops a similar position with regard to brigands: "[W]e must beware," Gentili warns, "of confounding a brigand with a military commander, and brigandage with war."[141] Again, he claims that this blunder has been made by numerous authors before him: "Justin speaking of Aristonicus, Frontinus of Viriathus, Appian of that same Spartacus and the pirates, of a certain Apuleius who was proscribed, and of Sextus Pompeius."[142] No matter how large or well-organized the group is, no matter how well they can actually challenge the "legitimate" power, and how scrupulously they might actually respect the laws of war,[143] these groups can never be seen as anything but illegal fighters that ought to be mercilessly destroyed.

---

[136] Gentili, *De iure belli*, Book I, Chapter 9, §65. For a more detailed analysis of Gentili's broader engagement with the Ottomans, see Malcolm, "Alberico Gentili and the Ottomans."

[137] Gentili, *De iure belli*, Book I, Chapter 25, §199.

[138] "Yet it is almost natural for us to war with the Turks, just as it was for the Greeks to contend with the barbarians. With the Saracens (who are Turks) we have an irreconcilable war. With other foreign peoples we have commercial relations, but certainly not war." Ibid., Book I, Chapter 12, §92. Gentili develops the part of his argument on the untrustworthiness of Turks at more length in *De legationibus*. For a brief analysis of this aspect, see Schröder, "Vitoria, Gentili, Bodin," 181. On Gentili and trust more broadly, see Schröder, *Trust in Early Modern International Political Thought, 1598–1713*, 14–44.

[139] On the fact that Gentili falls back onto more substantive and arguably religious arguments in his discussion of relations with the Turks, see also Malcolm, "Alberico Gentili and the Ottomans."

[140] Gentili, *De iure belli*, Book I, Chapter 4, §39.

[141] Ibid.

[142] Ibid., Book I, Chapter 4, §40.

[143] Ibid., Book I, Chapter 4, §41.

At this point, Gentili then comes to the clearest formulation of what distinguishes a legitimate enemy from a mere criminal: "The claim to the title of general will be justified not so much by the command of a regular army or by the capture of cities, as those writers and other historians seem to think, as by the assumption of a public cause [*adeptio publicae causae*]."[144] Without such a public cause, the fighters constitute a mere bellicose collectivity. Gentili stresses that the word *hostis* implies equality, like the word "war," and that while it has sometimes been wrongly extended to "those who are not equal, namely, to pirates, proscribed persons, and rebels" because "names are general and include several varieties," this can under no circumstances "confer the rights due to enemies, properly so called, and the privileges of regular warfare."[145] And in fact, Gentili further emphasizes elsewhere in *DIB* that "[b]ecause the jurist seems to have put the enemy and brigands on a par in his treatment, it must not be understood that the same craft is lawful against the enemy which is proper against brigands. For against subjects and violators of every law far more is allowed than against equals and observers of the same law."[146]

But what, then, is necessary for this element of "public cause," so central to Gentili's approach to the laws of war, to obtain? Gentili does not give an explicit definition of what he means, but it can be deduced from the examples he gives of who may or may not qualify as a proper enemy. Put simply, what seems to make the difference is whether a group of fighters have the license of an established sovereign. Gentili discusses various examples at the end of Chapter 4, ruling out large groups of well-organized fighters (with "leaders, camps, and standards") to be proper enemies and suggesting that this is because they have "no motive for war."[147] More specifically, what the key groups he dismisses as illegitimate fighters – Spartacus and his men as well as Charles Martel's "Saracens" – are lacking, and what the Frenchmen in the closing anecdote of the chapter manage to produce, is a license from an established sovereign.[148] "But history itself proves that they [the Frenchmen] were

---

[144] Ibid., Book I, Chapter 4, §§39–40.
[145] Ibid., Book I, Chapter 4, §41.
[146] Ibid., Book II, Chapter 3, §231. Here Gentili cites the unavoidable Bodin, *République* I, i, presumably referring to Bodin's seminal opposition between the Commonwealth and the "bands of thieves and pirates."
[147] Gentili, *De iure belli*, Book I, Chapter 4, §41.
[148] Ibid., Book I, Chapter 4, §§41–42. For this interpretation, I follow Rubin, *The Law of Piracy*, 29; Heller-Roazen, *The Enemy of All*, 108. It is worth noting that Gentili advances a different position in the *Hispanica advocatio*, this time suddenly condemning the granting of letters of war as a reprehensible custom of war, most likely because this was better suited to defending the interests of his client, the Spanish Crown. For an analysis of this shift, see Van der Molen, *Alberico Gentili and the*

not pirates," Gentili explains, "and I say this because of no argument derived from the number and quality of the men and the ships, but from letters of their king which they exhibited."[149] It is thus this license – the letter of marque in Gentili's time – which enables a belligerent to be an equal enemy protected by the laws of war. Those who lack such a license, in Gentili's approach, fall under a different category.

It is worth noting that Gentili does not discuss where sovereignty might lie, nor whether either the people or their representatives might be legally entitled to contest the authority of an established sovereign. Gentili's solution is simply to assert that only established sovereigns have the right to wage war. Anyone else who does so automatically falls into the category of enemies of mankind. This is clearly an approach that is heavily in favor of the status quo, and that reinforces the dominance of those already in power. In many ways, it is strikingly reminiscent of Ayala's own doctrine. And in fact, Gentili explicitly rejects Hotman's attempt to bring rebels under the protection of the laws of war. Beginning his discussion by arguing, contra Hotman, that the laws of war do not apply to runaway slaves and brigands, "for inasmuch as such men are the enemies of all mankind and spare absolutely no one ... they cannot ... enjoy the common law of all,"[150] he then also rejects Hotman's claim that the laws of war can be "extended to those who have revolted."[151]

Gentili's most detailed reflections about rebels come in a chapter on the destruction and sacking of cities and start off from specific considerations about individuals who rebel against their occupier after defeat.[152] In this context, Gentili concludes that rebellion constitutes the chief incentive to cruelty and that it cannot be excused, and he agrees with Josephus that "[h]e who has once been subjected and rebels again appears rather like an incorrigible slave than a lover of liberty."[153] This is a discussion of rebellion in the immediate aftermath of defeat, but Gentili then delves into what appears to be a discussion of the broader principle, taking as an example the rebellion of the Jews against the Roman Empire in the days of Titus. "The Jews," Gentili explains, "were under the sway of Rome from the days of Pompey and

Development of International Law, 174–76; Rech, *Enemies of Mankind*, 54–65. This sudden and obviously instrumental shift in position may well have contributed to limiting the direct impact of Gentili's work on later jurists.

[149] Gentili, *De iure belli*, Book I, Chapter 4, §36.

[150] Ibid.

[151] Ibid. Gentili reiterates his claim that rebels are akin to pirates and thus cannot be considered proper "enemies" in Ibid., Book I, Chapter 4, §41. I discuss this point in greater detail later.

[152] Ibid., Book III, Chapter 8.

[153] Ibid., Book III, Chapter 8, §521.

therefore their subsequent rebellion was a wicked one." He then states the following definition: "Rebels are those who although subjects, oppose the command or act of their superior; or at any rate those who resist a sovereign or an official of his in matters affecting the condition of the empire."[154] Giving a concrete example, he explains: "When I was asked whether those cities were rebels which became enemies of Henry the Fourth of France because they did not think that he was lawfully their king ... I replied that they were guilty as it were by the fault of their origin, since at birth they became legally subject to him."[155]

This is particularly interesting in the context of the late sixteenth century, amidst crucial debates about the locus of political authority,[156] the possibility of bundling and dividing various rights, and whether force could be used legitimately by entities other than the prince. The Monarchomachs had caused a stir when they had claimed – to put it somewhat crudely – that sovereignty rested not with the prince but with the people, as a self-standing legal subject assimilated to the medieval *universitas* and holding the right to use force under certain circumstances. But as Daniel Lee has shown, this was only the tip of the iceberg. Beyond these well-known arguments about popular rebellion as a last resort to limit the abuses of royal power, or the idea of the people as a "sleeping sovereign" awakening at critical moments to curtail royal power,[157] these debates were not merely about establishing the appropriate limits of public authority but about the more fundamental question of "what *constitutes* public authority, in the first place."[158] The complex constitutional structure of the Holy Roman Empire complicated these sovereignty debates, including with respect to who held the right to wage war.[159] And of course, the legal articulation of political authority took on a new dimension in the context of faraway imperial expansion, a point to which I will return in Chapter 5. Within this wider context, Gentili was adopting a particularly narrow stance, one that undermined alternative

---

[154] Ibid., Book III, Chapter 8, §522.
[155] Ibid.
[156] In general, for a foray into the way different kinds of nonstate communities – companies, churches, cities, etc. – were understood as bodies politic in early modern England, see Withington, *The Politics of Commonwealth*; Turner, *The Corporate Commonwealth*.
[157] The "sleeping sovereign" metaphor is from Tuck, *The Sleeping Sovereign*.
[158] Lee, *Popular Sovereignty in Early Modern Constitutional Thought*, 6 (emphasis in original). As Lee explains, with the rise of the sovereign nation-state, and especially after the Enlightenment, the question of the constitution of public authority receded into the background in favor of fully state-centered theories of modern constitutionalism. By contrast, before the seventeenth century, "the question of constituting public authority in the absence of a state was *the* major question" (7) (emphasis in original).
[159] Steiger, "Die Träger des *ius belli ac pacis* 1648–1806."

positions on the nature of public authority, the divisible character of sovereignty, and the legitimacy of popular rebellion.

There is nonetheless one passage in *DIB* where Gentili seems to be going in a completely different direction, contradicting himself on nearly everything else he has put forward regarding the nature of sovereignty, the right to wage war, and the legitimacy of revolts. This, unsurprisingly, is his chapter entitled "Defending the Subjects of Another Against Their Sovereigns,"[160] which would have been directly relevant to the question of whether it was legal for the English to support Dutch subjects in their rebellion against the Spanish. If anything, this chapter illustrates the extent to which Gentili's new framework for the laws of war put him in an awkward position vis-à-vis his own allegiances. Due to his circumstances, it was unthinkable for Gentili to dismiss the Dutch fighters as mere enemies of mankind in *DIB*, even if this meant contradicting himself quite extensively. He could perhaps have vested authority in England to authorize the Dutch rebels, but this could have raised some issues in light of the fact that the Dutch were nonetheless rebelling against their own sovereign. Instead, he appears to suddenly adopt a new vision of sovereignty, stating:

I say that a dispute concerns the commonwealth, when the number of subjects who are aroused to war is so great and of such a character, that since they defend themselves by arms, it is necessary to make war against them. For those who have so much power share as it were in the sovereignty [*in partem principatus*]; they are public characters and on an equality with the sovereign [*et publici et pares Principi sint qui tantum possunt*], just as one sovereign is said to be on an equality with another when he is able to resist the other in an offer of violence.[161]

---

[160] Gentili, *De iure belli*, Book I, Chapter 16.

[161] Ibid., Book I, Chapter 16, §120. Discussing these ideas only through English can often be misleading because translators tend to streamline opaque sentence constructions and sometimes use terms like "sovereignty" instead of the various more specific (and varied) concepts that were employed at the time. Yet the passage here leaves no doubt as to Gentili's willingness to acknowledge that the prince does not have a monopoly on public authority and that in certain cases rebels may in effect claim some of this authority for themselves. His language is, however, extremely prudent (note the "quasi" in the original), which is not surprising considering this undermines his own position quite spectacularly. The original Latin reads: "At quum incidit controuersia de republica: non iudices ulli in ciuitate sunt, nec esse possunt. Publicam uero dico rem, quando subditorum tanta ac talis mouetur pars, ut iam bello opus contra eos sit, qui se tuentur bello. Quasi uenerint isti in partem principatus, et publici et pares Principi sint qui tantum possunt: quemadmodum Princeps dicitur Principi par, qui alteri, utcunque maiori et potentiori, ium inferenti potest resistere." A more literal translation of the critical last sentence would read: "For those who have so much power share – as it were [quasi] – the sovereignty [principatus]; they are public characters and on equal terms with the sovereign/prince, just as one sovereign/prince is said to be on equal terms with another when he is able to defend himself against the latter's invasion, even if the other may be greater or more powerful [utcunque maiori et potentiori]."

While the first part of the citation is completely at odds with Bodinian understandings of sovereignty (most obviously on indivisibility), the last clause, for which Gentili cites Cephalus, directly contradicts his earlier repudiation of all the arguments that considered very large groups of well-organized fighters and seafarers who challenged Roman authority to be proper enemies rather than mere pirates, as well as his condemnation of the Jews who rebelled against the Roman Empire. Gentili goes on to defend at length the legitimacy of intervening on behalf of foreign subjects struggling against their sovereign, pushing the argument rather far and arguing that this is legal even if the subjects' cause is unjust, as "[w]e are right in protecting even unjust sons against the cruelty of a father."[162] In a remarkable move that clearly demonstrates the intrusion of reason of state considerations into Gentili's positions, he closes the chapter by explicitly legitimizing the defense of the Belgians,[163] quoting Justus Lipsius' "wise words" that "if that bulwark of Europe ... should be broken down by the Spaniards, nothing would be left as a bar against their violence."[164] This argument ultimately seems to have more to do with balance of power considerations than with any deep sympathy for the Dutch cause.

This chapter is fascinating because its content was so directly relevant to the main conflict of Gentili's time, and it neatly illustrates the tension between the framework Gentili was trying to develop and the political realities he had to personally navigate. It is hard to see how Gentili could have argued anything else on this particular topic. Obviously, claiming that in waging war, the Dutch did not have the license of an established sovereign and were thus violators of the law of nations (and therefore enemies of mankind) was simply not an option. Gentili had to perform an incongruous intellectual volte-face and quietly contradict himself for the sake of political *bienséance*.

This would not be the last time Gentili was left in an uncomfortable position because of his stark legal doctrine on war and political authority. As a lawyer in admiralty courts, he would end up contradicting himself numerous times on the distinction between pirates and privateers depending on his clients. (These contradictions have contributed to explanations of the neglect of his work in favor of that of Grotius.[165])

---

[162] Gentili, Book I, Chapter 16, §123.

[163] Belgians is the translation of *belgici*, which in modern Latin designates the Dutch.

[164] Gentili, *De iure belli*, Book I, Chapter 16, §127.

[165] While Gentili is often seen as a jurist of lesser importance for having had a less systematic method (see Nézard, "Albericus Gentilis"), he is also considered to have been "too much of a polemist and too much of an advocate" (Nussbaum, *A Concise History of the Law of Nations*, 101) and to have contradicted himself to suit the needs of his clients (although this is arguably what lawyers do). Grotius himself also made

More importantly, he would end up at even greater pains to justify the legitimacy of the Dutch Revolt in his later tract in defense of absolutism, awkwardly and rather unconvincingly trying to paint the issue as irrelevant. Ultimately, these difficulties highlight the extent to which the broader approach he developed in *DIB* was premised on an understanding of political authority and of the right to war that undermined the legitimacy of popular revolts and, correspondingly, cemented the power of established sovereigns.

3.4   The Initial Reception of Gentili's Writings

Throughout this chapter I have tried to place the significance of *DIB* within its own context. As a final step in this direction, it is worth asking how Gentili's contemporaries viewed him. Despite Gentili's important place in the history of international law, relatively little is known about the reception of his works in his own time, including his treatise on the laws of war.[166] In this final section of the chapter, I outline some elements to fill this gap in our knowledge of the reception of his work. In brief, after his death in 1608, Gentili was cited in passing within works on the *ius gentium* during the seventeenth century, and he also attracted some attention in the 1640s in light of his stark defense of absolutism, but his influence waned from the early eighteenth century until his rediscovery in the nineteenth.

The publication trajectory of *DIB* is revealing in itself. The treatise was first published in 1589 in short form, based on Gentili's lectures on the laws of war. The fully developed version, now considered Gentili's masterpiece, was published in 1598 as *De iure belli libri tres*, by Guilielmus Antonius in Hannover. All of Gentili's works were placed on the *Index librorum prohibitorum* [the List of Prohibited Books] from 1603 onward,

---

various derogatory and partly unfair remarks about Gentili's work, despite in fact owing much to the Italian jurist. As Schröder points out, in the first lines of *De iure belli* Gentili claims to be the first to make readily available the laws which can regulate the relations between different and potentially hostile polities, and Grotius would be at pains to circumvent this assertion in light of his own desire to claim the merit of developing the first systematic theory of interpolity relations; see Schröder, "Vitoria, Gentili, Bodin," 171.

[166] Gesina van der Molen's seminal monograph on Gentili merely mentions his revival in the late nineteenth century, without addressing the question of his earlier reception. Valentina Vadi's more recent monograph, despite its length, discusses the early reception of Gentili only in passing. The one piece that addresses the early reception of Gentili – and specifically of his *DIB* – in some depth is a chapter about Gentili's three references to the Hanseatic League in *DIB*, which essentially constitutes a side note within a broader research project on the legal aspects of the Anglo-Hanseatic controversies during the 16th century; see Wijffels, "Alberico Gentili and the Hanse."

an unsurprising feat considering *DIB* in particular was "full of anti-Spanish sentiment," including "the ultimate ignominy" of associating Spain, a fervently Catholic power rising into a position of hegemony in Europe, with Christianity's archenemy, the Turks.[167] Nonetheless, a second and third edition of *DIB*, which were "very much like the first,"[168] were published at Hannover by the successors of Antonius in 1604 and 1612 respectively. Efforts to republish Gentili's treatise on the laws of war then stopped for a century and a half, until a fourth edition of *De iure belli libri tres* was published within an incomplete and seldom mentioned 1770 edition of the "Opera Omnia" of Alberico Gentili.[169] The fifth, and most influential, republication of *DIB* happened in the late nineteenth century, to which I will turn in Chapter 4.

In light of the breadth of Gentili's various writings on the *ius naturae et gentium*, his name was nonetheless "respectfully mentioned" over the seventeenth century by the likes of Abraham De Wicquefort (1606–1682), Samuel von Pufendorf (1632–1694), Anthony Wood (1632–1695), Pierre Bayle (1647–1706), and Cornelis van Bynkershoek (1673–1743).[170] In fact, as Haggenmacher notes, his reputation was sufficiently established for Pierre Bayle to include an article about Gentili in his famous *Dictionnaire*.[171] The article in question, however, is not particularly laudatory, and its content is revealing in itself. Bayle informs us that Gentili's various works made him well known [*lui acquirent beaucoup de réputation*] but then merely notes that his three volumes on the laws of war "were not useless to Grotius," and that he "also did three *de Legationibus*." He then highlights "his disputations on the power of kings, and on the union of the kingdoms of Great Britain, and on the inherent injustice of resistance against kings" and notes that they "show even more clearly that he was not in favor of republican maxims" than the ten disputations he asked his son to dedicate to the Earl of Pembroke in 1607.[172]

---

[167] Koskenniemi, "International Law and raison d'état," 300. Gentili was soon to be joined by Grotius, who was placed on the Index for rebutting papal claims to imperium in *Mare Liberum*.

[168] Van der Molen, *Alberico Gentili and the Development of International Law*, 54.

[169] The publication was interrupted after two volumes due to the editor's death.

[170] Van der Molen, *Alberico Gentili and the Development of International Law*, 61.

[171] Haggenmacher, "Grotius and Gentili," 134.

[172] Bayle, *Dictionnaire historique et critique*, Vol. 7, 66. "Il a fait trois livres *de Jure Belli*, qui n'ont pas été inutiles à Grotius. Il en a fait aussi trois *de Legationibus*. Ses disputes sur le pouvoir absolu des rois, et sur l'union des royaumes de la Grande-Bretagne, et sur l'injustice inséparable de la résistance aux rois, *de vi civium in regem semper injusta*, marquaient encore plus clairement qu'il n'était pas pour les maximes républicains, que les dix disputes dont il fit présent à son fils, afin qu'il les dédiât, en l'an 1607, au comte de Pembrock, son patron."

Bayle's description shows the extent to which Gentili was remembered not primarily for his writings on the *ius gentium* but for his defense of absolutism. In England, Gentili went very much against the grain in putting forward such a defense, as "the early Stuart political nation was held together by an *anti*-absolutist consensus."[173] In this context, Burgess reminds us that, if anything, "the few who openly challenged that consensus were mainly of importance for the way in which they enabled everyone else to unite in disagreement against them."[174] Importantly, and "with the possible exception of Dr. John Cowell's *Interpreter* (1608),"[175] Gentili's defense did not raise much interest until the 1640s, when "it was used to reveal the real kernel of royalist belief in an anonymous parliamentarian tract of 1644."[176] The pamphleteer claimed that Gentili "had encouraged both James I and Charles I to advance the total prerogative at the expense of the people's liberty and to lead the country into civil war."[177] Even then, however, the revived Gentili did not attract much attention; no one responded to the anonymous parliamentarian's tract.[178] Ultimately, the impact of Gentili's defense of absolutism on English legal and political debates in the first half of the seventeenth century is questionable.[179] What is clear is that his reputation – at least from the 1640s onwards – was somewhat tainted, particularly in England, and sufficiently so to affect Bayle's remarks in his *Dictionnaire*.

More broadly, Gentili's reputation in the seventeenth century was deeply shaped by the meteoric rise of the man who would come to completely overshadow him after his death, Hugo Grotius. The "miracle of Holland" drew extensively from Gentili's writings – particularly from *DIB* in drafting his own *De iure belli ac pacis* – while not giving the

---

[173] Burgess, *Absolute Monarchy and the Stuart Constitution*, 18 (emphasis in original).

[174] Ibid.

[175] Ibid., 78. See also Levack, *The Civil Lawyers in England, 1603–1641*, 4. Cowell was the Regius Professor of Civil Law at Cambridge.

[176] Burgess, *Absolute Monarchy and the Stuart Constitution*, 78.

[177] Levack, *The Civil Lawyers in England, 1603–1641*, 4. The tract is entitled *"England's monarch, or a conviction and refutation by the common law of those false principles and insinuating flatteries of Albericus, delivered by way of Disputation, and after published, and dedicated to our dread Soveraigne King JAMES, in which he laboureth to prove by the Civill Law, our Prince to be an absolute Monarch; and to have a free and Arbitrary power over the lives and estates of his people."*

[178] Sharp, "Alberico Gentili's Obscure Resurrection as a Royalist in 1644," 299. For a detailed analysis of the tract, see Ibid., 288–89.

[179] For an in-depth discussion, see Burgess, *Absolute Monarchy and the Stuart Constitution*, 78–90. For his part, Diego Panizza argues that Gentili's arguments actually had an impact on Hobbes, who would have heard them during his time in Oxford and then transformed them into his *Leviathan*. Panizza, "Il pensiero politico di Alberico Gentili: religione, virtù e ragion di stato," 212–13.

Italian much credit.[180] Peter Haggenmacher has examined the respective positions of the two authors in the emergence of international law as a legal discipline at some length, with a particular emphasis on Gentili's influence on Grotius and an explicit analysis of their treatises on the laws of war, and I will not repeat his detailed analysis here.[181] The main point is that neither Gentili nor Grotius would have thought of themselves as the prophets of a new legal order or as "fathers" of international law; instead, "all they had in mind was a reformulation of the traditional *ius belli*."[182] Precursorism, or what Quentin Skinner has called "the mythology of prolepsis,"[183] that is, the endless search for "antecedents" or "origins" of ideas or practices, has led scholars to regard Gentili as having been at least as modern as Grotius when measured against the classical international law of the eighteenth century, notably the treatises of Moser and Vattel. This is very much anachronistic and of little help in determining why Grotius' work dethroned Gentili's in the seventeenth century. Essentially, Haggenmacher's suggestion is merely that "the philosophical substance and 'geometrical' construction of *De iure belli ac pacis* appealed more to the age of system-builders like Pufendorf, Spinoza, Leibniz, and Wolff than did the 'plain empirical approach of Gentili.'"[184]

A century after his death, discussions of Gentili's work began to wane altogether. Specifically, his reputation "suffered a severe set-back during the period following the Peace of Utrecht" of 1713.[185] Of course, his name "did not vanish altogether,"[186] and one can trace a thin but steady stream of superficial citations of his works from the early eighteenth to the mid-nineteenth century, the period during which Grotius was considered the sole founding father of the *ius naturae et gentium*.[187] In the eighteenth century, these citations include a separate paragraph on Gentili in Glafey's *Geschichte des Rechts der Vernunft* of 1723, a mention by Martens in one of his early works, the claim that Gentili is "the first scholar to have earned himself some merit in the promotion of the science of the Law of Nations" in Ompteda's *Litteratur* of 1785,

---

[180] On Grotius' relationship to Gentili, see notably Simmonds, "Hugo Grotius and Alberico Gentili."

[181] Haggenmacher, "Grotius and Gentili." On their respective treatises on the laws of war, see Ibid., 156–67.

[182] Ibid., 173–74.

[183] Skinner, "Meaning and Understanding in the History of Ideas," 73.

[184] Haggenmacher, "Grotius and Gentili," 174.

[185] Ibid., 134.

[186] Ibid.

[187] Although, as I will discuss in Chapter 4, Grotius' reputation may also not have been as solidly established as it has been assumed.

and a mention in Ward's famous *Enquiry* of 1795 as the one "who bore the palm from all the jurists before Grotius."[188] In the first half of the nineteenth century, he is notably mentioned in Hallam's *Introduction to the Literature of Europe* of 1839 as well as in Wheaton's *History of the Law of Nations* of 1841.[189] These references to Gentili generally consist of a paragraph at most, and often of a mere few words. The only known exceptions, apart from the incomplete 1770 "Opera Omnia" of Gentili's works, are the 1750 monograph of T. Begnigni, an antiquary from San Ginesio, Gentili's birthplace, and W. A. Reiger's doctoral thesis of 1867, which I will discuss in Chapter 4. Kaltenborn has also been deemed to have been "one of the first, if not the first, of scholars outside Italy to acquire a proper understanding of Gentili's work in relation to that of Grotius" in his *Die Vorläufer des Hugo Grotius* 1848, but it is also acknowledged that his work is "not usually listed in bibliographies relating to Gentili."[190]

In short, for nearly two and a half centuries after his death, Gentili did not attract much attention, and when he was remembered during this period, it was as much – if not more – for his controversial absolutist positions than for his writings on the laws of war.

3.5   Conclusion

To sum up, I have argued that in *DIB*, Gentili elaborated a stark dichotomy between "public violence" and violence carried out by enemies of mankind in order to develop and legitimize an absolutist approach to the laws of war. In doing so, he found a way to reconcile his absolutist leanings, his admiration for reason of state ideas, and his desire to make the law of nations an essential component of inter-sovereign relations. His construction of a constitutive other through the figure of the enemy of mankind enabled him to give supreme sovereigns an incentive to

---

[188] Glafey, *Vollständige Geschichte des Rechts der Vernunft*, Book III, §4, 58; Martens, *Primae lineae iuris gentium europaearum practici in usum auditorum adumbratae*, Prolegomena, §7, 6; Ompteda, *Litteratur des gesammten sowohl natürlichen als positiven Völkerrechts*, §49, 168–69; Ward, *An Enquiry into the Foundation and History of the Law of Nations in Europe*, Vol. 2, chapter 18, 608; but see also 612. All cited in Haggenmacher, "Grotius and Gentili," notes 6–12, 134–35. For an exhaustive bibliography of the works that cite Alberico Gentili (including the ones mentioned earlier), see Armigero Gazzera, *Alberico Gentili*.

[189] Hallam, *Introduction to the Literature of Europe in the Fifteenth, Sixteenth, and Seventeenth Centuries*, Vol. 2, chapter 4, §§90–92, 153–55; Wheaton, *Histoire des progrès du droit des gens en Europe et en Amérique*, Vol. 1, 49–53. Cited in Haggenmacher, "Grotius and Gentili," notes 13–14, 135.

[190] Vecchio, "The Posthumous Fate of Alberico Gentili," 664–65.

buy into his legal framework and bind themselves to a certain degree. Crucially, he posited that only established sovereigns could be legitimate belligerents, and in a move strikingly reminiscent of Ayala, he placed rebels in the same category as pirates and brigands, making them enemies of mankind as well.

In doing so, Gentili erected at the heart of his legal framework a very sharp distinction between war proper – a contest between two established sovereigns, narrowly defined – and the type of violence that would occur between sovereigns and nonsovereigns. In the latter case, the violence would not be considered a "war" legally speaking, and the laws of war would not protect the "illegitimate" belligerent. In fact, Gentili explicitly justified the use of extreme (and usually forbidden) measures by sovereigns against these types of fighters. Gentili's framework thus legitimized a type of violence that was not bilateral but instead served a purpose of punishment and pacification (or law enforcement, more broadly), obeying principles reminiscent of the logic of the just war. In short, Gentili's approach to the laws of war presents two sides. The first establishes war as a legal institution rather than a punitive endeavor, giving equal rights to belligerents on both sides and putting forth a number of clear rules. The second creates a space in which violence can be waged against certain opponents stripped of their rights in the name of defending some form of human community. In this sense, Gentili's work is as much about the moderation and the "humanization" of war as it is about entrenching a dehumanizing process of ruthless violence beyond the narrow sphere of "war," unleashed against those who dare to take up arms when they are not already established sovereigns. The latter stems from his absolutist stance and his resulting narrow understanding of who could claim to be a "public authority," a position that was not the norm at the time and that sought to discredit the legitimacy of armed rebellion.

Gentili's approach was not exactly congenial to the realities of his time. The Holy Roman Empire, with its patchwork of overlapping sovereignties, occupied the heart of Europe; the Wars of Religion, and particularly the Dutch Revolt, had given rise to numerous debates about the nature of sovereignty and the legitimacy of resistance; and the years following the publication of *DIB* would witness the creation of the East India Company (1600) and its Dutch counterpart, the Vereenigde Oost-Indische Compagnie (1602), powerful mercantile companies that operated private armies and raised further questions regarding political authority and the use of force. This pervasive murkiness may explain why Gentili's ideas fell into near oblivion following his death before being revived by a group of lawyers in the late nineteenth century.

Before we turn to this revival in Chapter 4, it is worth summing up what has been established by reading Gentili in the context of his own time. Clearly, Gentili was a rather complicated figure. His views on a number of methodological and substantive matters evolved drastically over the course of his career, making it difficult to view his writings as part of a systematic or coherent approach to the *ius gentium*. What we do know is that by the end of his career, Gentili was expounding such stark absolutist views that those who remembered him at all in the two centuries after his death tended to remember him for this. His advocacy on behalf of Catholic Spain made him all the more controversial, and this last chapter of his life provides a rather remarkable plot twist to the story of the persecuted Protestant who fled his Italian homeland for England.

We have also seen that *DIB* is a complex and sometimes contradictory work. Written just a few years before Gentili's defense of absolutist rule, it is at least partly an attempt to reconcile his absolutist leanings with his commitment to regulating relations between sovereigns through law. With it, Gentili intervened in several different debates, especially the question of the nature of political authority.[191] His position on this point, and especially in the context of war, explicitly departed from that of his predecessors. His general depiction of sovereignty owed much to Bodin's but went even further in concentrating power in the hands of the prince. As such, it was incompatible with many of the existing arrangements that underpinned the European political order at the time, most obviously those of the sprawling Holy Roman Empire. Within the context of war, Gentili took the rather radical step of granting virtually no recognition to rebels – except in the very specific and politically touchy case of the Dutch – and, regardless of their cause, power, or level of organization, allowing for them to be legally annihilated through extremely violent means. As Gentili acknowledges, this was an unusual position to take, and as such *DIB* constitutes a bold intervention in the debates of his time – one that has perhaps not been sufficiently acknowledged.

With this in mind, we can turn now to the way Gentili was revived in the late nineteenth century. We are now better prepared to appreciate the creativity of the story his revivers told about him – many aspects of which have, as we shall see, trickled down to the present.

---

[191] For a detailed overview of his other interventions, see Vadi, *War and Peace*.

Part II

Gentili's *De iure belli* and the Myth of "Modern War"

4   Unearthing the "True Founder" of International Law

The second part of this book tells the story of how Gentili was revived and came to be seen as the father of the modern laws of war. What it seeks to show is that the sixteenth-century Gentili became associated with the restriction of the right to wage war to states in a misguided and anachronistic way, which has trickled all the way down to us and has continued to cloud our understanding of when, why, and how the legal right to wage war actually became restricted to sovereign states. Gentili was cited out of context and selectively by nineteenth-century lawyers and then by the influential Carl Schmitt. As should be clear from the contextual discussion of Gentili's *De iure belli* in Part I, it did not make much historical sense for later Gentili enthusiasts to derive the notion of "public war" as "war carried out by sovereign states" from him. They could also have used much better sources to do so. Yet my point is that this is nonetheless precisely what they did, and that we have inherited their mistakes down the line.

This chapter tells the remarkable story of how, in the late nineteenth century, Gentili was revived and presented as a challenger to Grotius for the broad title of "true founder of international law." To avoid any misunderstanding, I do not mean to claim that Gentili then became as famous as Grotius – and later Vitoria – across the literature on the history of international law; I simply argue that he was pushed to center stage by a group of prominent individuals who claimed he was potentially the true founder of international law, and that, on this basis, he eventually came to occupy a newly important place, particularly within histories of the laws of war.

Unlike the chapters in Part I, those in Part II are less about the substantive content of Gentili's thought than the thinking and purposes of those who engaged him more than 250 years after his death. This chapter, in particular, moves almost entirely away from the substance of Gentili's ideas. Instead, it sheds light on why Thomas Erskine Holland (1835–1926) and other late nineteenth-century international lawyers approached the project of reviving Gentili the way they did. It focuses on the nineteenth-century move to establish the scientific credentials of international law as well as the stakes that were involved in doing so. As such, it is a sort of "outside account" of the revival, one that emphasizes the various external circumstances of the revival rather than examining what it was about Gentili's specific ideas that led to his canonization. The latter, what we might call the "inside account" of the revival, will be the focus of the beginning of Chapter 5.

This chapter homes in on the 1860s and 1870s and the emergence not just of the academic discipline of international law,[1] but of a narrative about its past.[2] The revival of Gentili began in 1874, a year after the establishment of the epoch-making Institut de droit international that essentially founded the discipline of international law proper. It involved many of the most important international lawyers of the period, split across three subcommittees working on the revival: an English one, an Italian one, and a largely fruitless Dutch one.[3] Even though the English committee ultimately had a much greater influence in shaping the narrative about Gentili beyond his Italian homeland, the more detailed work on this revival currently concerns its Italian counterpart.[4] The chapter therefore closely examines the Oxford-centered revival of Gentili, based on the virtually unexplored papers of the English subcommittee and particularly the papers of its leading figure, T. E. Holland.[5]

The chapter begins by placing the construction of the history of international law within its broader intellectual context. It emphasizes two interrelated developments: the proliferation of histories primarily based on narrating the achievements of a handful of "great men," and the emergence of teleological understandings of history rooted in linear narratives of progress. This provides some essential tools to understand why and – to some extent – how the history of international law as a new "science" and a professional academic field was constructed during the closing decades of the nineteenth century. International legal practices existed before, of course, but what exactly "international law" consisted of prior to its establishment as a "science" in the 1860s and 1870s came

---

[1] Koskenniemi, *Gentle Civilizer*; Nuzzo and Vec, *Constructing International Law*.
[2] Craven, "Invention of a Tradition," 364–65; Koskenniemi, "International Law and raison d'état," 298; Lacchè, "Monuments of International Law," 147.
[3] The principal achievement of the Dutch subcommittee was to erect the famous statue of Grotius if Delft, so it is safe to say that it remained a peripheral endeavor in the revival of the Italian jurist.
[4] Lacchè, "Monuments of International Law."
[5] *The Papers of Sir Thomas Erskine Holland*, Bodleian Library manuscripts, shelf mark MSS. Eng. Misc. c. 125–26; Ital. c. 20.

to be understood under a whole new light, with repercussions to this day in terms of how we study the history of the field.

Having established this context, the chapter turns to the revival of Gentili himself in order to begin understanding the making of his modern image. I begin by noting two elements of Gentili's revival that make it a particularly remarkable endeavor. The first is that Gentili was the very first jurist to be pulled back from the dead and thrust forward as a challenger to the already famous Grotius for the title of "founding father of international law." In other words, it is his revival that marked the beginning of what some have called "the contest of the putative fathers of the law of peoples" or the "battle of the founders of international law," a somewhat esoteric showdown that raged on until the mid-1930s.[6] Second, the revival of Gentili was a highly institutionalized affair in which many of the most important international lawyers of the period were involved. While it was a general trend to historicize new disciplines and to emphasize the importance of specific individuals in their making, this broader context fails to provide answers to a number of puzzling questions: Why did these prominent international lawyers turn specifically to Gentili? What did they emphasize in his work in trying to construct the history of their own endeavor? What does it tell us about their own motives? The chapter begins answering these questions, showing that the establishment of Gentili as the other great founder of international law was a central affair within the broader emergence of the discipline of international law and was driven by personal, institutional, and political motives all at once.

4.1   Context: Constructing the History of International Law

It is now a well-established fact that the late nineteenth century was a crucial turning point for international law.[7] Echoing the wider trend toward "scientization" and professionalization already visible in economics and in the social sciences,[8] international law was constituted as the formal academic discipline we now know. This process is generally associated with core milestones in the 1860s and 1870s, most notably the first attempts to codify the laws of war (Lieber Code of 1863, Geneva Convention of 1864, St. Petersburg Declaration of 1868); the

---

[6] Rasilla del Moral, "Francisco de Vitoria's Unexpected Transformations and Reinterpretations for International Law," 581–82.
[7] See most notably Koskenniemi, *Gentle Civilizer*.
[8] Ibid., 17.

foundation of the *Revue de droit international et de législation comparée* (1868),[9] the first scientific legal journal on an international basis; and the foundation in October 1873 of the Association for the Reform and Codification of the Law of Nations, later to become the International Law Association. The most famous turning point, however, was the foundation on September 8, 1873, of a permanent institution for the new discipline, the Institut de droit international, which ushered in the rise of international law as we know it today. Its purpose, broadly speaking, was to turn international law into a widely recognized science and a professional field of its own.

This period was a watershed moment not only for the emergence of the discipline of international law but also for the influential idea that this field was a consistent endeavor with a coherent history. While the substantial discontinuities between pre- and post-1870 international law have now been shown,[10] this disjuncture was obscured for over 100 years, hidden in the folds of a story of seamless continuity between the early modern period and the twentieth century. This story of continuity can be understood as having fulfilled several roles, from establishing the historical pedigree of a new academic discipline to masking the role of academics in determining the content of international law.[11] But most importantly, it was a product of the late nineteenth-century imagination, and we are only beginning to understand the extent to which it painted a misleading picture of the past that remains profoundly influential to this day. In the simplest sense, this newfound "historical consciousness fundamentally reshaped the conceptualization of what was to become known as 'international law'."[12]

---

[9] As Koskenniemi explains, "[e]stablishing professional journals was one means whereby the mid-Victorian generation institutionalized the various scientific disciplines – including economics and social sciences." Ibid. The *Revue* was a crucial step in the professionalization of international law and its coronation as a proper "science," and it became an organ of the Institut de droit international in 1875.

[10] Ibid.; Nuzzo and Vec, *Constructing International Law*. Although to moderate this narrative somewhat, see Benton and Ford, *Rage for Order*.

[11] As Amanda Alexander reminds us, "[i]t has long been noted that academics have an unusually important role in the determination of international law; Oppenheim made the point at the beginning of the last century and Ian Brownlie at the end. Nevertheless, the involvement of academics in legal change is often obscured – not least by the historical narratives and language of continuity they deploy." Alexander, "A Short History of International Humanitarian Law," 136.

[12] Craven, "Theorizing the Turn to History in International Law," 22. Craven specifies: "The significance of this, I argue, is not merely confined to an acknowledgement that publicists and jurists suddenly became interested in the past in a way that wasn't apparent before, but that this historical consciousness fundamentally reshaped the conceptualization of what was to become known as 'international law,' and placed at centre-stage the problem of historical method."

In the late eighteenth century, scholars had started writing the first accounts of the history of international law as a discipline and launching what would become the ubiquitous trend of beginning any international law textbook with a "historical introduction."[13] These historical inclinations deepened over the course of the nineteenth century, and they acquired a newfound degree of significance with the emergence of international law as a formal academic discipline in the 1870s. International lawyers and scholars of international law, who now came to form an unprecedently coherent epistemic community, increasingly coalesced around a professional identity grounded in a shared historical consciousness, a common trove of ancestors and genealogies. For the emergence of international law as a "science" did not depend exclusively on the renewal of concepts, methods, and purposes, but also on "the *invention of traditions*, centered around precursors, founders and followers."[14]

Noting this phenomenon, Martti Koskenniemi simply suggests that "[n]ineteenth-century international lawyers imagined a history to what they were doing because that was the habit of a historical age."[15] While this is perfectly plausible, it tells us very little about why this history took the form that it did. After all, there are always countless ways of piecing together the story of the past, and international law was no different in the plurality of histories it offered. One must therefore account not simply for the fact but also for the form of this "invention of tradition." In this respect, there are two particular features of this newfound history of international law that are especially striking.

The first was this history's emphasis on individuals, or specifically on "great men." Despite the fact that the more theoretical writings of prominent jurists did not necessarily affect the development of international law in practice,[16] the late nineteenth century marked the moment when international law's history became "penned as biographical accounts of European publicists."[17] The history of international law emerged not so much as a history of legal practices,[18] but as a history

---

[13] Craven, "Invention of a Tradition," 364–65. Of course, as Craven notes (366), this "is not to say ... that prior to this time, international lawyers were unaware of historical precedents or of the contribution made by earlier scholars." There simply was no such overarching story of historical continuity, or metanarrative of the development of the discipline in the sense elaborated in the nineteenth century.

[14] Lacchè, "Monuments of International Law," 147 (emphasis in original).

[15] Koskenniemi, "International Law and raison d'état," 298.

[16] See notably the critique in Benton and Ford, *Rage for Order*.

[17] Singh, "Book Review," 977.

[18] The turn toward more practice-based accounts of the development of international law has only emerged since the mid-2000s. See, for example, Benton and Ford, *Rage*

of ideas – those of a handful of glorified European men. This could have been different. Throughout the eighteenth century, compendia of treaties had been established,[19] and they could have served as the basis for the new historiography of international law. As scholars have noted in other contexts, the canonization of personal heroes is a particularly fruitful way to harness history's power as a reservoir for ideology,[20] and in the case of Gentili, I will show that the motivations for canonizing him were not purely ideological, but that ideologies of various kind were indeed a central component to both the fact and the form of his revival.

The second striking feature of this history is the attempt to demonstrate the existence of a very clear continuity between the *ius gentium* of early modern Europe and the international law of the nineteenth century. Scholars are now well into charting the creation of the canon of international law, notably the reenshrinement of Grotius' importance[21] and the establishment of Francisco de Vitoria as a founding father of international law.[22] Some unprecedented archival work has also been conducted into the conceptualization and establishment of the profoundly influential twenty-two-volume *Classics of International Law*, published between 1911 and 1950 by the Carnegie Endowment for International Peace under the general editorship of James Brown Scott.[23] These works all point to the great efforts that were made to tie the emerging discipline of international law in the late nineteenth and early twentieth centuries to an early modern precedent, as if one could draw a straight line from the writing of famous sixteenth- and seventeenth-century jurists through those of their eighteenth-century counterparts and all the way up to the present.

---

for *Order*; Keene, "A Case Study of the Construction of International Hierarchy"; Keene, "The Treaty-Making Revolution of the Nineteenth Century"; Lesaffer, *Peace Treaties and International Law in European History.*

[19] The most celebrated of these compendia was Dumont, *Corps universel diplomatique du droit des gens, contenant un recueil des traitez d'alliance, de paix, de trêve, de neutralité, de commerce, etc., qui ont été faits en Europe, depuis le règne de l'empereur Charlemagne jusques à présent.*

[20] Sylvest, *British Liberal Internationalism, 1880–1930*, 148–94.

[21] Van Ittersum, "Hugo Grotius."

[22] Orford, *What Is the Place of Anachronism in International Legal Thinking*; Amorosa, *Rewriting the History of the Law of Nations*; Smeltzer, "On the Use and Abuse of Francisco de Vitoria"; Somos and Smeltzer, "Vitoria, Suárez, and Grotius." Some noise had already been made about Vitoria in the 1860s, but his revival did not truly take off until decades later. On these earlier efforts, see Haggenmacher, "La place de Francisco de Vitoria parmi les fondateurs du droit international"; Rossi, *Broken Chain of Being.*

[23] For a detailed analysis, see Amorosa, *Rewriting the History of the Law of Nations.*

These two features naturally reflect broader trends of the period, particularly with regard to the wider construction of historical narratives. In the most obvious sense, and as I briefly discussed in the introduction of this book, the nineteenth century witnessed the emergence of what came to be known as "great men theory" and of the broader romantic idea of the genius, leading to the canonization of various men across the arts and sciences. The narratives that emerged around these men often reflected the desire to tie these individuals to specific breakthroughs into "modernity."[24] This search for origins and founding fathers went hand in hand with a second trend: the ascent of a more linear understanding of the development of modernity.

The nineteenth century famously marked the emergence of various teleological metahistories that depicted the development of the modern world as one moving inexorably toward various discernible endpoints, ranging from the victory of liberal ideas to the imminent revolt of the working class or the triumph of the white race. With regard to the history of international law specifically, a particularly important contextual element is the emergence, in the nineteenth century, of a particular way of telling the history of early modern international relations. While the disciplines of International Law and International Relations gradually came apart in the twentieth century,[25] they were deeply intertwined when they first emerged and strove to become proper "sciences," not least because they both attempted do to so in part by relying on "stylized histories populated by founding fathers and origin myths" and "a reliance on sovereignty as a foundation principle."[26] The most important foundational myth they both latched onto was the idea that the seventeenth century – and often specifically the 1648 Peace of Westphalia – had marked the emergence of the modern states-system, that is, an international system composed of formally equal sovereign states.

This story of the emergence of the modern international states-system was in large part the brainchild of early nineteenth-century historians. It developed as part of a broader emphasis on writing the history of Europe as that of nation-states, to the detriment of entities such as the Holy Roman Empire.[27] The so-called myth of Westphalia has been tied to different though related constructions of narratives about early

---

[24] On Leonardo da Vinci's newfound fame in the nineteenth century and the emergence of the idea of the "Renaissance man," see Bullen, "Walter Pater's 'Renaissance' and Leonardo da Vinci's Reputation in the Nineteenth Century."

[25] Koskenniemi, "Law, Teleology and International Relations."

[26] Pitts, "International Relations and the Critical History of International Law," 283.

[27] See the introduction of Wilson, *Heart of Europe*.

modern Europe. Some scholars have claimed that early nineteenth-century historians developed their narrative of the Thirty Years War as a struggle for the respect of state sovereignty against imperial overreach from seventeenth-century French and Swedish anti-Habsburg propaganda.[28] Others, not incompatibly, have pointed specifically to a group of counter-revolutionary German historians who sought to criticize Napoleon by emphasizing the soundness of the system they claimed he was seeking to overthrow.[29] The modern states-system, they argued, was one of the greatest achievements of European civilization, a beacon of stability and mutual respect that had to be preserved at all cost.

Regardless of where and how exactly this early nineteenth-century narrative originated, it was quickly taken up and fleshed out by lawyers working within the area of the law of nations. One particularly important development in this respect is the fact that the increasing popularity of the idea of early modern Europe as a world of formally equal sovereign states became closely intertwined with a surge in Emer de Vattel's readership.[30] Vattel had depicted states or nations as moral persons and, crucially, he had presented the model of an international community of equal sovereign states not as a mere normative aspiration, but, regardless of how much this jarred with the political realities of his time,[31] as an accurate description of the European world. By the late nineteenth century, when international law was formalized into an academic discipline, Vattel had become *the* major authority on the law of nations, and it was commonly accepted that the seventeenth century had marked the emergence of a system of formally equal sovereign states, constituting the cornerstone of modern international relations and a gift from Europe to the rest of the world. This broader context forms the background within which one can better understand the revival of Alberico Gentili.

4.2   The Revival of Alberico Gentili

I should begin with a word about why one should pay specific attention to the revival of this sixteenth-century Italian jurist. After all, he is now

---

[28] Osiander, "Sovereignty, International Relations, and the Westphalian Myth," 260–68. On the related construction of the idea of a "state of nature," see Jahn, *The Cultural Construction of International Relations*.

[29] Keene, *Beyond the Anarchical Society*, 19–29; Devetak, "Historiographical Foundations of Modern International Thought."

[30] On Emer de Vattel's reception in the nineteenth century, see Fiocchi Malaspina, "Emer de Vattel's 'Le droit des gens'"; Wallenius, "The Case for a History of Global Legal Practices."

[31] Whelan, "Vattel's Doctrine of the State," 76–77. I discuss this in greater detail in Chapter 5.

just one of many foundational figures in the field of international law. His revival, however, is particularly noteworthy for two main reasons. First, Gentili was the first jurist to be pulled back from the dead and presented as a challenger to Grotius for the title of "father of international law." In other words, while the pantheon of "the founders of international law" would gradually widen over the late nineteenth and the early twentieth centuries – notably with the celebration of Vitoria by James Brown Scott (1866–1943) and with Scott's broader efforts to establish a history to the discipline of international law – the revival of Gentili constituted "the first real challenge to Grotius' undisputed reputation as the founder of international law."[32] This was an unprecedented challenge, and it caused an earthquake in the community of international lawyers in a way that the further expansion of the pantheon of founding fathers of international law would not. These were the earliest days of the attempt to create the canon of the new discipline of international law and the revival of Gentili constituted the first conscious and sometimes controversial step in the process. As such, his revival constituted a remarkable move that certainly deserves an explanation.

4.2.1   Competing Fathers: Grotius and Gentili

The relationship between Grotius' and Gentili's respective canonizations remains clouded in a certain degree of mystery, not least because the trajectory of Grotius' own afterlife is still debated. While scholars once conventionally noted that "during the eighteenth and nineteenth centuries ... Grotius had come to be generally regarded as the sole founding father of the *jus naturae et gentium*,"[33] others later emphasized that Grotius' eighteenth-century canonization had happened primarily within the realm of moral philosophy, long before the broader rise of historicism in the nineteenth century and his canonization within the history of the law of nations.[34] Martine Julia van Ittersum has further complicated this picture by briefly charting the waxing and waning of Grotius' star over the same period. Grotius, she argues, has been many things to many people, his public image(s) evolving across time and space. He only became established as the "father of international law" in the late nineteenth century, as a result of three factors coming together in that period: the conceptualization

---

[32] Haggenmacher, "Grotius and Gentili," 133.
[33] Ibid., 134.
[34] Hochstrasser, *Natural Law Theories in the Early Enlightenment.*

of the Dutch past by American historians and government officials, the importance of the Dutch Golden Age for Dutch nation building, and the emergence of the Institut and of modern international law more broadly.[35] This canonization as the founder of international law made Grotius more important than ever before. Van Ittersum notes that as late as 1864, the Dutch government showed no interest in buying or preserving Grotius' manuscripts when his descendants lost control of his material legacy and his original writings were auctioned off in The Hague.[36] The turning points, for her, were his establishment as a Dutch national hero through the Grotius commemorations of 1883 and 1886 and his reburial in 1889,[37] and perhaps even more importantly, the great celebration organized in his honor by the U.S. delegation at the Hague Peace Conference of 1899.[38]

In light of the echoes between Grotius' and Gentili's respective canonizations in the late nineteenth century, it is worth outlining van Ittersum's argument in some further detail. At that point, she explains, Grotius stood for the Dutch as "a symbol of the country's civilizing mission": stuck with the problem of how to brand itself as a "small, truncated country in a continent dominated by big nation-states," Dutch liberals developed the idea that their kingdom had a manifest destiny in international politics through its internationalist commitment to peaceful conflict resolution.[39] They traced this tradition directly back to Grotius' *De iure belli ac pacis*, his presumed magnum opus despite the greater importance he himself reserved to his *Annotations on the Old and New Testament*,[40] and specifically to his presumed advocacy of international arbitration and attempt to limit the horrors of war.[41] As we will see, these two themes were the exact same ones that Gentili became

---

[35] Van Ittersum, "Hugo Grotius," 94. Van Ittersum has also carefully charted the use – and sometimes downright weaponization – of Grotius' memory in other domains, notably the appropriation of his legacy by parties on either side of the Dutch Patriot Revolt in the late eighteenth century. Van Ittersum, "Confronting Grotius' Legacy in an Age of Revolution." For a similarly fascinating study of the competing uses of Grotius in seventeenth-century England, see Barducci, *Hugo Grotius and the Century of Revolution, 1613–1718*. Again in the English context, Grotius was claimed both by resistance theorists and by royalists and absolutists.

[36] Van Ittersum, "Hugo Grotius," 87.

[37] Ibid., 87 and 94.

[38] On the American delegation's celebration of Grotius, see also Nabulsi, *Traditions of War*, 10–11. On Grotius' reception by twentieth-century international lawyers, see Rasilla del Moral, "Grotian Revivals in the Theory and History of International Law."

[39] Van Ittersum, "Hugo Grotius," 95.

[40] Ibid., 98.

[41] Ibid., 95.

celebrated for, a similarity that is far from coincidental and arguably says more about the interests of the "revivers" than about Grotius' and Gentili's own intentions in their time. As for the Americans, Van Ittersum contextualizes this sudden enthusiasm for Grotius within the broader importance that Holland acquired in the collective imagination of U.S.-based urban elites during the Gilded Age, particularly with the idea that Holland, not England, was "the mother of America."[42] Grotius, to them, was a mascot for the American characteristics and ideals that had originated in Holland and found their most elaborate form across the Atlantic, from Protestantism and religious tolerance to freedom and democracy.[43] In this context, different myths fed off each other in the 1880s and 1890s, converging at the Peace Palace in The Hague and leading to Grotius' canonization: U.S. nationalism and the American brand of manifest destiny, revamped Dutch nationalism in its internationalist guise, and, deeply intertwined with the latter, "the self-understanding of modern international law as a narrative of historical progress."[44]

Based on this confluence of circumstances in the late nineteenth century, Grotius' working papers were "rediscovered" and a major conversation ensued about how to adequately commemorate him. Should statues be erected of him for public consumption? Was it preferable to focus on republishing previously forgotten manuscripts for the perusal of legal scholars? Could both be pursued simultaneously? As we shall see, virtually identical questions arose in the case of Gentili.

Van Ittersum's account is extremely valuable, not least in adding a crucial facet to our understanding of the creation of international law's canon. Her claim that Grotius' modern image is "based on a highly selective reading of *De Jure Belli ac Pacis* and completely ignores the larger historical context of Grotius' work, particularly his hands-on involvement in Western imperialism and colonialism,"[45] dovetails with the themes of the present work. However, her chronology leaves space for some elements of debate. While she emphasizes the crowning of Grotius as the founder of international law in the 1880s and 1890s, the analysis that follows supports accounts that suggest there was already a clear sense, in the 1870s, that Grotius was the true founder of international law, and that this was not to be undermined by the revival of Gentili.

---

[42] Ibid., 90.
[43] Ibid., 90 and 92.
[44] Ibid., 96.
[45] Ibid., 84.

As such, there is perhaps an earlier history of Grotius' reception amongst international lawyers – and particularly those involved in the *Revue* and the Institut in the 1860s and 1870s – to be carefully traced as well. An important part of the question here is how to place the role of the Dutch subcommittee for the revival of Gentili within the canonization of Grotius. The committee was founded in 1875 along with its Italian and English counterparts (which I will discuss at more length later), and in a rather comical turn of fate, its ultimate achievement was to erect the famous statue of Grotius on Delft's market square in 1886. Rumor has it that the committee was "attacked" by a mysterious lawyer called Levy, who in the words of T. E. Holland, our main protagonist in the Gentili revival, was "too exclusive in his admiration of the Dutchman Grotius."[46] According to Holland, Levy's arguments were then refuted by the president of the Dutch subcommittee, Tobias Asser, "in the columns of the *Algemeen Handelsblad*."[47] While van der Molen considered that the controversy between Asser and Levy had still not been solidly established,[48] the online archive of the newspaper shows that there was indeed an exchange between the two men to this effect,[49] though why exactly the Dutch subcommittee collapsed afterwards is not entirely clear. Lots of questions thus remain as to what exactly the relationship between the canonization of Grotius and that of Gentili was in the 1870s and 1880s, but if anything, what the research that follows shows is that the lawyers involved in the revival of Gentili considered the celebration of the Italian to be a profound and eminently controversial challenge to Grotius' unopposed status up until that point.

Second, Gentili's revival was a remarkably institutionalized and high-profile endeavor, suggesting that late nineteenth-century lawyers perceived its stakes to be high. Operating loosely through the epoch-making Institut de droit international – almost all the key lawyers involved would soon become members – Gentili's revival was orchestrated from 1874 onward through a major international effort involving numerous major figures in the international legal scene of the period. At its heart was T. E. Holland, the newly appointed Chichele Professor of International Law at Oxford. His inaugural lecture as Chichele

---

[46] Holland, "Preface," 15. See also Rolin-Jaequemyns, "Quelques mots sur les hommages projetés à la mémoire de Grotius et d'Albéric Gentil, et sur les dernières publications y relatives," 690.

[47] Holland, "Preface," 15.

[48] Van der Molen, *Alberico Gentili and the Development of International Law*, 282, n. 27.

[49] Levy, "Alberigo Gentili"; Asser, "Alberigo Gentili." I thank Bastiaan Bouwman for bringing this to my attention.

Professor, entitled "An Inaugural Lecture on Albericus Gentilis" and delivered at All Souls College on November 7, 1874, was long considered the starting point of Gentili's spectacular revival.[50] In it, Holland outlined what he saw as Gentili's various contributions to the emergence of the law of nations, and though he admitted Grotius was superior to Gentili in many respects, he nonetheless boldly argued that it was Gentili who had taken "the first step towards making International Law what it is"[51] and that Grotius had simply "followed" Gentili on this path.[52] In the aftermath of the lecture, an umbrella-like International Committee was created to revive the Italian jurist and his work, which then branched out into three distinct subcommittees that formed the actual driving forces of the revival. The subcommittees were divided along national lines: there was an Italian one, an English one, and a Dutch one, each endowed with its share of eminent jurists and high-profile figures.

The dedication of these men to Gentili's momentous revival is rather remarkable, and one might indeed wonder why Alberico Gentili and his *DIB* suddenly benefited from such considerable attention on the part of prominent scholars and jurists. Why did these international lawyers turn specifically to Gentili, what did they emphasize in his work in trying to construct the history of their own endeavor, and what does it tell us about their own motives? These are the questions addressed in this chapter and the one that follows. In order to answer them, it is essential to place the revival of Gentili within the larger process of inventing "traditions" and within the conscious development of a historical pedigree for the arising "science" of international law. As suggested by Luigi Lacchè, whose work on the revival of Gentili constitutes a starting point for this analysis, the Alberico Gentili that emerged in the late nineteenth century was "of course far from his historical world, but perfectly functional on the building-site of the new international law."[53] The task, then, is to evaluate what shape this new Alberico Gentili took, in what became, in a way, a new context for the reading of his work.

Analyzing motives is not an easy task, and it is sometimes all too easy to paint individuals as unidimensional political creatures single-mindedly pushing forward a clear agenda. As I have already hinted,

---

[50] This is notably the case in van der Molen's biography, *Alberico Gentili and the Development of International Law.*

[51] Holland, *Inaugural Lecture*, 35.

[52] Ibid., 31. For a detailed outline and assessment of his various claims in the lecture, see Haggenmacher, "Grotius and Gentili."

[53] Lacchè, "Monuments of International Law," 208.

politics were indeed at the heart of Gentili's revival, but my analysis also seeks to highlight the extent to which the process of the revival was moved by personal, sociological, and institutional interests as well. More often than not, the reception of Gentili developed in an idiosyncratic way, with Gentili being pulled back from the dead almost accidentally. The motives for reviving him were neither clear nor homogeneous from the start, and the reasons behind the success of the revival and the form it took have much to do with a very specific set of circumstances. The fact that Gentili had been a professor at Oxford – giving him some particularly attractive credentials for those wishing to invoke his authority on international legal matters – and that a number of very influential international lawyers were based there in the 1870s and keen to add another jewel to the crown of their institution, is just one of the coincidences that made the celebration of the long-dead Italian jurist possible on such a large scale. Before examining the dynamics of the revival in England, however, I first outline Lacchè's existing work on the revival of Gentili in Italy, highlighting its main insights as well as its limitations in accounting for the shape the Italian jurist's revival took on the international stage.

4.2.2 The View from Italy: Sbarbaro and Gentili as the Father of International Arbitration

As another scholar intrigued by the sudden prominence Gentili acquired in the late nineteenth century, Lacchè has also sought to account for what he describes as the explosion of a "real *Gentilis cult*" or a *"Gentilis-mania"* in 1875.[54] Lacchè ties the resurgence of Gentili to a man called Pietro Sbarbaro (1838–1893), and specifically to his "very singular and eccentric personality," to his relationship with the famous Pasquale Mancini (1817–1888; the first president of the Institut and a prominent Italian statesman), and to the intellectual, political, and religious movements of the time.[55] Sbarbaro, upon whose life and writings Lacchè grounds his analysis, became a professor at the University of Macerata in 1874, where, the following year, he began pressing for the erection of a monument to Gentili. But beyond his position as a professor, Sbarbaro was a man deeply involved in the debates of his time, "an eclectic scholar of political economy and philosophy of law, journalist, polemicist, [who] taught in various universities in Italy and

---

[54] Ibid., 153 (emphasis in original).
[55] Ibid., 156. For an earlier, briefer account of this part of the story, see Vecchio, "The Posthumous Fate of Alberico Gentili."

was eternally at loggerheads with almost all of the ministers of education until he, in 1883, was dismissed,"[56] as well as a "monarchist and Mason, anticlerical, and a profoundly religious man, liberal conservative, [who] dedicated his life to the development of proletariat mutualism and international pacifism."[57]

The broad contextual element here is that Italian scholars of the nineteenth century rediscovered the works of Gentili – "in parallel to [T. E.] Holland" – within the crucial context of the political movement of the Risorgimento (Resurgence) that eventually led to the unification of Italy and the conquest of Rome in 1871.[58] However, according to Lacchè, the centrality of Sbarbaro in Gentili's Italian revival meant that the sudden enthusiasm for a monument to the long-dead jurist has to be understood specifically within the context of Italian nationalism and Unitarianism, as well as masonic pacifism, with the latter deemed "all too present in the trajectories of the Gentilis affairs, at an Italian and international level."[59] The "*most profound reasons*" for the surge of interest in Gentili, Lacchè reiterates, are to be found in the "cultural history of the Gentilis myth, made up of Risorgimento patriotism, anticlericalism, Mason *esprit*, nation building."[60] Put simply, Gentili became a remarkably popular figure as a son of the emerging nation, a name to brandish to remind Italians of the glorious achievements of their common ancestors. It is easy to understand how this made Gentili popular in Italy, but the argument has less traction when it comes to understanding Gentili's revival on an international level. Here, Lacchè also suggests that the revival of Gentili was directly intertwined with the successful advocacy efforts in favor of international arbitration.

Lacchè's analysis is based on the papers of Sbarbaro, who was indeed deeply involved in international arbitration efforts, and it provides an important piece of the puzzle for understanding the shape that Gentili took in his second context. Lacchè focuses his analysis on the period during which Sbarbaro was most active in establishing the International Committee for the revival of Gentili and ensuring that a monument in his honor would be erected, namely 1874–75. With his appointment at Macerata, Sbarbaro brought with him the issue of arbitration, as well as his network of high-profile figures working on the issue around Europe,

---

[56] Lacchè, "Monuments of International Law," 157.
[57] Ibid.
[58] Vadi, "Alberico Gentili on Roman Imperialism," 142. On the Risorgimento, see, for example, Riall, *The Italian Risorgimento*; Patriarca and Riall, *The Risorgimento Revisited*.
[59] Lacchè, "Monuments of International Law," 161.
[60] Ibid., 156 (emphasis in original).

and particularly, in Italy, the all-important Mancini. Clearly, Sbarbaro explicitly tried to make Gentili the "father of international arbitration," composing the first element of the new narrative about the long-dead jurist.

Lacchè's analysis stems from "a clue which has never been taken up until now,"[61] to be found in the initial 1875 proposal of the University of Macerata (the "Macerata Proposal") encouraging the university to commit itself to erecting a monument to Gentili in one of the towns of the Marche region. In this proposal, Gentili is depicted as being the forefather of the principle of international arbitration, a move that is "certainly the work of Sbarbaro."[62] Sbarbaro had been agitating in favor of arbitration, and it is unsurprising to find him trying to link Gentili to one of the hot topics of his day. Just a month after his appointment at Macerata, on July 11, 1874, Sbarbaro had published an anonymous article on the *Alabama* ruling and the broader topic of peace and arbitration, emphasizing the crucial importance of this mechanism and the noble role played by Richard Cobden (1804–1865) in England, who had been derided when he had first presented his proposal for international arbitration before the House of Commons.[63] England, Sbarbaro noted, had with the *Alabama* ruling now "accepted the utopia of Arbitration,"[64] and this mechanism was moving forward in great strides. Sir Henry Richards (1812–1899) picked up the mantle of Richard Cobden as one of England's most prominent advocates for arbitration, and Lacchè emphasizes that "we have no trace [of him] in the little Gentilis Panthéon, and yet his is a presence not to be ignored."[65] Lacchè makes very clear the close links between four figures in the movement for the promotion of international arbitration: Sbarbaro, Richards, Mancini – who would eventually champion the question of arbitration in the Italian Parliament, pushing the so-called Mancini motion – and Count Sclopis (1798–1878), the president of the *Alabama* arbitration college. He also provides some elements directly linking the work of this group with the initial efforts to revive Gentili, beyond the mere overlap in the names of the characters involved.

The most obvious set of evidence comes from Sbarbaro's own writings, and from what emerged out of the University of Macerata through his efforts. Lacchè finds a brief mention of Gentili in a speech of praise

[61] Ibid., 157–58.
[62] Ibid.
[63] Ibid., 158.
[64] Ibid., 159.
[65] Ibid.

Sbarbaro wrote for the Emperor of Russia, who had received members of the Peace Congress during his visit in London in June 1874. More importantly, the resolution of the council of the Macerata law faculty of March 23, 1875 – Lacchè's original clue – recognizes Gentili "unanimously as restorer and founder of modern international law," "founder of the true school of international law and forerunner of Grotius, as well as of the modern principle of international arbitration."[66]

Sbarbaro makes his point even more clearly in a strikingly lyrical 1886 pamphlet dedicated to the theologian "Socino" [Fausto Sozzini/Faustus Socinus] (1536–1604) and to one of the most famous figures of Italian unification, Giuseppe Mazzini (1805–1872).[67] Placing his work within "the century of great resurrections," he outlines the purpose of "a curious generation," "very avid to rebuild the past, to remake the history of great men and great things using more impartial criteria" and a "scientific method," a generation whose "unique intent and religion is the discovery of all truth."[68] "Never before," he explains, "did buried men and institutions ... present themselves to posterity in order to demand new examination, to implore ... a more just sentence on their character ... on the part played in carrying out human destinies and in the course of human history."[69] Gentili, Sbarbaro makes clear, is one of these great, buried men, with the institution of arbitration buried alongside him, and Italy has made this double resurrection possible. Though "thirsting for justice and peace among its various nations," Europe would never have

---

[66] Ibid., 181.

[67] Sbarbaro, *Da Socino a Mazzini*. Cited in Lacchè, "Monuments of International Law," 186. Sbarbaro appears to have been the only one to link the two men in his rather obscure work *Da Socino a Mazzini*. Fausto Socino was a sixteenth-century theologian, founder of Socinianism, and a noted figure of Unitarianism (the direct doctrinal descendants of Socianism are the Unitarian Christians of England and Transylvania). Sbarbaro, like many of his peers, saw liberal theology – and Unitarianism more specifically – as central to the project of the nation-state. He explains his reasoning in one of his speeches: "... che per salvare le nazioni dal doppio pericolo, dal doppio flagella della Superstizione Ortodossa e dell'Ateismo, non c'è altra via, altra formula di salute e di vita morale che il Cristianesimo Liberale di Parker, di Channing, del nostro grande Socino" [... that to save the nation from the double perils, the double scourges of Orthodox Superstition and Atheism, there is no other way, no other formula for salvation and for a moral life than the Liberal Christianity [liberal theology] of Parker, of Channing, of our great Socino]. Sbarbaro, *Da Socino a Mazzini*, 74. The writings of Channing, who became the leader of the Unitarian movement in the United States, were in fact translated into French and published in 1866 with an introduction by Édouard de Laboulaye, whom we will also encounter shortly. Reflecting the tensions of the age, Laboulaye emphasized the importance of Christian theology as a bulwark against "positivist philosophy" [philosophie positive].

[68] Sbarbaro, *Da Socino a Mazzini*, 10–13. Lacchè's translation.

[69] Ibid., 10–13.

traveled this road alone, were it not for "the Geneva Arbitration [the *Alabama* ruling] where Italy appears as peace-maker between two great nations by the sole mastery of pen and unarmed reason";[70] Italy needed to recount "to civilised Europe, the practical possibility of substituting war with that knowledge of peaceful Arbitration, which Gentilis, since the 16th century, invoked from God and greeted on the far away horizon of the future of mankind."[71] Gentili was revived at this particular moment, then, Sbarbaro judiciously observes, because – and here he cites the French historian Edgar Quinet (1803–1875), who played a key role in elaborating the myth of Leonardo da Vinci as the "first modern man"[72] – "the dead only return when they have something to teach the living."[73]

Sbarbaro's ideas, of course, spilt beyond his own writings. In both his efforts to promote international arbitration and his attempt to revive and glorify Gentili, he was drawing extensively on his Italian and international networks, amongst which were numerous international pacifists, including Emilio Castelar (1832–1899), Édouard de Laboulaye, François Laurent (1810–1887), Henry Richards, and Charles Lemonnier (1860–1930).[74] These individuals, probably thrilled to tie their endeavor to this rediscovered father of international law, were quick to adopt Sbarbaro's narrative. The letters he received from Richards, as well as from Charles Lemonnier and Armand Goegg (1820–1897), both representatives of the Central Committee of the International League for Peace and Freedom, all underline "the universal character of the message of Gentilis, to be collocated in the *Panthéon* of the founders of international law and of the fathers of Peace."[75] And indeed, the papers of T. E. Holland contain letters from the American Thomas Willing Balch (1866–1927), who would come to be known as the "father of arbitration," where Balch explains to Holland that he is attempting to raise the profile of Gentili across the Atlantic.[76] In addition, by what strikes even Lacchè as a "truly singular coincidence," Count Sclopis, who presided over the *Alabama* arbitration, had actually been studying the work of Gentili himself, a fact which certainly facilitated the development of links between the two endeavors.[77] Finally, one

---

[70] Ibid., 10–13.
[71] Ibid., 10–13.
[72] Bullen, "Walter Pater's 'Renaissance' and Leonardo da Vinci's Reputation in the Nineteenth Century," 273.
[73] Lacchè, "Monuments of International Law," 185–86.
[74] Ibid., 196.
[75] Ibid., 195.
[76] Balch, "Letter from Thomas Balch to Thomas Erskine Holland," October 27, 1911.
[77] Lacchè, "Monuments of International Law," 183.

particular piece of evidence makes it clear that this enthusiasm for arbitration was directly imported into the broader revival of Gentili, beyond the individual writings of Sbarbaro. The International Committee for the revival of Gentili opened its subscriptions for financing the Gentilis monument on September 14, 1875, the anniversary of the third Geneva arbitration judgment.[78]

As such, Lacchè explains, from 1875 "the picture of a Gentilis, apostle of Peace and announcer of a future international law which was desired to become the present, emerged very strongly."[79] For him, there is "no doubt" that "peace and arbitration since the beginning represent the main moving force that directs the protagonist of the Gentilis rebirth."[80] His main insights regarding the international popularity of Gentili concern the importance of the jurist for the international arbitration movement that Sbarbaro was deeply involved in. Indeed, Lacchè argues that "[i]t is only by being conscious of the work carried out by Sbarbaro at the beginning of the [1870s] in the movement for peace and international arbitration that the reasons for the Gentilis *renaissance* can be understood," with Sbarbaro constituting "the *trait d'union*" between Sir Henry Richard – the secretary of the Peace Society – and Mancini.[81] This is absolutely plausible, but a question arises: To what extent was this initial narrative of Gentili as the father of international arbitration maintained as the revival movement spread to England and to the broader international scene? Did this remain the focus of the narrative that emerged about him in his late nineteenth-century context?

While enlightening in a number of ways, Lacchè's analysis focuses specifically on the part of Gentili's revival that led to the erection of a statue in his honor in San Ginesio in 1908.[82] As a result, although he pays close attention to the links between Holland and Sbarbaro, his archival excavations reveal a tremendous amount about why Gentili became so remarkably popular in Italy, but they do not tell us as much about why his name and works became so important beyond his homeland. Yet it appears that the revival of Gentili took on a life of its own beyond Sbarbaro, beyond Italy, and beyond the specific issue of arbitration.

---

[78] Ibid., 194.
[79] Ibid., 183.
[80] Ibid., 194.
[81] Ibid., 170 (emphasis in original).
[82] The erection of his statue in Italy was delayed by disagreements over Gentili's beliefs. Catholic authorities were highly uncomfortable with the canonization of a man they saw as a Protestant renegade and they sought to discredit his work for some time. Vecchio, "The Posthumous Fate of Alberico Gentili"; Vadi, *War and Peace*, 24–27.

4.2.3   A Malleable Champion

Gentili's perceived vanguardism could indeed be used for a variety of purposes. In a letter to local newspapers in April 1875, Mancini had explained that Gentili's "life and teachings three hundred years ago foresaw the cult of the two greatest ideas of our century: *freedom of conscience* against theocratic despotism; *Justice and Peace among Nations* against the barbarities of war."[83] The latter could of course encompass the principle of international arbitration, but it could also stand, for instance, for the burgeoning attempts to regulate war. More broadly, the sort of anachronisms associated with the application of Gentili's ideas to the late nineteenth century made it easy to harness his work to different projects. In fact, the possibility of using Gentili for a wide range of political-legal endeavors was not lost on Sbarbaro and Mancini's contemporaries, and the many titles now bestowed upon the Italian jurist did occasionally raise some eyebrows.

The risk of Gentili being used both opportunistically and anachronistically was noted in a particularly perceptive way in an 1875 piece for the *Revue* on the revival of Gentili by Gustave Rolin-Jaequemyns, one of the most important figures of the period as – amongst others – a founder of the *Revue*, cofounder and first Secretary of the Institut, and one of the prime movers behind the codification of the laws of war.[84] First, Rolin-Jaequemyns is fairly skeptical of Sbarbaro's ideas about the "posthumous rehabilitation" of great thinkers, and particularly about the anachronistic attribution of titles to these long-dead figures. For instance, he explains regarding Gentili that "we doubt ... that it is rigorously accurate to represent the wise lawyer of the Spanish embassy as a sort of inspired apostle of peace," and more generally, he suggests that "to drape a great jurist from three centuries ago into such ultra-modern garments is not a good example for the artist who will be in charge of his statue."[85] He also explicitly points to the space that exists for varying

---

[83] Lacchè's translation, "Monuments of International Law," 155 (emphasis in original).

[84] Rolin-Jaequemyns, "Albéric Gentil. Hommages à sa mémoire." Rolin-Jaequemyns was the first secretary of the Institut under the presidency of Pasquale Mancini. He was also one of the key figures behind the codification of the laws of war, along with the three most famous architects of the codification, Johann Caspar Bluntschli, Francis Lieber, and Feodor Fedorovich de Martens. The latter had come to replace the French jurist Édouard de Laboulaye from 1870 – the one who would suggest the republication *of De iure belli* to T. E. Holland. Like many other members of the Institut, from the mid-1870s Rolin-Jaequemyns also became increasingly interested in the issue of the Congo, and King Leopold eventually appointed him member of the High Council for the independent state of the Congo Free State in 1889.

[85] Ibid., 142.

interpretations of the jurist's work and its contemporary relevance, and the fact that they have already taken different directions. He notes that the International Committee is made up of at least twenty vice-presidents, that Sbarbaro, the secretary, has no less than eight vice-secretaries, and that the Italian subcommittee is composed of about 200 members,[86] making the adoption of a single narrative about the importance of Gentili rather improbable. Even more importantly for our purposes, he explicitly underlines the fact that Holland and Sbarbaro have adopted different approaches in their efforts to revive the Italian jurist, seeing the differences between the English and the Italian approaches as "characteristic."[87] He makes it clear that he prefers the English approach for its "effectiveness and ... greater level of attention paid to scientific profile" over the "Italian rhetorical celebration."[88]

While this might come across as a somewhat caricatured comparison of the two approaches, it is true that the English subcommittee, unencumbered by the nationalist baggage involved in the Italian revival of Gentili, turned to a somewhat more active engagement with the works of the jurist. While the assessment of Gentili's importance drew on previous studies of his work in the early days of the revival, the republication of *DIB* in 1877, edited by T. E. Holland, unleashed a new phase in the revival of Gentili's work. The discussion that follows focuses on the work of the English subcommittee and the revival of Gentili's work within the Anglophone sphere. Accordingly, instead of relying primarily on the papers of Sbarbaro, as Lacchè does, it mainly relies on the papers of the English subcommittee, and particularly the papers of T. E. Holland, which have attracted virtually no scholarly attention thus far.

A note before I turn to the English subcommittee's work: while the British and the Italian subcommittees were regularly in touch and collaborated smoothly, especially Holland and Sbarbaro, determining who it is that truly revived the Italian jurist has generated some controversy. According to conventional accounts of the resurgence of Gentili,[89] his revival began on November 7, 1874, with the inaugural lecture given by Holland in his capacity as the newly appointed Chichele Professor of International Law at All Souls College, University of Oxford. Holland's lecture would then have been published by Macmillan (a traditional

---

[86] Ibid.
[87] Ibid., and again at 143.
[88] Ibid., also cited in Lacchè, "Monuments of International Law," 199.
[89] See, for instance, van der Molen's seminal biography of Gentili, *Alberico Gentili and the Development of International Law*, 61.

procedure), then sent by Sir Travers Twiss (1809–1897)[90] to Mancini, who would then have passed it on to Sbarbaro. This is in line with both Holland's and Twiss' own recounting of the story. Twiss indeed explains that Sbarbaro decided, upon reading a copy of Holland's lecture, to meet with his colleagues, and that together they decided to "form an International Committee to do fitting honour to the memory of their great countryman,"[91] while Holland claims that "[a] copy of the lecture was sent by Sir Travers Twiss in the February following, to Mancini, then Professor of International Law at Rome, who, much interested, communicated it to Professor Sbarbaro of Macerata."[92] However, Lacchè questions the validity of this timeline, pointing out that Sbarbaro had already begun agitating for the revival of Gentili in June 1874, "well before Holland's inaugural lecture."[93] He suggests that Sbarbaro merely used Holland's famous lecture as the "occasion" upon which he could draw momentum for his plans concerning Gentili, and that as such (and somewhat qualifying his statement), it was not "the inaugural lecture *alone* which rendered the birth of that real *Gentilis cult* ... possible."[94]

Whether this is true or not, Holland would certainly have been offended by such an affirmation; a letter from Coleman Phillipson (1875–1958) responding to what was apparently a rather angry letter from Holland suggests that the latter was indeed very attached to his status as the great reviver of Gentili. "I deeply regret the impression my article gave you," Coleman explains, referring to the draft of what would become his classic piece on Albericus Gentilis in the famous, Carnegie-funded *Classics of International Law* series. "It was far from my intention to belittle your work in connection with the Gentilis revival,"[95] he continues, noting in particular that he absolutely did not mean to place Henry Nézard, who wrote another key piece about Gentili in the Francophone *Les fondateurs du droit international*,[96] on

---

[90] Twiss' eventful life and involvement in international law has now been recounted in great detail by Andrew Fitzmaurice, whose work I have drawn on in Chapters 4 and 5. See Fitzmaurice, "The Resilience of Natural Law in the Writings of Sir Travers Twiss'"; Fitzmaurice, *King Leopold's Ghostwriter*.

[91] Twiss, "Albericus Gentilis on the Right of War," 145.

[92] Holland also puts forward this narrative in various places, notably in the preface he wrote to Ermelinda Armigero Gazzera's *Bibliografia*. Holland, "Preface," 12.

[93] Lacchè, "Monuments of International Law," 169.

[94] Ibid., 153 (emphasis in original).

[95] Phillipson, "Letter from Coleman Phillipson to Thomas Erskine Holland," October 3, 1911.

[96] Nézard, "Albericus Gentilis."

an equal footing with Holland. "When the contributions to the 'Great Jurists' series come to be collected, I shall gladly – and gratefully – avail myself of the opportunity to add such information as is wanting in my present paper."[97]

This exchange is interesting in what it tells us about the personal dynamics behind Gentili's revival and the stakes involved in claiming the credit for reviving his work. Lacchè briefly notes that in 1867, Groningen University had used, as the subject of one of its selection exams, "who between Gentilis and Grotius, should be held up as the founder of international law?" The winner of the exam, Wijbrand Adriaan Reiger (1842–1910), whose 1867 dissertation entitled *Commentatio de Alberico Gentili, Grotio ad condendam juris gentium disciplinam via præeunte* constituted the first "more profound study" of the Italian jurist and his work,[98] would later be nominated Knight of the Order of the Crown of Italy, an honor bestowed "as a sign of the gratitude owed to you by our country for that which you have done to claim the glory of Albericus."[99] The formulation of the exam question suggests Holland and Sbarbaro were not the first to pick up on Gentili's potential as a canonical figure for the emerging discipline of international law. In any case, this suggests that pinning the revival of Gentili onto a single person may well be as fraught with risk as pinning the origins of international law onto a single jurist.

4.2.4   The English Subcommittee for the Revival of Alberico Gentili

The English subcommittee was founded a few months after the Italian one, in November 1875. As Travers Twiss, himself a member of the English subcommittee, explains, "[t]he admirers of Gentilis in this country were unwilling to be left behind in making public a similar expression of their feeling towards one, who had brought honor upon England."[100] Importantly, while Gentili became seen as a national hero in Italy, with great emphasis placed on the erection of monuments in his honor, the Oxford-based English subcommittee had at its disposal many of the writings of the former Oxford professor, and its task

---

[97] Phillipson, "Letter from Coleman Phillipson to Thomas Erskine Holland," October 3, 1911.

[98] Van der Molen, *Alberico Gentili and the Development of International Law*, 61.

[99] Lacchè, "Monuments of International Law," 204–05. Lacchè suggests that "[t]he fact that a Dutchman rectified, with impartiality, the pretended wrongs towards the 'apostle of peace' – Albericus Gentilis – offered great support to the Gentilis movement which came about in Italy in 1875", 205.

[100] Twiss, "Albericus Gentilis on the Right of War," 145.

became a slightly more substantive one. This keen interest in the work of Gentili was certainly characterized by more than a touch of institutional pride, with Holland ending his inaugural lecture by emphasizing the remarkable achievements of "the adopted son of Oxford."[101]

T. E. Holland's seminal lecture occurred just a year after the founding of the Institut, and it is striking to note that the various steps initially taken to revive Gentili's work occurred within the exact same time frame as the period so crucial for the development of international law: Holland's lecture in 1874, the creation of the International Committee in 1875, the republication of *DIB* in 1877. In fact, Holland even gave his speech on Gentili again at the Institut's meeting in The Hague in 1877 and invited the Institut to meet in Oxford in 1880. Since the "men of 1873"[102] essentially ushered in the modern international legal profession, one inevitably wonders why they concentrated a nonnegligible chunk of their time and efforts trying to revive the works of a long-dead sixteenth-century jurist. Why, in their own words, did prominent international lawyers in England "care very much for the memory of Gentilis"?[103] Some contextual elements are helpful to begin answering this question.

The makeup of the English subcommittee – fifteen members in total, excluding the honorary president – points to three key features of Gentili's English revival: its high-profile character, its links with the development of international law as a professional discipline, and its relevance to circles that had a direct influence on policymaking.

While the Italian subcommittee benefited from the honorary presidency of Prince Umberto (1844–1900), the eldest son of King Victor Emmanuel (1820–1878), and future King of Italy himself, as well as the leadership of the famous Mancini, who was also the president of the Institut, the English subcommittee had Prince Leopold (1853–1884) – the youngest son of Queen Victoria – as its own prestigious honorary president, and as a whole, it was composed of a wider and more influential range of jurists than its Italian counterpart in the world of late nineteenth-century international law. It was also based in Oxford, which was a widely respected intellectual center "therefore at the heart of the international debate."[104]

---

[101] Holland, *Inaugural Lecture*.

[102] I borrow this phrase from Koskenniemi, *Gentle Civilizer*.

[103] T. E. Holland letter to P. Sbarbaro expressing the enthusiasm of himself and his colleague (Phillimore, Twiss, Deane, etc.), London, July 28, 1875, cited in Lacchè, "Monuments of International Law," 201, n. 157.

[104] Lacchè, "Monuments of International Law," 153.

The subcommittee consisted of "the Professors of the Oxford Faculty of Law, together with the surviving Oxford members of the (suppressed) College of Advocates practicing in the admiralty and ecclesiastical courts,"[105] a grouping whose nature I will explain shortly. Four of the five most notable members of the subcommittee either already were or would become prominent members of the Institut:[106] J. R. Phillimore (1810–1885, the chairman of the subcommittee),[107] Travers Twiss,[108] Mountague Bernard (1820–1882),[109] and T. E. Holland.[110] Travers Twiss had taught at King's College London from 1852 to 1855 before moving to Oxford to hold the Regius Chair of Civil Law in Oxford (the same chair as Gentili), a position he would keep until 1870.[111] Mountague Bernard had been the first to occupy the newly founded Chichele Chair of International Law and Diplomacy (1859), which was, crucially, the first professorship in international law to be established in England at the time,[112] and T. E. Holland was now his successor.[113] They were all well known both in England and in the increasingly important international law circles across Europe.[114]

The "surviving Oxford members of the (suppressed) College of Advocates practicing in the admiralty and ecclesiastical courts" were, in short, English civil lawyers. This is important both because English civil lawyers were closely involved in the emerging discipline of international law and because they were keen participants in matters of public policy.

While English common law was obviously the dominant system, civil law was still practiced in England in two institutions, just like it had

---

[105] Holland, "Preface," 16.

[106] The fifth, Henry Sumner Maine, was not a member of the Institut.

[107] Honorary member of the Institut 1883–85. For membership records, see Macalister-Smith, "Bio-Bibliographical Key to the Membership of the Institut de droit international, 1873–2001."

[108] Member of the Institut 1874–91, honorary member 1891–97.

[109] Member of the Institut 1873–82.

[110] Associate of the Institut 1875–78, member from 1878 onward.

[111] Koskenniemi, *Gentle Civilizer*, 33.

[112] Ibid. In addition to the Chichele Chairs at Oxbridge, James Lorimer (1818–1890) held the Chair in the Law of Nature and Nations in Edinburgh, a position that had been established as early as 1707.

[113] On the Dutch side, although the endeavor ultimately capsized, the subcommittee was constituted and presided over by Tobias Asser (1838–1913), one of the founders of the precursor to the Institut, the *Revue de droit international et législation comparée* (1868), with W. A. Reiger, the winner of the 1867 Groningen exam, as the secretary. Lacchè, "Monuments of International Law," 205.

[114] These circles would eventually include North American jurists as well, but this development only took off in earnest a couple of decades later.

been in Gentili's own time: the ecclesiastical courts and in the admiralty court.[115] In the mid-nineteenth century, these institutions were still served by the Doctors' Commons and by posts at Oxford and Cambridge. Prominent figures of the subcommittee, such as its president, Robert Joseph Phillimore, and one of its most vocal members, Sir Travers Twiss, were high-profile characters in international legal circles but they were professional civil lawyers, not international lawyers.[116] In fact, Twiss had succeeded Phillimore as Oxford's Regius Professor of Civil Law in 1855, and "although these university posts were supposedly moribund by the nineteenth century," Twiss personally "made great and persistent efforts to revive both the chairs and the role of civil law in the law curriculum of the universities," notably petitioning Oxford to reinvigorate the discipline.[117] The Doctors' Commons was dissolved in 1865 following the Court of Probate Act of 1857 transferring the authority in ecclesiastical matters from the College of Advocates to common law courts and a decision by College members to simply wind down the Doctors' Commons and profit from the sale of its property.[118] This happened just as international law was emerging as a formal discipline, and with the latter deeply indebted to Roman law, the reconversion of civil lawyers was an almost effortless process and civil law in England received "a new lease of life."[119]

As a consequence both of their singular position in England and of the mid-nineteenth-century reforms that came to affect their profession, these civil lawyers became particularly influential in policymaking at that point, along with the leading common lawyers of their day. I will explain the significance of this shift and provide some biographical elements to situate the main protagonists of the British part of the Gentili revival, notably in terms of the extent of their involvement in the affairs of their time and the links that existed between their academic interests and their involvement in practice.

In the second half of the nineteenth century, international lawyers "often played a significant role in public affairs, sitting on royal commissions which considered questions of international law, and advising government on international questions."[120] This was a particularly

---

[115] Fitzmaurice, *Sovereignty, Property and Empire, 1500–2000*, 219.
[116] Ibid.
[117] Ibid.
[118] Ibid., 220.
[119] Ibid.
[120] Lobban, "English Approaches to International Law in the Nineteenth Century," 72. On the broader context of British liberal internationalism and of the role of lawyers, see Sylvest, *British Liberal Internationalism, 1880–1930*, 61–91.

remarkable development in the British context, where, by 1865, the aforementioned series of reforms had marked the end of a separate body of civilian lawyers, the Doctors' Commons, famously described by Charles Dickens as "a cosey, dosey, old-fashioned, time-forgotten, sleepyheaded little family party."[121] The Doctors' Common has exercised a great amount of power because it served both the ecclesiastical courts, which focused on marriage, and – more importantly – the admiralty courts, which dealt with maritime law. The latter was absolutely crucial for Britain's maritime empire and meant these lawyers were involved in numerous international relations matters. The Queen's (or King's) Advocate General, in particular, was the equivalent position to that of Attorney General in the common law and consulted as the leading authority on maritime law matters.[122] Consequently, international law shifted from being the preserve of a specialist branch of the profession to becoming the preserve of a group of academic jurists, who were less concerned with the litigation of waning admiralty courts than with the political issues of their time.[123] This new approach to international law was developed first and foremost between Oxford and Cambridge, around the likes of Travers Twiss, Mountague Bernard, and T. E. Holland at Oxford, and William Whewell (1794–1866), William Harcourt (1827–1904), Henry Maine (1822–1888), and John Westlake (1828–1913) at Cambridge.[124]

Through this new approach to international law, prominent figures of English law, such as Holland and Westlake, and their counterparts in civil law, such as Twiss and Phillimore, came together to weigh in on various policy areas, two of which stand out. The first was the question of the regulation of war, which, as I will explain in Chapter 5, was the initial impetus behind the Institut. Relatedly, these prominent international lawyers were of course often involved in matters concerning international arbitration as well, as this was one of the most significant developments of the period.[125] Yet, in the eyes of many, including Holland – and by contrast with Sbarbaro – the codification of international law, and specifically of the laws of war, was even more important

---

[121] Fitzmaurice, *Sovereignty, Property and Empire, 1500–2000*, 230.

[122] Ibid.

[123] Lobban, "English Approaches to International Law in the Nineteenth Century," 69–70.

[124] Ibid., 70–71.

[125] For instance, John Westlake – who was not a direct member of the English subcommittee but was a regular commentator on Gentili's revival – was one of the British members of the International Court of Arbitration under the Hague Convention between 1900 and 1906.

than the development of international arbitration.[126] In the most basic sense, war and neutrality became "the most elaborately detailed parts of the whole of international law."[127] The second key area of interest for many of these lawyers was the expansion of the legal scaffolding of imperialism.

To illustrate these various points, four men are worth describing in a little more detail: T. E. Holland, Travers Twiss, Robert Phillimore, and John Westlake. T. E. Holland and Travers Twiss were the most prominent and most active figures of the subcommittee, while Robert Phillimore was its president. John Westlake was not actually on the English subcommittee, but as one of the most famous international lawyers of the period, he was part of the same circles and weighed in forcefully during the debates about Gentili's revival.

T. E. Holland, our self-proclaimed star of the revival, was a well-known figure with a particular interest in the development of the laws of war. He would become famous as a legal scholar from 1880 with the publication of *Elements of Jurisprudence*, which eventually underwent thirteen editions and became "widely regarded as the most successful book on jurisprudence ever written" during his lifetime.[128] Additionally, he was one of the founders of the *Law Quarterly Review*,

---

[126] Indeed, in a lecture looking back on his years at Oxford and the developments of international law during the period, Holland first talks about the progress made by international arbitration at some length and then concludes: "But by far the most notable fact in the history of the science, since I became its official representative here [at Oxford], has been the movement towards the substitution of written rules for the unwritten customs which previously constituted International Law." Specifically, he explains, this "process of quasi-legislation has been effected by means of Conferences ... [which] except in so far as they have endeavoured, by the means just described, to encourage the peaceful settlement of disputes, [have] been concerned with an elaboration and formulation of the laws of war." Holland outlines the key developments of the period on this front: the 1856 Treaty of Paris abolishing privateering, the 1864 Geneva Convention, the 1868 St. Petersburg Declaration, the 1899 Geneva Convention, and the Conventions established at the Hague in 1906–07 and in London in 1908–09. Together, he explains, these "may collectively be described as 'the Hague Code of War on Land'," a name he coined himself in *The Laws of War on Land*. This is not to say that Holland was not deeply interested in international arbitration as well. In fact, the two endeavors – international arbitration and the regulation of warfare – were very much linked, and in Holland's copy of the 1899 Hague Conference documents, he has underlined numerous passages about the modalities of third-party mediation and arbitration between dissenting states. Holland, *A Valedictory Retrospect (1874–1910)*, 9–10. See also Holland, *The Laws of War on Land*.

[127] Neff, *War and the Law of Nations*, 168.

[128] Although the influence of this work declined rapidly after Holland's death in 1926. Holland revised the thirteenth and final edition in 1924, at age eighty-nine. Cosgrove, "Holland, Sir Thomas Erskine (1835–1926)," 699.

the legal periodical that became the model for legal journals around the world, after which he became one of the original fellows of the British Academy and became a Queen's Counsel in 1901.[129] In the 1870s, however, and specifically in the field of international law, he was known less for his academic work than for being an active publicist and a prolific government consultant, two activities he would continue to pursue over the entire course of his academic career.

Holland became well known to the wider public through his regular letters to *The Times* on contemporary topics of international legal controversy, particularly regarding the laws of war.[130] He also worked remarkably closely with the admiralty and the war office and would come to publish numerous pieces on the laws of war both on land and at sea. Most notably, the war office eventually commissioned him to "prepare a Handbook, such as had been issued by authority in other countries, of 'the Laws and Customs of War on Land,' thousands of copies of which were issued to the army in 1904."[131] Following the Geneva Convention of 1906 – which Holland attended as one of the British plenipotentiaries – and The Hague Convention of 1907, he was instructed to bring this book, as well as the chapter on the subject in the *Manual of Military Law* also known as the "Red Book," up to date.[132] These handbooks for soldiers were one of the key requirements emerging out of the conferences on the codification of the laws of war. All countries had to transpose these laws into domestic legislation and issue clear instructions for those fighting on the ground to ensure these laws were being applied in practice.[133] Holland's hand in drafting the

---

[129] Ibid.

[130] Ibid., 700. These letters were eventually collected and published as *Letters to The Times on War and Neutrality* and underwent three editions (1909, 1914, 1921), the third of which covers the period 1881–1920.

[131] Holland, *A Valedictory Retrospect (1874–1910)*, 13.

[132] Ibid., 14. This, however, seems to have been somewhat compromised. Holland explains that "[t]he work was ... while in course of execution, taken out of my hands by certain military persons" but he notes – not without apparent satisfaction – that this was "[n]ot, however, till an edition of the 'Red Book' containing my entirely re-written chapter, had been issued by the Office in 1907), who were desirous of doing it in their own way, but have apparently found it necessary to obtain assistance outside of the War Office, and have not yet brought their labours to a conclusion." Ibid.

[133] Holland, "Lecture XIX: War. Measures of: Operations by Dolus," 290–91. Holland discusses these at some length, providing details on the manuals that had been published at the time: "These usages, growing out of sentiments of humanity, as also of personal honours, reinforced by considerations of general convenience, have till recently been preserved, for the most part, only by military tradition. Within the last forty years or so, however, such of these usages as commended themselves to the various Governments have been, not uncommonly, embodied in 'Manuals,' differing in many respects one from the other, issued by the authority of the

British manual neatly underlines his direct impact beyond the walls of the university.[134] Holland was also, expectedly, one of the commission members in charge of the drafting of the earlier "Oxford Manual" in 1880, alongside the likes of Johann Caspar Bluntschli (1808–1881), Feodor Fedorovich de Martens (1845–1909), and Gustave Moynier.

Similarly, Sir Travers Twiss was both a renowned scholar and an active participant in the politics of his day, both in matters of war and in colonial affairs.[135] By contrast with Holland, his most important work was actually in the field of international law. His most famous publication, *The Law of Nations Considered as Independent Political Communities*, was published in two parts in 1861–1863, and the translation into French by his friend Alphonse Rivier (1835–1898) became "a standard work on the continent."[136] In typical fashion for the period, half of the treatise concerned "the rights and duties of nations in time of war," while the other half focused on peace, and it is unsurprising that the former received more attention (with an earlier reedition, for instance), as in the words of Rivier, it was "characteristic of the time for the necessity to reprint the volume regarding war to have been felt first" in light of the ongoing conflicts, most notably the American Civil War and the Franco-Prussian War.[137]

---

several Governments, for the guidance of their respective armies." He cites manuals by the following countries: the United States (Lieber), 1863 (reissued 1898); the Netherlands (a textbook for officers), 1871; Russia (a catechism), 1877 (republished); Serbia (a manual), 1878; France (a manual), by M. Billot, 1878; Spain, 1882; Portugal, 1890; Italy, 1896. "Great Britain," Holland explains, "long hesitated to publish such a Manual, relying rather on 'the good sense of the British officer.' A chapter in the *Manual of Military Law*, first published in 1883, has no official authority, and expresses only the opinion of the compiler (Lord Thring); it is, moreover, now much out of date, and was struck out in the new edition completed in 1908." In light of the limitations of these endeavors, "[t]he task was then taken up by private effort [following Brussels 1874], and the labours of some years resulted in the publication, in 1880, at its Oxford meeting, by the Institut de droit international, of its *Manuel des lois et coutumes de la guerre sur terre* [the 'Oxford Manual'] – which was translated into most languages (including Chinese) – and adopted in Argentina for the instruction of the army. It was supplemented, at Cambridge in 1895, by resolutions on penalties for breach of the Geneva Convention [of 1864]." Eventually, these manuals would be made a binding requirement with the Hague injunction that signatories "issue instructions to their armed land forces which shall be in conformity with the Regulations." Hague Convention IV, 1907, article 1.

[134] For a more in-depth discussion of Holland's involvement in the British War Office's manual, see Brazil, "British War Office Manuals and International Law, 1899–1907."

[135] For a thorough examination of Twiss and his work, see Fitzmaurice, *King Leopold's Ghostwriter*.

[136] Lobban, "Twiss, Sir Travers (1809–1897)," 737.

[137] Rivier, "Review: The Law of Nationals Considered as Independent Political Communities," 699.

On a practical front, he was involved in various domestic legal affairs, notably sitting on a range of royal commissions, but more importantly for our purposes, he "was engaged in most of the prize cases which arose from captures made during the Crimean War,"[138] and he was appointed advocate-general to the admiralty in succession to Sir Robert Joseph Phillimore, the president of the English subcommittee. He would eventually succeed the latter again as Queen's Advocate-General on August 23, 1867, shortly before being knighted.[139] He was well connected internationally, serving as a Foreign Office consultant,[140] and rather remarkably enjoyed being "on familiar terms" with Prince Metternich.[141]

After a significant amount of personal drama in 1872 that irremediably damaged his reputation in England,[142] Twiss resigned all offices and turned almost exclusively to international law circles.[143] He became a prominent member of the Institut (he served as its vice-president thrice) and was increasingly involved in the crucial debate over the management of the Congo. His article "La libre navigation du Congo," which called for an international protectorate to be established over the area, caught the attention of King Leopold of Belgium,[144] who hired Twiss as a legal counsel.[145] During the famous Berlin Conference of 1884–85, whose exact aims are still debated but whose impact was undeniably the deepening of European control over the African continent,[146] Twiss was also asked to act as unofficial advisor to the British delegation, and along with Lord Selborne (1812–1895) and Sir Julian Pauncefote (1828–1902), Twiss "largely determined the legal aspects of British policy at Berlin."[147] Eventually, Twiss "drafted the constitution of the Congo Free State for Leopold, and in 1887 was made Grand Commander of the Order of Leopold."[148]

---

[138] Lobban, "Twiss, Sir Travers (1809–1897)," 738.
[139] Ibid.
[140] Koskenniemi, *Gentle Civilizer*, 33.
[141] Lobban, "Twiss, Sir Travers (1809–1897)," 737.
[142] His wife, who was supposed to be the orphaned daughter of a major-general in the Polish army, was outed as a prostitute by one of her lovers, who also pointed out she had been Twiss' mistress for three years prior to their marriage, a rather scandalous set of circumstances in Victorian England.
[143] He also carried out a brief but catastrophic stint in legal history, a field he then entirely abandoned to focus exclusively on international law.
[144] Lobban, "Twiss, Sir Travers (1809–1897)," 738.
[145] Koskenniemi, *Gentle Civilizer*, 133.
[146] For a brief overview of the debates, see Vergerio, "The Berlin and Hague Conferences." For a longer analysis, see Craven, "Between Law and History."
[147] Lobban, "Twiss, Sir Travers (1809–1897)," 738–39.
[148] Ibid., 739.

Our last key subcommittee member, Sir Robert Joseph Phillimore, the subcommittee's president, was a very famous legal figure at the time and a close friend of Prime Minister William Gladstone (1809–1898). In England, he was the last Judge of the High Court of Admiralty from 1867 to 1875.[149] Amongst international legal circles, he was known notably for his four-volume *Commentaries upon International Law*, and for holding the presidency of the Association for the Reformation and Codification of the Laws of Nations, where he gave the inaugural lecture at its annual conference in 1879.[150] Though not usually associated specifically with the codification of the laws of war, this was an area of international law that formed an important part of his work. His initial interest in the discipline, which eventually led to the *Commentaries*, had sprung from his time as a law officer during the American Civil War,[151] an element to which I will return in some detail in Chapter 5.

Finally, John Westlake also commented peripherally but nonetheless influentially on the Gentili revival. Initially famous amongst international jurists for *A Treatise on Private International Law* (1858), he was part of the original trio behind the idea of the *Revue*;[152] he took up the Whewell Chair of International Law at Cambridge (1888), where he published his two most renowned works in public international law – *Chapters on the Principles of International Law* (1894), and *International Law, Part 1: Peace* (1904) and *Part 2: War* (1907) – and he eventually presided the Institut (1895).[153] Westlake's writings on the laws of war and peace would become crucial resources for generations of scholars, particularly at a time when the laws of war were emerging out of a series of sometimes nebulous conferences. Westlake was also "[t]he most frequent commentator on the colonial process among members of the *Institut*,"[154] and by contrast with some of his contemporaries, his views were sharply against extending any sort of sovereignty – "a purely European notion" – to natives.[155] His *Chapters on the Principles of International Law* (1894) directly addresses many of the issues raised at the Berlin Conference around colonialism and sovereignty and is

---

149 This office disappeared after nearly 400 years of existence.
150 Twiss, "Les travaux de l'association pour la réforme et la codification du droit des gens pendant sa session du mois d'août 1879," 440.
151 Doe, "Phillimore, Sir Robert Joseph, Baronet (1810–1885)," 79.
152 Though he ultimately declined to assume a principal role in the project. Koskenniemi, *Gentle Civilizer*, 13. The other two were Rolin-Jaequemyns and Asser.
153 Wells, "Westlake, John (1828–1913)," 274–75.
154 Koskenniemi, *Gentle Civilizer*, 127.
155 Ibid.

"acutely sensitive to the theoretical and methodological challenges that appeared to confront all international lawyers at the time."[156]

To sum up, these various men were instrumental to the development of a new approach to international law and they were deeply involved in the political affairs of their day, especially the codification of the laws of war and the development of a legal architecture for renewed imperial expansion, two elements that will be discussed at length in Chapter 5 in order to further explain the form that Gentili came to take in his canonized form. For now, suffice it to say that from an institutional standpoint, given the prominence of civil lawyers on the English subcommittee, it is hardly surprising that its members latched onto Gentili as a great foundational figure of international law, seeing as he had himself been the Regius Professor of Civil Law at Oxford. In fact, in *Two Introductory Lectures on the Science of International Law* (1856) and *The Law of Nations* (1861), Twiss had pointed to Gentili's successor in the position, Richard Zouche, as the man who had developed, in 1650, "the distinction between natural law-based theory and the positive description of relations between states,"[157] which he then traced forward to the epochal split between positivism and natural law approaches to international law. Gentili's predecessor, and the first holder of the Chair in Civil Law, John Story, had not occupied the position for long, and after a rather eventful series of politico-religious incidents that led him to flee England, he was ultimately hanged, drawn, and quartered for treason under Elizabeth I; while he was beatified by Pope Leo XIII in 1886, he must not have been the most obvious candidate for canonization to the eyes of our civil lawyers. By contrast, the revival of the more straightforwardly canonizable Gentili could take the story of civil law and international law's shared destiny back half a century from Zouche and even provide a precursor to the more famous Grotius.

Thus, in the context of the emergence of international law as an academic discipline, Gentili was in an excellent position to be hailed as the founder of the newly established "science." He did not have Grotius' credentials as a child prodigy, but he had a colorful life story as a persecuted Protestant refugee from Italy, he could be seen as an authority via his position as Oxford's Regius Professor of Civil Law, and he had published a magnum opus, *DIB*, that was more than reminiscent of Grotius' famous *De iure belli ac pacis*. In light of this, the immediate purpose of the English subcommittee became the establishment of a memorial for Gentili in St. Helen's Church in London and the republication of *DIB*.

---

[156] Craven, "Invention of a Tradition," 369.
[157] Fitzmaurice, *Sovereignty, Property and Empire, 1500–2000*, 232.

The urgency of the English memorial stemmed from the fact that in his research about the Italian jurist, Holland had discovered the actual date of his death as well as his place of burial – the graveyard of St. Helen's Church; the Committee thus sought to place a "memorial tablet in the north aisle of St. Helen's, as near as possible to the spot indicated,"[158] which it eventually did during a ceremony attended by Prince Leopold, Robert Phillimore, T. E. Holland, the ambassador of Italy, and various other public figures.[159] The republication of *DIB* appears to have originally been suggested by another well-known jurist, Édouard de Laboulaye (1811–1883),[160] who, in a letter to Angelo Valdarnini (1847–1930)[161] written on April 25, 1875, specifically emphasized how great it would be to have a new edition of *DIB*, a suggestion next to which Holland put a note.[162] More importantly, though, the official explanatory booklet of the subcommittee states that its purpose was to "commemorate the services rendered by Albericus Gentili to International Law; of which science he was, in the opinion of many, the true founder."[163]

This qualification, "in the opinion of many," is a clear reference to the fact that Grotius had until then been considered the sole founder of international law. Positions regarding the hierarchy between the two great jurists varied; the most common argument was that Grotius' writings were more impressive, but that Gentili was the one who had opened the way for these writings to arise in the first place. As such, Holland concluded his inaugural lecture of November 1874 by explaining that he was "by no means concerned to place Gentilis on a level with his undeniably greater follower; or to say that his writings do not exhibit, in some degree, the faults with which they have been charged," but that he wanted to remind his audience that "the first step towards

---

[158] Holland, "Preface," 16. The exact location of Gentili's grave remains unknown to this day. The register of St. Helen's states: "Alberico Gentili, Doctor of Roman Law, was buried in the cemetery at the foot of the corner of the window where there stood the clump of gooseberry bushes, and less than two feet away from the nun's grating, on the 21st June, 1608." Cited in Del Vecchio, "The Posthumous Fate of Alberico Gentili." I also checked this myself on site. This proved problematic when Italy requested to have Gentili's remains returned to his homeland in order to bury him as a national hero.

[159] N. A., "Inauguration de la table commemorative d'Albéric Gentil," 293.

[160] Laboulaye is now more commonly remembered for his involvement in France's gift to the United States of the statue of liberty. See Viano, *Sentinel*.

[161] Valdarnini was an early Gentili scholar during the revival phase, publishing his main work on the jurist in 1875. Valdarnini, *Alberico Gentili fondatore del diritto internazionale [con una lettera di E. Laboulaye]*.

[162] Ibid.

[163] N. A., "Informational Booklet of the English Sub-Committee."

making International Law what it is, was taken, not by Grotius, but by the Perugian refugee, the adopted son of Oxford, Albericus Gentili."[164] With this lecture, which made a great splash at the time,[165] a profound challenge had thus been made to the orthodox understanding of international law's origins, and Travers Twiss expressed genuine concern at the risk of controversy developing over whether Gentili or Grotius was the greatest.[166] Twiss concluded his article diplomatically, suggesting that the republished work of Gentili, "without any pretense to rival the moral philosophic treatise of Grotius," would "contribute materially to enlarge the statesman's knowledge of the foundations, upon which the complicated system of the Public Law of Europe has been gradually built up."[167] Similarly, and in rather more flowery language, Gustave Rolin-Jaequemyns concluded that "Gentilis and Grotius are not, must not be two glories jealous of one another: they are two stars each endowed with a light of its own or rather which it borrows from a common center, that of eternal justice and truth."[168]

Yet the challenge persisted, not so much over the "greatness" of the jurists' works but over the title of "father of international law." Admirers of Gentili – in Italy, as one might expect, but also in England and in the United States – echoed the words of Holland and emphasized the primacy of Gentili over Grotius on this front. One of the clearest manifestations of this position would eventually be found in the writings of Coleman Phillipson, the man whom Holland would rebuke for not granting him sufficient credit for the revival of the Italian jurist. Phillipson was a barrister of the Inner Temple who published a few books on war and its laws, edited the fifth edition of Wheaton's *Elements of International Law*, and, crucially, wrote the influential introduction to the famous 1933 republication and English translation of *DIB* included in the aforementioned Carnegie series, *The Classics of International Law*. This introduction is an especially important text because it long constituted the standard gateway for engaging with

---

[164] These are the final words of the inaugural lecture. Holland, *Inaugural Lecture*, 35. Earlier on, Holland also explains: "It was left for Gentilis, starting from the doctrine of Natural Law as thus elaborated, to give it a practical application to the development of a Law of nations. In the path thus opening up, Grotius followed; and after him have come the whole series of writers on International Law." Ibid., 31.

[165] Rolin-Jaequemyns notes that Holland's inaugural lecture "a fait sensation." Rolin-Jaequemyns, "Albéric Gentil," 142.

[166] Twiss, "Albericus Gentilis on the Right of War," 159–60.

[167] Ibid., 161.

[168] Rolin-Jaequemyns, "Quelques mots sur les hommages projetés à la mémoire de Grotius et d'Albéric Gentil, et sur les dernières publications y relatives," 694. Rolin-Jaequemyns' assessment is cited again in Balch, "Albericus Gentilis."

DIB. In his 1911 piece first published in the *Journal of the Society of Comparative Legislation*,[169] then published in 1914 as part of a book on "The Great Jurists of the World,"[170] and eventually expanded into the 1933 introduction, Phillipson explained that Gentili was the "first great writer of *modern*[171] international law" [emphasis in original], and that "for this reason" it could "justifiably be claimed that – as the precursor of Grotius, and as the one who substantially prepared the way for him and greatly influenced his and all succeeding work – Gentilis is the real 'father' of the modern law of nations."[172] Earlier on, around the time of the republication of *DIB* (1877), various reviews of the work expressed similar attitudes, such as an anonymous piece from the *Saturday Review* of August 30, 1879, which argues that "[i]f any man can claim the honourable title of founder of international law, the name must be held to belong rather to Alberigo [*sic*] Gentili, the adopted son of Oxford, than to any of the later luminaries of the science."[173]

4.3   Conclusion

This chapter has told the remarkable story of how, from 1874, Gentili was revived and creatively hailed as the potential "true founder of international law," the first substantive challenge to the more famous Grotius. I have shown that to understand Gentili's revival, one has to place it back in the context of the emergence not just of the academic discipline of international law, but of a narrative about its past. The revival of Gentili began a year after the establishment of the epoch-making Institut de droit international in 1873, the institution that founded the discipline of international law proper. It involved many of the most important international lawyers of the period, split across three committees working on the revival: an English one, an Italian one, and a peripheral Dutch one. Despite the fact that the English committee

---

169 Phillipson, "Albericus Gentilis," 1911.
170 Phillipson, "Albericus Gentilis," 1914.
171 The claim that Gentili was more "modern" than Grotius can also be found, for example, in the work of the main Francophone Gentili expert of the period, Henry Nézard. Nézard indeed claims that Gentili's work was in fact more modern than Grotius' in some respects, as Gentili wrote extensively about the political events of his time – the struggle between François Ier and Charles Quint, the conflict between Spain and Holland, the Italian wars – instead of confining himself to classical examples. Nézard, "Albericus Gentilis," 90. I will discuss this "modernity" question in Chapter 5.
172 Phillipson, "Albericus Gentilis," 1911, 5.
173 *Saturday Review*, August 30, 1879, available in the *Papers of Sir Thomas Erskine Holland*.

ultimately had a much greater influence in shaping the narrative about Gentili beyond his Italian homeland, previous detailed work on Gentili's revival had focused almost exclusively on its Italian counterpart. This chapter has therefore closely examined the Oxford-centered revival of Gentili, showing the extent to which the establishment of Gentili as the other great founder of international law was a central affair within the broader emergence of the discipline of international law.

However, one key question remains: What was it, beyond the institutional factors stemming from the "Oxford connection," that made Gentili so great in the eyes of these jurists and commentators? What story was written about the nature of his greatness? With so many different figures involved in the revival across Italy and England, it is clear that his work was revived with various purposes in mind. The first, peace and international arbitration, has been analyzed at length by Lacchè based on Sbarbaro's papers. However, this is only part of the story, and not necessarily the most important one if one seeks to understand the form that Gentili's canonized figure eventually acquired in the twentieth century. The second, defining and regulating war, has remained virtually unexplored, and I turn to it in Chapter 5.

5 Constructing the History of the "Modern" Laws of War

Chapter 4 outlined the personal, institutional, and political dynamics that played a part in Alberico Gentili's nineteenth-century revival, in particular the emergence of the academic discipline of international law and the crafting of a historical narrative about its past. What we have yet to uncover is the specific story that emerged about Gentili's greatness in his nineteenth-century context. In Chapter 3, we saw that in the aftermath of his death, Gentili had been remembered primarily for his absolutist writings. Two and a half centuries later, what story did his revivers tell to justify celebrating him as a founder of international law?

This chapter will argue that nineteenth-century international lawyers painted Gentili as the man who had invented the modern definition of war. In doing so, they gave us a popular narrative about the history of the laws of war that has prevented us from appreciating the profound changes that occurred in the regulation of war in the course of the nineteenth century.

The English subcommittee and its affiliates emphasized the importance of *De iure belli* over all of Gentili's other works. Further building on the papers of T. E. Holland, this chapter tracks the emergence of a dominant narrative about the importance of Gentili, centered on a remarkably selective account of his treatise on the laws of war. What these lawyers specifically seized upon was Gentili's definition of war as a public contest of arms. They understood this to mean that Gentili was the originator of the concept of "public war" as "war between sovereigns" or "war between states," and thus of "modern war."

Importantly, the group of men involved in his revival did not read the text of *DIB* in any detail – when they read it at all – nor did they use any of Gentili's writings to support specific doctrinal moves. None of this would have been to their purpose; they were only interested in Gentili superficially.[1] What mattered to them was that they could

---

[1] In fact, the substantive reappraisal of Gentili's work only took off in the late twentieth century.

now gesture toward the Italian jurist to support a broad narrative about modernity and the monopolization of war by sovereign states. This was obviously deeply anachronistic – for one, as we saw in Part I, Gentili had no concept of the abstract "state" as such – but it was a narrative that made sense to them in their own context, and it would go on to acquire ever greater traction and ultimately give Gentili the prominent place he now holds in conventional accounts of the history of laws of war.

Once we take stock of how this anachronistic narrative emerged and became popularized, we can get a sense of what it has obscured. Specifically, we can begin to deconstruct the idea that, as early as the seventeenth century, the right to wage war became the sole prerogative of sovereign states. This is often taken for granted – and in Chapter 6 we will see how scholars such as Carl Schmitt contributed greatly to the enshrinement of this narrative – but here there are at least two contextual elements that should give us pause.

First, what was understood as a "state" in the early nineteenth century was still a complex matter. While there is now plenty of work on the changing meaning of "the state" in the sixteenth and seventeenth centuries,[2] the stability of the concept in later periods has long remained taken for granted, at least amongst scholars of international relations and international law. But a newly emergent area of scholarship has shed light on how complex and layered the meaning of "the state" and "sovereignty" remained at the beginning of the nineteenth century. It is not in the early modern period but rather over the course of the nineteenth century that Europe – and much of Latin America as well – witnessed a general transition toward polities that were far more centralized, bureaucratically supervised, territorially homogenized, and linearly bounded than ever before.[3] In other words, it is only in the second half of the nineteenth century that the modern sovereign state became the norm on the European continent. At that point, not only did "the state" gain a more dominant place in international law, but the criteria for what it meant to be "a state" also became more restricted with the rise of the ideology of the nation-state, as did the understanding of the concept of "sovereignty."[4] This ultimately popularized "a particular image of a state, as a discrete unit, situated in

---

[2] See especially Skinner, *Visions of Politics*. For an overview of earlier transformations, see Viroli, *From Politics to Reason of State*.

[3] On the nineteenth-century shift toward homogeneous and linearly bound territories in Europe, see Branch, *The Cartographic State*. On the diversity of polities in Europe pre-1848, see Schroeder, *The Transformation of European Politics, 1763–1848*.

[4] I will discuss these various points at length later.

space and enduring through time,"[5] normalizing what is usually termed "the modern sovereign state."

The second and related contextual element is the extent to which the meaning of the term "public" – and, with it, "public authority," "public actor," "public war" – changed over time. While the idea of a "public" act and of a broader distinction between private and public actors will be familiar to contemporary ears, its meaning in the sixteenth century was profoundly different from its meaning in the nineteenth, which itself is different from its contemporary instantiation.[6] In short, it has reflected the changing understandings of political authority over time. The occurrence of the term across different periods seems to have caused much confusion, especially in narratives that tie "modernity" to war becoming a "public" endeavor. By taking stock of the misunderstandings around the term, and especially those we inherited from the nineteenth century, we might eventually be able to tell a more accurate story about the relationship between public authority and the right to wage war.

One of the most important consequences of having a narrative that takes for granted the dominance of "the state" in the early modern period is that we have paid no attention to the simultaneous emergence of two parallel ways of thinking about war and its rules in the late nineteenth century: one for wars between actors considered modern sovereign states, in the narrow, late nineteenth-century sense of the term, and one for wars between modern sovereign states and actors not recognized as such. Wars amongst modern sovereign states became known as "regular wars," and they would come to fall under the ambit of the "laws of war" that lawyers began to codify in the 1860s and that eventually culminated in the 1949 Geneva Convention. The other type of warfare, between modern sovereign states and opponents denied that same status, became known as "small wars," and a parallel literature on how to conduct them – one almost entirely free of legal language – developed in small war manuals. The nonrecognized opponent, the actor denied the credentials of "public authority," could be a domestic one in the case of a popular revolt, or a foreign one in the case of a people resisting imperial expansion. These late nineteenth-century small war manuals began from the principle that the opponent was not a legitimate belligerent against whom the conventional laws of war could apply, and they have formed the basis of contemporary counterinsurgency strategies from 1950s Algeria to 2000s Iraq.

---

[5] Learoyd, "Semi-Sovereignty and Relationships of Hierarchy," 92.

[6] It is worth noting, by way of example, that the distinction between public and private international law is of a very recent vintage.

These two parallel ways of thinking were simultaneously enshrined in separate manuals for soldiers between 1870 and 1914. Yet, to my knowledge, nobody has ever explored whether their genesis might be substantially related. My claim here is that because we have failed to appreciate the extent to which the modern sovereign state triumphed in international law – and especially in the laws of war – in the late nineteenth century, we have missed the key contextual element that would allow us to bring these simultaneous developments together within a single explanatory framework. By providing a space for that connection to be made, this chapter provides a preliminary foray into the subject matter in the hope that further research might follow.

This chapter is divided into three sections. In the first, I examine the narrative that late nineteenth-century lawyers put forward about *DIB* and its importance. I track the emergence of the story of Gentili's "modernity" – especially vis-à-vis the more famous Grotius, whose thinking on war was now downgraded as "medieval" – and highlight the fact that Balthazar Ayala was briefly considered a better contender than Gentili for the title of founder of the modern laws of war, though it is the Oxford-based Italian who ultimately won that posterity contest. The second section of the chapter provides the critical context within which this narrative of Gentili's modernity can be understood: the emergence of the broader professional discipline of international law in the late nineteenth century, along with the triumph of the modern sovereign states in international law and in the laws of war. The final section of the chapter turns to the consequences of this triumph for imperial warfare, first by clarifying the relationship between "sovereignty" and "civilization," and second by shedding light on the explicit emergence of a bifurcated system of international violence during this period.

Before diving in, let me say a few words about what I do *not* argue. First, I am not claiming that, upon being revived, Gentili displaced Grotius as the perceived "true founder" of international law within the discipline at large. Rather, I show that important voices of the period canonized Gentili as the founder of the "modern" legal definition of war, breathing life into a narrative that would come to thrive in the twentieth century. Second, I do not argue that the nineteenth-century contrast between "small wars" and "regular wars" depended on Gentili. In order words, I am not making a causal claim that without Gentili's revival, there would have been no bifurcation of the regulation of "small wars" and "regular wars." I also do not wish to imply that nineteenth-century lawyers expressly needed to cite Gentili in order to make this distinction, nor that they needed to engage with his work to come up with the idea in the first place. My aim, based on the approach I laid out in Chapter 1, is to explain why we have a certain understanding of Gentili today – and what this understanding has obscured in our understanding of how warfare has been historically regulated.

5.1   Reading *De iure belli* in the Nineteenth Century: Gentili and Narratives of Modernity

In the most basic sense, Gentili was deployed by international lawyers in the 1870s in order to create a sense of continuity between the early modern period and their own endeavors. While Gentili was put to the service of various causes, the single most important element driving his revival on the international scene was his definition of war. International lawyers wove an increasingly popular – if historically questionable – narrative about Gentili as founder of the modern laws of war, emphasizing that he had limited war to sovereign states – a move these lawyers read as driving a wedge between a medieval world where war was an abysmal free-for-all and a modern world where war became a much more evolved and orderly institution. Importantly, these lawyers considered it essential to turn to Gentili on this front because they found Grotius' considerations on the matter deeply unsatisfactory.

5.1.1   A New Appreciation for DIB

Though the rest of Gentili's writings would later be published as well, the English subcommittee turned first and foremost to his writings on war and, specifically, to his *DIB*. To them, *DIB* was Gentili's masterpiece, and indeed, in his inaugural lecture, Holland had emphasized the importance of the latter over Gentili's other two most famous texts, *De legationibus* and the *Hispanica advocatio*.[7] Following the republication of *DIB* and the discussion that ensued amongst many of the most well-known lawyers of the period, the analysis of Gentili's relevance to the late nineteenth century thus became centered primarily on his writings on the laws of war. These lawyers put forward two broad reasons why *DIB* was so groundbreaking, which have remained commonplaces about Gentili's work to this day.[8]

---

[7] Holland, *Inaugural Lecture*, 33.

[8] These are summed up in a statement by Holland from his 1879 lecture entitled "The Early Literature on the Law of War": Gentili's "achievement was threefold. He got rid of question of tactics and of the discipline of armies; he reduced to reasonable dimensions the topic of private warfare; and he placed his subject upon a non-theological basis." Though important, the first point regarding the emancipation of the laws

The first claim was that in *DIB* Gentili had freed the science of international law from theology. This reading acquired a certain recognition with time and became a standard argument in favor of the Italian jurist. In his 1879 lecture, Holland emphasized the epoch-making break putatively constituted by *DIB*, pointing to the theological focus of his predecessors: "Up to this point the subject had been in the hands of Italians and Spaniards, who had always treated it with distinct reference to the doctrines of the Catholic Church."[9] Placing the Italian jurist at the heart of the shift away from theology, Holland drew a line between the literature on the laws of war that "took its rise in the thirteenth century, at Bologna" and "the literature which superseded it," dating "from the sixteenth century, more specifically from the year 1588" and having first seen "the light in the University of Oxford," a clear reference to Gentili's original draft of *DIB*, the lectures of 1588/89, and in passing, another indication of the institutional pride involved in Gentili's revival.[10] This idea – about the importance of Gentili as a secularizer of the laws of war and of international law more broadly – was popular across the board. For instance, in his lectures at the Athenaeum of Turin, the famous Mancini drew a striking parallel and explained that Gentili was "entitled at the hands of the Italian nation to a special recognition of his merits as having achieved for the Science of International Law a similar service to that, which Machiavelli had accomplished for the Science of Politics, by emancipating it from the trammels of theological casuistry."[11] These claims were then enshrined by Coleman Phillipson in his 1911 piece foreshadowing his highly influential 1933 introduction to the translated version of *DIB* in the Carnegie-funded series *Classics of International Law*.[12]

---

of war from other military considerations was not picked up on as assiduously by Holland's contemporaries, so I have focused on the other two. Holland, "The Early Literature on the Law of War," 57.

[9] Ibid., 55.

[10] Ibid., 57–58.

[11] Cited in Twiss, "Albericus Gentilis on the Right of War," 143. This chronology about the early modern secularization of international law by Protestant jurists is essentially a nineteenth-century myth; see the discussion in Chapter 3.

[12] Phillipson ("Albericus Gentilis," 1911) explains: "Notwithstanding various shortcomings – indeed, inevitable at the time he wrote – the entire work of Gentilis is manifestly superior to all previous productions, such as, for example, those of Ayala, Victoria, Soto, Belli, or Suarez," citing as the most important mark of Gentili's superiority the fact that all these earlier works had a theological basis. (5–6) Gentili, he later sums up – in rather anachronistic terms since Gentili knew no such thing as "international law" – "did more than any other writer to free international law from the besetting theological importations and the incubus of scholastic casuistry." (29) In his conclusion, he reiterates that Gentili "clearly marked out the respective spheres

This narrative about a shift away from theological concerns was well in line with contemporary understandings about the watershed quality of the 1648 Peace of Westphalia.[13] An article from the *Revue* of 1908 informs us that at the inauguration of the monument for Gentili in his native town of St. Ginesio that year, the Italian minister of public education gave a speech emphasizing Gentili's influence on his time, and the great progress that had been made less than half a century after his death, epitomized by the achievements of the Peace of Westphalia.[14] While it is unlikely that Gentili truly influenced the 1648 agreements, the attempt to make this connection bespeaks an effort to develop a convincing and consistent historical narrative of the development of a secular "science of International Law" and of its progressive impact over time.

The second – and, for our purposes, more important – claim that these lawyers made about Gentili pertained to what he had to say about war. In addition to couching Gentili as the founder of international law and tying his work to contemporary events, some jurists argued that he was also "the true father of the Science of the Right of War" (with *DIB*) and "of the Right of Peace" (with *De legationibus* and – though this is counterintuitive – *De armis romanis*).[15] More specifically, his definition of war was seen as groundbreaking and – crucially – more advanced than that of his great competitor, Grotius.

Grotius had defined war quite broadly as *status per vim certantium*, or the condition of those contending by force, and in *De iure belli ac pacis* he had discussed three distinct types of war: public wars, private wars, and mixed (public/private) wars.[16] The inclusion of the last two types made him deeply disappointing to late nineteenth-century international lawyers, who dismissed Grotius as having remained stuck in the Middle Ages on this point. Although, as Haggenmacher explains, Grotius'

---

of the international jurist and the theologian." (29) Phillipson, "Albericus Gentilis," 1911; Phillipson, "Introduction."

[13] For some examples, see notably Koch, *Histoire abrégée des traités de paix, entre les puissances de l'Europe, depuis la paix de Westphalie*; Heeren, *A Manual of the History of the Political System of Europe and Its Colonies.*

[14] Nys, 'L'inauguration du monument d'Albéric Gentil à San Ginesio.' For the actual speech, see Luigi Rava (Ministro Della Istruzione Pubblica), Alberico Gentili: Discorso pronunciato all' inaugurazione del monumento in San Ginesio, 26 Settembre 1908 (Roma, 1908).

[15] This interpretation of Gentili's work is most explicit in the work of Emerico Amari (1810–1870), cited by Travers Twiss alongside Mancini's comparison of Gentili and Machiavelli. Twiss, "Albericus Gentilis on the Right of War," 143. For a brief discussion of *De armis romanis*, see Chapter 2.

[16] Grotius, *De Iure Belli Ac Pacis*, Book I, chapter 3.

definition merely stemmed from a different methodological standpoint reflecting another approach to the laws of war,[17] the notion that Gentili was "more advanced" in defining war stuck with the lawyers of the time and, as I will discuss in Chapter 6, with their successors. Echoing this widely shared sentiment, one of the most commonly used textbooks of the period puts forward Gentili's famous formula,[18] *bellum est publicorum armorum iusta contentio*, noting that Gentili identified this issue of the necessarily public character of war "more than three centuries ago" and that this definition of war as an "armed struggle between states" is the one adopted "in general [by] all the moderns [*les modernes*]."[19] The authors then concede also to reproduce Grotius' "mediocre" definition, but only "due to the fame of its author."[20]

In his inaugural lecture, Holland had claimed that *DIB* constituted a crucial move forward in part because it "reduced to reasonable dimensions the topic of private warfare."[21] Gentili's exclusion of what he would have considered "private" and "mixed" wars from the ambit of "war" legally defined was indeed a bold move in his time, as I have discussed at some length in Part I, but not in the way these nineteenth-century lawyers described it.[22] In the late sixteenth century, this definition had left Gentili's *DIB* disconnected from the political realities of his time and subject to controversies about his absolutism. In the late nineteenth century, however, this definition could be extracted from its original context, stripped from any considerations about sixteenth-century debates about political authority and about Gentili's controversial absolutist stance, and turned into a manifesto for a new framework for regulating warfare. Gentili's approach was thus hailed as prescient, and his revivers quickly started slipping back and forth between "public war" as "war between sovereigns" and as "war between states."

As with many of the popular claims about Gentili, this idea would once again be most explicitly enshrined by Coleman Phillipson in his 1911 text on Gentili for the collection on *The Great Jurists of the World*. Phillipson claims that Gentili's definition of war is "the most precise that has ever been enunciated" and that his "grasp of the matter is here firmer than that of the Dutch jurist [Grotius]," whose definition of war

---

[17] Haggenmacher, "Grotius and Gentili," 169. See also Haggenmacher, *Grotius et la doctrine de la guerre juste*, 462, n. 94. Grotius' definition of war is merely more abstract, "accentuating its general and philosophical aspect."

[18] Koskenniemi, *Gentle Civilizer*, 73.

[19] Fauchille, *Traité de droit international public,* 1–2.

[20] Ibid.

[21] Holland, *Inaugural Lecture.*

[22] See Chapter 3, Section 5.1.1.

[parties maintaining a contest by force] "is too wide and indefinite, and may also imply conflicts like private or intestine war or single combats."[23] Phillipson further explains that Gentili's definition contains "the three essential elements: (1) a public contest between sovereigns ... (2) by force of arms ... (3) begun and conduced in a just and regular manner, in conformity with the law generally established and adopted by both belligerents."[24] The third condition is interesting because there were of course no codified laws of war for both parties to adopt in Gentili's time; it is merely a back-projection of the framework for regulating war that had emerged, as we will see shortly, from the 1860s onward.

Phillipson notes that this third condition entails that "irregular hostilities" are excluded from the definition, as in that case the belligerents do not constitute "regular enemies, iusti hostes."[25] Again, this question of "irregular hostilities" was at the forefront of the debate on the codification of the laws of war in the late nineteenth century, and clearly it seemed to these Gentili revivers that the Italian jurist could be of some help on this front. In the 1933 version of his piece, Phillipson reaffirms this point and, with it, Gentili's presumed superiority over Grotius on the matter. Indeed, to his former criticism of Grotius' definition as being "too wide and indefinite," he adds that Gentili critically distinguishes "warfare that is regular (i.e., begun and prosecuted according to rules by the sovereign authority) from the acts of marauders, pirates, &c., or insurgents. The Italian jurist's grasp of the matter is here firmer than that of the Dutch jurist."[26] The language of "insurgents" was again a nineteenth-century addition – Gentili had merely spoken of "rebels" in a very specific context – and its usage tells us much about what Gentili's revivers were hoping to use him for.

It is worth noting that some of these arguments could be found before Holland's inaugural lecture, suggesting that Gentili's definition of war

---

[23] Phillipson, "Albericus Gentilis," 1911, 19. Henry Nézard makes a similar assessment, pointing out that by defining war as *Status per vim certantium*, Grotius problematically continues to place public war and dueling in the same category, against the ideas that would form the basis of the classical laws of war; see Nézard, "Albericus Gentilis," 90.

[24] Phillipson, "Albericus Gentilis," 1911, 19. This was echoed in the United States around the same time by the aforementioned Thomas Willing Balch, who noted, in his piece on Alberico Gentili meant to elevate the jurist's profile across the Atlantic, that Gentili defines war as "a just contention of the public force" (citing the usual Latin) and that "he maintains that while pirates may imitate the usages of war and not those of assassins, nevertheless that does not make them enemies in the real meaning of the word." Balch, "Albericus Gentilis," 672–73.

[25] Phillipson, "Albericus Gentilis," 1911, 19.

[26] Phillipson, "Introduction," 33. Note the repetition between 1911 and 1933 of the idea that Gentili is more advanced than Grotius on this point.

already carried some appeal before his full-blown revival. For instance, in the first edition (1854) of his *Commentaries upon International Law*, hailed by Holland as "one of the most important books on international law,"[27] Robert Phillimore drew on Gentili for his definition of war. He explained that to fall into the category of war, violence must combine certain characteristics, and most importantly "[it] must be waged by the public authority of the State, and carried on through the agency of those who have been duly commissioned for that purpose by that authority."[28] He then explicitly and approvingly cites Gentili: "According to an early but very sound definition offered by *Albericus Gentilis*, the precursor of Grotius, 'Bellum est publicorum armorum iusta contentio'."[29]

This discussion remained identical in the later editions of Phillimore's *Commentaries* (1871, 1885). However, in light of the various efforts to flesh out Gentili's merits, the argument about the prescient character of his definition of war acquired new traction. In the war section of his later lectures on international law, Holland would similarly look first to Gentili, and then juxtapose Grotius' definition as an unsatisfactory foil: "Definitions throw some light on the character of War. War is defined by Gentilis as *Publicorum armorum iusta contentio*. For Grotius it is *Status per vim certantium*. His definition is more general than that of Gentilis, omitting therefrom '*publicorum*' and '*iusta*'."[30]

Gradually, Gentili's new reputation was cemented: He had provided the first "modern" definition of war and, in doing so, was not only a precursor to Grotius but actually far superior to the Dutchman. By 1898, Bonfils and Fauchille's much used[31] *Manuel de droit international public* of 1898 began its second volume – on war and neutrality – with a long discussion of the necessity of war between states who face no superior, as well as on the distinction between public and private war. The first author cited by Bonfils and Fauchille is Gentili, who is seen as having identified the present issue "more than three centuries ago."[32] The authors then emphasize the distinction between two conceptions

---

[27] Holland, "Review: Commentaries upon International Law, by Sir Robert Phillimore," 246 ["l'ouvrage du savant juge de la cour d'amirauté a pris dès longtemps sa place parmi les livres les plus importants sur le droit international"].

[28] Phillimore, *Commentaries upon International Law*, 100.

[29] Ibid (emphasis in original).

[30] These lectures and the research Holland had completed for them were collected in a posthumous volume, according to his will. Holland, "Lecture XVIII: War: Definition of and Effects of, in Lectures on International Law," 263.

[31] Koskenniemi, *Gentle Civilizer*, 73.

[32] Fauchille, *Traité de droit international public*, vol. 2, 1.

of war: The first, "by authors such as Grotius," encompasses "private wars, wars between individuals, and struggles between states"; the second, adopted "in general [by] all the moderns [*les modernes*]," only includes as "war, as a matter of international law," the "armed struggle between states, between international political entities."[33] To illustrate their point, the authors cite various definitions, including the one from the inescapable Grotius, which they deem "mediocre," as well as Gentili's now famous definition, alongside Vattel's, Bynkershoek's, and Massé's, as a token of what the "modern" conception of war entails.[34] "War" now meant war between sovereign states, and Gentili was the true originator of this deeply modern idea. This was all painfully anachronistic, but the claim would only become more popular thereafter.

At this point, it is natural to ask why Balthazar Ayala was not used in place of Gentili for these purposes. Also an absolutist, Ayala had put forward a similar definition of war that prioritized sovereign authority at all costs and that could have constituted another good source of inspiration for the "states only" club. In fact, Ayala did make an appearance during the discussions around Gentili's revival, briefly raising doubts as to whether Gentili was the right "father" to enthrone.

5.1.2   The Founder of Modern War: Gentili or Ayala?

Ayala's name began to be associated with the revival of Gentili from a fairly early point,[35] and a debate quickly emerged about their relative importance – specifically, about their respective definitions of war and their rationales for how to apply its laws. In his 1878 review of the republished *DIB*, John Westlake emphasized Ayala's superiority on this point quite forcefully. After noting the evolution of Gentili's definition from the rather vague *Bellum est contentio armata* (1588/89) to the famous *Bellum est publicorum armorum iusta contentio* (1598), he remarks that Ayala's own treatise was published around the same time

---

[33] Ibid., 1–2.

[34] Ibid., 2.

[35] For instance, in his brief review in the *Revue* of Holland's 1874 lecture, Alphonse Rivier – Rolin-Jaequemyns' close friend and collaborator, who took over as Secretary-General of the Institut while the latter was the Belgian Home Secretary during the period 1878–84 – points out that while Grotius is the father of international law, others contributed to opening the way for his own work. The two names he mentions are Ayala, who "in his own country, is not duly appreciated," and "especially Gentili, to whom the Italians are currently erecting a statue." Rivier, "Review: An Inaugural Lecture on Albericus Gentilis." ["Tel fut l'Anversois Ayala, qui, dans sa patrie, n'est pas estimé à sa juste valeur. Tel fut surtout Alberigo Gentili, auquel les Italiens érigent en ce moment une statue."]

and points out that "[i]t is interesting to compare the two writers on the cardinal question of the reason why the laws of war, which both admit to depend on its being a *justum bellum*, apply equally to both sides in a given contest." He explains – somewhat inaccurately, though understandably, given Gentili's muddled argument on this point – that Gentili understands *iustum* in the "popular sense" and that he "finds the reason in the fact that there is generally a show of justice on each side," while Ayala "repudiates the popular sense" and considers that "a war is technically just if undertaken by the proper authority." Westlake then goes on to express a strong preference for Ayala on this basis.[36]

Travers Twiss' defense of Gentili's superiority over Ayala in that same year (1878) suggests that there might well have been an explicit debate on these issues within the English subcommittee. Indeed, Twiss explains that "the Executive body has exercised, in our opinion, a judicious discretion in selecting the treatise of Gentilis 'De Jure Belli Libri tres' for republication at the Oxford Press. It is a word far in advance of the treatise of Balthazar Ayala."[37] On this initial point, Twiss avoids discussing the competing definitions of war and merely states that Ayala "had a more limited object in view, than was before the eyes of the Oxford professor," and that his work "was intended for the lettered soldier rather than for the learned jurist or the philosophic statesman."[38] Later on, however, Twiss notes the competing claims that have been made on behalf of Ayala, with specific respect to the question – phrased very much in nineteenth-century terms, since the modern concept of the nation would have been foreign to both Ayala and Gentili – of who was the first author to have "reduced systematically the practice of Nations in the conduct of warfare to juridical rules."[39] Twiss manages to shake off the challenge to Gentili's predominance by pointing to the existence of other writers who were also notable precursors to the Italian,[40] thus making space for other important thinkers before the

---

[36] Westlake, "Review: De iure belli libri tres."
[37] Twiss, "Albericus Gentilis on the Right of War," 154.
[38] Ibid.
[39] Ibid., 138.
[40] Here Twiss leans on Mancini, noting that the latter "has with commendable equality pointed out that Albericus Gentili did not lead the way, but was preceded by Pierino Bello of Alba in Piedmont, a name almost unknown to jurists North of the Alps," although he himself is reluctant to put Belli on too high a pedestal in light of the works of Vitoria and Soto before him. He concludes that he is "of accord with Professor Mancini in assigning to Pierino Bello ... a place amongst the earliest writers who have treated systematically of the Right of War," thus placing Belli alongside Ayala in a narrative where they simply open the way for the more important Gentili. Ibid., 138–39. Twiss is referring to Mancini, *Della nazionalità come fondamento del diritto delle genti*. I thank Jessica Marglin for bringing the original reference to my attention.

cherished "adopted son of Oxford" and placing them, Ayala included, in a narrative where they are mere precursors to the greater Gentili.[41]

These debates confirm that within the English context, Gentili was seen as a jurist of great importance primarily because of his definition of war as public, which – in the anachronistic interpretation of nineteenth-century lawyers – was understood to mean that he had intended to restrict the right to wage war to sovereign states. There is little in the writings of Holland, Twiss, or other members of the English subcommittee or its direct interlocutors on the importance of Gentili as the father of international arbitration. In the English context, Gentili was celebrated primarily in light of his writings on war, and particularly because his writings appeared to have foreshadowed some developments that were central to the thinking of those who revived his work, who were all involved in contemporary efforts to codify the laws of war.

Indeed, international lawyers drew explicit parallels between the writings of the Italian jurist and their own efforts to codify the laws of war in a remarkable variety of ways. Often, as twentieth- and twenty-first-century scholars were later to do as well,[42] they pointed to similarities between the wars of religion of the sixteenth and seventeenth centuries and the wars of their own lifetime. Twiss, for instance, explained that *DIB* had "been reclaimed from oblivion at an opportune moment, when Eastern Europe is involved in a war, which, as regards its motives and its possible results, is hardly second in importance to the Great War, which desolated Central Europe in the early part of the seventeenth century."[43] In his letter to Valdarnini in which he had suggested republishing *DIB*, Édouard de Laboulaye somewhat ghoulishly asked, "if Gentili could come out of his tomb, wouldn't he be proud to think that we still remember his efforts to moralize war? And have we ever faced

---

[41] The main international law manuals of the late nineteenth century would further enshrine these ideas, as well as the centrality of Gentili. For instance, Thomas Alfred Walker's (1862–1935) massive *A History of the Law of Nations* of 1899 gives Gentili pride of place and presents him as Grotius' most important rival, extensively describing both of their works on the laws of war. After spending about ten pages on medieval writers, a dozen on "moral theologians" – including Vitoria, merely described as a "worthy forerunner of Grotius" – and another dozen on "politicians and political philosophers," Walker begins a separate section on the "forerunners" of international law proper, in which he gives a page to Conradus Brunus, two pages to Francisco Vasquez, a mere three pages to Ayala, and a whopping thirty pages to Gentili, before turning to the last and classic "forerunner," Grotius, for a solid sixty pages of description. Walker, *A History of the Law of Nations*, 203–336.

[42] See, perhaps most famously, Leo Gross' article drawing an explicit parallel between the seventeenth-century wars of religion and the two world wars. Gross, "The Peace of Westphalia, 1648–1948." A more recent example is Milton, Axworthy, and Simms, *Towards A Westphalia for the Middle East*.

[43] Twiss, "Albericus Gentilis on the Right of War," 137.

a more pressing need to return to this terrible subject, when today an entire school predicates law on victory and success?"[44] In fact, in the first part of his 1898 *Studies on International Law* dedicated to the laws of war, Holland would seamlessly combine his inaugural lecture on Gentili and some additional research he had completed on the jurist with various pieces on contemporary codification efforts, as if they were merely two sides of the same coin.[45]

For these international lawyers, linking their way of thinking about war back to the work of Gentili gave it a certain historical pedigree; it was a form of mythopoeic historical genealogy that helped legitimize what I will argue constituted one of the most important – yet surprisingly underappreciated – political and legal projects of the period: the monopolization of the right to wage war by polities recognizing each other as sovereign states. Evidently, the Gentili they reinvented, stripped of his absolutism[46] and thoroughly decontextualized, was "far from his historical world, but perfectly functional on the building-site of the new international law."[47] Through this new narrative about Gentili, the strict limitation of war, as a legal concept, to sovereign states could now be associated with the "modernity" that had putatively given us Westphalia and the states-system, a core shift that Grotius was perceived as having somehow completely missed.

5.2   International Law and the Laws of War in the Late Nineteenth Century

What conditions help explain the emergence of a narrative centered on this particular idea of "modernity"? It is notable that the revival of Gentili and the republication of *DIB* occurred at the same time as

---

[44] Valdarnini, *Alberico Gentili fondatore del diritto internazionale [con una lettera di E. Laboulaye]*, 9. ["Si Gentili pouvait sortir de sa tombe, ne serait-il pas fier de penser qu'on se souvient encore de ce qu'il a tenté pour moraliser la guerre? Et avons-nous jamais eu plus grand besoin de revenir sur ce terrible sujet qu'aujourd'hui ou toute une école fait de la victoire et du succès la source du droit?"].

[45] Holland, *Studies in International Law*. The most explicit linking of Gentili to contemporary events is perhaps to be found in a now rarely mentioned 1917 book by Ermelinda Armigero Gazzera, which remained for many years the standard bibliography listing both Gentili's writings and the works that had cited him. As Holland notes in his preface to the book, Gazzera's volume contains two preliminary chapters in addition to the bibliography, one of which "deals with the relation of Gentili's views to the events of the present day." Gazzera's chapter is an extremely lyrical – and creative, to say the least – ode to Gentili's contemporary import. Armigero Gazzera, *Alberico Gentili*, 9.

[46] His revivers restored Gentili's reputation on this front by claiming that his characterization as an absolutist was mere slander from his Catholic opponents.

[47] Lacchè, "Monuments of International Law," 208.

the Institut's early attempts to codify the laws of war, which culminated in the "Oxford Manual" of 1880 and would eventually lead to the Hague Conferences of 1899 and 1907. These events were not only contemporaneous but intimately linked. The Oxford Manual acquired that name because the Institut met in Oxford that year by invitation of Holland himself. More broadly, as we saw in Chapter 4, many of the people driving the revival of Gentili – both within and beyond the English subcommittee – were involved in the efforts to codify the laws of war, along with those to hash out the legal architecture of empire.[48] The debates they entered into over Gentili's famous treatise, as well as the parallels they drew between his writings and their own efforts, provide crucial insights into what it was that made them so keen to revive the long-dead Italian writer, and to what use they sought to put his work.

The revival of Gentili took place within the development of a broader narrative about the rise of European nation-states. The link between the two is not surprising, for one of the ways that origin myths acquire traction over others[49] is through their ability to connect with other narratives in order to form clusters or "constellations."[50] The broader narrative about nation-states pulled together stories of a shared past – of long-existing nations waiting for an institutional vehicle to finally allow them to thrive as such – with stories of a shared future, narratives meant to bring multiple modernities together into a single unifying story. The story of Gentili resonated because it harmonized with an already dominant theme: the inevitable and desirable triumph of the modern state form as the core unit of the international order.

As such, Gentili's revival reflects a critical but underappreciated set of developments: the triumph of the modern sovereign state in international law, and especially in the laws of war. In order to shed light on these developments, I will proceed in three steps. First, I will explain how central the laws of war were to the broader emergence of

---

[48] The link between the development of the laws of war and the legislation of empire is an area that has remained surprisingly under-researched, and I will return to this point separately in the final section of the chapter. One exception is Mégret, "From 'Savages' to 'Unlawful Combatants'." Apart from that, the literature is remarkably thin. For a preliminary foray into the links between the Berlin Conference of 1884–85 and the Hague Conferences of 1899 and 1907, see Vergerio, "The Berlin and Hague Conferences."

[49] Not all origin stories are born equal – consider, for instance, the European Union's tale of a virgin rebirth after the atrocities of World War II and the extent to which it erased the competing take of an EU born out of an imperialist "Eurafrica" project. See Hansen and Jonsson, "Building Eurafrica."

[50] For a discussion, see Shiller, *Narrative Economics*.

the discipline of international law in the 1860s and 1870s, and to what extent these new laws were shaped by the main conflicts of the period. Having outlined this context, I will then turn to the profound shift that was taking place in the conceptualization of sovereignty and, finally, to how it changed the nature of the legal concept of war.

5.2.1   The Centrality of the Laws of War to the Emergence of Modern International Law

The "science" of international law, enshrined most explicitly over the period 1873–85, emerged out of a decade of political and military turmoil. The 1860s witnessed the first attempts to codify the laws of war (Lieber Code of 1863, Geneva Convention of 1864, St. Petersburg Declaration of 1868) and the foundation of the *Revue de droit international et de législation comparée* (1868), the precursor to the Institut. As I noted earlier, the codification of the laws of war was at the heart of the Institut's efforts, and as Koskenniemi puts it, "the laws of war have perhaps never before nor since the period between 1870 and 1914 been studied with as much enthusiasm."[51]

More specifically, however, the creation of the Institut was intimately linked to the conflicts of the time, particularly to the Franco-Prussian War of 1870–71 and, to a somewhat lesser extent, the American Civil War of 1861–65. Ultimately, it was the failure of both sides in the Franco-Prussian War to abide by the terms of the 1864 Geneva Convention that kick-started the emergence of the professional discipline of international law. Dismayed by this failure, Gustave Rolin-Jaequemyns (1835–1902) and Gustave Moynier (1826–1910), with the encouragement of Francis Lieber (1800–1872, the author of the famous Lieber Code of 1863), decided to create a conference and eventually a permanent institution or an academy of international law.[52] As such, in its earliest days, the discipline of international law grew specifically out of the pressing need to regulate the most prominent conflicts of the period.[53]

A central question in this context was how to distinguish between combatants and noncombatants. This issue acquired additional importance once it was paired with the positivist urge to spell out clear and coherent legal rules on various international legal matters, including – crucially – the

---

[51] Koskenniemi, *Gentle Civilizer*, 87.
[52] Ibid., 158–59.
[53] On the lasting impact of the Franco-Prussian War on the Institut's internal politics, see Genin, "The Institute of International Law's Crisis in the Wake of the Franco-Prussian War (1873–1899)."

conduct of war. Francis Lieber's 1863 *Instructions for the Government of Armies of the United States in the Field*, written in the context of the American Civil War and often known as the "Lieber Code," was the first document to attempt to clearly lay out such rules, and it came to provide the foundation for later efforts. One of the most vexing legal questions of the conflict was how to conceptualize the legal status of the Confederates. Since they did not constitute a formally recognized state, various issues had emerged regarding the application of the law of neutrality, notably vis-à-vis Confederate ships (the crux of the landmark *Alabama* arbitration case of 1872). However, since the problem pertained to what was essentially a civil war rather than an international conflict involving a foreign invasion and occupation, lawyers were able to address these issues by developing and refining the concepts of quasi-insurgency and quasi-belligerency. These concepts enabled them to adapt the emerging laws of war to conflicts that did not involve two clear state entities when a context of civil war made it absolutely necessary,[54] and they provided the necessary legal flexibility to resolve the question of belligerents' status within that conflict.

The matter could not be so easily resolved in the context of the Franco-Prussian War, which became the most important conflict on the mind of those trying to codify the laws of war. The central legal issue had been the participation of French militias, the *francs-tireurs* or "free shooters,"[55] who were not formally part of the army but were eventually placed under the orders of generals in the field. Despite this indirect link, they were executed by the German side as irregular, armed noncombatants rather than recognized as combatants entitled to the protection of the emerging laws of war (particularly the First Geneva Convention of 1864). The issue of these insurgents' legal status dragged on over the following years.[56] Holland would eventually

---

[54] Neff, *War and the Law of Nations*, 258–73.

[55] The term refers to members of a *corps franc* or *Freikorps* in German, that is, civilian combatants who may or may not be linked to a regular army.

[56] The status of insurgents led to explosive debates amongst jurists during the 1874, 1899, and 1907 conferences, as discussed extensively in Nabulsi, *Traditions of War*. Some important legal distinctions existed, for instance between unorganized "spontaneous" insurgencies, which were considered illegal, and organized partisan warfare, in which the fighters wore military uniforms, carried arms openly, and abided by the laws of war. The latter, which formed militia and voluntary corps, were considered legitimate combatants alongside armies; see Best, *Humanity in Warfare*, 196–99. Moreover, insurgency was ruled out against an occupier, but some form of it was allowed against an invader; Ibid., 199. However, these clauses still left most insurgents – particularly civilians taking up arms against occupying forces – unprotected by the laws of war. These issues led to fierce debates at Brussels (1874) and The Hague (1899, 1907), with serious attempts to create laws that would be less

describe the controversy over the question of a distinction between lawful and unlawful combatants as the reef that had shipwrecked the Brussels conference of 1874.[57] Twenty years later, it would again lead to fierce debates at The Hague in 1899 and 1907.

I argue here that this debate was part of a still broader and profoundly important set of developments. To make this case, I build on the literature that highlights the resilient heterogeneity of polity forms in the first half of the nineteenth century, including in Europe. Many of these problems arose as a result of the attempt to limit formally the legal definition of war to armed conflicts between sovereign states narrowly defined – a highly significant, if surprisingly underexamined, move in the late nineteenth century that occurred within a broader narrowing down of the concept of sovereignty.

5.2.2   The Triumph of the Modern Sovereign State in International Law

For all the existing criticisms of the "myth of Westphalia,"[58] many scholars continue to claim that the rise of the state as the primary – even the only – subject of international law happened around 1648,[59] and that prior to the twentieth century, the state was the only subject of international law.[60] There is now growing evidence, however, that it is only in the late nineteenth century that international lawyers came to place the sovereign state – at the cost of all its competitors and with very few exceptions – at the heart of their new edifice.[61]

---

favorable to occupying forces, but ultimately, "although [these debates] were passionate and long, they made little mark on the 'status of belligerent' part of the texts originally before the conferences ... between the Brussels Code [1874] and the Hague Regulation in their final, 1907, form, that crucial definition of the lawful belligerent, given double emphasis by being moved up from ninth to first place, remained adamantly almost the same." Ibid., 199–200.

[57] Holland, *Lectures*, 5. Cited in Nabulsi, *Traditions of War*, 8, n. 18.

[58] See, for instance, Teschke, *The Myth of 1648*; Osiander, "Sovereignty, International Relations, and the Westphalian Myth"; Osiander, *Before the State*.

[59] To take but one example, see Cassese, "States."

[60] It is common to find assertions such as the following: "Up to the beginning of the twentieth century, sovereign states were the only actors recognized by international law." Anghie, "Colonialism and the Birth of International Institutions," 514. In fact, the latest edition of one of the most widely used international law textbooks explains that: "The main subjects of international law are states, and for centuries states were held to be the only subjects of international law, save perhaps for a few oddities (the Holy See, the Maltese Order) which would be considered subjects of international law for historic reasons and, it seems, because states generally treated them as subjects." Klabbers, *International Law*, 72.

[61] In most cases, these exceptions entailed reinviting nonstate actors after they had been booted out of the club. On the resilience of private empires and their use as a precedent to create artificial legal persons in the late nineteenth century, see Press, *Rogue Empires*; Fitzmaurice, *King Leopold's Ghostwriter*.

This chronological discrepancy may be rooted in a tendency to tell the history of international law through the thought of those who were retrospectively identified as its "founders," notably through the famous *Classics of International Law* collection. Not only have the relevant texts often been read anachronistically, but many of them were more concerned with making normative statements about how international law should operate than with descriptive accuracy about the actual operation of international law at the time. In some cases, these writers developed their ideas with little regard for the realities unfolding around them; in other cases, they tried to squeeze their world into Procrustean categories that we have nonetheless taken at face value.

Take the work of the famous Emer de Vattel (1714–1767). In practice, Vattel's native Neuchâtel "epitomized the dependence of many states on outside powers and the heterogeneity of states in post-Westphalian Europe."[62] Indeed, Neuchâtel formally fell under the legal authority of the King of Prussia. Yet, in *Le droit des gens* (1758), Vattel argued that "Neuchâtel was a perfectly free and independent sovereign state."[63] As Frederick Whelan has noted, Vattel's characterization was "a rather daring act of the theoretical imagination,"[64] and it left many unanswered questions as to how his framework could actually be applied in practice. The world Vattel described tells us much about how he wished international law to operate, not how it functioned in reality.[65] Polities were in fact too heterogeneous to allow a bright line to be drawn between those that were legally "sovereign states" and those that were not.[66]

---

[62] Pitts, *Boundaries of the International*, 88.

[63] Vattel, *Le droit des gens*, Book I, chapter 1, §9. Cited in Pitts, *Boundaries of the International*, 88.

[64] Whelan, "Vattel's Doctrine of the State," 76–77. Cited in Pitts, *Boundaries of the International*, 89.

[65] Ultimately, when Vattel published *Le droit des gens* in the mid-eighteenth century, the practice of international law was more heavily based on treaties and other practical legal instruments than on the musings of individual jurists. As such, the awkward discrepancies between the world he described in his treatise and the political realities of his time did not necessarily have a major impact on actual legal practices. That being said, Vattel's treatise eventually did become widely popularized and was relied on both as a guidebook for diplomats and consuls and as a textbook for international lawyers in the nineteenth century. By then, however, the European world was moving toward a more homogeneous arena of sovereign states, and Vattel's treatise was no longer so at odds with the political world it sought to apply to. The tendency to overestimate the impact of these individuals on international legal practice is a broader issue that is now beginning to be addressed more systematically. See Wallenius, "The Case for a History of Global Legal Practices." On the surge in Vattel's popularity in the nineteenth century, see Fiocchi Malaspina, "Emer de Vattel's 'Le droit des gens'"; Fiocchi Malaspina, "Le droit des gens di Emer de Vattel."

[66] More broadly, as one scholar puts it, while it is "perhaps a cliché of the twentieth century historiography of international law to decry its statist orientation, its reification of state-will, and its understanding of the order of international law as constituted

Of course, popular early nineteenth-century textbooks by the likes of Georg Friedrich von Martens (1756–1821) and Johann Ludwig Klüber (1762–1837) spoke of what would later be called "international law" as law among "states," language we might consider on par with contemporary understandings of statehood and international law. But there are now a number of works that unpack what exactly the "state" was meant to signify in those contexts and how complex the concept of sovereignty remained in the early nineteenth century. We tend not to problematize the concept of "the state" in the eighteenth and nineteenth centuries, but in fact, for jurists like Martens and Klüber, the term was used generically to encompass all sorts of heterogeneous polities within which sovereign rights and duties were still subject to a degree of division. Martens wrote of "demi-sovereign states" that were part of larger "composed states" and dealt extensively with the question of whether demi- or semi-sovereign states were to be understood as fully "sovereign" from a legal standpoint, and thus as "subjects of international law" in later parlance. There were still numerous "semi-sovereign" states in the nineteenth century, from Belgium and the states of the German and Swiss confederations, to the Kingdom of Poland, Cracow (separately), Egypt, the Transvaal, and the Indian "Princely" States.[67] What exactly it meant for only "states" to be "sovereigns" and thus "subjects of international law" was still far from crystal clear – indeed, it was hotly debated – at the beginning of the nineteenth century.[68]

---

through the free will of its privileged subject, the state," we now know that this "characterization of international law as a system of states, or an "anarchical society" of self-contained state orders bound together solely through contractual or consensual ties, takes shape not contemporaneous with the Treaties of Westphalia, but in the last decade of the eighteenth century and first two decades of the nineteenth century – in particular after the Congress of Vienna." Bhuta, "State Theory, State Order, State System," 405, drawing on Jouannet, *The Liberal-Welfarist Law of Nations*, 115–34.

[67] The most in-depth study of semi-sovereignty is currently Learoyd, "Semi-Sovereignty and Relationships of Hierarchy." See also Learoyd, "Configurations of Semi-Sovereignty in the Long-Nineteenth Century."

[68] In fact, exceptions to the sovereign/nonsovereign binary remained in the twentieth century. In the case of membership to international organizations, see the work of Ellen Ravndal: "From an Inclusive to an Exclusive International Order"; Ravndal, "Acting Like a State"; Ravndal, "Colonies, Semi-Sovereigns, and Great Powers." Fascinatingly, Ravndal explains that "it was the newly independent states of Africa and Asia, alongside the older former colonial states of Latin America, which led the charge against an inclusive membership policy. The newly independent states, clinging to the notion of sovereignty, sought to expel anyone not sovereign. Sovereignty and sovereign equality was their only claim to actorhood on the international stage and membership of the international order. Having to prove to themselves and others that they belong, the newest members of a club often become the most conservative and traditionalist." Ravndal, "From an Inclusive to an Exclusive International Order," 23.

The issue underwent remarkable shifts over time. As David Kennedy explains, "over the course of the nineteenth-century, legal scholars placed the authority of sovereigns at the center of a reimagined legal order replete with formal distinctions."[69] More specifically, there appear to have been two related developments. First, what had long been a sort of spectrum based on differing degrees and forms of sovereignty was increasingly turned into a stark binary – sovereign or nonsovereign. Second, considerations about the rights and duties of sovereigns broadly speaking were increasingly replaced by discussion over the rights and duties of sovereign states.

As is well known, the nineteenth century saw the emergence of the nation-state as the most important actor – alongside empires – in international relations, particularly with Germany (1871), Italy (1871), and, to a lesser extent, Belgium (1830) and Greece (1830) emerging as new players on the European international scene. The flip side of this coin was the gradual demise of other forms and theories of political organization, ranging from alternatives to the nation-state that had the new concept of the nation at their heart[70] to composite polities such as the Holy Roman Empire[71] and the German Confederation (1806/66) and mercantile "company-states,"[72] most notably the Dutch East India Company (VOC) (1800) and the British East India Company (1858/74). While empires and their various jurisdictional arrangements remained a central feature of the international order throughout the period and beyond, these developments constituted a significant reconfiguration of the international system's main units, particularly on the European continent.

Despite the wide-ranging literature on these developments, the profound challenges they posed for the emerging discipline of international law have not attracted as much attention. The chronology of

---

[69] Kennedy, *Of War and Law*, 61.

[70] On early nineteenth-century nation-based alternatives to the nation-state, see Vick, *The Congress of Vienna*, 266–67. For mid-century developments, see Cole, *Different Paths to the Nation*.

[71] The Holy Roman Empire is often treated as a mere exception despite the fact that it formed the geographical core of the European continent throughout the early modern period. In fact, while historians long dismissed the Empire as a medieval "misfit" in the early modern world, the new historiography of the Empire is now overturning this idea and showing the extent to which the Empire was central to the continent's broader development, a fact that was long lost upon contemporary historians because their nineteenth-century predecessors, eager to establish teleological accounts of the formation of nation-states, struggled to reconcile the thousand-year Empire with their narratives and consequently minimized the Empire's historical importance. See especially Wilson, *Heart of Europe*.

[72] Stern, *The Company-State*; Cavanagh, "A Company with Sovereignty and Subjects of Its Own?"; Weststeijn, "The VOC as a Company-State"; Sharman and Phillips, *Outsourcing Empire*; Fitzmaurice, *Humanism and America*.

these changes, in particular, remains rather hazy. For example, in the brief account Kennedy provides of this seminal shift, he considers that the practice of placing the authority of the sovereign at the center of the international legal order is a general nineteenth-century phenomenon to be contrasted with the early modern period. Thus, for him, early modern authors "from Grotius to Vattel" were distinct from their nineteenth-century counterparts in that they "rarely spoke of 'sovereigns' at all."[73] "For them," he continues, "[a]ll sorts of entities had rights – rulers of many different kinds, individuals, citizens, pirates, merchants ... The key elements in the system were *rights* and *wrongs*, not sovereigns."[74] By contrast, "by the late nineteenth century," international lawyers "*begin* their analysis with the sovereign act" [emphasis in original]. Turning to his primary field of interest, war, he then notes: "In such a world, it was easy to suggest that all wars publicly declared by a sovereign were just; the point was to discover if this was the sovereign, and if the war was the product of his public act."[75] There are two notable issues with this characterization.

First, the disjuncture between the early modern period and the nineteenth century is not entirely compelling. It is true that many jurists in the early modern period made space for individuals (though certainly not pirates), merchants, and other presumably "private" actors to have rights in their treatises, including, in certain cases, the right to use force. However, one of the core debates throughout this period turned precisely on the question of how far the boundaries of public authority could be stretched. Indeed, Kennedy's depiction of late nineteenth-century international lawyers who "*begin* their analysis with the sovereign act" plainly echoes Gentili's position. It is in this early modern context that all sorts of entities deemed sufficiently "public" had rights, notably those Kennedy calls "rulers of many different kinds." In a world in which sovereignty was still widely considered divisible, identifying who could either carry out or commission "public" acts was a tremendous source of controversy. There were thus multiple strands of argumentation for the legality of an act of international violence – some based on the idea that the act had to be conducted by a "public" authority to be legal,[76] others based on claims about the rights of "private" actors to use force. Grotius' defense

---

[73] Kennedy, *Of War and Law*, 61–62.
[74] Ibid.
[75] Ibid., 62.
[76] In that context, the problem of establishing a link between the act of aggression and an effectively "public" commission was often at the top of the agenda in prize cases, particularly as privateers regularly displayed tendencies to interpret the mandate within their letter of marque quite generously.

of the Dutch East India Company in the *Santa Catarina* case exemplifies this duality: In typical lawyerly fashion, Grotius develops separate arguments on the basis of the company being considered either as an agent of a public authority (the King of Johore) or as a private actor.[77] Grotius would similarly develop a number of arguments about the right of the Dutch polity to wage a public war against Spain despite its continuing *de jure* subordination to the Spanish Crown through much of the Dutch Revolt.[78] The picture is thus much more complex than the dichotomy offered by Kennedy. Most importantly, there were already numerous arguments made on the basis of the importance of sovereign authority in the early modern period, though what exactly this meant would come to change in the nineteenth century.

Second, because Kennedy anchors his chronological narrative in a broad disjuncture between the early modern period and the nineteenth century, he obscures one of the most intriguing features of the shift at hand: It was not decisively complete until *late* into the nineteenth century. In fact, the most radical shifts took place not between the early modern period and the nineteenth century, but rather within the nineteenth century itself, particularly before and after the emergence of the discipline of international law in the 1870s.

One of the most remarkable such shifts was the gradual disappearance of "demi-sovereigns" and "semi-sovereigns" as subjects of international law, a topic that has remained remarkably under-researched.[79] Over the course of the nineteenth century, lawyers moved steadily to exclude all entities other than fully sovereign states from the ambit of international law. One might understand this process as part of the broader "shrinking" of international society suggested by Charles Alexandrowicz.[80] In the past, attention had been primarily focused on the exclusion of non-European polities that had previously interacted with Europeans on relatively equal terms and, in the course of the nineteenth century, had become relegated to the bottom of the international social and legal hierarchy[81] or even considered unfit to participate in international society altogether, for instance through the signing of legal treaties. But this shrinking also took place in terms of the type

---

[77] Keene, *Beyond the Anarchical Society*, 40–59. More broadly, on Grotius and the *Santa Catarina*, see especially Borschberg, "The Seizure of the Sta. Catarina Revisited."

[78] Keene, *Beyond the Anarchical Society*, 40–59.

[79] For an attempt to remediate this gap, see Learoyd, "Semi-Sovereignty and Relationships of Hierarchy"; Learoyd, "Configurations of Semi-Sovereignty in the Long-Nineteenth Century."

[80] Alexandrowicz, *The Law of Nations in Global History*.

[81] See notably Keene, "A Case Study of the Construction of International Hierarchy."

of political entities that were considered eligible members of international society. This was the case for demi- or semi-sovereign states, but also for actors such as the Church or chartered companies. As Andrew Fitzmaurice notes, while these entities continued to wield power on the international stage, sovereign states started increasingly to restrict their powers in both practice and theory, and these actors experienced an important decline in the late eighteenth and early nineteenth centuries. While these developments took their course, various controversies emerged as lawyers questioned this new "very restrictive understanding of international society" and wondered whether "non-state artificial persons, such as chartered companies and organisations like the International Red Cross, could be admitted once again to international society."[82]

Some exceptions remained through the mid-nineteenth century and beyond, with authors such as Henry Wheaton (1785–1848) and William Beach Lawrence (1800–1881) pointing to cases where individuals or nonstate actors could be accorded legal subjectivity. But "more and more exclusively, the entities it became permissible to talk about were states,"[83] and what "states" meant became defined much more narrowly. The criteria for statehood indeed shrank, yielding "a particular image of a state, as a discrete unit, situated in space and enduring through time,"[84] an image much closer to the ideal type of the modern nation-state than what had been considered the norm in the late eighteenth century. It is in this context that mid-nineteenth-century lawyers and commentators began referring to entities that had been a staple of the international political landscape a few decades earlier – company-states,[85] semi-sovereigns[86] – as mindboggling anomalies that belonged to the distant past.

---

[82] Fitzmaurice, *King Leopold's Ghostwriter*, 7.

[83] Learoyd, "Semi-Sovereignty and Relationships of Hierarchy," 91–92.

[84] Ibid., 92.

[85] For example, in 1833, Thomas Babington Macaulay, an author, statesman, and employee of the East India Company, expressed his dismay: "It is strange, very strange, that a joint stock company of traders ... which, judging a priori from its constitution, we should have said was as little fitted for imperial functions as the Merchant Tailors' Company or the New River Company, should be intrusted with the sovereignty of a larger population, the disposal of a larger clear revenue, [and] the command of a larger army, than are under the direct management of the Executive Government of the United Kingdom." Cited in Stern, *The Company-State*, 3. Similarly, Adam Smith called the company a "strange absurdity" and Edmund Burke "a state in disguise of a merchant." But as Stern reminds us, there was nothing strange about it: The company was typical of "an early modern world filled with a variety of corporate bodies politic and hyphenated, hybrid, overlapping, and composite forms of sovereignty." (3)

[86] Travers Twiss considered that the concept was a relic from "another system of political law," concerned primarily with the modalities of the Germanic Empire. Twiss, *The Law of Nations Considered as Independent Political Communities*, Vol. 1, 25. Cited in Learoyd, "Semi-Sovereignty and Relationships of Hierarchy," 93.

Importantly, this development was not necessarily generalized beyond international law. Various international governmental organizations continued to include colonies and semi-sovereigns as members deep into the twentieth century, with the modern sovereign state only triumphing as the sole legitimate member of these organizations in the decades after World War II.[87] After all, until then, the world at large remained one of empires, so it is not exactly surprising that institutions of the international order maintained their relatively inclusive stand on the recognition of polities that could have international standing. International lawyers, if anything, were rather unusual in their attempt to squeeze the world into an ill-fitting shoe. The result of their efforts was the development of a highly exclusionary framework, and nowhere was this more apparent than in the crown jewel of the emerging discipline: the laws of war.

5.2.3   The Triumph of the Modern State in the Laws of War

The crucial shift of the late nineteenth century in terms of how international lawyers conceptualized war was that they not only emphasized the exclusively "public" character of war with a new fervor, but also that they redefined "public" to mean "states" in the narrow, modern sense of the term.

The renewed importance of the public character of war in the late nineteenth century has already been highlighted in the literature. Rotem Giladi points to Francis Lieber's seminal Code of 1863,[88] a document upon which those codifying the laws from the late 1860s to World War I would draw heavily. Though Lieber was not the first to draw a distinction between public and private war, Giladi explains, "his treatment of modern war as exclusively public ... became, in time, a foundational concept of the 19th Century effort to modernize and humanize the laws of war."[89] Giladi then perceptively emphasizes the legacies of this nineteenth-century shift, reminding us that to this day, the principle of the public nature of war "remains embedded, albeit implicitly, in contemporary international humanitarian law and its paradigmatic interstate war outlook."[90] Yet the slippage between "public war" and "interstate war" deserves closer scrutiny.

The term "public" – whether as in "public actor," "public authority," or "public war" – seems to have caused much confusion. As we saw in

---

[87] Ravndal, "Colonies, Semi-Sovereigns, and Great Powers."
[88] Giladi, "Francis Lieber on Public War."
[89] Ibid., 448.
[90] Ibid.

Part I, it was also relevant in Gentili's time; the question of who could wield "public" authority was an important debate into which Gentili had intervened. Yet this idea meant something radically different in the nineteenth century. It is true that, in both periods, the concept effectively restricted the kind of actors who could claim to be legally resorting to war. But Gentili's distinction reflected the much more fluid nature of political authority in the early modern period. Nineteenth-century lawyers, by contrast, sought to associate "public" with the modern sovereign state, in the very specific form it adopted over the course of the nineteenth century – a form that would have been entirely unimaginable for the likes of Gentili.

This shift did not unfold over the nineteenth century as a whole, but rather during its last three and a half decades, with the emergence of the discipline of international law. Over that period, the idea of war as an exclusively public endeavor became enshrined in the various conventions and treatises that were emerging in an attempt to codify international law and systematize what had otherwise been a field that since the early eighteenth century relied primarily on collections of treaties.[91] However, what exactly this meant has remained largely underconceptualized. As I have noted, Gentili was revived by late nineteenth-century lawyers precisely because he defined war as a just and *public* contest of arms, a move which they considered prescient. Yet the meaning of "public" had significantly evolved by then. As a result, whereas Kennedy explains that "[p]rivate armies, mercenaries, privateers – all these were outmoded ... because they did not fit with the new, exclusively *public* nature of sovereign war,"[92] Gentili had made plenty of space in his own theory of "public" war for privateers and other private actors fighting on behalf of a those he deemed to be public authorities. The change was thus as much in defining that war was to be a public endeavor as in defining what a "public" actor entailed.

Kennedy hints at a crucial subtext for late nineteenth-century international lawyers: the idea of "one sovereign, one military."[93] As he notes, privateering – another staple of earlier times – became considered problematic, but this was not, contrary to what he claims, because it was one of the "private modes of warfare associated with the old regime."[94] Privateers were very much considered to be partaking in public war throughout the early modern period and into the nineteenth century, as

---

[91] Notably the compilations of Dumont and Mably.
[92] Kennedy, *Of War and Law*, 64.
[93] Ibid., 61.
[94] Ibid.

long as their acts had effectively been commissioned by a public authority. More precisely, Kennedy suggests that privateering, abolished in
1856, was simply "incompatible with new legal conceptions of sovereignty that stressed its legal status as a unitary public authority exercis-
ing a monopoly of military force."[95] In light of the standard delays in
communication, especially overseas, the old phenomenon of privateering had often stretched the meaning of "public" control and authority
rather thin, but it is only with the emergence of the modern nation-state
and the expansion of the powers of central governments – particularly
through the growing competence in administration from the 1840s –
that privateering became seen as truly anomalous. While this centralization process only peaked in the 1890s, the international lawyers of the
1870s were – like other members of the elite involved in the development
of new international institutions[96] – already actively pushing this agenda
forward. There is perhaps no better embodiment of this link than the
Swiss jurist and politician Johann Caspar Bluntschli, whose writings
were just as central to the legitimization of the strengthening nation-
state as to the codification of international law and of the laws of war.[97]

It is in this context that the real shift happened, one which Gentili could
never have foreseen. War was now to be the exclusive legal prerogative of
polities recognizing each other as modern sovereign states, and anyone
who was not part of a recognized state's formal army was now to be considered an illegal combatant. The radical shift was the seemingly inno-
cent slip from Gentili's focus on sovereigns to the later focus on states,
and the narrowing down, over the course of the nineteenth century, of
the idea of what "a state" was. This would be enshrined in the emerging laws of war, with consequences both immediate and long-lasting.
And to legitimize this new approach, international lawyers pointed to
Gentili to show that there was a long tradition of restricting the right to
wage war to sovereign states, in a rather questionable feat of historical
reconstruction that nonetheless perfectly served their purposes.

This new approach brought about some significant changes. First,
this is when the practice of war became a well-regulated mechanism of
state interaction. As such, it acquired a new standing, reaching "its pin-
nacle of legal prestige" and attaining the exalted status of an "institution
of international law."[98] It was the central pillar of codified international

---

[95] Ibid. Although this was not the only reason behind the abolition of the practice, see
Lemnitzer, *Power, Law and the End of Privateering.*

[96] Murphy, *International Organization and Industrial Change,* 53–54.

[97] See especially his two most famous works in these fields, *The Modern Law of War*
(1866) and *The Theory of the State* (1875).

[98] Neff, *War and the Law of Nations,* 161.

law, and it made clear the rules of a new system in which only mutually recognizing modern sovereign states could participate.

Second, this shift meant that the laws of war "came to refer exclusively to the regulation of the *conduct* of hostilities."[99] What mattered was whether you were recognized as a sovereign state, not whether there was any legitimacy to your cause, for instance as an indigenous armed group resisting a foreign invasion. The new idea of war as the exclusive prerogative of sovereign states led to a near-exclusive focus on the *ius in bello* (the rules that determine how to conduct hostilities during war) at the cost the of *ius ad bellum* (the rules that determine whether entering into war is permissible in the first place), which "shriveled into virtual nothing."[100] This division between *ius in bello* and *ius ad bellum* would long remain a debated point amongst both international lawyers and political philosophers.[101] Yet the idea that war is the legal prerogative of sovereign states and that *ius ad bellum* considerations should be absolutely minimal continues to be central both to contemporary international humanitarian law and to contemporary just war theorizing.[102] Before we move forward in time in Chapter 6, I examine the significant but underappreciated role this shift would play within the context of late nineteenth-century imperial expansion.

5.3   "Modern War" and Empire

The idea that war was the prerogative of recognized sovereign states, and that only such states could be protected by the emerging laws of war, was developed within the European context, but it also impacted the imperial stage. While there is now extensive literature on the relationship between international law and empire in the late nineteenth century,[103] this particular aspect has not been examined in much detail, perhaps owing again to the false sense of continuity that has persisted regarding the exclusive primacy of the sovereign state as a bearer of the right to wage war. Ultimately, questions about sovereignty and about

---

[99] Ibid., 163.

[100] Ibid. See also Nabulsi, *Traditions of War*, 4.

[101] This debate arose particularly fiercely in the twentieth century, notably regarding the United Nations. See Neff, *War and the Law of Nations*, Chapter 9, particularly 342–43. See also Nabulsi, *Traditions of War*, Conclusion.

[102] The seminal example is still Walzer, *Just and Unjust Wars*.

[103] See notably Pitts, *Boundaries of the International*; Sylvest, "Our Passion for Legality"; Fitzmaurice, "Liberalism and Empire in Nineteenth Century International Law"; Nuzzo, *Origini di una scienza*; Craven, "Colonialism and Domination." For the seminal piece on the relationship between international law, positivism, sovereignty, and civilization, see Anghie, "Finding the Peripheries."

the "public" character of actors taking part in warfare played an important role in the colonial context, with which many of the men reviving Gentili were also deeply involved.

In this final section of the chapter, I examine a particularly significant development in this regard, the interaction between two forms of hierarchies in determining the applicability of the emerging laws of war: the civilized/uncivilized divide, and the sovereign/nonsovereign divide.

5.3.1   Sovereignty or Civilization?

It is often assumed that the emerging codified laws of war had a restricted range of application based on which countries were deemed to be civilized. As Martti Koskenniemi puts it, if war was now an institution, a duel regulated by all sorts of written rules, "[t]he rules of such dueling, it goes almost without saying, appl[ied] only to combat between the civilized."[104] It is easy to come to this conclusion on the basis of the broader idea that international law only applied within the so-called family of civilized nations. Indeed, in a pertinent example of what was taught to actual officers at the time, the 1912 *Manual for British Officers* states that "the rules of International Law apply only to warfare between civilized nations, where both parties understand them and are prepared to carry them out" and that they "do not apply in wars with uncivilized States and tribes, where their place is taken by the discretion of the commander and such rules of justice and humanity as recommend themselves in the particular circumstances of the case."[105]

Yet the picture was more complicated. As Koskenniemi also notes, "if the distinction between the civilized and the uncivilized did structure colonial international law at the end of the nineteenth century, it did so accompanied by considerable doubts about its adequacy."[106] Indeed, one may even say that the dichotomy between civilization and barbarism was "riddled with contradictions and ambiguities."[107] Even more importantly, this binary underpinned but one conception of global order amongst many, one that could be "complemented, supplanted, and occasionally undermined by other attempts to classify and order the world."[108] As such, determining the domain of the application of the laws of war was not necessarily as straightforward as it is sometimes made

---

[104] Koskenniemi, *Gentle Civilizer*, 86. See also Mégret, "From 'Savages' to 'Unlawful Combatants'."
[105] Edmonds, *Land Warfare*, 14.
[106] Koskenniemi, *Gentle Civilizer*, 131.
[107] Bell, "Empire and International Relations in Victorian Political Thought," 283.
[108] Ibid.

out to be. In many ways, the issue was that while some principles could appear very simple in theory, the enduring diversity of polities made their practical application much more difficult. In recent years, much crucial light has been shed on the late nineteenth-century relationship between international law and empire, but the overwhelming emphasis on the evolution of the civilized/uncivilized distinction has tended to obscure the equally important changes that the concept of sovereign statehood underwent as a standalone criterion. While the two were often connected, they also obeyed their own logic and the hierarchies they created were a complex web rather than a clear set of dichotomies.

International lawyers of the period directly grappled with the problem of defining the boundaries of international law's sphere of operation. In doing so, they sought to root the new "science" of international law and its various principles in "facts, not speculation."[109] Both the Institut and the Association for the Reform and Codification of the Laws of Nations "placed the question of the scope of International Law at the center of their agenda,"[110] and in 1875, the Institut had thus explicitly attempted to clarify the issue of international law's realm of application by launching a study under the chairmanship of Travers Twiss "on the possibility of applying customary (European) international law 'in the Orient'."[111] The lengthy summary of the Commission's work[112] published in the *Revue* illustrates the extent to which this issue raised thorny questions for international lawyers. Discussing the existing treaties between countries such as the United States and "organized states and semi-organized tribes," such as Turkey, China, Japan, Persia, Siam, Madagascar, Borneo, Muscat, Lew Chew, Morocco, Algiers, Tripoli, and Tunis, the commission notes that "[t]his state of things raises a good number of serious questions and creates much confusion."[113] For indeed, if these polities had previously signed such treaties, then they must have been considered as international legal actors in their own right. More broadly, numerous societies seemed to fall in a liminal space between the categories of civilized and barbarian. This was not only the case in "the Orient"; polities such as "Russia, the Ottoman empire, the newly independent republics of Latin America, even the countries of southern Europe ... all presented difficulties and generated debate."[114]

---

[109] Lobban, "English Approaches to International Law in the Nineteenth Century," 88.
[110] Pitts, *Boundaries of the International*, 68.
[111] Koskenniemi, *Gentle Civilizer*, 132.
[112] Its members were Asser, Field, De Holtzendorff, Lorimer, Martens, Rivier, and Twiss.
[113] Field, "De la possibilité d'appliquer le droit international européen aux nations orientales," 663.
[114] Bell, "Empire and International Relations in Victorian Political Thought," 283.

Under these circumstances, the concept of civilization did a significant amount of work in international relations, but its relevance to applying the laws of war was effectively limited.[115] It was not clear how to draw the line between civilized and uncivilized actors. Indeed, this divide certainly was not equivalent to a distinction between Europeans and non-Europeans. For example, China, Mexico, Japan, Persia, Siam, and Turkey all sent delegates to the 1899 Hague Conference, joined by the Argentine Republic, Bolivia, the United States of Brazil, Chile, Colombia, Cuba, the Dominican Republic, Ecuador, Guatemala, Haiti, Nicaragua, Panama, Paraguay, Peru, Salvador, Uruguay, and the United States of Venezuela in 1907.[116] The famous "Standard of Civilization"[117] was a notoriously moving target – not least because one of its criteria was conforming to the rather vague "accepted norms and practices of 'civilized' international society"[118] – and the broader concept of "civilization" was far from operational within the new legal edifice that required clarity, consistency, and coherence.

Given these difficulties, international lawyers came to focus on a second distinction as a clearer means to determine the realm of application of the laws of war. Indeed, there were other forms of social stratification that operated within nineteenth-century international order beyond the criterion of civilization.[119] The one that became at least equally relevant for these international lawyers was the question of whether one qualified as a modern sovereign state.[120]

Two elements are worth highlighting about this process. First, the overlap of these different forms of hierarchy meant that it was possible

---

[115] For an in-depth discussion of this problem in the case of international law at large, and through an analysis of Travers Twiss himself, see Fitzmaurice, "Equality Between European and Non-European Nations in International Law." For an emphasis on the civilization aspect with regards to the laws of war, see Bartelson, *War in International Thought*, chapter 4; Mégret, "From 'Savages' to 'Unlawful Combatants'."

[116] On the ambiguous status associated with post-independent Latin American states, see notably Fawcett, "Between West and Non-West."

[117] See the literature on the "standard of civilization," notably Gong, *The Standard of Civilization in International Society.*

[118] Ibid., 15.

[119] For a typology of the different forms of social stratification characterizing the international order of the nineteenth century, see Keene, "The Standard of 'Civilisation', the Expansion Thesis and the 19th-Century International Social Space."

[120] This had in fact already been a source of debate in the seventeenth and eighteenth centuries concerning the case of the Barbary corsairs. See Rech, *Enemies of Mankind*, 49–104. For a similar argument about the murkiness of the legal regime on the use of force in the nineteenth century and the importance of the distinction between, on the one hand, violence amongst sovereign states and, on the other hand, violence between sovereign states and other entities not recognized as such, see von Bernstorff, "The Use of Force in International Law Before World War I."

to be considered a sovereign state but not an entirely civilized one or a civilized polity but not an entirely sovereign state. As such, while it is often assumed that international law and the laws of war simply applied to sovereign states within the "family of civilized nations," the picture was rather more complicated. A state such as Belgium was considered civilized, of course, but the fact that it could not wage any offensive wars because it was formally neutralized meant for most international lawyers that its status fell short of a complete sovereign.[121] Conversely, Latin American states were considered sovereign, but deep into the nineteenth century they were still not considered to be entirely civilized.[122] In theory, the recognition of a polity's sovereign statehood was very much separate from its recognition as a member of the "Family of civilized nations," although in practice these distinctions often collapsed into each other, creating a remarkably muddled field.[123] In any case, in determining whether or not to apply the emerging laws of war to countries that did not fall squarely within the clear category of "civilized sovereign states," the emphasis was placed as heavily on whether they were considered to be "sovereign states" as on whether they were deemed "civilized."

Second, and crucially, the enshrinement of these ideas during the development of the "science" of international law and the codification of the laws of war overlapped exactly with the period known as European "high imperialism" (1870–1914).[124] It is thus natural to ask whether these questions about sovereignty might have played an important role in the colonial context as well. In fact, as we saw, there is a remarkable amount of overlap between the men who established and then led the Institut, those who pushed forward the codification of the laws of war, those who were involved in the revival of Gentili, and those who helped develop the legal infrastructure of colonialism. Though examining the details of this network is beyond the scope of this book,[125] one particularly noteworthy figure is Sir Travers Twiss, who was thrice the vice-president of the Institut, a leading member of the English committee to revive Gentili, the author of a standard work of international law on

---

[121] Belgium "always tended to regard neutralization as an unjustified limitation on its sovereignty imposed as a condition of its independence." Black, *Neutralization and World Politics*, 25.
[122] Schulz, "Civilisation, Barbarism and the Making of Latin America's Place in 19th-Century International Society."
[123] Gong, *The Standard of Civilization in International Society*, 33–34.
[124] For an overview, see Hopkins, "Overseas Expansion, Imperialism, and Empire 1815–1914."
[125] For a preliminary foray into the overlap between those involved in the Berlin and Hague conferences, see Vergerio, "The Berlin and Hague Conferences."

the laws of war and peace, and the author of the constitution of King Leopold's Congo.

To my knowledge, the precise relationship between debates over the nature of sovereignty and the right to wage war and attempts to operationalize the concept of civilization for legal purposes has not been examined in any meaningful way, despite the fact that the same group of writers took up both issues. One critical link, I suggest in the following section, was the emergence of the first counterinsurgency manuals, or, in the parlance of the time, of "small wars" manuals.

5.3.2   The Rise of a Bifurcated System: Small Wars and Regular Wars

Though ample literature exists on the emergence of the laws of war,[126] and another, more limited set of works exists on the emergence of small war manuals[127] – which were in fact the first modern counterinsurgency manuals – virtually nothing has been written about the relationship between the two. This is in spite of the fact that the first small wars manuals and the first manuals on the laws of war appeared over the same period, they were both taught to officers in military academies, and they were covering broadly similar questions about the appropriate behavior to adopt on the battlefield in different contexts.

The neglect of this relationship is all the more puzzling in view of complaints from contemporary legal scholars that while counterinsurgency has become the dominant or even defining type of conflict of our age, the laws of war seem "undesigned for it"[128] or even entirely "undefined."[129] An essential part of the problem is the lack of agreement as to what laws should apply in wars involving nonstate actors.[130] As a result, soldiers involved in counterinsurgency operations often act on the basis of "various operational rules that supply rough guidance" promulgated by commanders and legal advisors attempting to palliate for the lack of any clear legal requirements.[131] The more historically inclined literature points out that modern counterinsurgency operations have unfolded for over 150 years, meaning that the contemporary laws of war cannot be said to be merely "lag[ging] behind changes

---

[126] See notably Howard, Andreopoulos, and Shulman, *The Laws of War*; Nabulsi, *Traditions of War*; Neff, *War and the Law of Nations*; Witt, *Lincoln's Code*.
[127] Owens, *Economy of Force*; Porch, "Bugeaud, Gallieni, Lyautey"; Porch, *Counterinsurgency*; Whittingham, "Savage Warfare."
[128] McLeod, *Rule of Law in War*, 60.
[129] Banks, *Counterinsurgency Law*, xii.
[130] Ibid., x; McLeod, *Rule of Law in War*, 60.
[131] Banks, *Counterinsurgency Law*, xi.

in armed conflict."[132] In fact, insurgencies and irregular warfare have long informed[133] and even been at the very heart of the development of the modern laws of war.[134] It is thus natural to ask whether the historical context can help to explain at least part of the problem we face today. Indeed, the incompatibilities between the two areas today arguably trace back to their very origins in this period.

As I noted earlier, it has conventionally been suggested that the laws of war only applied to conflicts between the civilized.[135] Our understanding changes, I suggest, if we view the rise of counterinsurgency manuals alongside manuals on the laws of war within the context of the late nineteenth-century efforts to restrict the legal concept of "war" to a practice carried out by modern sovereign states and their formal armies. The emerging laws of war were meant first and foremost to apply solely to such conflicts, opening up a separate space for determining which rules were to prevail in conflicts that fell outside the now narrowed-down legal sphere of "war." Since the laws of war would not apply in those cases, a separate set of rules of conduct emerged, unburdened by legal considerations and therefore of a more directly strategic kind. In short, the classic divide between what became known as the distinction between "regular war" and "small war" was intertwined with the changing ideas about what exactly "war" entailed in legal terms. Most obviously, the laws of war were built around a sharp distinction between civilians and combatants, generally prohibiting the targeting of civilians altogether, whereas "small war" strategies were designed with the civilian population placed at the very heart of the war effort, as opposed to constituting a mere sideshow to the actual war theater.

Of course, "small wars" had been part of European military jargon for some time already, but the meaning of the term changed from the late eighteenth century onward. The American War of Independence is generally considered to have marked a turning point toward a new type of conflict that would come to dominate the nineteenth century,[136] both within and outside Europe. These new conflicts were insurgencies with a strong ideological component, and they were qualitatively different from the "small wars" of the past. Until then, "small wars" had constituted tactical parentheses within broader conflicts between

---

[132] Ibid., viii.
[133] McLeod, *Rule of Law in War*, 63.
[134] Nabulsi, *Traditions of War*, 4–18.
[135] Koskenniemi, *Gentle Civilizer*, 86; Mégret, "From 'Savages' to 'Unlawful Combatants'."
[136] Heuser, "Small Wars in the Age of Clausewitz," 149.

major European sovereigns. The new small wars, by contrast, constituted a separate form of conflict altogether, pitting the forces of a recognized sovereign state against those of an entity not recognized as
such, in either domestic or international conflicts.[137] Small wars thus
came to acquire both a qualitatively different nature and an unprecedented importance. The trend originating with the American War of
Independence would be strengthened by the French Revolutionary and
Napoleonic wars, which Clausewitz distinguished as "People's Wars."[138]
Following these developments, the term "small war" came to acquire
a new meaning, which is still the one familiar to military theorists and
practitioners today: guerrilla warfare – coined after the invasion of
Spain by France in 1808 and the subsequent Spanish resistance – and
the attempt to defeat insurgents in these contexts, now referred to as
counterinsurgency.

From this moment on, it became essential for military officers to
make two determinations: first, whether a conflict was a "regular war"
or a "small war" (i.e., whether it was fought against a recognized sovereign state's army), and second, in the case of a "small war," whether
it was of a "savage" or of a "civilized" kind. In this context, the dual
hierarchy – sovereign statehood versus civilization – became particularly evident and raised a number of questions about how the emerging
laws of war were to deal with these new configurations. In the closing decades of the nineteenth century, the default assumption was that
against those not recognized as civilized sovereign states, the emerging
laws of war would simply not apply. But how were the numerous liminal
cases dealt with?

Crucially, the nineteenth-century term "small war," sometimes used
interchangeably with "irregular warfare,"[139] pertained to both domestic
and international conflicts. In the case of the latter, it generally referred
to conflicts involving indigenous forces resisting a foreign invader but
not considered those of a "sovereign state." In other words, in both

---

[137] In the sixteenth, seventeenth, and eighteenth centuries, small war, *Kleinkrieg*, or *la
petite guerre* referred to a form of warfare that was part of broader military campaigns,
akin to today's special operations; Deruelle, "The Sixteenth-Century Antecedents of
Special Operations 'Small War'"; Fonck and Satterfield, "The Essence of War." The
"irregular" fighters of *la petite guerre* commonly fought within the broader context
of wars waged by regular standing armies. They were generally used to gather intel-
ligence about the enemy, and sometimes to harass enemy forces in sudden attacks
before swiftly retreating. During the early modern period, small wars were thus an
auxiliary part of wars between standing armies, a sideshow to the main confronta-
tions; Heuser, "Small Wars in the Age of Clausewitz," 149.

[138] Scheipers, *Clausewitz on Small War*; Scheipers, "The Most Beautiful of Wars."

[139] Scheipers, *Unlawful Combatants*.

cases, "small wars" involved a recognized sovereign state fighting against forces deemed to belong to a "nonstate" actor. Eventually, these new types of wars came to be divided by military theorists and jurists into two categories: "civilized small wars" and "savage small wars."[140] But the line between intra-European and colonial small wars remained thin in the most famous writings on the subject. Thus, Callwell, who is sometimes called "the Clausewitz of colonial warfare,"[141] wrote his magnus opus *Small Wars: Their Practices and Principles* mostly about "uncivilised" or "savage" warfare, but he also discusses partisan warfare in "civilised" countries.[142] His definition of "small wars" speaks for itself:

Practically it may be said to include all campaigns other than those where both the opposing sides consist of regular troops. It comprises the expeditions against savages and semi-civilised races by disciplined soldiers, it comprises campaigns undertaken to suppress rebellions and guerilla warfare in all parts of the world where organized armies are struggling against opponents who will not meet them in the open field, and it thus obviously covers operations very varying in their scope and in their conditions.[143]

This overlap was at least partly a result of the fact that it was often the same individuals who were involved in both types of struggles. For example, Thomas Bugeaud – the "father" of counterinsurgency, cited by all the main later authors of small war manuals in both the French and the British context – first developed these ideas with two core experiences in mind: the "pacification" of Algeria, that is, his brutal and successful campaign against the forces of Abd el-Kader (1808–1883) between 1835 and 1847, and also the repression of the 1848 uprisings in Paris, for which he served as one of the strategic architects.[144] The primary thrust of these new military doctrines was thus the general repression of armed groups fighting against the military apparatus of a recognized sovereign state.

---

[140] The classic statement regarding this division is Callwell, *Small Wars*.

[141] Porch, "Introduction," xii.

[142] Callwell, *Small Wars*, 21–22. See also Whittingham, "Savage Warfare," 592. Although Callwell's work is often seen as the starting point of the history of the British approach to counterinsurgency (Whittingham, "Savage Warfare," 592), his work "reflected prevailing opinion as much as it influenced it" (Anglim, "Callwell versus Graziani," 592) and he was part of a much broader "school" of theorist-practitioners working on small wars that had emerged in the late nineteenth century.

[143] Callwell, *Small Wars*, 21–22.

[144] Ideville, *Le Maréchal Bugeaud, d'après sa correspondance intime et des documents inédits, 1784–1849.*

The overlap between savage and civilized small war has mostly been overlooked,[145] probably due to the extensive focus of small wars on imperial conflicts from the late nineteenth century onward. Indeed, with the peak of European imperial expansion after 1870s, these counterinsurgency doctrines would come to focus primarily on repressing insurgencies in the imperial theater. The great majority of "small" wars that occurred in the final decades of the nineteenth century were in fact not civil wars[146] but rather conflicts waged between a state and native people resisting foreign invasion or colonial conquest.[147] However, the term "small wars" continued to refer to war against "nonstate" actors more broadly. If anything, the military theorist-practitioners (or "warrior scholars"[148]) who wrote about "small wars" during the nineteenth century were merely shifting their focus from "civilized" to "savage" small wars following the events of their day. In the first half of the century, they focused on the American and European insurgencies, but by the late nineteenth century, they wrote primarily about imperial warfare.

In imperial and colonial conflicts, the goal of conquering and socially engineering overseas territories in the name of civilization meant that extreme levels of violence could be carried out against resisting natives.[149] States could thus eschew the usual restraints placed on warfare, such as the bans on the extermination of populations or on the use of particularly murderous weapons, such as the explosive dum dum bullets.[150] In other words, methods of warfare that were being explicitly outlawed in the codified laws of war could be legally used against natives. Within Europe, the lower propensity to think of one's opponents as racially inferior limited some of the worst excesses found in colonial warfare,[151]

---

[145] Two exceptions stand out. The first is Sibylle Scheipers' *Unlawful Combatants*, particularly chapter 5, "War in the Colonies," and her related article "Counterinsurgency or Irregular Warfare?" Scheipers, however, tends to juxtapose the two types of warfare and only to provide an overview of some of the ways they were linked, rather than systematically explore the connection between the two. The second is Mégret's aforementioned chapter "From 'Savages' to 'Unlawful Combatants'" but by virtue of its limited length and scope, it constitutes a helpful starting point rather than a full inquiry into the question

[146] On the newfound importance of whether or not a conflict could legally be termed a "civil war" following the juridification of war in the nineteenth century, see Armitage, *Civil Wars*.

[147] Kalyvas, "The Changing Character of Civil Wars," 207.

[148] Mumford and Reis, *The Theory and Practice of Irregular Warfare*.

[149] Scheipers, *Unlawful Combatants*, 182.

[150] Mégret, "From 'Savages' to 'Unlawful Combatants'"; Spiers, "The Use of the Dum Dum Bullet in Colonial Warfare."

[151] There were of course various manifestations of racial thinking within intra-European conflicts, both during the nineteenth century and obviously through World War II, but these were comparatively less prominent than in the context of imperial expansion.

but the same type of logic nonetheless applied. In legal terms, the repression of insurgents resisting foreign occupation in the aftermath of their country's formal defeat seems to have been generally couched as a campaign of law enforcement, existing in a sphere separate from the proper "war" that had occurred between two sovereign states. As a result, insurgents were for the most part denounced as mere criminals and could not benefit from any of the privileges of lawful belligerency and the protection of the laws of war.[152] Worse, their actions could lead to the collective punishment of the civilian population.[153]

Ultimately, it is not a coincidence that the explosion of people's wars in Europe, the peak of aggressive European imperialism, and the attempt to restrict the concept of war to conflict between the armies of mutually recognized sovereign states all happened within a relatively small window of time. The "small wars" unfolding in Europe and overseas shared a number of features, most importantly the fact that they fell outside the new legal concept of war as a military conflict between two recognized sovereign states. As such, they raised some fundamental questions regarding the rules that ought to apply to the conduct of violence. The development of manuals on the conduct of "small wars," and the incompatibilities their strategies presented vis-à-vis the emerging laws of war, can be understood as part of this broader picture.

5.4   Conclusion

This chapter has sought to account for the particularities of the shape that Gentili took on in his nineteenth-century incarnation – and what that revival has obscured.

As we saw in Chapter 4, in the Italian context, and at the very beginning of the revival in 1874, Gentili's name and his newly glorified reputation were harnessed to the cause of international arbitration, as an additional motor to push forward an increasingly successful endeavor. However, once the revival acquired traction in England, where the subcommittee ended up focusing more precisely on the republication

---

[152] On the debate around the characterization of insurgents and the exceptions that could be made, see *supra* note 56.
[153] Although the Hague Regulations restricted the customary method of applying collective penalties to civilians (Article 50), occupying forces were still allowed to carry out reprisals against the population in case acts of illegitimate warfare were committed by enemy individuals not belonging to the armed forces, as confirmed in Oppenheim, *International Law: A Treatise*, 175–76. These forms of collective punishment were applied both in Europe and in the colonies; see Scheipers, *Unlawful Combatants*, 178.

of *DIB*, Gentili was not only pulled out of the context of the Italian Risorgimento and placed within a more universal framework character- istic of the period, but he also became harnessed to a different interna- tional cause, that of the codification of the laws of war. That is when the story of Gentili as the father of the modern laws of war began to emerge.

I have argued that in order to understand the way Gentili was can- onized, and especially his association with the modern laws of war, we have to place his revival back within the underappreciated context of the late nineteenth century, one in which a new form of state was triumphing over all the other forms of political entity on the continent: the modern nation-state understood as a unitary authority with control over a linear and homogeneous territory and a much stricter monopoly over the use of force than ever before. International lawyers sought to enshrine this new understanding of the state as the basis for interna- tional law. Doing so entailed a remarkable narrowing down of the con- cept of "the state" and "sovereignty," and the establishment of sharp dichotomies between state/nonstate and sovereign/nonsovereign where earlier there had been much more fluid spectra. This was most explicit within the field at the heart of the emerging "science" of international law, the laws of war, which were being codified for the first time. In this context, international lawyers were able to tell a story about Gentili that helped legitimize granting the right to wage war only to polities recog- nizing each other as modern sovereign states. This effort was destined to be anachronistic, since Gentili possessed no notion of "the sover- eign state," of "international law," nor of "subjects of international law." Only by confronting these anachronisms head-on can we put these issues on a firmer foundation.

This is not to say that nineteenth-century lawyers had no good rea- son to return to Gentili. While Sbarbaro quoted Quinet's idea that "the dead only return when they have something to teach the living,"[154] the story is usually more complicated. Figures from the past return dressed in a variety of novel ways by those who wish to speak with them – whether because they have something to learn from the work of the past, or because calling upon its dusty authority can strengthen their own claims in the present. For our lawyers, considerations about both empire and the laws of war were front and center in their work, and there is no doubt that in their attempt to develop new regulations for the conduct of warfare they heard some direct echoes between their mission and Gentili's.

---

[154] Sbarbaro citing Quinet in Lacchè, "Monuments of International Law," 185–86.

Indeed, in his own time, Gentili had also sought to restrict the meaning of "public," in line with his absolutist leanings and an almost caricatured understanding of Bodin's *République*. The crucial difference was the conflation of "public" actors with sovereign states in the late nineteenth century. In light of the broader move toward excluding all nonstate actors – or those not recognized as proper sovereign states – from the right to wage war and from the protection of the laws of war, Gentili's definition provided a convenient way for international lawyers to legitimize their approach, even where this reading missed drastic changes in the meaning of the underlying ideas. The strict limitation of war to sovereigns could now be associated with the "modernity" that had presumably given us Westphalia and the states-system, a core shift that Grotius was perceived as having somehow completely missed. This narrative about Gentili, war, the state, and modernity would be further enshrined in the twentieth century, during which, as we will see in Chapter 6, the repetition of this particular story about Gentili irrevocably crowned him as the father of the modern laws of war.

The changes that occurred in the nineteenth century in terms of the conceptualization of statehood, sovereignty, and the right to wage war have in large part been obscured by the efforts of the international lawyers of the period to depict their system as the mere continuation of well-established principles, something which they did explicitly through the revival of Gentili. But in fact, the shift that took place in the nineteenth century had a profound impact on the way the laws of war were applied in a variety of conflicts, both in Europe and in the context of the "high imperialism" of 1870–1914, an impact which I have tried to begin recovering here, with the intent to open up a space for further research.

Let me end by reiterating that I do not mean to suggest that Gentili, though he was himself a proponent of empire,[155] foresaw any of these nineteenth-century developments with regard to the triumph of the modern sovereign state or the emergence of a legal vacuum around "small wars," nor that nineteenth-century lawyers drew their arguments directly from him or depended on him in any essential way. Instead, the point I wish to stress is that Gentili's revival occurred at a timely juncture, and the account that emerged about his importance should be understood within the world of these lawyers and their preoccupations, particularly regarding war and its laws both within Europe and in the context of empires. Framing the newly celebrated Gentili as

---

[155] Pagden, *The Burdens of Empire*, 75–96.

the intellectual father of their project gave a certain historical pedigree to the exclusionary triumph of the modern sovereign state in international law and in the laws of war. And through this process, these lawyers gave us a narrative about Gentili, the modern state, and war that would be further amplified and popularized in the twentieth century, to which I now turn.

6 Carl Schmitt and the Entrenchment of the Myth

Gentili's revival in the 1870s was followed by the establishment of a broad canon of "founders of international law," enshrined in the twenty-two-volume *Classics of International Law* collection, published between 1911 and 1950 by the Carnegie Endowment for International Peace under the general editorship of James Brown Scott.[1] Within this broadening of the international law pantheon, however, Gentili, the original challenger of Grotius' unquestioned supremacy, remained – to this day – seen as a particularly important figure, especially within the realm of the laws of war. There have been various reasons for this continued enthusiasm for Gentili's work, much of it building off the narratives that were developed about his "greatness" during his late nineteenth-century revival. Yet one particular twentieth-century scholar stands out in how influential he was in ensuring Gentili's position as a key protagonist in the history of international law: Carl Schmitt (1888–1985), the "most controversial German legal and political thinker of the twentieth century."[2]

Despite his status as the perceived "Crown Jurist" of the Reich between 1933 and 1936, Schmitt remained highly influential amongst West German conservative intellectuals until his death in 1985, as well as abroad through clandestine channels.[3] His *Der Nomos der Erde*, specifically, had a significant (if unspoken) impact on the works of two German post-war historians of international law,[4] Karl-Heinz Ziegler (*Völkerrechtsgeschichte*, 1996) and, more importantly, Wilhelm Grewe

---

[1] For a detailed analysis of the creation of this collection, see Amorosa, *Rewriting the History of the Law of Nations*.

[2] Schwab, "Introduction," in *Political Theology: Four Chapters on the Concept of Sovereignty*, ed. and trans. George Schwab (Chicago: University of Chicago Press, 2006), xxxvii. The main work on Schmitt's thought in English is still Balakrishnan, *The Enemy*. For a critique, see Teschke, "Decisions and Indecisions." For an earlier critique of critical theorists' turn to Schmitt, see Neocleous, "Friend or Enemy." For a thorough biography, see Mehring, *Carl Schmitt*.

[3] Müller, *A Dangerous Mind*.

[4] Koskenniemi, "International Law as Political Theology," §6.

(*Epochen der Völkerrechts*, written during World War II but first published in 1984),[5] whose *Epochs of International Law* remains to this day the main work on the matter, "with no successor being in sight."[6] The history of international law garnered little interest in the English-speaking academy until the 1990s,[7] but when the field eventually took off, both Grewe's and Schmitt's *magna opera* were translated into English – in 2001 and 2003, respectively – and came to form the foundations of the discipline.[8] Schmitt's influence on Grewe is unmistakable, to the point where it can be said that the "most widely used textbook on the history of international law, Wilhelm Grewe's *The Epochs of International Law*, is a Schmittian book."[9] In fact, Grewe's "book reads almost like a commentary, or expansion, of Schmitt's *Der Nomos der Erde*."[10]

Beyond the recent interest in the history of international law, Schmitt's influence has also been felt widely in the discipline of IR. This is unsurprising, as beyond his critiques of liberalism, his *Nomos*, specifically, is a history not just of international law, but of international relations more broadly.[11] This influence can be felt in two main respects. First, it has been pointed out that through the work of Hans Morgenthau (1904–1980), Schmitt's ideas became "absolutely central" for the development of realism in IR.[12] Second, while the translation of *The Concept of the Political* unleashed a first wave of "Schmittiana" in the 1980s, focused on Schmitt's critique of liberalism and anchored in the field of political theory (epitomized by the

---

[5] For an in-depth analysis of the context in which Grewe wrote his *Epochen*, including Grewe's relationship to Schmitt, see Fassbender, "Stories of War and Peace." Grewe was also strongly influenced by Wolfgang Windelband's *The Foreign Policy of Great Powers in Modern Times: From 1494 to the Present*; see Fassbender, "Stories of War and Peace," 505.

[6] Fassbender, "Stories of War and Peace," 480. A potential candidate is now Neff, *Justice among Nations*.

[7] The main text until then was Arthur Nussbaum's *Concise History of the Law of Nations*. He, too, emphasizes the importance of Gentili, though not quite as much as Schmitt. He explains: "Gentili's work on international law covers, for the first time, practically all pertinent problems of the period." On the laws of war, "[h]is treatment is far more comprehensive than that of the scholastics, including Suarez, who came after him." Ibid., 95.

[8] This period also saw the establishment of the *Journal of the History of International Law* (1999).

[9] Koskenniemi, "Carl Schmitt and International Law," 593. See also Fassbender, "Stories of War and Peace." As Fassbender notes, "Carl Schmitt is one of the most frequently (and usually approvingly) quoted authors in the *Epochen*." Fassbender, "Stories of War and Peace," 504. Nonetheless, Fassbender is less categorical than Koskenniemi in his assessment of Schmitt's influence on Grewe in terms of the latter's "analysis of specific developments and events in the history of international law but also the general concept of his book" (504).

[10] Koskenniemi, "The Epochs of International Law," 747.

[11] Koskenniemi, "International Law as Political Theology," §6.

[12] See most notably Koskenniemi, "Out of Europe."

work of Chantal Mouffe), the publication by Telos Press of an English version of the *Nomos* in 2003 gave rise to a second wave of Schmitt-related studies,[13] stemming this time from International Law (IL)[14] and IR.[15] In particular, critical theorists in IR have made much of the power of Schmitt's historical analysis, going as far as suggesting that Schmitt should be one of the household names in the IR canon.[16] The *Nomos*, we are told, "offers perhaps the most compelling history of the development of international law from the ashes of the Middle Ages to the beginning of the Cold War" and constitutes "a fully-fledged alternative historical account of international relations, of the genesis, achievements and demise of 'international society,' often referred to as the 'Westphalian system' in the field of IR."[17]

In the narrative put forward in the *Nomos*, Schmitt is categorical about Gentili's importance for international law and international relations: he considers him, and his less famous Oxford successor and intellectual follower, Richard Zouche (1590–1660), to be "the true founders of European international law,"[18] remarkably bracketing Grotius out. Schmitt's central claim in this regard is reminiscent of the nineteenth-century narrative about Gentili: The Italian jurist, he tells us, ushered in the "modern" concept of war, which would constitute one of the pillars of the European *nomos* until World War I. By contrast, Schmitt criticizes Grotius' "line of argument" on these same matters as "unsteady and uncertain."[19] He remarks that for Grotius "a private war was still war in the sense of international law," but that despite this fact he "is commonly thought to be the true founder of 'modern international law'," a title Schmitt clearly disapproves of.[20] Reiterating his criticism, he explains

---

[13] The left's appropriation of Schmitt after years of criticism (notably by Jürgen Habermas) and of monopolization by archconservatives has led to numerous debates about the wisdom of this move. For a discussion, see Specter, "What's 'Left' in Schmitt?"

[14] As Koskenniemi notes, "[t]he book was published in Germany only in 1984, but as soon as the English translation came out in 2000 it ascended to the status of leading general treatment of its topic." Koskenniemi, "Carl Schmitt and International Law," 593.

[15] Chandler, "The Revival of Carl Schmitt in International Relations." For a critical response to Chandler's assessment of the revival's value in IR, see Odysseos and Petito, "Vagaries of Interpretation." See also the special issue of *South Atlantic Quarterly* on "World Order: Confronting Carl Schmitt's The Nomos of the Earth," 104:2 (2005).

[16] Odysseos and Petito, *The International Political Thought of Carl Schmitt*, 1; Petito and Odysseos, "Carl Schmitt"; Hooker, *Carl Schmitt's International Thought*, 3.

[17] Odysseos and Petito, *The International Political Thought of Carl Schmitt*, 1.

[18] Koskenniemi, "International Law as Political Theology," 309.

[19] Ibid., 160.

[20] Schmitt, *Nomos of the Earth*, 160.

that Grotius "seriously confuses the concepts of 'war in form' and just war," and that by contrast with Gentili and Ayala, Grotius' arguments are "[s]till completely in line with traditional theological expressions of the Middle Ages."[21] To clarify the incoherent character of Grotius' claims, he explains, "we need examine only how Gentili dealt with this matter in practical terms, as in booty and prize law."[22]

Schmitt thus positions himself very starkly within the debate on determining the "true founder of international law," emphatically choosing Gentili over Grotius on the basis of his supposedly superior definition of war, walking in the footsteps of Gentili's nineteenth-century revivers. In fact, Schmitt celebrated this nineteenth-century revival of Gentili as "a shining example of the history of great thinkers in international law."[23] Ultimately, Schmitt's *Nomos* and Grewe's heavily Schmitt-indebted *Epochs of International Law* associate Gentili with a key shift from medieval warfare to a more humane form of "modern" war. As a result, Gentili has continued to occupy this space in histories of the laws of war in the twentieth century and up to this day as a way to legitimize certain ideas about war and sovereignty, most importantly the idea that limiting war to states is what has enabled the "moderation" and the "humanization" of war, a development seen as characteristic of the "modern" era.

Yet Gentili's influence on Schmitt has attracted remarkably little attention, particularly when compared with the extensive analyses of Schmitt's use of Bodin, Hobbes, and Vitoria.[24] Apart from one monograph on Schmitt which notes in passing that in arguing against the concept of just war "Schmitt's stance is resonant of Alberico Gentili, whom Schmitt often mentions with admiration,"[25] the one exception is a piece by Peter Schröder that examines the influence of Bodin, Hobbes, *and* Gentili on Schmitt. In this piece, Schröder argues that while Schmitt certainly appropriates Bodin's and Hobbes' theories of sovereignty, Gentili is in fact "pivotal" for his argument once he turns to the consequences of these theories for international law.[26] This raises a number of questions: Why did Schmitt turn to Gentili so enthusiastically? How did he use him in developing his influential historical narrative, particularly regarding war? Which elements of Gentili's theory did he perceive as critical, which ones did he leave out, and why? How

21 Ibid., 161.
22 Ibid.
23 Ibid., 158.
24 On Vitoria, see Smeltzer, "On the Use and Abuse of Francisco de Vitoria."
25 Slomp, *Carl Schmitt and the Politics of Hostility, Violence and Terror*, 99. See also p. 105.
26 Schröder, "Carl Schmitt's Appropriation of the Early Modern European Tradition of Political Thought on the State and Interstate Relations," 349.

should we approach the claims about Gentili's importance that we have inherited from his broader narrative?

This chapter argues that Schmitt's influential emphasis on Gentili is not simply a mere inheritance of nineteenth-century narratives. Rather, Schmitt places Gentili at the heart of his history of the development of international law and the evolution of the concept of war in a move that should be understood as part of his broader attempt to defend authoritarian rule. In particular, I argue that placing so much emphasis on Gentili provided Schmitt with a way to make absolutist forms of rule seem normatively desirable. Schmitt came to associate absolutism with the humanization and the rationalization of warfare, not through an analysis of historical facts (which would have made the endeavor difficult) but through a partial interpretation of the works of some "great" thinkers, most importantly Gentili's treatise on war.

Once more, Gentili was brought to center stage in order to defend a particular political project, to legitimize it through the construction of a story of historical continuity. Through this remarkable act of historical invention, Schmitt put forward a seductively straightforward narrative about the emergence of the modern concept of war, of the sovereign territorial state, and of a secular European international law, pointing to Gentili's treatise on the laws of war as the pillar of this new "modern" European order and giving it a normative twist by suggesting it had allowed for the containment or the "bracketing" of the horrors of war. Standing in Schmitt's long shadow, various late twentieth-century IR and IL scholars, from Wilhelm Grewe, Hedley Bull, Kalevi Holsti, and Ian Brownlie to more recent advocates of the "new wars" thesis, have continued to enshrine this mythical account of our past. To tell this story, the chapter begins by providing the main contextual elements within which to read the *Nomos*. It then outlines the narrative Schmitt elaborated about Gentili, highlighting both what he emphasized and what he omitted. The following section seeks to explain what Schmitt was trying to achieve with his historically questionable narrative. Finally, the chapter discusses the legacy of Schmitt's ideas, particularly in the discipline of IR.

6.1   Reading the *Nomos*

While the *Nomos* is occasionally described as Schmitt's "most idiosyncratic book,"[27] it is more commonly considered to be a broad history

---

[27] Müller, *A Dangerous Mind*, 88.

of international law and international relations[28] that provides "the missing substantive historical-juridical backbone" of *The Concept of the Political*,[29] and it has even been claimed – quite compellingly – to be Schmitt's single most important piece of writing, the "dominant summit from which one can see the surrounding lands."[30] In fact, Schmitt himself retrospectively considered it to be his most important work.[31] In many ways, it can be seen as the culmination of his thinking, tying together the different themes of his career into a single narrative whose various elements Schmitt would then continue to deepen until the publication of his last article in 1978.[32]

While the chronology of the writing of the book is still debated, it appears to have been written mainly between 1943 and 1945, building on various themes that Schmitt had already developed in the 1930s, particularly in his essays on war. Schmitt seems to have then reworked the book at some length between 1947 and 1948, editing various parts and possibly adding entirely new passages as well.[33] The book was finally published in 1950. It is, in many ways, a product of its time, written when the German literature on international law turned increasingly toward historical arguments.[34] It pulls together over twenty years of Schmitt's thinking on international law, and it comes across first and foremost as "an elegy on the passing of the Eurocentric world order associated with the sixteenth-century conquest of the New World and the seventeenth-century development of the European territorial nation-state system," or, in other words, the so-called Westphalian order.[35]

At its core, and in a way reminiscent of most international law textbooks, Schmitt's narrative describes the development of international law in three stages: the medieval *Respublica Christiana*, the rise of the territorial state, and the age of discoveries. The *Respublica Christiana* is the foil against which the "modern," "secular" international order arises. The rise of the territorial state marks the sharp break from Church authorities, the separation between religion and secular jurisdiction,

---

[28] Koskenniemi, "International Law as Political Theology," §6.

[29] Teschke, "Fatal Attraction," 180.

[30] Haggenmacher, *Préface*, 2. "Il occupe en effet une position clé au milieu d'une œuvre abondante, tel un sommet dominant d'où se perçoit l'ensemble d'une vaste contrée."

[31] Ibid., 1.

[32] Ibid., 1–2.

[33] Ibid., 26 and 29.

[34] This was the case after 1933 and even more so after 1938. Fassbender, "Stories of War and Peace," 496.

[35] Rasch, "Introduction," 179.

and the rise of the *ius publicum Europeaum* to regulate the relationship between states, replacing papal authority. Finally, the great discoveries are depicted as the event that fostered the consolidation of the *ius publicum Europeaum* by enabling unlimited land-taking overseas and thus acting as a stabilizing mechanism for Europe internally. For Schmitt, "the great merit ... of this system lay in the manner it was able to limit inter-European warfare by conceiving it as a public law status between formally equal sovereigns."[36]

One cannot overemphasize the importance of war and its laws for Schmitt's ideas. The first revival of his works focused on his critique of liberalism, giving his writings on war, that is, "what must count as the neuralgic center of Schmitt's thought, especially in midcareer,"[37] little explicit attention. Since then, the publication of English translations of the *Nomos* (1950/2003) and the *Theory of the Partisan* (1975/2007)[38] have placed war back at the center of Schmitt studies. This unleashed a new series of translations of some of his lesser known tracts: *Forms of Modern Imperialism in International Law* (1933/2011), *The Turn to the Discriminatory Concept of War* (1937/2011), *The Großraum in International Law with a Ban on Intervention for Spatially Foreign Powers* (1939/2011), *Großraum versus Universalism: The International Legal Struggle over the Monroe Doctrine, The International Crime of Aggression and the Principle "nullum crimen, nulla poena sine lege"* (1945/2011),[39] and more recently *The Changing Structure of International Law* (1943/2016), in which Schmitt first explains the concept of the *nomos*, beginning with the statement: "War has become global: its meaning and purpose are nothing less than the *nomos* of our planet."[40] The centrality of war to his worldview, and particularly to his understanding of the history of international law, is undeniable. In fact, he explains forcefully that "the history of international law is a history of the concept of war."[41] In the *Nomos*, Schmitt does not simply understand the concept of war to be at the center of the international legal order; one can actually understand the entire book as a "giant projection of this central problem [defining the concept of war] over a succession of geo-juridical decors

---

[36] Koskenniemi, "International Law as Political Theology," §8.
[37] Teschke, "Carl Schmitt's Concepts of War," 367.
[38] Schmitt, *Theory of the Partisan.*
[39] Schmitt, "Forms of Modern Imperialism in International Law"; Schmitt, "The Turn to the Discriminating Concept of War"; Schmitt, "The Großraum in International Law with a Ban on Intervention for Spatially Foreign Powers"; Schmitt, "Großraum versus Universalism."
[40] Schmitt, "The Changing Structure of International Law," 310.
[41] Schmitt, "The Turn to the Discriminating Concept of War," 31.

spread out over time."[42] Although Schmitt does also discuss the question of spatial order extensively, it is still the debate about the concept of war that provides the "real cohesion" behind the book.[43]

In light of this, it is critical to note what Schmitt understands to be the key shift in the regulation of war in his history of international law and international relations. Put simply, the turning point, for him, was the replacement of the medieval just cause approach with a new, formal concept of war, the just enemy (*iustus hostis*), which placed all legitimate belligerents on equal footing and turned war into a form of "duel," that is, a rule-based procedure for resolving inter-European rivalries. According to Schmitt, this move came to underpin the entire system of warfare during the absolutist age, which he depicts as Europe's golden era, as opposed to the liberal way of war, which he sees as emerging with the rise of Britain and the United States (1890–1918) and a sea-based and economy-driven Anglo-American universalism.[44] It is in this context that his reliance on Gentili becomes quite remarkable.

6.2   Schmitt's Story About Gentili

Schmitt interpreted Gentili's work – focusing overwhelmingly on *De iure belli* – based not only on the original text but also on what nineteenth-century international lawyers had said about it. He worked with the Carnegie reprint and English translation of *DIB*, which contained Coleman Phillipson's introduction. He also makes explicit references to the revival process, mentioning T. E. Holland by name and evoking the formation of "a committee … in Oxford, under the chairmanship of Sir Robert Phillimore" and the ironic fate of its Dutch counterpart, interestingly making no mention of the Italian subcommittee. His citations are made in fairly broad brushstrokes – he often simply cites entire chapters of *DIB* – but he does approvingly bring up Henry Nézard in the text, whose chapter on Gentili in *Les fondateurs du droit international* (1904) drew on the various themes put forward by Gentili's revivers. As we will now see, many of the tropes he developed about Gentili and his importance for international law were, in some way, inflated versions of what nineteenth-century lawyers had read into his work.

---

[42] Haggenmacher, *Préface*, 41. "On pourrait considérer *Le nomos de la terre* tout entier comme une gigantesque projection de ce problème central sur une suite de décors géo-juridiques échelonnés dans le passé."
[43] Ibid.
[44] Koskenniemi, *Gentle Civilizer*, 416.

6.2.1   *Gentili As the Key Thinker of the Modern World*

Having established the exceptional nature of Europe's system of warfare during the absolutist age, Schmitt categorically establishes Gentili as its intellectual originator. According to him,

> It was Gentili who succeeded in creating a new concept of war based on the sovereign state—on the *aequalitas* of the *justi hostes*—rather than on the justice or injustice of the reasons for war offered by either side. This was the decisive turning point, at least in the thinking of the intellectual vanguard at that time.[45]

Schmitt does note the similarities between Gentili and Ayala, sometimes seemingly veering toward presenting Ayala as the more important jurist. He oscillates somewhat awkwardly on this point throughout his discussion of Gentili's Spanish contemporary. Schmitt finds both Ayala and Gentili to be particularly noteworthy because of their reliance on Bodin. He considers that in their writings on war, they built on a number of ideas that were already present in late medieval doctrine, but that they gave these ideas "groundbreaking and world-historical power in international law" through their reliance on Bodin's concept of state sovereignty.[46] "Many medieval authors," he tells us, had promoted the idea that war must be "public" and must be conducted by a "prince or emperor."[47] But they still designated private war as war. By contrast, he explains, "when Ayala and Gentili said that 'war must be public on both sides,' this meant that it must be between states."[48] While, as we have seen, the latter is historically misleading, it makes for an appealingly clean-cut transition from messy medieval wars between various actors to modern rule-based wars between states.

As a result of this move, Schmitt boldly seeks to reappraise the importance of Ayala and Gentili relative to Grotius and Pufendorf, whom he acknowledges as "the two most celebrated and influential teachers of 17th century international law."[49] He is categorical on this point: "By no means were [the latter] pioneers of the new international law among states, least of all the new concept of war. This honor goes to … Ayala and Gentili."[50] Surprisingly in light of the conventional celebration of Grotius for his groundbreaking method, Schmitt claims that he was

---

[45] Schmitt, *Nomos of the Earth*, 158–59.
[46] Ibid., 154.
[47] Ibid., 158.
[48] Ibid.
[49] Ibid., 134.
[50] Ibid.

"no trailblazer" and considers his method to be "a scientific regression" in comparison with "Bodin's conceptual clarity."[51] Compared with Bodin, Ayala, Gentili, and Zouche, "Grotius had a strong general pathos for justice, but no juridical and scientific awareness of the problem."[52] In fact, Schmitt suggests, "[t]his may explain his irrepressible popularity" since "[f]rom the standpoint of propaganda, this served a practical purpose for him, which we do not wish to dispute."[53]

He then hesitates in his assessment of the Spaniard vis-à-vis the Italian. Drawing directly on nineteenth-century debates, he tells us that "John Westlake has asserted that Ayala is more a teacher than a thinker" and that "[g]enerally this is true,"[54] suggesting that Ayala is primarily useful in revealing "the transparent effect of Bodin's legal expertise in general and of his new, state-centered concept of sovereignty in particular."[55] This reliance on John Westlake is fairly ironic considering Westlake was particularly vocal in defending Ayala's conceptualization of war over Gentili's, and if anything, it underlines Schmitt's propensity to cherry-pick the writings of those he cites. In any case, Schmitt then seems to veer in a different direction, emphasizing that Ayala sometimes does show himself to be a real thinker as well, and even calling him, on one occasion, "the founder of the new international law among states" in his discussion of Ayala's reliance on the humanistic jurists Alciatus and Budaeus.[56] Elsewhere, he again designates Ayala, Gentili, and Zouche as "the juridical founders of modern interstate international law," singling them out for having "divorced the question of *bellum justum* proper from that of *justa causa belli*, and made war into a mutual relations between sovereign states."[57] As I discussed in Chapter 3, the overlaps between Gentili and Ayala are indeed striking, with Ayala having defended a position that actually came much closer to the sort of "war in form" that Schmitt has in mind here.

Ultimately, though, Schmitt dismisses the challenge to Gentili's primacy constituted by Ayala, arguing that Gentili's formulations "were much more determined and deliberate than were Ayala's, and had far greater juridical power of form, given their convinced humanistic rationalism and their striking linguistic style."[58] He adds that "Gentili also

---

[51] Ibid., 134–35.
[52] Ibid., 135.
[53] Ibid.
[54] Ibid., 152.
[55] Ibid.
[56] Ibid., 153.
[57] Ibid., 124.
[58] Ibid., 159.

presented these formulations in an exceedingly lively manner, with numerous examples from classical antiquity, the Old Testament, and contemporary history,"[59] and that "Henry Nézard was right in saying that Gentili was the first to designate private war as non-war, even though Ayala did so almost simultaneously."[60] As such, Schmitt singles out Gentili as the most important protagonist in his story and notes in passing that "the great historical interest in Gentili is completely understandable."[61]

Through this association of Gentili with a new concept of war, Schmitt attributes two crucial developments to the Italian jurist. First, he singles him out for secularizing both the concept of war and international law more broadly. Here, Schmitt blows up the nineteenth-century association of Gentili with the secularization of international law and refers to what has since become Gentili's most famous quote along with his definition of war: *Silete theologi in munere alieno!* Schmitt tells us that Gentili utters this exclamation "in order to remove theologians from the discussion of the concept of war and to rescue a non-discriminatory concept of war."[62]

This is a misreading of Gentili's text, as the now famous quote is in fact taken out of its context. As Noel Malcolm rightly notes, Gentili's exclamation pertains to a specific issue – understanding the nature of Ottoman behavior – and by no means entails that theologians should not be concerned with politics at all. Gentili is responding to a specific claim made by the theologians about the Ottomans, which he believes to have been misguided.[63] Nonetheless, Schmitt cites this formulation again multiple times, turning it into something akin to a secularist mantra. He argues, rather boldly, that being "[a] true jurist of this transitional period, Gentili ... formulated the battle cry and coined what may be considered to be the slogan of the epoch in terms of the sociology of knowledge: *Silete theologi in munere alieno!*"[64] And again, serving as the brief introduction to Schmitt's crucial third chapter on land

---

[59] Ibid.
[60] Ibid.
[61] Ibid.
[62] Ibid.
[63] As Malcolm explains, "[i]n this context, the phrase does not really bear all the significance that later interpreters of Gentili have tried to give it; 'in munere alieno' here does not mean the whole business of political theory or just war theory, but refers rather to the sort of political knowledge, about the true nature of Ottoman behaviour and Ottoman policy – which, once properly taken into account, would show up the inadequacy of one particular set of claims that the theologians made." Malcolm, "Alberico Gentili and the Ottomans," 138.
[64] Schmitt, *Nomos of the Earth*, 121.

appropriation in Part II on "The Land Appropriation of a New World": "The new European international law began with Gentili's entreaty that theologians should remain silent with respect to the question of just war: *Silete theologi in munere alieno!*"[65]

Echoing some contemporary narratives, Schmitt thus draws a very sharp line between the "theologians" and the "humanists," and correspondingly between medieval and modern international law, warning that "[b]y no means should [Vitoria] be associated intellectually with the likes of Balthazar Ayala, Alberico Gentili, or Richard Zouche, all of whom, being jurists of international law, eschewed theological arguments."[66] Schmitt's treatment of Grotius vis-à-vis Gentili on this front is once again instructive. Gentili is a "primarily true jurist" who "refers frequently to Vitoria without appropriating his arguments in any systematic way."[67] Schmitt reiterates the cleavage: "In contradistinction to the theologians, Gentili is too much the secular jurist."[68] Grotius, however, "is a different matter."[69] Indeed, Schmitt tells us, "[h]e also distinguished himself from theologians, but he was inclined to use their arguments,"[70] thus leaving him, for Schmitt, with a foot in the Middle Ages.[71] As we saw in Part I, it is a real stretch to draw such a sharp line between the two and, along with it, a wedge between the medieval and the modern periods. While Gentili's argumentative style was indeed different from that of theologians like Vitoria, he nonetheless drew heavily on canon law and theological writings and considered the *ius gentium* and the *ius naturale* to be the expression of divine will, so he can hardly be understood to have "secularized" international law in the broad sense of the term. In fact, it is now well established that the idea of the sudden secularization of international law by early modern Protestant jurists is very much a nineteenth-century myth.[72] Here Schmitt was building on

---

[65] Ibid., 126.
[66] Ibid., 110.
[67] Ibid., 116.
[68] Ibid.
[69] Ibid.
[70] Ibid.
[71] Schmitt approvingly cites a certain Paulo Manual Merea, "who rightly says that Grotius (*volens, nolens*) remains within the tradition of the scholastic Middle Ages." Ibid., 160, n. 13.
[72] As Haggenmacher reminds us, "Gentili's position is Protestant especially through its lack of precision: it deliberately identifies *ius gentium* with *ius naturale*, both being in turn an expression of divine will – which, incidentally, makes it a rather unfortunate choice as a 'secular' conception, despite Gentili's often quoted sentence reminding theologians to stay within their bounds." The idea of an "enlightened and secularized natural law theories of Protestant jurists, in opposition to the scholastic and obscurantist 'casuistry' of Catholic theologians" is very much an "all too simple nineteenth-century cliché." Haggenmacher, "Grotius and Gentili," 170.

elements of the nineteenth-century myth and streamlining them into a powerful but grossly anachronistic story.

Second, and relatedly, Schmitt associates this new, secular concept of war to the emergence of the concept of the state in a striking manner. He is adamant about the very close link between the two and even makes the shift in the concept of war appear as the more important of the two developments: "It must be remembered that the historical significance of the modern state consists in its having ended the whole struggle over *justa causa*."[73] The "historical and intellectual accomplishment of the sovereign decision," according to Schmitt, was to designate an entity that could "decide authoritatively on all the obvious, but impenetrable questions of fact and law pertinent to the question of *justa causa*."[74] Tying this to the secular turn, Schmitt tells us that "[t]he state was established as the new, rational order, as the historical agency of detheologization and rationalization" and that "[t]he first stage of its juridical self-consciousness was attained in the thinking of two jurists: Bodin and Gentili."[75]

The importance Schmitt assigns to Gentili is remarkable, as are the analytical approximations and presentist back-projections that characterize his argument. He insists that what Gentili and Ayala – "humanist jurists" according to him – meant when they stated that war on both sides must be conducted by "princes" was that "it must be fought by sovereign territorial states."[76] This echoes the conceptual slips of the late nineteenth century between "sovereigns" and "sovereign states" and, again, it is quite obviously anachronistic, as the concept of the "sovereign state" in the modern sense did not emerge until at least half a century after the publication of *DIB*,[77] as did its modern territorial conceptualization.[78] Yet Schmitt attempts to drive the point home in a very forceful manner:

Everything that can be said about the legitimacy of state wars lay in this new concept of "state," a non-public war is a non-state war. Not only was it illegitimate; it was no longer war in the sense of the new international law. It could be anything else—rebellion, mutiny, breach of the peace, barbarism, and piracy— but not war in the sense of the new European international law.[79]

---

[73] Schmitt, *Nomos of the Earth*, 157.
[74] Ibid.
[75] Ibid., 159. Schmitt thus casts Ayala aside entirely.
[76] Ibid., 158.
[77] Hobbes being conventionally considered as the turning point in thinking about "the state" in the abstract terms that underpin the concept of the "sovereign state." See most notably Skinner, *Visions of Politics*.
[78] See notably Branch, *The Cartographic State*.
[79] Schmitt, *Nomos of the Earth*, 158.

Schmitt thus seamlessly weaves together a remarkably coherent and seductively simple story about the emergence of the concept of non-discriminatory war, of the sovereign territorial state, and of a secular European international law. Our modern world, we are tempted to believe, sprung almost entirely formed from the fertile mind of a Bodinian Gentili.

There is also a strong normative element to Schmitt's narrative about this key shift toward modernity. Compared with the "wars of annihilation" of the past, "wherein the enemy is treated as a criminal and a pirate," the new, modern and European form of war "signified the strongest possible rationalization and humanization of war."[80] In other words, what can be semi-satisfactorily translated as a "bracketing"[81] of war "was achieved for 200 years."[82] This, for Schmitt, was the great moral achievement of the state, one which he believed to be deeply underappreciated in his own time: "All definitions that glorify the state, and today no longer generally are understood, hark back to this great accomplishment, whether or not they later were misused and now appear to have been displaced."[83] Glorifying the state, allowing it to tower over all other forms of organization and monopolize the right to use force, is what allowed Europeans to tame war, to make it less inhumane. And since Gentili is the presumed originator of this way of regulating war, this is where he emerges – again, in remarkably anachronistic fashion – as an avant-garde humanitarian.

6.2.2   Glossing Over the Pandora's Box of the Pirate

As Schröder points out, what is particularly striking in Schmitt's use of Gentili in the *Nomos* is that while Schmitt extolled the qualities of Gentili's concept of war, he "flatly denied and deliberately ignored" the "crucial ambiguity of Gentili's notion of the pirate."[84] In *Nomos*, Schmitt

---

[80] Ibid., 142.

[81] As Schröder explains, "it is admittedly difficult to render the German 'Hegung des Krieges' into English. The suggestion by G.L. Ulmen to translate this all-important concept as 'bracketing of war' does not fully do justice to the inherent richness of the German noun 'Hegung' which is derived from the verb 'hegen', which has up to twelve meanings. [...] The second of these [meanings] is relevant for Schmitt's use of 'Hegung des Krieges', which in my view is best rendered as 'circumscribing war' and backed by the explanations in Grimm's *Wörterbuch*." Schröder, "Carl Schmitt's Appropriation of the Early Modern European Tradition of Political Thought on the State and Interstate Relations," 359, n. 40.

[82] Schmitt, *Nomos of the Earth*, 120–21.

[83] Ibid., 142.

[84] Schröder, "Carl Schmitt's Appropriation of the Early Modern European Tradition of Political Thought on the State and Interstate Relations," 367.

barely mentions Gentili's use of the concept of the enemy of mankind and his reliance on the figure of the pirate. This is surprising for three reasons. First, Schmitt talks about the political use of the figure of the pirate on a number of occasions in the *Nomos*, particularly to denounce the fact that Britain and the United States are treating their legitimate enemies like pirates and thus undermining the entire system of "war in form."[85] Second, by the time he was writing the *Nomos*, Schmitt had already engaged in a written debate with Hersch Lauterpacht on the malleability of the concept of piracy,[86] and on its political use by the Allies to treat German submarine operators as criminals.[87] Third, he would come to discuss the figure of the pirate extensively in some of his other works, most notably in his *Theory of the Partisan*. In fact, since 9/11 and the beginning of the War on Terror, there has been a surge of interest in the concept of the enemy of mankind embodied by the figure of the pirate, and much of it draws directly on Schmitt's writings.[88]

As I argued in Chapter 3, not only is the notion of the pirate "an incredibly charged political tool" for Gentili,[89] it is in fact one of the two pillars of the way he elaborates his famous concept of war, the other being, of course, the limitation of the right to war to "princes." Schmitt's silence on this front is thus doubly striking. He does note that pirates were not always considered "enemies of mankind" in the ancient world,[90] and in the case of Ayala, he mentions that "war" was now opposed to a broad sphere of violence that did not only pertain to pirates and brigands: "Everything else was criminal prosecution and suppression of robbers, rebels, and pirates."[91] Schmitt does not pick up at all, here, on what the considerable political implications that making rebels "enemies of mankind" would have had at the time, which was in fact precisely Ayala's intention.[92] He mentions this idea once more in his discussion of Zouche: "Traitors and rebels who pursue war against their princes or their state, and pirates on the high sea have no *jura belli*,"[93] again leaving it at that, with no consideration of the implications

---

[85] See, for instance, Schmitt, *Nomos of the Earth*, 43–44, 65, 122, 124, 153, 174, 309.
[86] Schmitt, "The Concept of Piracy (1937)."
[87] Rech, "Rightless Enemies."
[88] See notably Zolo, *Invoking Humanity*; Heller-Roazen, *The Enemy of All*; Policante, *The Pirate Myth*. Daniel Heller-Roazen is one of the translators into English of the work of Giorgio Agamben, who has heavily contributed to the revival of Schmitt's writings across disciplines.
[89] Schröder, "Carl Schmitt's Appropriation of the Early Modern European Tradition of Political Thought on the State and Interstate Relations," 367.
[90] Schmitt, *Nomos of the Earth*, 44.
[91] Ibid., 153.
[92] See Chapter 3.
[93] Schmitt, *Nomos of the Earth*, 164.

this would have had at the time. Oddly, he makes no similar comment in his discussion of Gentili, despite the fact that it is he who dedicates an entire chapter to the idea that "brigands do not wage war."

Essentially, Schmitt leaves little room for any discussion of the instrumentalization of the figure of the pirate and the concept of the "enemy of mankind" in the early modern period, making it seem as if determining who fell into that dreaded category was not a matter of debate. The juxtaposition of this ellipsis with his extensive engagement with the instrumentalization of that figure in his own time is remarkable. Why would an otherwise well-informed Schmitt say nothing about the importance that these debates on the status of pirates and rebels took in the context of that period, particularly in light of the Dutch Revolt? Why make no reference to Gentili's discussion of the matter, including his adoption of Ayala's stance on rebels, as well as his inclusion of Indians, Turks, and atheists in his "enemy of mankind" category?

It may be that Schmitt was simply not aware of these debates or of Gentili's chapter on the matter. However, this does seem unlikely in light of how prominent this discussion is in *DIB*, which Schmitt cites in both its Latin and its English editions.[94] In addition, it is hard to believe that Schmitt could have written so extensively about the period without any idea of the debates about sovereignty within which Bodin had published what is considered his masterpiece, debates which became ever more pressing with the escalation of the Dutch Revolt. As a result, I wish to suggest here that Schmitt intentionally omitted to discuss this point in order not to endanger his broader narrative. In doing so, I follow Schröder in supposing that Schmitt "deliberately misrepresented and simplified the political and philosophical complexities of the early modern discourse on inter-state relations."[95]

Schmitt's story of the limitation, humanization, and rationalization of war is questionable in a number of respects. A compelling case has been made for why European state warfare was far from "limited" in the absolutist age, in the sense that its "magnitude, frequency, duration, intensity, and costs" were actually magnified over the period.[96] Schmitt's analysis, in other words, "is not based on a concrete analysis of European societies in 1599–1900, and even less on the reality of

---

[94] Ibid., 158–59, ns. 10 and 12.

[95] Schröder, "Carl Schmitt's Appropriation of the Early Modern European Tradition of Political Thought on the State and Interstate Relations," 371.

[96] Teschke, "Carl Schmitt's Concepts of War," 18. This is a different claim from that of eighteenth-century warfare being a form of trial with a lawful verdict, achieved through the victory of one of the sides; see Whitman, *The Verdict of Battle*.

European warfare during that time."[97] The case I wish to make here, however, is that Schmitt also deliberately obscured the extent to which the division between "war" and all other forms of violence was established to legitimize wars of annihilation, not only against uncontroversial criminals but also against inconvenient political enemies. Schmitt may well have found this palatable in itself, but in his celebration of the "golden age" of Europe and its "bracketing" of war, and particularly in his praise of Gentili, he does not delve into the issue at all, letting us believe that the "bracketing" of war came at no cost, simply taking away the rights of those who essentially did not deserve them in the first place.

What makes Schmitt's silence particularly interesting is its juxtaposition with the extensive discussion of the figure of the enemy of mankind as a political tool in his critique of liberal warfare. Indeed, one of Schmitt's key goals in the *Nomos* was to draw "attention to a silent transformation in the concept of war, inaugurated by the war guilt clause in the Versailles treaty,"[98] and the putative reemergence of the "medieval" discriminatory concept of war. Schmitt decried the tendency of the latter to "bring into existence – in fact allow only the existence of – wars on behalf of humanity, wars in which enemies would enjoy no protection, wars that would necessarily be total."[99] In this context, the fact that he decided to remain entirely silent on the politics that animated the struggle over the concept of war in the early modern period is surprising.

Ultimately, in placing Gentili at the heart of his narrative about the humanization of war, the emergence of the state, and the secularization of international law, Schmitt ignored the explicitly exclusionary purpose of Gentili's move, and the controversial violence that his restrictive definition of war sought to legitimize. This omission made his story of the humanization of war in the early modern period both compellingly simple and evidently misleading. However, it appears to have fitted very well with the story he was trying to tell in support of his ideological views, and in light of this proximity, its continued popularity should give us pause for thought.

6.3   Deciphering Schmitt's Instrumentalization of Gentili

Schmitt's intentional effort to shape concepts and traditions as part of his political struggle is no secret. In a famous speech of 1933, he explained:

In the political struggle, concepts and conceptual words are anything but empty sound. They are an expression of sharp and precise elaborate opposites

---

[97] Koskenniemi, "International Law as Political Theology," §10.
[98] Koskenniemi, *Gentle Civilizer*, 418.
[99] Ibid., 419. The reference is to Schmitt, *Nomos of the Earth*, 298–99.

and friend-enemy constellations. Thus understood, the content of world history accessible to our consciousness has always been a struggle for words and concepts. These are, of course, not empty, but energetic words and concepts and often very sharp weapons.[100]

It is thus, as Schröder suggests, "particularly important to clarify Schmitt's use and instrumentalization of these concepts and traditions."[101] Why, then, would Schmitt have placed so much importance on Gentili while purposely ignoring central aspects of his thought? I would like to suggest that Schmitt's use of Gentili can be understood as part of what, some have argued, was an attempt by Schmitt to legitimize his longstanding defense of domestic authoritarianism.

One of the main challenges in interpreting Schmitt's turn to the history of international law and international relations is determining the extent to which his goal was to justify Nazi policies. Benno Teschke, who has offered the most elaborate analysis of this turn, suggests that Schmitt's "reinterpretation of the history of international law during the 1930s and 1940s is bound to the concrete situation of the intellectual and political crisis of legitimacy generated by Hitler's spatial revolution" and that Schmitt "offered the most incisive and comprehensive politico-jurisprudential justification" of the latter through his concrete-order-thinking.[102] In other words, Schmitt developed his story to justify Hitler's spatial revolution and the Nazi wars of conquest – notably by grounding his reinterpretation of Europe's geopolitical history in the practice of land appropriations. This is a compelling suggestion to some extent, as Schmitt was, as mentioned earlier, once perceived as the "Crown Jurist" of National Socialism, a zealous defender of the regime who used his acuity as a legal thinker to justify political assassinations.[103] Yet one must take into account his falling out with the regime in 1936, and the chronology behind the writing of the *Nomos*. Could he still have been defending the regime in the early 1940s, after being lambasted for being a Catholic and a two-faced opportunist and eventually being demoted from his position as *Reichsfachgruppenleiter*

---

[100] This is from his inaugural speech at the University of Cologne; see Schmitt, "Reich – Staat – Bund." The original German reads: "Im politischen Kampf sind Begriffe und begrifflich gewordene Worte alles andere als leerer Schall. Sie sind Ausdruck scharf und präzis herausgearbeiteter Gegensätze und Freund-Feind-Konstellationen. So verstanden, ist der unserem Bewusstsein zugängliche Inhalt der Weltgeschichte zu allen Zeiten ein Kampf um Worte und Begriffe gewesen. Das sind natürlich keine leeren, sondern energiegeladene Worte und Begriffe und oft sehr scharfe Waffen."

[101] Schröder, "Vitoria, Gentili, Bodin," 371.

[102] Teschke, "Fatal Attraction," 187.

[103] Schmitt, "Der Führer schützt das Recht."

(Reich Professional Group Leader)? And could this also have been the case when he was reworking the manuscript in 1947–48, long after the regime's defeat?

The extent to which Schmitt endorsed and justified the Nazis is widely debated, as are the reasons why he was willing to associate himself with them in the first place. Some suggest that Schmitt was indeed a merciless opportunist who did not share the ideological vision of the regime,[104] while others have made a strong case for why Schmitt was ideologically predisposed to support the Nazi regime, pointing to his anti-liberal legal writings and his vehement anti-Semitism.[105] Perhaps tellingly, even historians who speak of Schmitt in laudatory terms point to the significant degree of continuity in his writings from the 1920s onward,[106] rejecting the suggestion that Schmitt was moved merely by opportunistic motives.[107] In the analysis that follows, I suggest that Schmitt's use of Gentili can be understood as part of Schmitt's consistent defense of domestic authoritarianism. While he may not have explicitly been actively trying to legitimize Hitler's regime and its policies, he defended its abstract form, consistently with his unwavering personal ideology.

Schmitt's turn to the history of international law and international relations is best assessed in the context of his broader works. Importantly, it followed a long period focused on constitutional law, peaking with his involvement in the debates over Article 48 of the Weimar Constitution on executive government by emergency decrees. In his engagement with the issue of constitutional crises, Schmitt developed his political decisionism, according to which such a crisis required "an extra legal and eminently political decision by a single authority for the reassertion of order, grounded in the state's right to self-preservation."[108] His political decisionism was a fierce attack on legal positivism, which he considered grounded in norms that applied

---

[104] Bendersky, *Carl Schmitt, Theorist for the Reich*, 195–242; Schwab, *The Challenge of the Exception*. See also Fassbender, "Carl Schmitt (1888–1985)."

[105] Dyzenhaus, *Legality and Legitimacy*, 85–101; Scheuerman, *Carl Schmitt*.

[106] Haggenmacher describes Schmitt as "one of the most eminent masters of German juridical thought in the twentieth century," discusses the "beauty" of his texts, and suggests that Schmitt was simply turned into a scapegoat after 1945 in light of his brief Nazi period. The latter claim is hard to square with the fact that Schmitt remained notoriously unrepentant about his involvement with the regime after 1945. Haggenmacher, *Préface*, 2, 17, and 42.

[107] Ibid., 13. "Malgré les nouvelles directions qu'elle prenait, sa pensée restait ainsi essentiellement continue par ses options fondamentales," as opposed to constituting "un pamphlet de circonstance venant aplanir la voie des chars allemands."

[108] Teschke, "Carl Schmitt's Concepts of War," 377.

only under normal circumstances and were thus incapable of dealing with situations of emergency. However, in the 1930s, Schmitt switched strategy. He turned to international law and international history in an attempt to rewrite the history of international law as an anti-liberal tract.[109]

Schmitt's *Nomos* is a fascinating case of the attempt to build a picture of history based largely on thinkers, cherry-picking their works to achieve the desired result. For all its "scientific" veneer, the *Nomos* is an "eminently personal" work based less on rigorous historical investigation than on intuitions stemming from Schmitt's own life.[110] The debates he is genuinely interested in are not those of the early modern period but those of the twentieth century. The Glossarium, his personal journal, sheds much light on the link between the themes raised in the *Nomos* and the contemporary concerns that are at stake in Schmitt's historical narrative.[111] Most explicitly, Schmitt experienced the treatment of Germany, defeated in both world wars, as a personal tragedy.[112] He would denounce it as a misguided shift away from the established order of things and continue to defend the validity of "nondiscriminatory war" and of authoritarian forms of government. This is the context within which one can better understand his use of Gentili.

The *Nomos*, it is clear, "is not at all derived from what takes place in the international social world."[113] As I noted earlier, Schmitt's narrative about the evolution of the concept of war has little to do with reality. He is nostalgic about what he depicts as a period of absolutism that constituted Europe's golden age, "an imaginary period somewhere before the Revolution when wars were supposedly waged as 'cabinet wars' in a restrained way between adversaries that regarded each other as *justus hostes*."[114] Unable to turn to the historical facts in order to tell his story, he instead proceeds "at the level of a de-contextualized interpretation of a selection of political theorists, eclectically mobilized to construct an ideal-type of absolutism and the attendant *ius publicum*."[115] This ode to Europe's absolutist age, however, was not merely meant to celebrate a past that was putting the present to shame; it could also help legitimize an absolutist form of government within Schmitt's contemporary context. The *Nomos* is thus grounded in "a political theology conceived in

---

[109] Ibid., 378.
[110] Haggenmacher, *Préface*, 41.
[111] Ibid., 40.
[112] Ibid.
[113] Koskenniemi, "International Law as Political Theology," §22.
[114] Koskenniemi, "The Epochs of International Law," 749.
[115] Teschke, "Fatal Attraction," 197.

support of domestic absolutism."[116] Schmitt relies on the notion of the *nomos* to give "the impression of describing a 'concrete order'" when in fact "he is simply describing the logical corollaries of a theory of domestic absolutism."[117]

Bodin and Hobbes provided useful sources, of course, particularly once Schmitt had stripped their arguments of the elements that did not suit him.[118] In the case of Hobbes, for instance, Schmitt draws on the figure of the Leviathan, the strong sovereign able to counteract the inherently crooked tendencies of man, but he conspicuously ignores the foundational importance that Hobbes attaches to the social contract as a source of legitimacy for state power.[119] He interprets Hobbes merely as a decisionist, a precursor to his own approach, even though Hobbes' insistence on the importance of the contract – and thus of the individual as a bearer of rights – in fact "supplies a premise for any liberal political theory."[120] Sir Robert Filmer, one of the most prominent defenders of absolutism who drew heavily on Bodin for his theories, had in fact strongly criticized Hobbes for his contractual approach, which he saw as a way to undermine both divine right and secular royal absolutism.[121] Schröder suggests that Schmitt could coopt Filmer's criticism, but that he "knew that absolute authority could no longer reasonably be argued for by reference to thinkers like Filmer or Bossuet."[122] It is thus not entirely surprising that in his eventual turn to international law and international relations, and in his attempt to tell the story of the changing concept of war, Schmitt ended up turning to Gentili, a key

---

[116] Koskenniemi, "International Law as Political Theology," §22.

[117] Ibid., §10. This is in line with Schmitt's 1922 dictum that "[a]ll significant concepts of the modern theory of the state are secularized theological concepts." Schmitt, *Political Theology*, 36.

[118] On Hobbes, see especially Schröder, "Carl Schmitt's Appropriation of the Early Modern European Tradition of Political Thought on the State and Interstate Relations," 350–59; Foisneau, "Security As a Norm in Hobbes's Theory of War"; McCormick, "Teaching in Vain."

[119] Schröder, "Carl Schmitt's Appropriation of the Early Modern European Tradition of Political Thought on the State and Interstate Relations," 351–52.

[120] Ibid., 355.

[121] Ibid. As Schröder notes, "in contrast to Filmer, who identifies and exposes it, Schmitt deliberately ignored the individualistic and liberal potential of Hobbes's theory when commenting upon and using it." Ultimately, Schröder continues, "Schmitt polarized the debate and took Hobbes fully in his own camp against the liberal tradition." Ibid., 356. In light of Schmitt's influence on the development of IR through Morgenthau and other German refugees, one might wonder whether this is at all related to IR's tendency to equate Hobbes with "realism" as opposed to "liberalism."

[122] Ibid., 358. Bossuet wrote one of the classic texts on divine-right absolutism in the late 1670s, *Politics Drawn from the Very Words of Holy Scripture*.

precursor of Filmer,[123] who, unlike Hobbes and Bodin, had helpfully written explicitly both about the laws of war and about the great virtues of absolutism.

Whether or not Schmitt had actually encountered Gentili's *Regales disputationes*,[124] his *DIB* is sufficiently anchored in absolutist principles for Schmitt to have been resolutely drawn to him, and to have chosen Gentili as the greatest figure of international law.[125] As I discussed in Part I, Gentili was one of the fiercest proponents of absolutism in late sixteenth-century England, and in his *DIB* he had drawn heavily on Bodin and sought to create a legal framework for war in a way that gave pride of place to an absolutist conception of sovereignty. Crucially, his conception of war allowed almost no exceptions to the indivisible character of sovereignty as put forward by Bodin, and it made no compromises in favor of those who rebelled against their sovereign. Rebels, like pirates and brigands – as Schmitt notes in the case of both Ayala and Zouche without further comment – were enemies of mankind too. Schmitt was quick to link to his own political vision an approach to war that made the justice of the cause dependent entirely on the sovereign's will: Empowered by Bodin's concept of sovereignty, he explains, "any true jurist" would dismiss relativistic claims about the just cause and confront it "with a *decisionist* formulation" [emphasis in original] seeking to establish where the authority to decide lies.[126]

In a way, Gentili's ideas were as ill-suited for their time and place as they were useful for what Schmitt was trying to achieve: attaching normative value to domestic absolutism, by couching it as a form of government that had historically ensured the humanization of warfare. The argument he is able to put forward – one which has endured to this day – is that moving away from the "nondiscriminatory" concept of war would draw us back into the violence of the Middle Ages. Schmitt's narrative of a shift from a medieval to a modern concept of war in the

---

[123] In the sense that Gentili, along with John Conwell, was "chiefly responsible for importing Continental ideas of sovereignty into English constitutional thought." Lee, *Popular Sovereignty in Early Modern Constitutional Thought*, 275. It may also be said that Gentili started a trend of distorting Bodin's ideas within the English debates: Like Gentili, "Robert Filmer, too, used Bodin in a very one-sided way to emphasize an absolutism far more vulgar than anything Bodin had ever formulated." Straumann, *Crisis and Constitutionalism*, 293. For a broader discussion on the use of Bodin by English royalist writers, see Burgess, "Bodin in the English Revolution."

[124] One may at least guess that he knew about them, since he cites Gesina Van der Molen's seminal biography of Gentili, which discusses Gentili's famous defense of absolutism at length.

[125] The same can be said of Schmitt's admiration of Ayala.

[126] Schmitt, *Nomos of the Earth*, 156.

late sixteenth century, enshrined at Westphalia half a century later, is a trope that will be familiar to most IR and IL scholars. And yet, it is crucial to remember that Schmitt had no use for "a meticulous history of war doctrines";[127] instead, he created two ideal types – medieval discriminatory war and modern nondiscriminatory war – and misleadingly identified a profound shift from one to the other in the late sixteenth century through Ayala and Gentili, when in fact the two visions he identified coexisted between the thirteenth and the eighteenth centuries.[128] The peculiar depiction of Gentili as some sort of avant-garde humanitarian, a man concerned with the "bracketing" of war and the limitation of violence for the sake of human welfare, is just one of the liberties Schmitt took in his instrumental engagement with the past.

6.4   The Legacy of Schmitt's Celebration of Gentili's Ideas

Schmitt's take on Gentili is, of course, not the only interpretation of the jurist's writings and of their importance in the history of international law. A more substantive reception of Gentili's oeuvre took off in earnest much later, mostly from the 1980s and originally through the work of Diego Panizza. This later reception has added much nuance to our understanding of Gentili's works, and this book draws heavily on its intellectual fruits. But before this substantive reception came about, Schmitt had already roped in the superficial nineteenth-century reading of the Italian jurist for his own purposes and put forward a story with a life of its own. By crowning Gentili as the great intellectual founder of modern interstate warfare, Schmitt picked up and enhanced the narrative that had been put forward by nineteenth-century lawyers, providing an account of war and modernity that would become particularly influential both in the discipline of IR and in the institutionalized academic subfield of the history of international law that emerged in the 1990s.

Schmitt's narrative about the development of international law did not materialize out of thin air. For one, it was the product of his political theology. Schmitt interpreted political events past and present as part of a great "struggle between Christ and Antichrist in a world whose historical horizon was constituted not by progress but by salvation."[129] It is

---

[127] Haggenmacher, *Préface*, 40. "Or, pour ses fins il n'avait en réalité que faire d'une histoire méticuleuse des doctrines de la guerre."

[128] Ibid.

[129] Koskenniemi, "Carl Schmitt and International Law," 604. For a more detailed analysis of how the *Nomos* is based on "a political theology conceived in support of domestic absolutism," though one that is not explicitly articulated in the text, see Koskenniemi, "International Law as Political Theology."

in this context that he juxtaposed the "public law of Europe" with the
unhinged violence outside the sphere of that civilizational frame. More
broadly, and more importantly for our present purposes, Schmitt's narrative was the product of the political realism that was characteristic
of his own time and place, a worldview centered on the immense value
of statehood and the desirability of a calculated form of internal and
external state-led brutality. One also finds various iterations of these
ideas in the works of Max Weber (1864–1920), Wilhelm Grewe, and,
of course, in IR, Hans Morgenthau (1904–1980).[130] Schmitt's history
of international law and international relations, however, stands out in
terms of the impact it continues to have today – particularly through
its influence on Grewe and since the translation of the *Nomos* – not
only on conventional understandings of the development of the modern
states-system and of international law, but also on narratives about the
evolution of war and its laws.

At the time Schmitt wrote, the elaboration of grand narratives about
the history of modern international relations was not new, nor was it
new for the form of these narratives to be driven by political motives.
The idea of a "states-system" constituted of mutually independent
states that recognized each other's territorial sovereignty had been
"developed by late eighteenth and early nineteenth-century conservative historians" seeking to "present a picture of European public order
that would legitimize their efforts to contain the French Revolution
and undermine the Napoleonic imperial system."[131] These historians,
the "Göttingen" or "German historical" school, plastered this narrative
onto the sixteenth and seventeenth centuries without much respect for
the historical facts, nonetheless inventing a history of the shift from the
"medieval" to the "modern" world that has remained prevalent today
in IR and beyond.[132]

Schmitt's story recycled various elements from the Göttingen narrative but gave them a new twist, in line with his ultimate goal of critiqu-
ing Anglo-American liberalism, particularly regarding its impact on
the conduct of warfare. As I mentioned earlier, the Schmittian claim
about the demise of a "bracketed" way of war, with Gentili as its most

---

[130] Koskenniemi, "The Epochs of International Law," 747.
[131] Keene, *Beyond the Anarchical Society*, 14. As Keene notes, this is not to say that
the entire narrative was false: "Like all good propaganda, the historical concept of
the states-system contained a substantial kernel of truth, but presented in a distorted way." Ibid., 16. See also Devetak, "Historiographical Foundations of Modern
International Thought."
[132] A number of studies have notably undermined the assumption that there was a shift
toward a stark form of absolutism, especially in France, during the early modern
period. See, for instance, Henshall, *The Myth of Absolutism*.

celebrated intellectual architect, hinges on a misrepresentation of history, a myth debunked by various scholars. It was nonetheless picked up almost unaltered and expanded upon by Grewe, who merely brought more nuance to the section of the story on the nineteenth century, which, despite Schmitt's best attempt, clearly could not be presented as a mere continuation of "bracketed" warfare, particularly in light of Napoleon's attempt to conquer the entire European continent. Like Schmitt, Grewe praises Gentili lavishly as the originator of the idea of "war as a duel."[133] Grewe's history of international law has rightly been criticized as a blatant piece of propaganda, a "problematic, even disturbing book."[134] Unlike Schmitt, he had the chance to add an epilogue to it when it was published in 1984, covering the period from 1944 to the present. A notable detail highlighting the rather tendentious character of the narrative is that his brief discussion of World War II makes no mention of the Holocaust, "not even euphemistically."[135]

Schmitt's influential narrative, as echoed and expanded upon by Grewe, has had numerous ramifications in the disciplines of IL and IR. Over the past few decades, Gentili has been regularly invoked as a key thinker of international relations and international law and even celebrated as "the founder of modern thought about international relations."[136] What is described as his "famous diatribe against the theologians" – *silete theologi in munere alieno* – is still used to mark the origin of modern international law.[137] The claim, directly reminiscent of Schmitt, is that Gentili's famous – and, as we have seen, misinterpreted – formulation marks the break between the medieval and the modern age and the beginning of a distinctly modern way of thinking about international law and international relations. For instance, Arthur Nussbaum, in what long remained the main English-language textbook on the history of international law, depicted Gentili as "the originator of the secular school of thought in international law."[138] In his seminal work on the laws of war, *International Law and the Use of Force by States*, on the laws of war, Ian Brownlie celebrates Gentili as "the first writer to develop a system of norms for state relations which was secular and legal in origin."[139]

---

[133] Grewe, *The Epochs of International Law*, 210–13.
[134] Koskenniemi, "The Epochs of International Law," 746.
[135] Ibid., 748.
[136] Forsyth, Keens-Soper, and Savigear, *The Theory of International Relations*, 15.
[137] Koskenniemi, "International Law and raison d'état," 297.
[138] Nussbaum, *A Concise History of the Law of Nations*, 101.
[139] Brownlie, *International Law and the Use of Force by States*, 11.

In IR, one of the earliest texts to latch onto Gentili's credentials, Forsyth, Keens-Soper, and Savigear's *The Theory of International Relations: Selected Texts from Gentili to Treitschke*, is remarkable in its resemblance to both the nineteenth-century narrative put forward in Coleman Phillipson's introduction to *DIB* in the Carnegie translation – in fact, the authors recognize being "heavily indebted" to the *Classics of International Law* series[140] – and the even more inflated Schmittian narrative about Gentili's importance. Gentili is presented as "the founder of modern thought about international relations" because of "his determination to examine the subject from a secular rather than a theological standpoint."[141] And then comes the classic quote and creative extrapolation: "His celebrated cry '*Silete theologi in munere alieno*' – Let theologians keep silence about matters outside their province! – marks Gentili sharply off from his scholastic predecessors and expresses the advent of a new era."[142] More recent contributions have drawn equally strikingly on this myth. For example, Travers Mcleod claims, in *The Rule of Law in War: International Law and United States Counterinsurgency in Iraq and Afghanistan*, that "[t]he present epoch of LOAC [law of armed conflict] dates back to Albericus Gentili's 1598 *De Jure Belli*," citing none other than our English subcommittee member Travers Twiss and drawing on his claim that "Gentilis' pioneering work represented the first attempt to separate the jurisprudence of war from theology."[143] While neither Gentili – nor Grotius for that matter – would ever have thought of himself as a modern jurist attempting to secularize international law,[144] the myth has now grown deep roots and it clearly serves enough of a purpose to be repeated *ad nauseam*.

What could the purpose of this myth be? The most obvious element of it has been the critique of contemporary warfare based on its comparison with practices of the past. This critique has been put forward by scholars with divergent agendas, from liberals to political realists to critical theorists. Perhaps most noticeably, Schmitt's work has been accepted rather uncritically by those who seek to use it as an attack on liberal warfare, particularly – and controversially – in the discipline of IR.[145] This has indirectly given Gentili's thought yet a new context

---

[140] Forsyth, Keens-Soper, and Savigear, *The Theory of International Relations*, 11.

[141] Ibid., 16.

[142] Ibid., 16. Still completely in line with the preexisting myth, the authors conclude that "it is wrong to see Gentili merely as a forerunner of the Dutch writer" because "in several respects Gentili is both clearer and more 'modern' than Grotius."

[143] McLeod, *Rule of Law in War*, 36–37.

[144] Haggenmacher, "Grotius and Gentili," 174.

[145] Teschke, "Carl Schmitt's Concepts of War," 368.

in which to thrive, as the jurist who presumably provided us with a less destructively moralistic approach to regulating warfare. As we have seen, however, this interpretation of Gentili's framework should be taken with a significant grain of salt. And yet, despite the wave of studies on the figure of the pirate and the concept of the enemy of mankind today,[146] and despite the studies that explicitly examine the history of the figure and concept through a Schmittian lens,[147] few scholars have ventured to question Schmitt's interpretation of Gentili. The fact that, in his influential narrative, Schmitt placed so much emphasis on Gentili's conceptualization of war without addressing his seminal use of the concept of the enemy of mankind may well be linked to the broader disjuncture between the study of this concept's history and the study of the history of war and its laws. In Schmitt's story, the unspoken element is that discriminatory war is not at all neutralized – it is simply displaced onto those who cannot claim the title of "sovereign state." Perhaps we should reflect on the fact that the *Nomos* was published in 1950, right before the surge in national liberation struggles and the attempt by imperial occupiers to denounce them as mere criminals against whom no actual "war" could be fought.[148] A war, the reasoning went, could only be fought between mutually recognizing sovereign states. Everything else belonged to "imperial policing" or to the murky, seemingly extra-legal realm of "small wars."[149]

More broadly, the Schmittian narrative about the emergence, development, and eventual collapse of a state-based system of "bracketed war" first elaborated by Gentili appears to be of significant import for works about the changing nature and purpose of war in the international order. Ultimately, Schmitt tells a story about the value of the controlled "anarchy" of this system, one in which the great powers agree to come together to determine the trajectory of the international order, and occasionally to settle their disagreements about limited spatial

[146] Alfert, "Hostes Humani Generis"; Burgess Jr, "Hostis Humani Generi"; Garibian, "Hostes Humani Generis"; Greene, "Hostis Humani Generis"; Thorup, "Enemy of Humanity"; Ambos, "The New Enemy of Mankind."

[147] See, notably, Zolo, *Invoking Humanity*; Heller-Roazen, *The Enemy of All*; Policante, *The Pirate Myth*.

[148] The most notorious case is perhaps France's unwillingness to recognize the Algerian War of Independence as a war, maintaining that it was an "internal problem" instead. It was not until 1999 that the French National Assembly adopted a law to replace the phrase "operations for the maintenance of order in Northern Africa" [*opérations de maintien de l'ordre en Afrique du Nord*] with "Algerian war" [*guerre d'Algérie*] in official state documentation. Grosjean, "La « guerre d'Algérie » reconnue à l'assemblée. Les députés adoptent la proposition de loi officialisant cette expression."

[149] On "imperial policing" and small wars, albeit in the interwar period, see Moreman, "'Small Wars' and 'Imperial Policing'."

claims through relatively contained warfare.[150] This lens, centered on the concept of "anarchy," will of course be familiar to all IR scholars, and most of all to IR realists. In fact, the emergence of "realism" as an IR approach is in no small part "the story of the importation of German traditions of political thinking into an American academic context,"[151] with Morgenthau being the single most famous data point in a broader story of German émigrés shaping the early discipline of IR.[152] And within this broad heritage, one can directly trace the "absolutely central" impact of Schmitt's ideas on Hans Morgenthau and on the wider development of realism in IR.[153] As international lawyers failed to address Schmitt's critiques of their normative systems, the discipline of IR grew into a newly important field by incorporating Schmittian insights into its professional identity.[154]

In particular, IR scholars thoroughly internalized the idea that war became "modern" once the right to wage it became the prerogative of sovereign states who from now on would drop considerations of just and unjust cause and simply consider each other as equals, a development generally associated with Gentili and with the humanization of warfare.[155] This has been developed by two main groups of IR scholars: those interested in the historical trajectory of the international order, and those who seek to establish the specificity of contemporary warfare by contrasting it with the "old wars" of the modern period.

Amongst scholars who seek to analyze the international order in its *longue durée*, one finds, of course, the English School and those who operated within its wider intellectual sphere between the 1950s and the 1980s. These scholars sought to retain both intellectual history and diplomatic history as pillars of the discipline in the midst of the shift toward approaches inspired by economics, and to this day they continue to act as an inspiration or a foil – or sometimes both – for scholars within the subfield of historical IR that developed after the "historical turn" of the early 2000s.[156] As such, they have given many current historical

---

[150] Haggenmacher, *Préface*, 32.

[151] Bell, "Political Realism and International Relations," 9, n. 5.

[152] On this émigré context and Morgenthau's place within it, see Rösch, *Power, Knowledge, and Dissent in Morgenthau's Worldview*.

[153] See most notably Koskenniemi, "Out of Europe," 424. On the intellectual links between Morgenthau, Schmitt, and Grewe, see also Fassbender, "Stories of War and Peace," 507–08.

[154] Koskenniemi, "Carl Schmitt, Hans Morgenthau, and the Image of Law in International Relations," 424.

[155] For some classic examples of the "humanization of warfare" narrative, see Best, *Humanity in Warfare*; Baxter, *Humanizing the Laws of War*.

[156] Bell, "International Relations."

IR scholars their narratives about the development of the international system, as well as a canon of thinkers to analyze and critique. While "international thought" is now a booming intellectual field, with an ever expanding list of relevant authors to examine and a critical eye for dated interpretations, one of the earliest efforts to compile classic texts on international relations, Forsyth, Keens-Soper, and Savigear's *The Theory of International Relations*, took Gentili as its starting point and reproduced the mythical story of his impact almost verbatim: Schmitt's nineteenth-century-inspired story is echoed in their work, with the recurring idea that the most significant function of the modern institution of war was to enable sovereign states to resolve their differences despite the absence of a higher authority. Similarly, Hedley Bull's[157] "understanding of the modern institution of war," as Barry Buzan succinctly summarizes, is that "war is by definition about narrowing the right to use force by giving the state monopoly powers over it."[158] While the English School is of course more famous for its obsession with Grotius, Bull explicitly links this development to Gentili, singling him out as the only "early internationalist" who came to terms with "the idea that is the foundation of later attempts to accept war between states as an institution of international society, that war may have a just cause on both sides, not merely 'subjectively' but objectively."[159]

Beyond the English School, one finds these ideas in the leading works on the history of IR theorizing. In *History of International Relations Theory*, for instance, Torbjørn Knutsen explains that Gentili "approaches the modern notion that only public authorities are entitled to wage war and that only states can be considered such authorities"

---

[157] Bull, *The Anarchical Society*, 186–89. For a further exploration of Hedley Bull's framework, see Pejcinovic, *War in International Society*. Pejcinovic builds on Bull's idea of war as an institution of international society, that is, as a "mechanism for order," and investigates the justifications that have underpinned the legitimization of warfare at different points in time. She focuses on the political justifications for warfare in what she terms the "late medieval" period (though the analysis is mainly on the sixteenth and early seventeenth centuries), the long nineteenth century, and the twentieth century. Curiously in light of Pejcinovic's focus on war as an institution of international society, the history of international law and its role in the regulation of warfare goes virtually unmentioned.

[158] Buzan, "The English School," 135.

[159] Bull, *The Anarchical Society*, 29. In fact, a doctoral thesis from the 1990s, which was edited and published posthumously by Cambridge University Press in 2017 in light of the surging interest in the history of international thought, explicitly sought to give Gentili a more central position within the English School's canon. The author draws on all the usual tropes: *Silete theologi in munere alieno* and the idea of Gentili as a great secularizer of international law, as well as the claim that Gentili was not a mere predecessor to Grotius but in fact was more "modern" than the Dutchman. Vollerthun and Richardson, *The Idea of International Society*, 15–16, 57.

and that he "sketches a distinctly modern outline of interstate relations as an anarchical society."[160] Here one finds the common slippage between "sovereigns," "public authorities," and "states," as well as the association of Gentili with a new, modern world in which international society became an "anarchical society" of sovereign states.

If we dig more deeply into these types of comments, we can see that there is a long tradition within IR of examining the historical relationship between war and international order that further reiterates the Schmittian story. One finds it in the profoundly influential works of Kalevi Holsti,[161] but also within more recent contributions on the modern concept of war, such as Jens Bartelson's *War in International Thought*.[162] Bartelson's narrative is deeply intertwined with the history of international law and of the laws of war,[163] and in its analysis of early modern jurists and of the transition from "medieval" to "modern" war it is unmistakably Schmittian. In drawing on this periodization, either explicitly or implicitly via IR sources such as Morgenthau or Bull, these scholars have unreflectively reproduced a popular but increasingly criticized narrative about the contrast between the "old" type of war – a contained state-to-state affair associated with, seemingly interchangeably, the early modern period, the absolutist eighteenth century, and the writing of Carl von Clausewitz (1780–1831) – and the "new" type of war, a form of conflict characterized by the participation of nonstate actors and associated with the twentieth century and especially with the post-1945 (or sometimes post-1990) era.

This narrative has forced political realism into a moral nostalgia about an absolutist age of "bracketed" war that appears to have never truly existed,[164] and it now thrives amidst the remarkably influential

---

[160] Knutsen, *A History of International Relations Theory*, 71–72.

[161] Holsti, *The State, War, and the State of War*; Holsti, *Peace and War*; Holsti, *Taming the Sovereigns*.

[162] Bartelson, *War in International Thought*.

[163] One of the central purposes of the book is to "freshly assess the transition from war as law enforcement to wars [*sic*] as an armed contest between legal equals" and to understand what was at stake in this transition under a new light (Ibid., 19). While he discusses not only international law but also early modern histories of state formation and the rise of territorial sovereignty, his overarching engagement appears to lie mainly with scholars working on the history of international law; see Ibid., 5–7.

[164] Koskenniemi, "The Epochs of International Law," 749. Some scholars have described the eighteenth century as the age of "cabinet wars" or "wars of princes," emphasizing the importance of pitched battles and of their limited scope. See notably Whitman, *The Verdict of Battle*. However, conflicts such as the War of the Spanish Succession (1701–14) and the Seven Years War (1756–63) dragged on for years, led to what were at the time enormous numbers of casualties, and are often considered

theorizing about the "old wars" and the "new wars."[165] The latter have been heavily criticized from a historical standpoint, with scholars notably debunking the "old wars" trope as an ahistorical, hollow construct;[166] I will not go into the details of their historical critique here, but if anything, the fact that in the original account the historical periods associated with the "old wars" and "new wars" ideal types are so inconsistent should give us pause. It is also striking to note that the main proponents of this narrative almost systematically conflate the question of who had the legal right to wage war – Schmitt's concern – with the question of who actually used force.[167] This has severely muddled the field, for the two are very different questions indeed. While there is an ongoing debate about the monopolization of external violence by sovereign states in practice,[168] much less has been written on the question of when sovereign states became the only entities legally allowed to wage war. The assumption is often that the shift happened in the seventeenth century – the 1648 Peace of Westphalia is the obvious hook to hang this development onto – but considering how much the concept of the sovereign state was yet to change over the course of the eighteenth and nineteenth centuries, as discussed in Chapter 5, the story of how sovereign states came to monopolize the legal right to wage war is likely to be more complicated than that.

The idea that modern war was a rule-based institution that allowed sovereign states to resolve their differences and that excluded nonstate actors from its ambit continues to "profoundly affec[t] our thinking about war and dominat[e], even today, the way policy-makers conceive of national security."[169] Determining the extent to which Schmitt's writings directly came to underpin the development of the "new wars" theory is beyond the scope of this project, but it would be an interesting

---

to have constituted the first "world wars." Whitman acknowledges this catch in his narrative (56) but claims that "it remains the view of most specialists that the eighteenth century was indeed 'an era of limited war' by comparison with previous centuries, and even by comparison 'with almost any other era'," citing a single brief passage from the somewhat dated Weigley, *The Age of Battles*, 168.

[165] See, most notably, Kaldor, *New and Old Wars*.

[166] See, for instance, Berdal, "The 'New Wars' Thesis Revisited"; Newman, "The 'New Wars' Debate"; Heuser, "Misleading Paradigms of War."

[167] Van Creveld, *The Transformation of War*, 41; Kaldor, *New and Old Wars*, 19; Münkler, *The New Wars*, 64.

[168] Tilly, "War Making and State Making as Organized Crime"; Tilly, *Coercion, Capital, and European States, AD 990–1992*; Thomson, *Mercenaries, Pirates, and Sovereigns*. On the continued importance of mercenaries, privateers, and mercantile companies in modern warfare, see, for instance, Colás and Mabee, *Mercenaries, Pirates, Bandits and Empires*; Scheipers, *Unlawful Combatants*; Percy, *Mercenaries*.

[169] Kaldor, *New and Old Wars*, 17.

avenue to explore.[170] In the meantime, what is clear is that his seductively simple story about the emergence of the modern concept of war, of the sovereign territorial state, and of a secular European international law, all tied back to Gentili's treatise on the laws of war, remains remarkably influential to this day through the broader influence it has had within the discipline of IR.

What this story does, ultimately, is to confer significant inherent normative value to the modern sovereign state and to an international system that gives this particularly type of polity a legal monopoly over the use of force at the cost of all its competitors, be they indigenous peoples, secessionist groups, or transnational movements. Carefully examining whether this is a desirable state of affairs and what the better alternatives might look like is, again, beyond the scope of this book, but what I hope to have made clear is that we should not simply take it for granted that this is simply the "modern" way of organizing the international system, that it allowed us to limit or "bracket" the destructive character of war, and that the modern sovereign state is, ultimately, a great stabilizing factor in the international order.

6.5   Conclusion

While Gentili was revived in the 1870s, his reputation gradually solidifying amidst a growing pantheon of "founders of international law" over the late nineteenth and early twentieth centuries, his importance in the narrative about the development of modern international law and modern international relations was most clearly enshrined in Carl Schmitt's deeply influential *The Nomos of the Earth*. This chapter has shed light on Carl Schmitt's remarkable reliance on Gentili, on his crowning of the Italian jurist as one of the – if not *the* – greatest thinkers of the modern states-system, and on the extent to which Schmitt squeezed Gentili's thought into a frame of his own making in order to support a politically motivated historical narrative. Through Schmitt's impact

---

[170] As a starting point, Teschke notes that Herfried Münkler's 1992 piece, "Gewalt und Ordnung," constituted an exception in being perhaps the only work that examined Schmitt's war writings during the first Schmittiana wave, and that although this first piece "is restricted to a summary of Schmitt's argument," Münkler's later work, "which introduces the distinction between Old Wars and New Wars, relies on Schmitt's conception of early modern wars as classical state-to-state affairs." Teschke, "Carl Schmitt's Concepts of War," 395, n. 1. Teschke is referring to Münkler, *Die neuen Kriege*, 68, 114. Münkler's work, translated into English as *The New Wars*, forms one of the pillars of the New Wars approach, along with Mary Kaldor's *Old and New Wars*, and Martin van Creveld's *The Transformation of War*. Münkler, *The New Wars*; Van Creveld, *The Transformation of War*.

on the discipline of IR via Morgenthau and the broader internalization of Schmitt's historical account, it has become a commonplace to think that war became "modern" once the right to wage it became the legal prerogative of states and that this happened somewhere between the late sixteenth and the mid-seventeenth century, between the thought of Alberico Gentili and the putative emergence of the states-system at Westphalia.

This final incursion into the reception of Gentili's thought demonstrates the extent to which his canonization and his continued prominence need to be understood in light of the political contexts that drove the receptions of his work. More specifically, it is not just the fact of his canonization that needs to be critically examined, but also the form that his canonization took, and the reasons why some parts of his thinking may have been highlighted whereas others were explicitly omitted. In Schmitt's case, Gentili's pedigree was used to develop and strengthen a historically questionable narrative about the development of the modern states-system and the so-called bracketing of war. Some elements of this story were already present after the nineteenth-century revival, but Schmitt took them in a more definitive direction, giving us what remains one of the most pervasive narratives about the development of the international order in the discipline of IR.

There is no question that Schmitt's historical narrative is deeply flawed. His purpose, anyway, was not to provide a careful and rigorously researched account of the past, but to cherry-pick whatever he needed from famous texts in order to speak to twentieth-century debates. Of course, one could argue that to some extent, this is what incursions into the history of legal and political thought always involve. But Schmitt took it to extremes, and in the case of Gentili, he put forward an interpretation of his writings on war that were clearly tendentious. Claiming that Gentili allowed for war to become more "limited" by only granting the right to wage it to sovereign states was both anachronistic – since Gentili could not have had the modern, abstract concept of the sovereign state in mind – and substantively misguided at best, considering Gentili's approach to war opened up a space of unrestrained violence against those deemed not to have the right to wage war, now considered enemies of all mankind. In Schmitt's narrative, "discriminatory war" only emerged with liberalism, following a long period of "limited war"; but this is without counting the fact that Schmitt's champion of the concept of limited war merely displaced unlimited violence to a realm falling outside a now narrowed-down definition of war. In the system Schmitt puts forward, war between those who recognize each other as sovereign states may be more limited, but any group or polity not recognized as such can be obliterated outside the legal realm of "war" and its rules of conduct. What this system does, without Schmitt ever admitting it explicitly, is support his own obsession with the normative desirability of unbridled state power. It also demonstrates a clear bias in favor of already established states and empires, against whom any resistance is criminalized.

The fact that IR scholars have largely accepted and internalized this narrative should give us pause. To return to Bull's phrasing of what is still a widespread assumption of the discipline, "[w]e are accustomed ... to contrast war between states with peace between states; but the historical alternative to war between states was more ubiquitous violence."[171] Was this truly the historical alternative, though? What should we make of the sphere of violence not legally called "war" that opened up once it was deemed that the latter was an exclusively interstate affair? There has been a recent move in the emerging field of Critical War Studies toward problematizing the ontology of war,[172] grounded on the observation that countless forms of violence are ignored in the study of war in international relations because they do not fit the conventional definition of what "war" is.[173] This is an important point, but these scholars treat the concept of war as an analytical category that can be molded according to their needs rather than as a historical category that has developed contingently to serve specific purposes. What this critical reading of Schmitt and his instrumentalization of Gentili shows is the extent to which the way we have defined war, historically, has shaped our understanding of how the modern world order developed, providing the major narratives that continue to ground our analyses to this day.

---

[171] Bull, *The Anarchical Society*, 178–79.

[172] See most notably Barkawi, "Decolonising War." See also Balibar, "What's in a War?"; Barkawi and Brighton, "Conclusion: Absent War Studies?"; Barkawi and Brighton, "Powers of War"; Sylvester, "War Experiences/War Practices/War Theory"; Holmqvist, "Undoing War"; Nordin and Öberg, "Targeting the Ontology of War." Even *The Economist* has picked up on this issue of ontology: "What Makes It a War?"

[173] This problematization of the ontology of war has also begun to emerge amongst historians and political scientists. For instance, Beatrice Heuser has argued for the concept of war to be adjusted in order to "include the mass-killing of non-combatants [including by their own state] and to put more emphasis on civil wars and insurgencies," while Wimmer and Min argue that the change in the institutional form of states – from empire to nation-state – is a major cause of war, and that this is overlooked by the existing quantitative literature on war because the latter "takes the independent nation-state as the self-evident unit of analysis and largely excludes other political types from consideration." Heuser, "Misleading Paradigms of War," 4; Wimmer and Min, "From Empire to Nation-State," 867.

Conclusion

This book has sought to question one of the most foundational narratives of International Relations and International Law: that war became "modern" once the right to wage it was restricted to sovereign states, that this restriction was put in place in order to limit the horrors of warfare, and that this development hinged in large part on Alberico Gentili's 1598 *De iure belli*. In order to deconstruct this influential narrative, I have critically examined its emergence and evolution, focusing on its intellectual anchor, Gentili. The book has put forward three sets of claims.

First, I have argued that far from being an avant-garde humanitarian tract, Gentili's famous treatise on the laws of war can be understood as the work of an absolutist – one deeply influenced both by Bodin and by the reason of state tradition – who was attempting to elaborate, popularize, and defend a controversial approach to war and its laws. Gentili dedicates a significant portion of *DIB* to those who cannot wage war and to how they ought to be dealt with by sovereigns if they attempt to do so. He claims that a conflict between an established sovereign and a group of individuals that cannot claim – or is actively denied – the same status is not a "war" proper. In this case, considerations of "just cause" come back under a new guise. Instead of raising questions about which party to the conflict has moral superiority on its side, the "just cause" systematically rests with the established sovereign as the only legitimate belligerent in the conflict. Gentili applies this exclusionary logic to a heterogeneous set of groups: pirates, brigands, atheists, the Turks, and, crucially, rebels, delving into the debates of his time about the locus of sovereignty in a context in which the concept of the sovereign state was not yet on the intellectual map. He argues that these groups fall under what he (wrongly) considers to be a well-established legal category with a traceable legacy in Roman law and a clear set of implications: that of enemies of mankind, or *hostis humani generis*. In making this argument, Gentili created a space for a type of international violence that was not "bilateral" and based on mutual respect but that instead served a purpose of punishment and law enforcement, obeying principles reminiscent of the medieval, discriminatory logic of just war that was supposedly left behind with the advent of the modern states-system. This remarkable exclusionary move is not merely present in his theory of the laws of war – it is one of its very foundations.

Second, I have shown that the conventional narrative about Gentili as the father of the modern laws of war and as an avant-garde humanitarian only emerged in the late nineteenth century. This marked the beginning of the process through which Gentili would turn into a cipher for a particular view of international law and modernity, and it came out of a very specific context. In addition to the personal and institutional factors that shaped the revival of Gentili, the form that his revival took should be understood in light of the political factors that made harnessing Gentili's name more or less useful based on the story that could be crafted about the Oxford-based Italian jurist. If the Italian context saw Gentili couched as a national hero as part of the Risorgimento and as the "father of international arbitration" thanks to Pietro Sbarbaro, the work of the English subcommittee, which would ultimately have a much greater influence on the international memorialization of Gentili, took a different turn. The revival of Gentili in England, driven by a group of men who were heavily involved in the codification of the laws of war and in the legislation of empire, came to echo their own concerns and became centered on his definition of war. At a time when they were seeking to limit the legal right to wage war only to entities that recognized each other as sovereign states, turning to Gentili allowed them to claim that their project was simply the continuation of a long-established "modern" way of thinking about war and its regulation. Of course, this was only possible through a fair amount of creative misinterpretation: They understood "public" to designate "sovereign states," they dismissed the critiques of Gentili as an absolutist, and they omitted to mention the exclusionary side of his framework for regulating war. Through this skewed reading of Gentili, they planted the seeds of what would become the narrative we now know.

Excavating the process through which Gentili was canonized in the late nineteenth century highlights the extent to which the belated triumph of the modern sovereign state in the laws of war – and in international law more broadly – was obscured by deeply influential myths about the continuities between early modern and late nineteenth-century international law. Once these myths are seen as myths, it becomes essential to look beyond the now well-established hierarchy between those deemed civilized and those deemed uncivilized in the context of late nineteenth-century international law, and to examine how central a narrowed-down understanding of sovereignty became at that point, particularly with respect to the regulation of warfare. The idea of war as the legal prerogative of sovereign states was developed within the European context, but it also appears to have had an underappreciated impact in the colonial one. As a preliminary foray into this issue, I have begun to show the extent to which sovereign statehood came to play an unprecedented role in determining how the laws of war were to be applied, highlighting the ramifications of this hierarchical trope for the conduct of conflicts conceptualized as "small wars." Between 1860 and 1874, a bifurcated system emerged: The newly codified laws of war would now exclusively apply to conflicts between mutually recognized sovereign states, while all other conflicts explicitly fell into a legal vacuum. Over the same period, a parallel literature emerged on how to conduct such conflicts: the "small wars" manuals that eventually came to form the basis of contemporary counterinsurgency practices.[1] I have begun to show that these developments cannot be understood separately from one another: They all happened as part of a single shift toward a concept of war based on the supremacy of the modern sovereign state.

Finally, I showed how the nineteenth-century story of Gentili's importance was picked up, accentuated, and ultimately reshaped by Carl Schmitt, who, in *The Nomos of the Earth* (1950), turned to Gentili with an agenda of his own. Schmitt's remarkable celebration of Gentili as the most important early modern thinker of the modern states-system – alongside Jean Bodin – has not attracted much attention, and yet it is absolutely central to a broader narrative about the development of war, the modern state, sovereignty, and international law that remains deeply influential to this day. I argued that Schmitt's interpretation of Gentili was, like his interpretation of other early modern thinkers, based on a highly tendentious reading of Gentili's work, driven first and foremost by Schmitt's involvement in the debates of his time. In concentrating so much power into Gentili's *DIB*, Schmitt's main purpose was to weave a seductively simple story

---

[1] One can indeed draw a direct line from the writings of late nineteenth- and early twentieth-century thinker-practitioners, such as C. E. Callwell, Hubert Lyautey, and Joseph Gallieni (along with the earlier Thomas Bugeaud), through to David Galula, who wrote one of the most famous counterinsurgency manuals based on his experience in Algeria and in other French colonies, and finally to contemporary manuals such as the United States' 2007 Field Manual on Insurgencies and Countering Insurgencies (FM 3-24), which was the first of its kind since the Vietnam War and informed US counterinsurgency operations in Iraq.

about modernity, the rise of the state, and the taming of war in the international system. This historical narrative, then, could form the basis for his defense of domestic authoritarianism and his critique of liberal powers who, according to him, had enabled the return of discriminatory war in the twentieth century. Just like nineteenth-century lawyers, Schmitt had to gloss over the discriminatory side of Gentili's treatise on the laws of war in order for it to fit his story, a rather remarkable omission considering his own extensive engagement with the political usages of the figure of the pirate as an enemy of mankind in other contexts. Ultimately, his narrative traveled all the way down to us through the likes of Wilhelm Grewe in IL and Hans Morgenthau in IR,[2] providing us with a misleading understanding of how and when the "modern" concept of war emerged.

What does this leave us with? If we are to take full stock of these findings, we need to consider them in light of broader discussions about canonization, periodization, and the regulation of warfare in the international system. As far as canons are concerned, I hope this story will contribute to sounding the alarm in terms of how the disciplines of IL and IR have engaged with their "great thinkers." We already know that, more often than not, our conventional narratives about these thinkers are not grounded in a rigorous analysis of their writings but in the way nineteenth- and twentieth-century scholars interpreted their work, based on their own personal, social, and especially political agendas.[3] This has led to a new, deeper engagement both with the writings on these thinkers in their context and with the way these writings were later received and interpreted. In IR, as we saw in Chapter 1, a number of works have emerged on specific thinkers who later became part of the IR canon.[4] While these provide important insights, the ad hoc nature of these studies can make it difficult to reflect on this corpus of authors as a whole. This fragmentation is of course partly due to the fact that the IR canon emerged rather haphazardly, especially by contrast to the IL canon that was monolithically enshrined in the *Classics of International Law* collection. In IL, a more coherent literature is emerging on the creation of the discipline's canon in the

---

[2] It is worth specifying that these later scholars did not share Schmitt's absolutist political project; they only adopted the historical narrative it was based on.

[3] Hutchings et al., "Critical Exchange," 389; Bell, "What Is Liberalism?"

[4] See, inter alia, Keene, "The Reception of Thucydides in the History of International Relations"; Easley, *The War Over Perpetual Peace*; Guilhot, "The First Modern Realist"; Bell, "What Is Liberalism?"; Molloy, *Kant's International Relations*; Jeffery, *Hugo Grotius in International Thought*; Keene, "Images of Grotius"; Bain, "Grotius in International Relations Theory."

late nineteenth and early twentieth centuries, when international law became professionalized.[5]

In the most specific sense, this book contributes to these literatures by providing a missing part of the existing canon-making story and by bringing together the sometimes artificially siloed considerations of IR and IL in these matters.[6] I have told the story of the first concrete attempt to widen the pantheon of the "founders of international law," focusing on the early days of the Institut and on the developments that occurred in England, three decades before the take-off of American international law.[7] While James Brown Scott, through his work as the general editor of the Carnegie series on the *Classics of International Law*, obviously played a crucial role in the construction of IL's canon,[8] what this book has sought to provide is the missing, earlier part of the story in the case of Gentili, the first challenger to Grotius for the title of "father of international law." I have shown how Gentili came to be considered as a key figure to include in that series in the first place, and how the narrative about his importance regarding the laws of war developed, before its final enshrinement in 1933 in Coleman Phillipson's introduction to the Carnegie series reedition and translation of *DIB*. I have also explained how, far from being the preserve of the discipline of IL, the narrative about Gentili, the state, and "modern war" traveled to the closely related discipline of IR, with a lasting impact to this day.

This study, however, is not primarily about examining the trajectory of a single canonical thinker; it is about the politics and the consequences of canon-making. In other words, what I have tried to do in

[5] Rossi, *Broken Chain of Being*; Orford, "What Is the Place of Anachronism in International Legal Thinking"; Amorosa, *Rewriting the History of the Law of Nations*; Craven, "Invention of a Tradition"; Nuzzo and Vec, *Constructing International Law*; Somos and Smeltzer, "Vitoria, Suárez, and Grotius." On the rise of the American Institute of International Law and the links between the development of American international law and imperialism in Latin America, see Scarfi, *The Hidden History of International Law in the Americas*.

[6] The reception of thinkers such as Grotius continues to be treated separately in the fields of IL and IR despite the significant amount of overlap between these processes; see, for instance, Bain, "Grotius in International Relations Theory"; Rasilla del Moral, "Grotian Revivals in the Theory and History of International Law." For an attempt to bridge the IL/IR divide in this respect, see Amorosa and Vergerio, "Historicizing the Canon in International Law and International Relations."

[7] This take-off included the foundation of the *American Journal of International Law* (1907), of the Carnegie Endowment for International Peace (1910) – of which Elihu Root was the president and James Brown Scott the secretary – and of the American Institute for International Law (1912), cofounded by the same James Brown Scott.

[8] As I discussed earlier, this has been the focus of the IL literature thus far. See, for instance, Amorosa, *Rewriting the History of the Law of Nations*; Somos and Smeltzer, "Vitoria, Suárez, and Grotius." An important exception is the work of Martina van Ittersum on Grotius, "Hugo Grotius: The Making of a Founder of International Law."

this book is to show what is at stake in critically examining the canon. We may well be sounding an alarm when we warn fellow scholars that conventional understandings of great thinkers are questionable and when we painstakingly historicize reception processes to show where the dubious interpretations came from, but why exactly this should be alarming to anyone other than the historicists among us is rarely fleshed out. Yet this is not merely a matter of niche interest in the history of political thought. It is part of a broader conversation within the humanities and the social sciences about the politics of disciplinary canons and the possibility for disciplinary reinvention. For a long time, canons were both ubiquitous and unquestioned. We now know that more often than not, a disciplinary canon tells us more about the agenda of those who dominated the discipline when the canon was established than about the intrinsic greatness of the works at hand. As such, as long as we uncritically accept old interpretations of canonical texts, we are bound not only to have little understanding of what insights these "great thinkers" might potentially provide us with, but also – and much more importantly – we are condemned to follow the political agendas of their interpreters and the deceptive historical narratives these interpreters left us with.

In spite of this, some canons continue to exist relatively undisturbed, notably in disciplines like IR and IL. They live on in our collective consciousness, providing us with many of our underlying assumptions about how the world works. They are the invisible anchor of our dominant theories; they typologize the different worldviews that are available to us as scholars. In this context, telling the history of how our canon came about is a powerful way to subvert some of the most deep-seated assumptions and categories of our discipline in order to make space for new discussions to emerge. When we map out the processes through which these various men came to be seen as quintessential theorists of the core concepts in our discipline, when we excavate the genealogies we inherited and examine them with newly critical eye, we open the way for challenging these narratives and for writing our own more accurate ones about where we have come from and where we might be going.

In the case of Alberico Gentili, what is most importantly at stake is the story we tell about the emergence of the "modern" concept of war. Many of the old assumptions of the disciplines of IL and IR have been shaken up, especially in the aftermath of the debunking of the myth of Westphalia.[9] Yet some assumptions remain remarkably untouched,

---

[9] Osiander, "Sovereignty, International Relations, and the Westphalian Myth"; Teschke, *The Myth of 1648*; Beaulac, "The Westphalian Model in Defining International Law."

notably around the regulation of war in the international system. The difference between the putatively "medieval" and "modern" concepts of war is expressed in the literature through a dizzying array of terms: Scholars speak of an opposition between, on the one hand, "just war," "medieval war," or "discriminatory war" in the Schmittian sense, and, on the other hand, "modern war," "regular war," "nondiscriminatory war," "bilateral war," "limited war," "normal war," "legal war," or "war in due form."[10] Whichever terms are used, the opposition is always the same, and the narrative is always broadly one of a shift from the medieval to the modern, and of a move away from uncontrollable violence in the international system.

Regardless of the exact linguistic terms they choose, what scholars of international relations and international law draw on when they uncritically rely upon this narrative can be divided into four interrelated claims. The first concerns the nature of war: War became "modern" because the right to wage it was restricted to sovereign states. The second is normative: This was done in an effort to limit the horrors of warfare. The third concerns chronology: This restriction happened in the course of the seventeenth century, following the emergence of a new framework for regulating war in Gentili's *DIB* of 1598 and alongside the presumed emergence of the states-system at Westphalia fifty years later. The fourth is an assertion of constancy: There is a significant amount of continuity between this way of regulating war and the laws of war we have today, that is, the Geneva Conventions of 1949, the basis of which we inherited from nineteenth-century international lawyers. What this book suggests is that almost every part of this is wrong and that we need to dramatically rethink our historical narrative about "modern war" and its regulation.

While it may be tempting to associate the restriction of the right to wage war to sovereign states with Gentili's *DIB* and with the Treaties of Westphalia, there are ample reasons to be skeptical of this move. As this book has shown, the part about Gentili is clearly a retrospective construction of history that took many liberties with the actual text and with assumptions about its impact in practice. The Italian jurist's *DIB* is hardly a compelling chronological marker of this crucial legal shift, and it is only known to us as such because periodizing the emergence of "modern war" in this way was useful to lawyers centuries down the

---

[10] Somewhat confusingly, the latter also underpins much of the current literature on "just war" theory that does away with questions of cause and focuses instead on the *ius in bello*, that is, the conduct of warring parties assuming only sovereign states possess the legal prerogative to wage war.

line. This is a classic problem with telling the history of international relations and international law through a series of great men whose thought we tend to retrofit into categories of our own making. And yet, telling history in this way is incredibly attractive when one is trying to make sense of the chaos of the past.

Canonical figures play a crucial role as chronological markers: They allow us to periodize. This is at least partly the source of their tremendous popularity. For nineteenth-century lawyers and even more importantly for Carl Schmitt, Gentili was the most important canonical marker used to establish the divide between medieval and modern war, and at the heart of their story lies the emergence of an international order centered around the concept of the sovereign state. Yet once we shed light on the shortcomings of their narrative constructions, we are bound to reconsider the validity of their broader periodization as well. In fact, the recent interest across history, IR, and IL in periodization as such, along with the critiques of both the medieval/modern divide and the centrality of the concept of the sovereign state in metanarratives about the development of the international order, dovetail neatly with the story this book has sought to tell.

Ten years ago, one scholar rightly noted that periodization was one of "the most fundamental and most underestimated questions of historiography of international law."[11] Since then, a number of works have emerged on this question, drawing our attention to the power that lies behind the necessary but never neutral division of the past into delineated historical periods.[12] Similar concerns have bubbled under the surface in IR for some time, with scholars recently picking up older reflections on the use of history,[13] casting a critical glance on conventional benchmark dates,[14] and addressing the politics of periodization head-on.[15] Together with other landmark works on periodization in the field of history,[16] this literature encourages us not only to reevaluate the soundness of existing periodizations in general, but also to be especially skeptical both of the conventional medieval/modern divide and of the association of the "modern" period with the concept of "state sovereignty."

[11] Digelmann, "The Periodization of the History of International Law," 998.
[12] Lesaffer, "The End of the Cold War as an Epochal Event in the History of International Law?"; Rasilla del Moral, "The Shifting Origins of International Law"; Rasilla del Moral, "The Problem of Periodization in the History of International Law."
[13] Walker, "History and Structure in the Theory of International Relations," esp. 169–72.
[14] Buzan and Lawson, "Rethinking Benchmark Dates in International Relations"; Carvalho, Leira, and Hobson, "The Big Bangs of IR."
[15] Guillaume, "Historical Periods and the Act of Periodization."
[16] See especially Kathleen Davis' much-discussed *Periodization and Sovereignty*.

In general, the distinction between the medieval and the modern is the "most powerful (and suspicious) epistemic rupture"[17] that scholars work with across the social sciences and the humanities. For all the critiques of teleological narratives that depict history as a succession of stages, the medieval/modern divide has been exceptionally resilient. There have nonetheless been a number of provocative pushbacks against it: Perhaps the Middle Ages lasted until the late eighteenth century,[18] perhaps we have never been modern at all,[19] perhaps the dichotomy is simply an artificial construct that served as a justification for colonialism and the civilizing mission.[20] Three elements of this discussion are particularly useful here.

The first is that our conventional understanding of the "Middle Ages" stems from categories that were developed much later and served particular political projects, from the enshrinement of a specific, state-based idea of political authority to the justification of European colonialism.[21] The second is that there is definitely much more continuity than was once assumed between the "medieval" and the "modern" worlds.[22] In fact, an increasing number of works point to the late eighteenth or even early nineteenth centuries as the more compelling turning point toward a new, presumably "modern" political era.[23] This harmonizes with what Cary Nederman has called the "continuity thesis," that is, the idea that a more compelling periodization for IR scholars would entail placing the key moments of discontinuity in the twelfth and eighteenth centuries rather than in the sixteenth or seventeenth, "with the period in between constituting a single, continuous historical epoch unbroken by any medieval/modern Great Divide."[24]

The third and final element is that the idea of a great medieval/modern divide became particularly prominent in the nineteenth century,

---

[17] Ingham, "Kathleen Davis," 1436.

[18] This was famously the periodization suggested by the medieval historian Jacques Le Goff. See notably Le Goff, *Faut-il vraiment découper l'histoire en tranches?*

[19] Latour, *Nous n'avons jamais été modernes.*

[20] See the works of, for instance, Kathleen Biddick, Robert M. Stein, Michelle Warren, and John M. Ganim. These scholars generally take up Dipesh Chakrabarty's cue that historicism "came to non-European peoples in the nineteenth century as somebody's way of saying 'not yet' to somebody else." Chakrabarty, *Provincializing Europe*, 8.

[21] Davis, *Periodization and Sovereignty.*

[22] The literature on this point is vast. In IR, see notably Bain, *Medieval Foundations of International Relations*; Bain, *Political Theology of International Order*. For an insightful overview of how to think more accurately about the "Middle Ages" from an IR perspective, see Costa Lopez, "International Relations in/and the Middle Ages."

[23] Bayly, *The Birth of the Modern World, 1780–1914*; Osterhammel, *The Transformation of the World*; Buzan and Lawson, *The Global Transformation.*

[24] Latham, "Political Theology of International Order," 815.

and that it was deeply intertwined both with legal narratives and, at this point, with the concept of the so-called sovereign "Westphalian" state.[25] As Davis puts it, "the history of periodization is juridical, and it advances through struggles over the definition and location of sovereignty."[26] Yet what sovereignty meant changed considerably over time, and as we saw in Chapter 5, it is only in the nineteenth century that "the state" exclusively came to signify "the sovereign state" in its homogenized, centralized, and territorial form. Nineteenth-century lawyers papered over the momentous disjunction this constituted by telling a story of continuity back to the early modern period. As Emmanuelle Jouannet reminds us, the idea of international law as a system of states, or – to use IR language – as an anarchical society of "self-contained state orders bound together solely through contractual or consensual ties"[27] did not emerge in the vicinity of 1648 but at the turn of the nineteenth century and especially after the Congress of Vienna of 1815.[28] But the damage was done, and one of the clichés of the twentieth-century historiography of international law is to "decry its statist orientation, its reification of state-will, and its understanding of the order of international law as constituted through the free will of its privileged subject, the state,"[29] even though this iteration of interpolity law was of a remarkably recent vintage.[30] To this day, the "state-centric" approach to the periodization of international law – and, through it, of international relations – remains the "most foundational one" because "it underlies the vast majority of grand narratives of the history of international law, either because it is consciously used, because it is implicit, or because it is contested."[31]

---

[25] For a fascinating foray into the distinction between "the ancients" and "the moderns" in the context of the British Empire of the nineteenth century, see Mantena, "Social Theory in the Age of Empire."

[26] Davis, *Periodization and Sovereignty*, 6. Beyond this legal dimension, there is of course a broader intellectual conversation about thinking historically and about our general propensity to prefer the achievements of modernity to those of "the ancients." Many thanks to Tomas Wallenius for bringing this wider context back into my field of vision.

[27] Bhuta, "State Theory, State Order, State System,"405.

[28] Jouannet, *The Liberal-Welfarist Law of Nations*.

[29] As summarized in Bhuta, "State Theory, State Order, State System,"405.

[30] On the use of "interpolity law" as a more accurate substitute for "international law" prior to the late nineteenth century, see Benton, "Interpolity Law."

[31] Lesaffer, "The End of the Cold War as an Epochal Event in the History of International Law?" 7. Famously, the International Court of Justice noted in the landmark ruling *Nicaragua v. United States of America* that "state sovereignty" is "the fundamental principle ... on which the whole of international law rests." Military and Paramilitary Activities (Nicaragua v. United States of America), Merits (1986) ICJ Rep 14, para. 263.

The myth of Gentili and modern war dovetails perfectly with these elements: It takes off in the nineteenth century, the temporal locus of many of the most important myths that continue to shape the disciplines of IR and IL, it features state sovereignty at its very heart, it is amplified and enshrined in the twentieth century by Schmitt within the particular context of the 1930s and 1940s,[32] and it narrates a shift from the medieval to the modern that is conceptually seductive but seemingly impossible to locate within the temporality associated with it. It is, ultimately, a remarkably clear manifestation of the various trends identified earlier, yet it has remained surprisingly unchallenged to this day.

Of course, one might suggest that even if the story about Gentili is wrong, we can still try to salvage the other elements about the emergence of "modern war" in the seventeenth century. This is a sensible impulse, for we would not want to risk throwing the proverbial baby out with the bathwater. Yet what the analysis in Chapter 5 points to is the extent to which the international legal order prior to the mid-nineteenth century had made space for polities other than the modern sovereign state to possess various rights associated with sovereignty, including the right to wage war. While determining how exactly this right was allocated in the early modern period is beyond the scope of this book, what is clear is that there was a qualitative change in the regulation of warfare with the emergence of a much more dichotomous understanding of the concept of sovereignty in nineteenth-century international law. The fact that we inherited a story of continuity between the early modern period and the twentieth century and have proceeded to draw uncritically on its core elements is perhaps one of the reasons why we have yet to take full stock of the profound changes that late nineteenth-century international lawyers brought about, along with their impact.

What does it mean for us to remain welded to the old story of Gentili, the state, and "modern" war? As is sometimes noted, "one of the many successful projects of international law was (and still is) the ambition to order the world through histories."[33] This story of Gentili, the state, and modern war has served to buttress a particular vision of international order, one in which only established sovereign states have the legal right to use force. Therein lies its single most powerful consequence, and as long as we fail to appreciate it, we will remain the uncritical Atlases of the world it helped establish.

---

[32] The impact of this period on the evolution of some of our core political concepts has been widely discussed. For instance, on liberalism, see Bell, "What Is Liberalism?"

[33] Iurlaro, *The Invention of Custom*, 14.

Today, the laws of war – now called international humanitarian law (IHL) – seem woefully ill-equipped to regulate international armed conflicts that involve insurgency and counterinsurgency operations. While after 1945, the restrictive language of "war" was replaced with broader categories of "armed conflict," IHL's conflict classifications have remained remarkably narrow. The contemporary framework for regulating war is divided between a large body of rules for "international armed conflicts," that is, conflicts amongst states, and a smaller body of rules for "noninternational armed conflicts," that is, conflicts in which at least one side is a nonstate actor, presumably within a domestic context.[34] This binary has obviously created numerous problems because of the many conflicts in which a state is fighting against a nonstate actor but the nonstate actor is not of a domestic kind.

Since the end of the Cold War, IHL has thus increasingly come under fire for being a mere relic from the bygone days of interstate warfare, a rulebook that simply does not suit an age where the participation of nonstate actors in armed conflict has become the rule rather than the exception. The problem, we are told, is that the laws of war "have been outmoded by a new and messier political reality."[35] We are putatively hampered by our outdated "Westphalian" lens, a nearly 400-year-old way of conceptualizing – and stabilizing – the international order that is becoming increasingly irrelevant as we march inexorably into a "post-Westphalian era." This idea is pervasive across the literatures both on the "new wars" and on the regulation of "extra-state wars,"[36] that is, wars pitting a state against a nonstate actor outside its borders.[37] And yet, these "messier" types of conflicts are hardly new; in fact, scholars have noted how prominent they were in the nineteenth century.[38] If anything, until recently, we had simply failed to take notice of their ubiquity over the past 200 years.[39]

---

[34] In addition, the famous though fairly superficial (and rather haphazardly honored) Common Article 3 of the Geneva Convention legally applies across all armed conflicts regardless of the actors involved.

[35] Schöndorf, "Extra-State Armed Conflicts," 2.

[36] On the regulation of extra-state wars, see notably Ibid.; Lubell, *Extraterritorial Use of Force against Non-State Actors.*

[37] The language of interstate, intrastate, and extra-state wars comes for the famous Correlates of War (COW) database.

[38] See, for instance, Berdal, "The 'New Wars' Thesis Revisited."

[39] The authors of the COW database once noted that these conflicts had received remarkably little attention, even though they "have been associated with one of the most important cyclical transformations of the modern international system – first the spread of imperialism, and then the emergence of independent new nations," 648, note 4. Sarkees, Wayman, and Singer, "Inter-State, Intra-State, and Extra-State Wars." In fact, Amitav Acharya reminds us that the COW's inclusion of extra-state (or extra-systemic) wars is itself a recent addition: "[T]he [COW] project, when it was founded

What this book shows, then, is that the current tension between IHL and "extra-state wars" or "extra-state armed conflicts" is in fact a direct inheritance of the late nineteenth century, when a conscious decision was made to exclude all actors not recognized as modern sovereign states from the ambit of the laws of war. We know, of course, that the question of which polities were deemed "civilized" played a central role as well, but the newfound importance of a narrow understanding of sovereign statehood as a standalone criterion has received scant attention. Yet if "civilization" was undermined as an explicit tool for ordering the international system after World War II,[40] sovereign statehood triumphed for good in the same period, when, with decolonization, the whole world first truly became a patchwork of unified territorial sovereign states (at least in name).[41] Our problem, then, is not that conflicts between sovereigns states and foreign insurgents are new and thus that IHL is lagging behind; instead, the issue is that we have inherited a system of laws that explicitly gave carte blanche to recognized states fighting against these types of actors. IHL's "failure" on this front is voluntary. In fact, one could say the system is working exactly as it was intended.

Ultimately, our existing narrative has helped those who already have the right to wage war as recognized sovereign states to undermine any attempts to challenge this established way of allocating the legal use of force. One important change did take place in 1977, when the movement led by George Abi-Saab won the battle to recognize struggles "in which peoples are fighting against colonial domination and alien occupation and against racist regimes in the exercise of their right of self-determination" as "international armed conflicts"

at the University of Michigan in 1963, coded wars since 1816 but neglected 'extra-state' wars, that is, imperial and colonial wars. It was criticized for reflecting a 'historical legacy of Western imperialism and racism that simply did not regard non-Western groups as civilized or as human beings equal to whites' and thus 'did not bother to record in any systematic way the fatalities sustained by non-national groupings in imperial wars of conquest or pacification' ... The COW database later added 129 extra-state wars, with the help of revised methodology and new historical research ... but 'there is probably still an undercount.'" Acharya, "Global International Relations (IR) and Regional Worlds." A significant amount of research is now emerging within the field of history on insurgencies and counterinsurgencies in the context of empire, notably through the work of the *Understanding Insurgencies: Resonances from the Colonial Past* network based at the University of Exeter's Center for the Study of War, State and Society and the work of KITLV, the Royal Netherlands Institute of Southeast Asian and Caribbean Studies.

[40] Keene, *Beyond the Anarchical Society*, 120–44.

[41] Naturally, "sovereignty" continued to be a malleable concept as powerful states found new justifications for intervening in the affairs of others. For a classic take on the question, see Krasner, *Sovereignty*.

for the purposes of IHL.[42] This amounted to "classifying liberation movements as legal subjects on a par with the colonizer,"[43] a radical change in international law. Tellingly, when faced with this push to consider the morality of certain struggles and allow that to trump matters of status, Western powers accused Third World delegates of seeking a return to the Middle Ages.[44] Any consideration of cause, they submitted, risked plunging us back to the senseless chaos of the pre-Westphalian world.

The Protocol went through thanks to its sheer number of supporters – a remarkable victory in itself – but it ultimately had a limited impact in practice, as decolonization was almost entirely over by then and states within which national liberation movements were still active had the option simply not to ratify the Protocol at all.[45] More importantly, this victory was in some ways a tragic one, to the extent that many of the newly independent states latched onto "all the negative endowments of European statehood," including narrow ideologies of nationalism along with "excessive militarism" and "the employment of the repressive (proto-) state structures left by the colonizers."[46] In other words, it ended up cementing a system of all-powerful states indebted to the political imagination of the late nineteenth century. What we have been left with is a world in which those already recognized as sovereign states have the right to use force while all other actors – including indigenous peoples, oppressed minorities, and groups who failed to secure their own state during the decolonization period[47] – are considered criminals if they take up arms. Strikingly, the language around "combating terrorism" also evolved significantly in the context of the Additional Protocols and foreshadowed various unsuccessful efforts to legislate the issue in the 1980s.[48] It would eventually allow established states – most importantly the United States – to reclaim ownership over morality in war, mainly through the appropriation of a loose "just war tradition."[49] Along with this, it ironically served to disqualify all nonstate actors

---

[42] This is the 1977 Additional Protocol I to the Geneva Convention. For an overview of this process, see Bernstorff, "The Battle for the Recognition of Wars of National Liberation."

[43] Ibid., 70.

[44] Whyte, "The 'Dangerous Concept of the Just War'," 316.

[45] Notable exceptions include Israel (the only country that voted against the Protocol instead of abstaining), Turkey, the United States, Iran, Pakistan, and India.

[46] Bernstorff, "The Battle for the Recognition of Wars of National Liberation," 70.

[47] On the latter, see Walker, "Decolonization in the 1960s."

[48] Bernstorff, "The Battle for the Recognition of Wars of National Liberation," 66–69.

[49] Whyte, "The 'Dangerous Concept of the Just War'."

resorting to violence, regardless of their cause, their means, or any other contextual elements underlying their struggle.[50]

All in all, what these developments have triggered is the enshrinement of a system in which only recognized sovereign states have the right to use force, at the cost of all other actors regardless of the legitimacy of their struggle. This is not an intuitive way of ordering the world. Of course, critics will rush to point to the subjectiveness of moral claims and to the potential pitfalls of a free-for-all when it comes to the use of force, and these are certainly valid concerns. But surely the validity of these concerns should not preclude attempts to improve a system that is also riddled with problems. For one, our current way of allocating the right to wage war generates conspicuous injustices. And if is it true that justice and order are two desirable elements that are perpetually in tension in the international system, it is not clear that this has brought us much in the way of order either. This book has suggested that the shift toward making the right to wage war the sole prerogative of actors recognized as sovereign states potentially happened much later than we conventionally assume, and that it mainly placed numerous forms of ruthless violence – notably imperial expansion and the later "policing" of empires – outside the legally regulated category of "war." If this is true, then the restriction of the right to wage war to sovereign states may have been followed not by the relatively peaceful days of an imaginary golden age of absolutism but by the late nineteenth-century surge in imperial violence and the two world wars of the early twentieth century.

This book does not seek to provide final certainties on any of these broader points. It does, however, open up a new discussion about the regulation of violence in the international system. If our story of "modern war" and its stabilizing impact is largely a myth, and if we are instead trapped in a late nineteenth-century imaginary sprinkled with Schmittian accents, then surely there should be space for us to reevaluate our models and to broaden what we deem possible in regulating the conflicts of tomorrow.

---

[50] Klabbers, "Rebel with a Cause?" More broadly, see Martineau, "Concerning Violence."

Bibliography

Acharya, Amitav. "Global International Relations (IR) and Regional Worlds." *International Studies Quarterly* 58, no. 4 (2014): 647–59.

Alexander, Amanda. "A Short History of International Humanitarian Law." *European Journal of International Law* 26, no. 1 (2015): 109–38.

Alexandrowicz, Charles Henry. *The European–African Confrontation: A Study in Treaty Making.* Leiden: Sijthoff, 1973.

Alexandrowicz, Charles Henry. "Introduction." In Gesina H. J. Van der Molen, *Alberico Gentili and the Development of International Law: His Life, Work and Times.* Leiden: Albertus Willem Sijthoff, 1968.

Alexandrowicz, Charles Henry. *An Introduction to the History of the Law of Nations in the East Indies (16th, 17th and 18th Centuries).* Oxford: Clarendon Press, 1967.

Alexandrowicz, Charles Henry. *The Law of Nations in Global History,* edited by Jennifer Pitts and David Armitage. Oxford: Oxford University Press, 2017.

Alfert, Robert. "Hostes Humani Generis: An Expanded Notion of US Counterterrorist Legislation." *Emory International Law Review* 6, no. 1 (1992): 171–214.

Ambos, Kai. "The New Enemy of Mankind: The Jurisdiction of the ICC over Members of 'Islamic State'." EJIL: Talk!, November 26, 2015.

Amorosa, Paolo. *Rewriting the History of the Law of Nations: How James Brown Scott Made Francisco de Vitoria the Founder of International Law.* Oxford: Oxford University Press, 2019.

Anghie, Antony. "Colonialism and the Birth of International Institutions: Sovereignty, Economy, and the Mandate System of the League of Nations." *NYU Journal of International Law and Politics* 34, no. 3 (2001): 513–633.

Anghie, Antony. "Finding the Peripheries: Sovereignty and Colonialism in Nineteenth-Century International Law." *Harvard International Law Journal* 40, no. 1 (1999): 1–80.

Anglim, Simon. "Callwell versus Graziani: How the British Army Applied 'Small Wars' Techniques in Major Operations in Africa and the Middle East, 1940–41." *Small Wars & Insurgencies* 19, no. 4 (2008): 588–608.

Aquinas, Thomas. *Summa Theologiae: Existence and Nature of God.* Cambridge: Cambridge University Press, 2006.

Armigero Gazzera, Ermelinda. *Alberico Gentili: Bibliografia.* Tolentino: Francesco Filelfo, 1917.

Armitage, David. *Civil Wars: A History in Ideas*. London: Yale University Press, 2017.

Armitage, David. "The Fifty Years Rift: Intellectual History and International Relations." *Modern Intellectual History* 1, no. 1 (2004): 97–109.

Armitage, David. *Foundations of Modern International Thought*. Cambridge: Cambridge University Press, 2012.

Armitage, David. *The Ideological Origins of the British Empire*. Cambridge: Cambridge University Press, 2000.

Armitage, David. "What's the Big Idea? Intellectual History and the Longue Durée." *History of European Ideas* 38, no. 4 (2012): 493–507.

Armitage, David, and Jo Guldi. "The Return of the Longue Durée: An Anglo-American Perspective." *Victoria* 70, no. 2 (2014): 219–47.

Asser, Tobias Michael Carel. "Alberigo Gentili." *Algemeen Handelsblad*, February 6, 1877.

Ayala, Balthazar. *De jure et officiis bellicis et disciplina militari libri tres*. Washington, DC: Carnegie Institution of Washington, 1912.

Bain, William. "Grotius in International Relations Theory." In *The Cambridge Companion to Hugo Grotius*, edited by Randall Lesaffer and Janne E. Nijman, 597–618. Cambridge: Cambridge University Press, 2021.

Bain, William, ed. *Medieval Foundations of International Relations*. London: Routledge, 2016.

Bain, William. *Political Theology of International Order*. Oxford: Oxford University Press, 2020.

Bain, William, and Terry Nardin. "International Relations and Intellectual History." *International Relations* 31, no. 3 (2017): 213–26.

Balakrishnan, Gopal. *The Enemy: An Intellectual Portrait of Carl Schmitt*. London: Verso, 2000.

Balch, Thomas Willing. "Albericus Gentilis." *The American Journal of International Law* 5, no. 3 (1911): 665–79.

Balch, Thomas Willing. "Letter from Thomas Balch to Thomas Erskine Holland," Papers relating to Albericus Gentilis, held at the Bodleian Library, University of Oxford, October 27, 1911.

Balibar, Etienne. "What's in a War? (Politics as War, War as Politics)." *Ratio Juris* 21, no. 3 (2008): 365–86.

Banks, William. *Counterinsurgency Law: New Directions in Asymmetric Warfare*. New York: Oxford University Press, 2013.

Bann, Stephen. *Romanticism and the Rise of History*. New York: Twayne Publishers, 1995.

Barducci, Marco. *Hugo Grotius and the Century of Revolution, 1613–1718: Transnational Reception in English Political Thought*. Oxford: Oxford University Press, 2017.

Barkawi, Tarak. "Decolonising War." *European Journal of International Security* 1, no. 2 (2016): 199–214.

Barkawi, Tarak, and Shane Brighton. "Conclusion: Absent War Studies? War, Knowledge and Critique." In *The Changing Character of War*, edited by Hew Strachan and Sibylle Scheipers, 524–42. Oxford: Oxford University Press, 2011.

Barkawi, Tarak, and Shane Brighton. "Powers of War: Fighting, Knowledge, and Critique." *International Political Sociology* 5, no. 2 (2011): 126–43.

Bartelson, Jens. *War in International Thought.* Cambridge: Cambridge University Press, 2017.

Baxter, Richard. *Humanizing the Laws of War: Selected Writings of Richard Baxter,* edited by Detlev F. Vagts, Theodor Meron, Stephen M. Schwebel, and Charles Keever. Oxford: Oxford University Press, 2013.

Bayle, Pierre. *Dictionnaire Historique et Critique.* Paris: Beuchot, 1820.

Bayly, Christopher Alan. *The Birth of the Modern World, 1780–1914: Global Connections and Comparisons.* Oxford: Blackwell, 2004.

Beaulac, Stéphane. "The Westphalian Model in Defining International Law: Challenging the Myth." *Australian Journal of Legal History* 8, no. 2 (2004): 181–213.

Bell, Duncan. "Empire and International Relations in Victorian Political Thought." *The Historical Journal* 49, no. 1 (2006): 281–98.

Bell, Duncan. "International Relations: The Dawn of a Historiographical Turn?" *British Journal of Politics & International Relations* 3, no. 1 (2001): 115–26.

Bell, Duncan. "Language, Legitimacy, and the Project of Critique." *Alternatives: Global, Local, Political* 27, no. 3 (2002): 327–50.

Bell, Duncan. "Political Realism and International Relations." *Philosophy Compass* 12, no. 2 (2017): 1–12.

Bell, Duncan. "Political Theory and the Functions of Intellectual History: A Response to Emmanuel Navon." *Review of International Studies* 29, no. 1 (2003): 151–60.

Bell, Duncan. "What Is Liberalism?" *Political Theory* 42, no. 6 (2014): 682–715.

Bendersky, Joseph W. *Carl Schmitt, Theorist for the Reich.* Princeton, NJ: Princeton University Press, 1983.

Benton, Lauren. "Beyond Anachronism: Histories of International Law and Global Legal Politics." *Journal of the History of International Law/Revue d'histoire du droit international* 21, no. 1 (2019): 7–40.

Benton, Lauren. *A Search for Sovereignty: Law and Geography in European Empires, 1400–1900.* Cambridge: Cambridge University Press, 2009.

Benton, Lauren, and Lisa Ford. *Rage for Order: The British Empire and the Origins of International Law 1800–1850.* Cambridge, MA: Harvard University Press, 2016.

Berdal, Mats. "The 'New Wars' Thesis Revisited." In *The Changing Character of War,* edited by Hew Strachan and Sibylle Scheipers, 109–33. Oxford: Oxford University Press, 2011.

Bernstorff, Jochen von. "The Battle for the Recognition of Wars of National Liberation." In *The Battle for International Law: South–North Perspectives on the Decolonization Era,* edited by Philipp Dann and Jochen von Bernstorff, 52–70. New York: Oxford University Press, 2019.

Bernstorff, Jochen von. "The Use of Force in International Law before World War I: On Imperial Ordering and the Ontology of the Nation-State." *European Journal of International Law* 29, no. 1 (2018): 233–60.

Best, Geoffrey. *Humanity in Warfare: The Modern History of the International Law of Armed Conflicts.* London: Weidenfeld & Nicolson, 1980.

Bevir, Mark. "The Contextual Approach." In *The Oxford Handbook of the History of Political Philosophy*, edited by George Klosko, 11–25. Oxford: Oxford University Press, 2011.

Bevir, Mark. "Contextualism: From Modernist Method to Post-Analytic Historicism?" *Journal of the Philosophy of History* 3, no. 3 (2009): 211–24.

Bevir, Mark. *The Logic of the History of Ideas*. Cambridge: Cambridge University Press, 1999.

Bevir, Mark. "On Tradition." *Humanitas* 8, no. 2 (2000): 28–53.

Bhuta, Nehal. "State Theory, State Order, State System: Jus Gentium and the Constitution of Public Power." In *System, Order, and International Law: The Early History of International Legal Thought from Machiavelli to Hegel*, edited by Stefan Kadelbach, Thomas Kleinlein, and David Roth-Isigkeit, 398–417. Oxford: Oxford University Press, 2017.

Binns, J. W. *Intellectual Culture in Elizabethan and Jacobean England: The Latin Writings of the Age*. Leeds: Francis Cairns, 1990.

Black, Cyril E. *Neutralization and World Politics*. Princeton, NJ: Princeton University Press, 1968.

Black, Jeremy. *European Warfare, 1494–1660*. London: Routledge, 2002.

Blane, Alexis, and Benedict Kingsbury. "Punishment and the ius post bellum." In *The Roman Foundations of the Law of Nations*, edited by Benedict Kingsbury and Benjamin Straumann, 241–67. Oxford: Oxford University Press, 2010.

Bodin, Jean. *On Sovereignty: Four Chapters from the Six Books of the Commonwealth*. Cambridge: Cambridge University Press, 1992.

Bodin, Jean. *Six Books of the Commonwealth*. Translated by Michael J. Tooley. Oxford: Blackwell's Political Texts, 1955.

Bodin, Jean. *Les six livres de la république*. Paris: Fayard, 1986.

Borschberg, Peter. "The Seizure of the Sta. Catarina Revisited: The Portuguese Empire in Asia, VOC Politics and the Origins of the Dutch–Johor Alliance (1602–c.1616)." *Journal of Southeast Asian Studies* 33, no. 1 (2002): 31–62.

Botting, Eileen Hunt, and Ariana Zlioba. "Religion and Women's Rights: Susan Moller Okin, Mary Wollstonecraft, and the Multiple Feminist Liberal Traditions." *History of European Ideas* 44, no. 8 (2018): 1169–88.

Boucher, David. *Appropriating Hobbes: Legacies in Political, Legal, and International Thought*. Oxford: Oxford University Press, 2018.

Bourke, Richard, and Quentin Skinner. *Popular Sovereignty in Historical Perspective*. Cambridge: Cambridge University Press, 2016.

Branch, Jordan. *The Cartographic State: Maps, Territory and the Origins of Sovereignty*. Cambridge: Cambridge University Press, 2014.

Brazil, Lia. "British War Office Manuals and International Law, 1899–1907." In *Empire and Legal Thought: Ideas and Institutions from Antiquity to Modernity*, edited by Edward Cavanagh, 548–77. Leiden: Brill Nijhoff, 2020.

Brett, Annabel S. *Changes of State*. Princeton, NJ: Princeton University Press, 2011.

Brown, Chris. "Political Thought, International Relations Theory and International Political Theory: An Interpretation." *International Relations* 31, no. 3 (2017): 227–40.

Brownlie, Ian. *International Law and the Use of Force by States*. Oxford: Clarendon Press, 1963.

Bull, Hedley. *The Anarchical Society: A Study of Order in World Politics*. Basingstoke: Palgrave, 2002.

Bull, Hedley. "The Grotian Conception of International Society." In *Diplomatic Investigations: Essays in the Theory of International Politics*, edited by Herbert Butterfield and Martin Wight. London: Allen & Unwin, 1966.

Bullen, Barrie. "Walter Pater's 'Renaissance' and Leonardo da Vinci's Reputation in the Nineteenth Century." *The Modern Language Review* 74, no. 2 (1979): 268–80.

Burgess, Douglas R., Jr. "Hostis Humani Generi: Piracy, Terrorism and a New International Law." *University of Miami International & Comparative Law Review* 13, no. 2 (2005): 293.

Burgess, Glenn. *Absolute Monarchy and the Stuart Constitution*. London: Yale University Press, 1996.

Burgess, Glenn. "Bodin in the English Revolution." In *The Reception of Bodin*, edited by Howell A. Lloyd, 387–408. Leiden: Brill, 2013.

Burke, Martin J., and Melvin Richter. *Why Concepts Matter: Translating Social and Political Thought*. Leiden: Brill, 2012.

Burke, Peter. *The Fortunes of the Courtier: The European Reception of Castiglione's Cortegiano*. University Park, PA: Penn State Press, 1996.

Burke, Peter. "The History and Theory of Reception." In *The Reception of Bodin*, edited by Howell A. Lloyd, 21–38. Leiden: Brill, 2013.

Burke, Peter. "Tacitism, Scepticism, and Reason of State." In *The Cambridge History of Political Thought, 1450–1700*, edited by James H. Burns and Mark Goldie, 477–98. Cambridge: Cambridge University Press, 1991.

Buzan, Barry. "The English School: A Neglected Approach to International Security Studies." *Security Dialogue* 46, no. 2 (2015): 126–43.

Buzan, Barry, and George Lawson. *The Global Transformation: History, Modernity and the Making of International Relations*. Cambridge: Cambridge University Press, 2015.

Buzan, Barry, and George Lawson. "Rethinking Benchmark Dates in International Relations." *European Journal of International Relations* 20, no. 2 (2014): 437–62.

Callwell, Charles Edward. *Small Wars: Their Principles and Practice*. London: HM Stationery Office, 1903.

Canning, Joseph. "The Medieval Roman and Canon Law Origins of International Law." In *Medieval Foundations of International Relations*, edited by William Bain, 102–16. Abingdon: Routledge, 2016.

Carlyle, Thomas. *On Heroes, Hero-Worship, and the Heroic in History*. London: Chapman and Hall, 1840.

Carvalho, Benjamin de, Halvard Leira, and John M. Hobson. "The Big Bangs of IR: The Myths That Your Teachers Still Tell You about 1648 and 1919." *Millennium–Journal of International Studies* 39, no. 3 (2011): 735–58.

Cassese, Antonio. "States: Rise and Decline of the Primary Subjects of the International Community." In *The Oxford Handbook of the History of International Law*, edited by Bardo Fassbender and Anne Peters, 49–70. Oxford: Oxford University Press, 2012.

Cavanagh, Edward. "A Company with Sovereignty and Subjects of Its Own? The Case of the Hudson's Bay Company, 1670–1763." *Canadian Journal of Law & Society/La Revue Canadienne Droit et Société* 26, no. 1 (2011): 25–50.

Certeau, Michel de. *L'invention du quotidien*. Paris: Union générale d'éditions, 1980.

Chakrabarty, Dipesh. *Provincializing Europe: Postcolonial Thought and Historical Difference*. Princeton, NJ: Princeton University Press, 2009.

Chandler, David. "The Revival of Carl Schmitt in International Relations: The Last Refuge of Critical Theorists?" *Millennium* 37, no. 1 (2008): 27–48.

Chernilo, Daniel. "The Critique of Methodological Nationalism: Theory and History." *Thesis Eleven* 106, no. 1 (2011): 98–117.

Church, William. "The Decline of the French Jurists as Political Theorists, 1660–1789." *French Historical Studies* 5, no. 1 (1967): 1–40.

Church, William. *Richelieu and Reason of State*. Princeton, NJ: Princeton University Press, 1972.

Cicero, Marcus Tullius. *De officiis*. London: W. Heinemann, 1961.

Colás, Alejandro, and Bryan Mabee, eds. *Mercenaries, Pirates, Bandits and Empires: Private Violence in Historical Context*. New York: Columbia University Press, 2010.

Cole, Laurence. *Different Paths to the Nation: Regional and National Identities in Central Europe and Italy, 1830–70*. Basingstoke: Palgrave Macmillan, 2007.

Collini, Stefan. "What Is Intellectual History?" *History Today*, October 1985. www.historytoday.com/stefan-collini/what-intellectual-history.

Comparato, Vittor Ivo, and Diego Quaglioni. "From Machiavellism to the End of the Seventeenth Century." In *European Political Thought, 1450–1700: Religion, Law and Philosophy*, edited by Howell A. Lloyd, Glenn Burgess, and Simon Hodson, 55–101. London: Yale University Press, 2007.

Cosgrove, Richard. "Holland, Sir Thomas Erskine (1835–1926)." In *Oxford Dictionary of National Biography* (online ed.). Oxford: Oxford University Press. https://doi.org/10.1093/ref:odnb/33944.

Costa Lopez, Julia. "International Relations in/and the Middle Ages." In *The Routledge Handbook of Historical International Relations*, edited by Julia Costa Lopez, Halvard Leira, and Benjamin de Carvalho, 408–18. Abingdon: Routledge, 2021.

Costa Lopez, Julia, Benjamin de Carvalho, Andrew A. Latham, Ayse Zarakol, Jens Bartelson, and Minda Holm. "In the Beginning There Was No Word (for It): Terms, Concepts, and Early Sovereignty." *International Studies Review* 20, no. 3 (2018): 489–519.

Craven, Matthew. "Between Law and History: The Berlin Conference of 1884–1885 and the Logic of Free Trade." *London Review of International Law* 3, no. 1 (2015): 31–59.

Craven, Matthew. "Colonialism and Domination." In *The Oxford Handbook of the History of International Law*, edited by Bardo Fassbender and Anne Peters, 862–89. Oxford: Oxford University Press, 2012.

Craven, Matthew. "The Invention of a Tradition: Westlake, The Berlin Conference and the Historicisation of International Law." In *Constructing International Law: The Birth of a Discipline*, edited by Luigi Nuzzo and Miloš Vec, 363–403. Frankfurt am Main: Vittorio Klostermann, 2012.

Craven, Matthew "Theorizing the Turn to History in International Law." In *The Oxford Handbook of the Theory of International Law*, edited by Anne Orford and Florian Hoffmann, 21–37. Oxford: Oxford University Press, 2016.

Daston, Lorraine and Peter Galison. *Objectivity*. Brooklyn, NY: Zone Books, 2007.

Davis, Kathleen. *Periodization and Sovereignty: How Ideas of Feudalism and Secularization Govern the Politics of Time*. Philadelphia: University of Pennsylvania Press, 2008.

Deruelle, Benjamin. "The Sixteenth-Century Antecedents of Special Operations 'Small War'." *Small Wars & Insurgencies* 25, no. 4 (2014): 754–66.

Devetak, Richard. "'The Battle Is All There Is': Philosophy and History in International Relations Theory." *International Relations* 31, no. 3 (August 8, 2017): 261–81.

Devetak, Richard. "Historiographical Foundations of Modern International Thought: Histories of the European States-System from Florence to Göttingen." *History of European Ideas* 41 (2014): 1–16.

Devetak, Richard. "A Rival Enlightenment? Critical International Theory in Historical Mode." *International Theory* 6, no. 3 (2014): 417–53.

Digelmann, Oliver. "The Periodization of the History of International Law." In *The Oxford Handbook of the History of International Law*, edited by Bardo Fassbender and Anne Peters, 997–1011. Oxford: Oxford University Press, 2012.

Doe, Norman. "Phillimore, Sir Robert Joseph, Baronet (1810–1885)." In *Oxford Dictionary of National Biography* (online ed.). Oxford: Oxford University Press. https://doi.org/10.1093/ref:odnb/33944

Domingo, Rafael, and Giovanni Minnucci. "Alberico Gentili and the Secularization of the Law of Nations." In *Christianity and Global Law*, edited by Rafael Domingo and John Witte, Jr., 98–111. Abingdon: Routledge, 2020.

Doran, Robert. "Editor's Introduction: Choosing the Past: Hayden White and the Philosophy of History." In *Philosophy of History after Hayden White*, edited by Robert Doran, 1–34. New York: Bloomsbury Academic, 2013.

Doyle, Michael. *Ways of War and Peace: Realism, Liberalism, and Socialism*. New York: W. W. Norton, 1998.

Dumont, Jean. *Corps universel diplomatique du droit des gens, contenant un recueil des traitez d'alliance, de paix, de trêve, de neutralité, de commerce, etc., qui ont été faits en Europe, depuis le règne de l'empereur Charlemagne jusques à présent.* Amsterdam: P. Brunel, R. and J. Wetstein, and G. Smith, Henri Waesberge, and Z. Chatelain, 1726.

Dunn, John. *The History of Political Theory and Other Essays*. Cambridge: Cambridge University Press, 1996.

Dunne, Timothy. "Mythology or Methodology? Traditions in International Theory." *Review of International Studies* 19, no. 3 (1993): 305–18.

Dyzenhaus, David. *Legality and Legitimacy: Carl Schmitt, Hans Kelsen and Hermann Heller in Weimar*. Oxford: Oxford University Press, 1997.

Easley, Eric S. *The War over Perpetual Peace: An Exploration into the History of a Foundational International Relations Text*. New York: Palgrave Macmillan, 2004.

Edelstein, Daniel. "Hostis Humani Generis: Devils, Natural Right, and Terror in the French Revolution." *Telos* 2007, no. 141 (2007): 57–81.

Edmonds, James E. *Land Warfare: An Exposition of the Laws and Usages of War on Land, for the Guidance of Officers of His Majesty's Army.* London: HM Stationery Office, 1912.

Engster, Daniel. "Jean Bodin, Scepticism and Absolute Sovereignty." *History of Political Thought* 17, no. 4 (1996): 469–99.

Fabre, Cécile. "In Defence of Mercenarism." *British Journal of Political Science* 40, no. 3 (2010): 539–59.

Farneti, Roberto. *Il canone moderno. Filosofia politica e genealogia.* Turin: Bollati Boringhieri, 2002.

Fassbender, Bardo. "Carl Schmitt (1888–1985)." In *The Oxford Handbook of the History of International Law,* edited by Bardo Fassbender and Anne Peters, 1173–78. Oxford: Oxford University Press, 2012.

Fassbender, Bardo. "Stories of War and Peace: On Writing the History of International Law in the Third Reich and After." *European Journal of International Law* 13, no. 2 (2002): 479–512.

Fauchille, Paul. *Traité de droit international public.* Edited by Henri Bonfils. Paris: Rousseau, 1898.

Fawcett, Louise. "Between West and Non-West: Latin American Contributions to International Thought." *The International History Review* 34, no. 4 (2012): 679–704.

Field, Dudley. "De la possibilité d'appliquer le droit international européen aux nations orientales." *Revue de droit international et de législation comparée* 7 (1875): 293–94.

Fiocchi Malaspina, Elisabetta. "Le droit des gens di Emer de Vattel: La genesi di un successo editoriale secolare." *Nuova Rivista Storica* 98, no. 2 (2014): 733–54.

Fiocchi Malaspina, Elisabetta. "Emer de Vattel's 'Le droit des gens': Its Circulation and Reception in the 19th Century." *Materiali per una storia della cultura giuridica* 43, no. 2 (2013): 303–20.

Fiocchi Malaspina, Elisabetta, and Nina Keller-Kemmerer. "International Law and Translation in the 19th Century." *Rechtsgeschichte-Legal History* 22 (2014): 214–26.

Fitzmaurice, Andrew. "Context in the History of International Law." *Journal of the History of International Law/Revue d'histoire du droit international* 20, no. 1 (2018): 5–30.

Fitzmaurice, Andrew. "Equality between European and Non-European Nations in International Law." In *International Law in the Long Nineteenth Century,* edited by Inge van Hulle and Randall Lesaffer, 75–104. Leiden: Brill Nijhoff, 2019.

Fitzmaurice, Andrew. *Humanism and America: An Intellectual History of English Colonisation, 1500–1625.* Cambridge: Cambridge University Press, 2003.

Fitzmaurice, Andrew. *King Leopold's Ghostwriter: The Creation of Persons and States in the Nineteenth Century.* Princeton, NJ: Princeton University Press, 2021.

Fitzmaurice, Andrew. "Liberalism and Empire in Nineteenth Century International Law." *The American Historical Review* 117, no. 1 (2012): 122–40.

Fitzmaurice, Andrew. "The Resilience of Natural Law in the Writings of Sir Travers Twiss." In *British International Thinkers from Hobbes to Namier*, edited by Ian Hall and Lisa Hill, 137–59. London: Palgrave Macmillan, 2009.

Fitzmaurice, Andrew. *Sovereignty, Property and Empire, 1500–2000*. Cambridge: Cambridge University Press, 2014.

Foisneau, Luc. "Security as a Norm in Hobbes's Theory of War: A Critique of Schmitt's Interpretation of Hobbes's Approach to International Relations." In *War, the State and International Law in Seventeenth-Century Europe*, edited by Peter Schröder and Olaf Asbach, 163–80. Farnham: Routledge, 2017.

Fonck, Bertrand, and George Satterfield. "The Essence of War: French Armies and Small War in the Low Countries (1672–1697)." *Small Wars & Insurgencies* 25, no. 4 (2014): 767–83.

Forst, Rainer. *Toleration in Conflict: Past and Present*. Cambridge: Cambridge University Press, 2013.

Forsyth, Murray Greensmith, Maurice H. A. Keens-Soper, and Peter Savigear. *The Theory of International Relations: Selected Texts from Gentili to Treitschke*. London: Allen & Unwin, 1970.

Franklin, Julian H. *Jean Bodin and the Rise of Absolutist Theory*. Cambridge: Cambridge University Press, 1973.

Franklin, Julian H. *Jean Bodin and the Sixteenth-Century Revolution in the Methodology of Law and History*. London: Columbia University Press, 1963.

Franklin, Julian H. "Sovereignty and the Mixed Constitution: Bodin and His Critics." In *The Cambridge History of Political Thought, 1450–1700*, edited by James H. Burns and Mark Goldie, 298–323. Cambridge: Cambridge University Press, 1991.

Freeden, Michael. *Ideologies and Political Theory: A Conceptual Approach*. Oxford: Clarendon Press, 2008.

Fulgosius, Raphaël. "Just War Reduced to Public War." In *The Ethics of War: Classic and Contemporary Readings*, edited by Gregory M. Reichberg, Henrik Syse, and Endre Begby, 227–30. Oxford: Blackwell Publishing, 2006.

Garibian, Sévane. "Hostes Humani Generis: Les pirates vus par le droit." *Critique*, no. 6 (2008): 470–79.

Garnsey, Peter. *Thinking about Property: From Antiquity to the Age of Revolution*. Cambridge: Cambridge University Press, 2007.

Genin, Vincent. "The Institute of International Law's Crisis in the Wake of the Franco-Prussian War (1873–1899)." In *International Law in the Long Nineteenth Century*, edited by Inge van Hulle and Randall Lesaffer, 214–32. Leiden: Brill Nijhoff, 2019.

Gentili, Alberico. *Il diritto di guerra (de iure belli libri III, 1598)*. Edited by G. Marchetto and C. Zendri, translated by P. Nencini, with an introduction by Diego Quaglioni. Milan: A. Giuffrè, 2008.

Gentili, Alberico. *De iure belli libri tres*. Edited by James Brown Scott, translated by John Carew Rolfe, with an introduction by Coleman Phillipson. Oxford: Clarendon Press, 1933.

Gentili, Alberico. *Lectionum et Epistolarum quæ ad ius civile pertinent Libri I–IV*. Londini: Iohannes Wolfius, 1583.

Gentili, Alberico. *De legationibus libri tres.* Edited by James Brown Scott, translated by Gordon J. Laing, with an introduction by Ernest Nys. New York: Oxford University Press, 1924.

Gentili, Alberico. *Regales disputationes tres: id est, de potestate regis absoluta. De vnione regnorum Britanniæ. De vi ciuium in regem semper iniusta.* Hanau: W. Antonius, 1605.

Gentili, Alberico. *The Wars of the Romans: A Critical Edition and Translation of De armis romanis.* Edited by Benedict Kingsbury and Benjamin Straumann, translated by David A. Lupher. Oxford: Oxford University Press, 2011.

Giesey, Ralph E. "Medieval Jurisprudence in Bodin's Concept of Sovereignty." In *Jean Bodin*, edited by Julian H. Franklin, 105–22. Abingdon: Routledge, 2006.

Giladi, Rotem. "Francis Lieber on Public War." *Goettingen Journal of International Law* 4 (2012): 447–77.

Glafey, Adam Friedrich. *Vollständige Geschichte des Rechts der Vernunft.* Leipzig: Neudruck der Ausgabe, 1739.

Goldie, Mark. *The Reception of Locke's Politics: From the 1690's to the 1830's.* London: Pickering & Chatto, 1999.

Gong, Gerrit. *The Standard of Civilization in International Society.* Oxford: Clarendon Press, 1984.

Gould, Harry. "Cicero's Ghost: Rethinking the Social Construction of Piracy." In *Maritime Piracy and the Construction of Global Governance*, edited by Michael J. Struett, Jon D. Carlson, and Mark T. Nance, 23–46. Abingdon: Routledge, 2012.

Greene, Jody. "Hostis Humani Generis." *Critical Inquiry* 34, no. 4 (2008): 683–705.

Greenwood, Christopher. "International Law and the 'War against Terrorism'." *International Affairs* 78, no. 2 (2002): 301–17.

Grewe, Wilhelm Georg. *The Epochs of International Law.* Berlin: Walter de Gruyter, 2000.

Grimm, Gunter. *Rezeptionsgeschichte: Grundlegung einer Theorie: mit Analysen und Bibliographie.* Munich: WFink, 1977.

Grosjean, Blandine. "La « guerre d'Algérie » reconnue à l'assemblée. Les députés adoptent la proposition de loi officialisant cette expression." *Libération*, June 1999. www.liberation.fr/france/1999/06/11/la-guerre-d-algerie-reconnue-a-l-assemblee-les-deputes-adoptent-la-proposition-de-loi-officialisant-277134.

Gross, Leo. "The Peace of Westphalia, 1648–1948." *American Journal of International Law* 42, no. 1 (1948): 20–41.

Grotius, Hugo. *De iure belli ac pacis libri tres.* Edited and with an introduction by James Brown Scott, translated by Francis Kelsey with the collaboration of Boak, Sanders, Reeves and Wright. New York: Oceana, 1964.

Grotius, Hugo. *The Rights of War and Peace.* Edited and with an introduction by Richard Tuck, from the edition by Jean Barbeyrac. Indianapolis, IN: Liberty Fund, 2005.

Guicciardini, Francesco. *Dialogue on the Government of Florence.* Translated by Alison Brown. Cambridge: Cambridge University Press, 1994.

Guilhot, Nicolas. "The First Modern Realist: Felix Gilbert's Machiavelli and the Realist Tradition in International Thought." *Modern Intellectual History* 13, no. 3 (2016): 681–711.

Guilhot, Nicolas. *The Invention of International Relations Theory: Realism, the Rockefeller Foundation, and the 1954 Conference on Theory.* New York: Columbia University Press, 2011.

Guillaume, Xavier. "Historical Periods and the Act of Periodization." In *The Routledge Handbook of Historical International Relations*, edited by Julia Costa Lopez, Halvard Leira, and Benjamin de Carvalho, 562–70. Abingdon: Routledge, 2021.

Guldi, Jo, and David Armitage. *The History Manifesto.* Cambridge: Cambridge University Press, 2014.

Haggenmacher, Peter. "Il diritto della guerra et della pace di Alberico Gentili." In *Atti del convegno quarta giornata gentiliana 21 settembre 1991.* Milan: A. Giuffrè, 1995.

Haggenmacher, Peter. "Grotius and Gentili: A Reassessment of Thomas E. Holland's Inaugural Lecture." In *Hugo Grotius and International Relations*, edited by Hedley Bull, Benedict Kingsbury, and Adam Roberts, 133–76. Oxford: Oxford University Press, 1992.

Haggenmacher, Peter. *Grotius et la doctrine de la guerre juste.* Paris: Presses universitaires de France, 1983.

Haggenmacher, Peter. "La place de Francisco de Vitoria parmi les fondateurs du droit international." In *Actualité de la pensée juridique de Francisco de Vitoria: Travaux de la journée d'études organisée à Louvain-La-Neuve par le centre Charles de Visscher*, edited by Antonio Truyol y Serra, Henry Mechoulan, Antonio Ortiz-Arce, Primitivo Marino, Peter Haggenmacher, and Joe Verhoeven, 27–36. Bruxelles: Bruylant, 1988.

Haggenmacher, Peter. "Préface." In *Le nomos de la terre*, by Carl Schmitt. Paris: Presses universitaires de France, 2012.

Hall, Ian. "The History of International Thought and International Relations Theory: From Context to Interpretation." *International Relations* 31, no. 3 (2017): 241–60.

Hall, Ian, and Mark Bevir. "Traditions of British International Thought." *The International History Review* 36, no. 5 (2014): 823–34.

Hallam, Henry. *Introduction to the Literature of Europe in the Fifteenth, Sixteenth, and Seventeenth Centuries.* Paris: John Murray, 1839.

Hansen, Peo, and Stefan Jonsson. "Building Eurafrica: Reviving Colonialism through European Integration, 1920–1960." In *Echoes of Empire: Memory, Identity and Colonial Legacies*, edited by Kalypso Nicolaïdis, Berny Sèbe, and Gabi Maas. London: I.B. Tauris, 2014.

Heeren, Arnold Hermann Ludwig. *A Manual of the History of the Political System of Europe and Its Colonies: From Its Formation at the Close of the Fifteenth Century, to Its Re-Establishment upon the Fall of Napoleon.* Oxford: DA Talboys, 1834.

Heller-Roazen, Daniel. *The Enemy of All: Piracy and the Law of Nations.* New York: Zone Books, 2009.

Henshall, Nicholas. *The Myth of Absolutism: Change and Continuity in Early Modern European Monarchy.* London: Longman, 1992.

Heuser, Beatrice. "Misleading Paradigms of War: States and Non-State Actors, Combatants and Non-Combatants." *War & Society* 27, no. 2 (2008): 1–24.

Heuser, Beatrice. "Small Wars in the Age of Clausewitz: The Watershed Between Partisan War and People's War." *The Journal of Strategic Studies* 33, no. 1 (2010): 139–62.

Hobsbawm, Eric, and Terence Ranger. *The Invention of Tradition.* Cambridge: Cambridge University Press, 1992.

Hochstrasser, T. J. *Natural Law Theories in the Early Enlightenment.* Cambridge: Cambridge University Press, 2000.

Hoekstra, Kinch. "Hobbes's Thucydides." In *The Oxford Handbook of Hobbes*, edited by Aloysius Martinich and Kinch Hoekstra, 547–74. New York: Oxford University Press, 2016.

Hoekstra, Kinch. "A Source of War: Gentili's Thucydides." Milan: A. Giuffrè, 2008.

Holden, Gerard. "Who Contextualizes the Contextualizers: Disciplinary History and the Discourse about IR Discourse." *Review of International Studies* 28, no. 2 (2002): 253–70.

Holland, Thomas Erskine. "The Early Literature on the Law of War." In *Studies in International Law.* Oxford: Clarendon Press, 1879, 40–58.

Holland, Thomas Erskine. *An Inaugural Lecture on Albericus Gentilis, Delivered at All Souls College, November 7, 1874.* London: Macmillan, 1874.

Holland, Thomas Erskine. *The Laws of War on Land (Written and Unwritten).* Oxford: Clarendon Press, 1908.

Holland, Thomas Erskine. "Lecture XIX: War. Measures of: Operations by Dolus." In *Lectures on International Law*, edited by Thomas Alfred Walker and Wyndham Legh Walker, 286–98. London: Sweet & Maxwell, 1933.

Holland, Thomas Erskine. "Lecture XVIII: War: Definition of and Effects of, in Lectures on International Law." In *Lectures on International Law*, edited by Thomas Alfred Walker and Wyndham Legh Walker, 263–85. London: Sweet & Maxwell, 1933.

Holland, Thomas Erskine. "Preface." In *Alberico Gentili: Bibliografia*, by Ermelinda Armigero Gazzera. Tolentino: F. Filelfo, 1917.

Holland, Thomas Erskine. "Review: Commentaries upon International Law, by Sir Robert Phillimore." *Revue de droit international et de législation comparée* 12 (1880): 246–47.

Holland, Thomas Erskine. *Studies in International Law.* Oxford: Clarendon Press, 1898.

Holland, Thomas Erskine. *A Valedictory Retrospect (1874–1910): Being a Lecture Delivered at All Souls College, June 17, 1910.* Oxford: Clarendon Press, 1910.

Holmqvist, Caroline. "Undoing War: War Ontologies and the Materiality of Drone Warfare." *Millennium Journal of International Studies* 41, no. 3 (2013): 535–52.

Holsti, Kalevi. *Peace and War: Armed Conflicts and International Order, 1648–1989.* Cambridge: Cambridge University Press, 1991.

Holsti, Kalevi. *The State, War, and the State of War.* Cambridge: Cambridge University Press, 1996.

Holsti, Kalevi. *Taming the Sovereigns: Institutional Change in International Politics.* Cambridge: Cambridge University Press, 2004.

Holub, Robert. *Reception Theory: A Critical Introduction*. London: Methuen, 1984.

Holub, Robert. "Trends in Literary Theory: The American Reception of Reception Theory." *The German Quarterly* 55, no. 1 (1982): 80–96.

Hooker, William. *Carl Schmitt's International Thought: Order and Orientation*. Cambridge: Cambridge University Press, 2009.

Hopkins, A. G. "Overseas Expansion, Imperialism, and Empire 1815–1914." In *The Nineteenth Century: Europe 1789–1914*, edited by T. C. W. Blanning, 210–40. Oxford: Oxford University Press, 2000.

Howard, Michael, George J. Andreopoulos, and Mark R. Shulman, eds. *The Laws of War: Constraints on Warfare in the Western World*. London: Yale University Press, 1994.

Hunter, Ian. "The History of Philosophy and the Persona of the Philosopher." *Modern Intellectual History* 4, no. 3 (2007): 571–600.

Hunter, Ian. "The History of Theory." *Critical Inquiry* 33, no. 1 (2006): 78–112.

Hutchings, Kimberly, Jens Bartelson, Edward Keene, Lea Ypi, Helen M. Kinsella, and David Armitage. "Critical Exchange: Foundations of Modern International Theory." *Contemporary Political Theory* 13, no. 4 (2014): 387–418.

Ideville, Henry d. *Le Maréchal Bugeaud, d'après sa correspondance intime et des documents inédits, 1784–1849*. Paris: Librairie de Firmin-Didiot et Cie, 1882.

Ingham, Patricia Clare. "Review: Kathleen Davis. Periodization and Sovereignty: How Ideas of Feudalism and Secularization Govern the Politics of Time." *The American Historical Review* 115, no. 5 (2010): 1436–38.

Iser, Wolfgang. *Der Akt des Lesens: Theorie ästhetischer Wirkung*. Munich: WFink, 1984.

Iurlaro, Francesca. *The Invention of Custom: Natural Law and the Law of Nations, CA. 1550–1750*. Oxford: Oxford University Press, 2021.

Iurlaro, Francesca. "Pirati, barbari e pastori: Tre figure al limite dell'humanitas nel pensiero di Alberico Gentili (1552–1608)." *Historia et Ius* 10 (2016): 1–11.

Jahn, Beate. *The Cultural Construction of International Relations: The Invention of the State of Nature*. London: Palgrave Macmillan, 2000.

Jahn, Beate. "Introduction." In *Classical Theory in International Relations*, edited by Beate Jahn, 1–25. Cambridge: Cambridge University Press, 2006.

Jauss, Hans Robert. *Literaturgeschichte als Provokation*. Erstausgabe. Frankfurt am Main: Suhrkamp, 1970.

Jeffery, Renée. *Hugo Grotius in International Thought*. New York: Palgrave Macmillan, 2006.

Jeffery, Renée. "Tradition as Invention: The 'Traditions Tradition' and the History of Ideas in International Relations." *Millennium: Journal of International Studies* 34, no. 1 (2005): 57–84.

Johnson, James Turner. *Ideology, Reason, and the Limitation of War*. Princeton, NJ: Princeton University Press, 1975.

Johnson, James Turner. *Just War Tradition and the Restraint of War*. Princeton, NJ: Princeton University Press, 1981.

Johnston, David, Nadia Urbinati, and Camila Vergara, eds. *Machiavelli on Liberty and Conflict*. Chicago: University of Chicago Press, 2017.

Jouannet, Emmanuelle. *The Liberal-Welfarist Law of Nations: A History of International Law*. Cambridge: Cambridge University Press, 2012.

Kadelbach, Stefan, Thomas Kleinlein, and David Roth-Isigkeit. *System, Order, and International Law: The Early History of International Legal Thought from Machiavelli to Hegel*. Oxford: Oxford University Press, 2017.

Kaldor, Mary. *New and Old Wars: Organised Violence in a Global Era*. Cambridge: Polity Press, 2012.

Kalyvas, Stathis. "The Changing Character of Civil Wars: 1800–2009." In *The Changing Character of War*, edited by Hew Strachan and Sibylle Scheipers, 202–19. Oxford: Oxford University Press, 2011.

Keen, Maurice Hugh. *The Laws of War in the Late Middle Ages*. London: Routledge, 1965.

Keene, Edward. *Beyond the Anarchical Society: Grotius, Colonialism and Order in World Politics*. Cambridge: Cambridge University Press, 2002.

Keene, Edward. "A Case Study of the Construction of International Hierarchy: British Treaty-Making against the Slave Trade in the Early Nineteenth Century." *International Organization* 61, no. 02 (2007): 311–39.

Keene, Edward. "Images of Grotius." In *Classical Theory in International Relations*, edited by Beate Jahn, 233–52. Cambridge: Cambridge University Press, 2006.

Keene, Edward. "International Intellectual History and International Relations: Contexts, Canons and Mediocrities." *International Relations* 31, no. 3 (September 1, 2017): 341–56.

Keene, Edward. *International Political Thought: A Historical Introduction*. Cambridge: Polity Press, 2005.

Keene, Edward. "The Reception of Thucydides in the History of International Relations." In *A Handbook to the Reception of Thucydides*, edited by Christine Lee and Neville Morley, 355–72. Chichester: Wiley Blackwell, 2015.

Keene, Edward. "The Standard of 'Civilisation', the Expansion Thesis and the 19th-Century International Social Space." *Millennium–Journal of International Studies* 42, no. 3 (2014): 651–73.

Keene, Edward. "Three Traditions of International Theory." In *Guide to the English School in International Studies*, edited by Cornelia Navari and Daniel Green, 171–83. New York: John Wiley & Sons, 2013.

Keene, Edward. "The Treaty-Making Revolution of the Nineteenth Century." *The International History Review* 34, no. 3 (2012): 475–500.

Kelley, Donald R. "The Development and Context of Bodin's Method." In *Jean Bodin: Verhandlungen der internationalen Bodin-Tagung*, edited by Horst Denzer, 123–50. Munich: C. H. Beck, 1973.

Kelley, Donald R. *Foundations of Modern Historical Scholarship: Language, Law, and History in the French Renaissance*. London: Columbia University Press, 1970.

Kelley, Donald R. "The Rise of Legal History in the Renaissance." *History and Theory* 9, no. 2 (1970): 174–94.

Kelly, John M. *A Short History of Western Legal Theory*. Oxford: Clarendon Press, 1992.

Kennedy, David. *Of War and Law*. Princeton, NJ: Princeton University Press, 2009.

Kingsbury, Benedict. "Confronting Difference: The Puzzling Durability of Gentili's Combination of Pragmatic Pluralism and Normative Judgment." *American Journal of International Law* 92, no. 4 (1998): 713–23.

Kingsbury, Benedict. "A Grotian Tradition of Theory and Practice: Grotius, Law, and Moral Skepticism in the Thought of Hedley Bull." *Quinnipac Law Review* 17 (1997): 3–33.

Kingsbury, Benedict, and Benjamin Straumann, eds. *The Roman Foundations of the Law of Nations: Alberico Gentili and the Justice of Empire.* Oxford: Oxford University Press, 2010.

Klabbers, Jan. *International Law.* Cambridge: Cambridge University Press, 2017.

Klabbers, Jan. "Rebel with a Cause? Terrorists and Humanitarian Law." *European Journal of International Law* 14, no. 2 (2003): 299–312.

Kloppenberg, James T. *Toward Democracy: The Struggle for Self-Rule in European and American Thought.* New York: Oxford University Press, 2016.

Knutsen, Torbjørn L. *A History of International Relations Theory.* Manchester: Manchester University Press, 1997.

Koch, Christophe de. *Histoire abrégée des traités de paix, entre les puissances de l'Europe, depuis la paix de Westphalie.* Paris: Chez Gide fils, 1817.

Koskenniemi, Martti. "Carl Schmitt and International Law." In *The Oxford Handbook of Carl Schmitt,* edited by Jens Meierhenrich and Oliver Simons, 592–611. Oxford: Oxford University Press, 2017.

Koskenniemi, Martti. "Carl Schmitt, Hans Morgenthau, and the Image of Law in International Relations." In *The Role of Law in International Politics: Essays in International Relations and International Law,* edited by Michael Byers, 17–34. Oxford: Oxford University Press, 2001.

Koskenniemi, Martti. "The Epochs of International Law." *International and Comparative Law Quarterly* 51, no. 3 (2002): 746–51.

Koskenniemi, Martti. *The Gentle Civilizer of Nations: The Rise and Fall of International Law 1870–1960.* Cambridge: Cambridge University Press, 2001.

Koskenniemi, Martti. "International Law and raison d'état: Rethinking the Prehistory of International Law." In *The Roman Foundations of the Law of Nations,* edited by Benedict Kingsbury and Benjamin Straumann, 297–339. Oxford: Oxford University Press, 2010.

Koskenniemi, Martti. "International Law as Political Theology: How to Read Nomos Der Erde?" *Constellations* 11, no. 4 (2004): 492–511.

Koskenniemi, Martti. "Law, Teleology and International Relations: An Essay in Counterdisciplinarity." *International Relations* 26, no. 1 (2012): 3–34.

Koskenniemi, Martti. "Out of Europe: Carl Schmitt, Hans Morgenthau, and the Turn to 'International Relations'." In *The Gentle Civilizer of Nations: The Rise and Fall of International Law 1870–1960,* 413–509. Cambridge: Cambridge University Press, 2001.

Koskenniemi, Martti. "Vitoria and Us." *Rechtsgeschichte–Legal History* 22 (2014): 119–38.

Krasner, Stephen. *Sovereignty: Organized Hypocrisy.* Princeton, NJ: Princeton University Press, 1999.

Lacchè, Luigi. "Monuments of International Law: Albericus Gentilis and Hugo Grotius in Constructing a Discipline (1875–1886)." In *Constructing International Law: The Birth of a Discipline*, edited by Luigi Nuzzo and Miloš Vec, 147–250. Frankfurt am Main: Vittorio Klostermann, 2012.

Lane, Melissa. "Doing Our Own Thinking for Ourselves: On Quentin Skinner's Genealogical Turn." *Journal of the History of Ideas* 73, no. 1 (2012): 71–82.

Latham, Andrew. "Political Theology of International Order: William Bain." *Cambridge Review of International Affairs* 33, no. 5 (2020): 814–16.

Latour, Bruno. *Nous n'avons jamais été modernes: essai d'anthropologie symétrique.* Paris: La découverte, 2013.

Lauterpacht, Hersch. "The Grotian Tradition in International Law." *British Yearbook of International Law* 23 (1946): 1–53.

Le Goff, Jacques. *Faut-il vraiment découper l'histoire en tranches?* Paris: Le Seuil, 2014.

Learoyd, Arthur. "Configurations of Semi-Sovereignty in the Long-Nineteenth Century." In *De-Centering State Making: Comparative and International Perspectives*, edited by Jens Bartelson, Martin Hall, and Jan Teorell, 155–74. Cheltenham and Camberley: Edward Elgar, 2018.

Learoyd, Arthur. "Semi-Sovereignty and Relationships of Hierarchy." D.Phil. Thesis, University of Oxford, 2017.

Lee, Christine, and Neville Morley, eds. *A Handbook to the Reception of Thucydides.* Oxford: John Wiley & Sons, 2014.

Lee, Daniel. *Popular Sovereignty in Early Modern Constitutional Thought.* Oxford: Oxford University Press, 2016.

Lee, Daniel. *The Right of Sovereignty: Jean Bodin on the Sovereign State and the Law of Nations.* Oxford: Oxford University Press, 2021.

Lehmann, Hartmut, and Melvin Richter, eds. *The Meaning of Historical Terms and Concepts: New Studies on Begriffsgeschichte.* Washington, DC: German Historical Institute, 1996.

Lemnitzer, Jan. *Power, Law and the End of Privateering.* Basingstoke: Palgrave Macmillan, 2014.

Lesaffer, Randall. "Alberico Gentili's ius post bellum and Early Modern Peace Treaties." In *The Roman Foundations of the Law of Nations*, edited by Benedict Kingsbury and Benjamin Straumann, 210–40. Oxford: Oxford University Press, 2010.

Lesaffer, Randall. "The Classical Law of Nations (1500–1800)." In *Research Handbook on the Theory and History of International Law*, edited by Alexander Orakhelashvili, 408–40. Cheltenham: Edward Elgar, 2011.

Lesaffer, Randall. "The End of the Cold War as an Epochal Event in the History of International Law?" *Tilburg Working Paper Series on Jurisprudence and Legal History* 10 (2010): 1–25.

Lesaffer, Randall. *Peace Treaties and International Law in European History: From the Late Middle Ages to World War One.* Cambridge: Cambridge University Press, 2004.

Lesaffer, Randall. "Peace Treaties and the Formation of International Law." In *The Oxford Handbook of the History of International Law*, edited by Bardo Fassbender and Anne Peters, 71–93. Oxford: Oxford University Press, 2012.

Levack, Brian. *The Civil Lawyers in England, 1603–1641: A Political Study.* Oxford: Clarendon Press, 1973.

Levack, Brian. "Law and Ideology: The Civil Law and Theories of Absolutism in Elizabethan and Jacobean England." In *The Historical Renaissance: New Essays on Tudor and Stuart Literature and Culture*, edited by Heather Dubrow and Richard Strier, 220–41. London: University of Chicago Press, 1988.

Levy, J. A. "Alberigo Gentili." *Algemeen Handelsblad*. February 3, 1877.

Li, Darryl. *The Universal Enemy: Jihad, Empire, and the Challenge of Solidarity.* Stanford, CA: Stanford University Press, 2019.

Lifschitz, Avi. *Engaging with Rousseau: Reaction and Interpretation from the Eighteenth Century to the Present.* Cambridge: Cambridge University Press, 2016.

Liu, Glory M. "Rethinking the 'Chicago Smith' Problem: Adam Smith and the Chicago School, 1929–1980." *Modern Intellectual History* 17, no. 4 (2020): 1041–68.

Lobban, Michael. "English Approaches to International Law in the Nineteenth Century." In *Time, History and International Law*, edited by Matthew Craven, Malgosia Fitzmaurice, and Maria Vogiatzi, 65–90. Leiden: Martinus Nijhoff, 2007.

Lobban, Michael. "Twiss, Sir Travers (1809–1897)." In *Oxford Dictionary of National Biography* (online ed.). Oxford: Oxford University Press. https://doi.org/10.1093/ref:odnb/33944

Lopez, Julia Costa. "Political Authority in International Relations: Revisiting the Medieval Debate." *International Organization* 74, no. 2 (2020): 222–52.

Lorenz, Chris, and Stefan Berger. *Nationalizing the Past: Historians as Nation Builders in Modern Europe.* New York: Palgrave Macmillan, 2010.

Luard, Evan. *War in International Society: A Study in International Sociology.* London: Yale University Press, 1987.

Luban, David. "A Theory of Crimes against Humanity." *Yale Journal of International Law* 29 (2004): 85–167.

Lubell, Noam. *Extraterritorial Use of Force against Non-State Actors.* Oxford: Oxford University Press, 2010.

Lupher, David. "The De armis romanis and the Exemplum of Roman Imperialism." In *The Roman Foundations of the Law of Nations: Alberico Gentili and the Justice of Empire*, edited by Benedict Kingsbury and Benjamin Straumann, 85–100. Oxford: Oxford University Press, 2010.

Macalister-Smith. "Bio-Bibliographical Key to the Membership of the Institut de droit international, 1873–2001." *Journal of the History of International Law* 5, no. 1 (2003): 77–160.

Machiavelli, Niccolò. *The Prince.* Edited by Angelo Codevilla. London: Yale University Press, 1997.

MacIntyre, Alasdair. *A Short History of Ethics.* New York: Macmillan, 1966.

MacKay, Joseph, and Christopher David LaRoche. "The Conduct of History in International Relations: Rethinking Philosophy of History in IR Theory." *International Theory* 9, no. 2 (July 2017): 203–36.

McMahon, Darrin. *Happiness: A History.* New York: Grove Press, 2005.

McMahon, Darrin. *Divine Fury: A History of Genius.* New York: Basic Books, 2013.

Malcolm, Noel. "Alberico Gentili and the Ottomans." In *The Roman Foundations of the Law of Nations: Alberico Gentili and the Justice of Empire*, edited by Benedict Kingsbury and Benjamin Straumann, 127–45. Oxford: Oxford University Press, 2010.

Malcolm, Noel. "Hobbes' Theory of International Relations." In *Aspects of Hobbes*, edited by Noel Malcolm, 433–55. Oxford: Clarendon Press, 2002.

Malcolm, Noel. *Useful Enemies: Islam and the Ottoman Empire in Western Political Thought, 1450–1750*. New York: Oxford University Press, 2019.

Mancini, Pasquale. *Della nazionalità come fondamento del diritto delle genti*. Milan: Tipografia Eredi Botta, 1854.

Mantena, Karuna. "Social Theory in the Age of Empire." In *Empire and Modern Political Thought*, edited by Sankar Muthu, 324–50. Cambridge: Cambridge University Press, 2012.

Marchand, Suzanne. "Intellectual History Confronts the Longue Durée." *History and Theory* 59, no. 3 (2020): 482–89.

Martens, Georg Friedrich von. *Primae lineae iuris gentium europaearum practici in usum auditorum adumbratae*. Gottingen: Dietrich, 1785.

Martineau, Anne-Charlotte. "Concerning Violence: A Post-Colonial Reading of the Debate on the Use of Force." *Leiden Journal of International Law* 29, no. 1 (2016): 95–112.

Martines, Lauro. *Lawyers and Statecraft in Renaissance Florence*. Princeton, NJ: Princeton University Press, 1968.

Mattingly, Garrett. *Renaissance Diplomacy*. Mineola, NY: Courier Corporation, 1955.

McCormick, John. "Teaching in Vain: Carl Schmitt, Thomas Hobbes, and the Theory of the Sovereign State." In *The Oxford Handbook of Carl Schmitt*, edited by Jens Meierhenrich and Oliver Simons, 269–90. Oxford: Oxford University Press, 2017.

McLeod, Travers. *Rule of Law in War: International Law and United States Counterinsurgency in Iraq and Afghanistan*. Oxford: Oxford University Press, 2015.

McMahon, Darrin, and Samuel Moyn. *Rethinking Modern European Intellectual History*. New York: Oxford University Press, 2014.

Mégret, Frédéric. "From 'Savages' to 'Unlawful Combatants': A Postcolonial Look at International Humanitarian Law's 'Other'." In *International Law and Its Others*, edited by Anne Orford, 265–317. Cambridge: Cambridge University Press, 2006.

Mehring, Reinhard. *Carl Schmitt: A Biography*. Cambridge: Polity Press, 2014.

Menchi, Silvana Seidel. *Erasmo in Italia, 1520–1580*. Turin: Bollati Boringhieri, 1987.

Meron, Theodor. "Common Rights of Mankind in Gentili, Grotius and Suarez." *American Journal of International Law* 85, no. 1 (1991): 110–16.

Milton, Patrick, Michael Axworthy, and Brendan Simms. *Towards A Westphalia for the Middle East*. Oxford: Oxford University Press, 2019.

Minnucci, Giovanni. *Alberico Gentili tra mos italicus e mos gallicus: l'inedito commentario ad legem juliam de adulteriis*. Bologna: Monduzzi Editore, 2002.

Minnucci, Giovanni. "Per una rilettura del metodo gentiliano." In *Alberico Gentili: La tradizione giuridica perugina e la fondazione del diritto internazionale*, edited by Ferdinando Treggiari, 29–56. Perugia: Università degli Studi di Perugia, 2008.

Molloy, Seàn. *Kant's International Relations*. Ann Arbor: University of Michigan Press, 2017.

Moreman, Tim R. "'Small Wars' and 'Imperial Policing': The British Army and the Theory and Practice of Colonial Warfare in the British Empire, 1919–1939." *The Journal of Strategic Studies* 19, no. 4 (1996): 105–31.

Moyn, Samuel, and Andrew Sartori. *Global Intellectual History*. New York: Columbia University Press, 2013.

Muldoon, James. *Empire and Order: The Concept of Empire, 800–1800*. Basingstoke: Macmillan Press, 1999.

Müller, Jan-Werner. *A Dangerous Mind: Carl Schmitt in Post-War European Thought*. London: Yale University Press, 2003.

Mumford, Andrew, and Bruno C. Reis. *The Theory and Practice of Irregular Warfare: Warrior-Scholarship in Counter-Insurgency*. Abingdon: Routledge, 2013.

Münkler, Herfried. *Die neuen Kriege*. Reinbek: Rowohlt, 2002.

Münkler, Herfried. *The New Wars*. Cambridge: Polity Press, 2005.

Murphy, Craig. *International Organization and Industrial Change: Global Governance since 1850*. Europe and the International Order. Cambridge: Polity Press, 1994.

N. A. "Inauguration de la table commemorative d'Albéric Gentil." *Revue de droit international et de législation comparée* 9 (1877): 293–94.

N. A. "Informational Booklet of the English Sub-Committee," 1875. L.Ital. A55d2. Bodleian Law Library.

Nabulsi, Karma. *Traditions of War: Occupation, Resistance, and the Law*. Oxford: Oxford University Press, 1999.

Nabulsi, Karma, and Sudhir Hazareesingh. "Using Archival Sources to Theorize about Politics." In *Political Theory: Methods and Approaches*, edited by David Leopold and Marc Stears, 150–70. Oxford: Oxford University Press, 2008.

Neff, Stephen C. *Justice among Nations: A History of International Law*. Cambridge, MA: Harvard University Press, 2014.

Neff, Stephen C. *War and the Law of Nations: A General History*. Cambridge: Cambridge University Press, 2005.

Neocleous, Mark. "Friend or Enemy: Reading Schmitt Politically." *Radical Philosophy* 79 (1996): 13–23.

Newman, Edward. "The 'New Wars' Debate: A Historical Perspective Is Needed." *Security Dialogue* 35, no. 2 (2004): 173–89.

Nexon, Daniel H. *The Struggle for Power in Early Modern Europe: Religious Conflict, Dynastic Empires, and International Change*. Princeton, NJ: Princeton University Press, 2009.

Nézard, Henry. "Albericus Gentilis." In *Les fondateurs du droit international: leurs œuvres, leurs doctrines*, edited by Joseph Barthélemy, 37–92. Paris: V. Giard & E. Brière, 1904.

Nordin, Astrid H. M., and Dan Öberg. "Targeting the Ontology of War: From Clausewitz to Baudrillard." *Millennium Journal of International Studies* 43, no. 2 (2015): 392–410.

Nussbaum, Arthur. *A Concise History of the Law of Nations.* New York: Macmillan, 1947.

Nuzzo, Luigi. *Origini di una scienza: diritto internazionale e colonialismo nel XIX secolo.* Frankfurt am Main: Klostermann Vittorio, 2012.

Nuzzo, Luigi, and Miloš Vec, eds. *Constructing International Law: The Birth of a Discipline.* Frankfurt am Main: Vittorio Klostermann, 2012.

Nys, Ernest. "L'inauguration du monument d'Albéric Gentil à San Ginesio." *Revue de droit international et de législation comparée* Series 2, Vol. 10 (1908): 645–47.

O'Driscoll, Cian, and Daniel Brunstetter, eds. *Just War Thinkers: From Cicero to the 21st Century.* New York: Routledge, 2017.

Odysseos, Louiza, and Fabio Petito. *The International Political Thought of Carl Schmitt: Terror, Liberal War and the Crisis of Global Order.* London: Routledge, 2007.

Odysseos, Louiza, and Fabio Petito. "Vagaries of Interpretation: A Rejoinder to David Chandler's Reductionist Reading of Carl Schmitt." *Millennium* 37, no. 2 (2008): 463–75.

Oestreich, Gerhard. *Neostoicism and the Early Modern State.* Cambridge: Cambridge University Press, 1982.

Ompteda, Dietrich Heinrich Ludwig von. *Litteratur des gesammten sowohl natürlichen als positiven Völkerrechts.* Regensberg: Johann Leopold Montags Erben, 1785.

Oppenheim, Lassa Francis. *International Law: A Treatise.* London: Longmans, Green, and Co, 1912.

Orford, Anne. "On International Legal Method." *London Review of International Law* 1, no. 1 (2013): 166.

Orford, Anne. "What Is the Place of Anachronism in International Legal Thinking." Université Paris 1, 2013. www.sam-network.org/video/what-is-the-place-of-anachronism-in-international-legal-thinking.

Osiander, Andreas. *Before the State: Systemic Political Change in the West from the Greeks to the French Revolution.* Oxford: Oxford University Press, 2007.

Osiander, Andreas. "Sovereignty, International Relations, and the Westphalian Myth." *International Organization* 55, no. 2 (2001): 251–87.

Osterhammel, Jürgen. *The Transformation of the World.* Princeton, NJ: Princeton University Press, 2014.

Owens, Patricia. *Economy of Force: Counterinsurgency and the Historical Rise of the Social.* Cambridge: Cambridge University Press, 2015.

Pagden, Anthony. *The Burdens of Empire: 1539 to the Present.* New York: Cambridge University Press, 2015.

Pagden, Anthony. "Gentili, Vitoria, and the Fabrication of a 'Natural Law of Nations'." In *The Roman Foundations of the Law of Nations*, edited by Benedict Kingsbury and Benjamin Straumann, 340–62. Oxford: Oxford University Press, 2010.

Pagden, Anthony. *The Languages of Political Theory in Early-Modern Europe.* Cambridge: Cambridge University Press, 1987.

Pallant, Anne. "Scipione Gentili: A Sixteenth Century Jurist." *Kingston Law Review* 14 (1984): 97.

Palonen, Kari. *Politics and Conceptual Histories: Rhetorical and Temporal Perspectives.* London: Bloomsbury, 2014.

Palonen, Kari. "Rhetorical and Temporal Perspectives on Conceptual Change." *Finnish Yearbook of Political Thought* 3 (1999): 60–73.

Panizza, Diego. "Alberico Gentili's De armis romanis: The Roman Model of the Just Empire." In *The Roman Foundations of the Law of Nations: Alberico Gentili and the Justice of Empire*, edited by Benedict Kingsbury and Benjamin Straumann, 53–84. Oxford: Oxford University Press, 2010.

Panizza, Diego. "Alberico Gentili's De iure belli: The Humanist Foundations of a Project of International Order." In *Atti dei convegni nel quarto centenario della morte 2008*, 557–86. Milan: A. Giuffrè, 2010.

Panizza, Diego. "Il pensiero politico di Alberico Gentili: religione, virtù e ragion di stato." In *Alberico Gentili: politica e religione nell'età delle guerre di religione: atti del convegno, seconda giornata gentiliana, San Ginesio, 17 Maggio 1987*, edited by Diego Panizza, 57–213. Milan: A. Giuffrè, 2002.

Panizza, Diego. "Political Theory and Jurisprudence in Gentili's De iure belli: The Great Debate between 'Theological' and 'Humanist' Perspectives from Vitoria to Grotius." In *The Roots of International Law/Les fondements du droit international: Liber amicorum Peter Haggenmacher*, edited by Pierre-Marie Dupuy, Vincent Chetail, and Peter Haggenmacher, 211–47. Leiden: Martinus Nijhoff, 2013.

Patriarca, Silvana, and Lucy Riall, eds. *The Risorgimento Revisited: Nationalism and Culture in Nineteenth Century Italy.* Basingstoke: Palgrave Macmillan, 2012.

Pejcinovic, Lacy. *War in International Society.* London: Routledge, 2013.

Pennington, Kenneth. *The Prince and the Law, 1200–1600: Sovereignty and Rights in the Western Legal Tradition.* Berkeley: University of California Press, 1993.

Peralta, Jaime. *Baltasar de Ayala y el derecho de la guerra.* Madrid: Ínsula, 1964.

Percy, Sarah. *Mercenaries: The History of a Norm in International Relations.* Oxford: Oxford University Press, 2007.

Petito, Fabio, and Louiza Odysseos. "Carl Schmitt." In *Critical Theorists and International Relations*, edited by Jenny Edkins and Nick Vaughan-Williams, 305–16. London: Routledge, 2009.

Phillimore, Robert. *Commentaries upon International Law.* London: W. Benning, 1854.

Phillips, Andrew, and J. C. Sharman. *International Order in Diversity: War, Trade and Rule in the Indian Ocean.* Cambridge: Cambridge University Press, 2015.

Phillipson, Coleman. "Albericus Gentilis." *Journal of the Society of Comparative Legislation* 12 (1911).

Phillipson, Coleman. "Albericus Gentilis." In *Great Jurists of the World*, edited by John Macdonell and Edward Manson, 109–43. Boston: Little, Brown, and Company, 1914.

Phillipson, Coleman. "Introduction." In *Alberico Gentili, De iure belli libri tres*, edited by James Brown Scott, translated by John Carew Rolfe, 9–51. London: Clarendon Press, 1933.

Phillipson, Coleman. "Letter from Coleman Phillipson to Thomas Erskine Holland," Papers relating to Albericus Gentilis, held at the Bodleian Library, University of Oxford, October 27, 1911.

Pitts, Jennifer. *Boundaries of the International: Law and Empire*. Cambridge, MA: Harvard University Press, 2018.

Pitts, Jennifer. "International Relations and the Critical History of International Law." *International Relations* 31, no. 3 (2017): 282–98.

Pocock, J. G. A. *The Machiavellian Moment: Florentine Political Thought and the Atlantic Republican Tradition*. Princeton, NJ: Princeton University Press, 1975.

Pocock, J. G. A. *Political Thought and History: Essays on Theory and Method*. Cambridge: Cambridge University Press, 2009.

Pocock, J. G. A. *Politics, Language and Time: Essays on Political Thought and History*. London: Methuen, 1972.

Poirson, Martial. *Ombres de Molière: naissance d'un mythe littéraire à travers ses avatars du XVIIe siècle à nos jours*. Paris: Armand Colin, 2012.

Policante, Amedeo. *The Pirate Myth: Genealogies of an Imperial Concept*. Abingdon: Routledge, 2015.

Porch, Douglas. "Bugeaud, Gallieni, Lyautey: The Development of French Colonial Warfare." In *Makers of Modern Strategy from Machiavelli to the Nuclear Age*, edited by Peter Paret, Gordon A. Craig, and Felix Gilbert, 376–407. Oxford: Oxford University Press, 1986.

Porch, Douglas. *Counterinsurgency: Exposing the Myths of the New Way of War*. Cambridge: Cambridge University Press, 2013.

Porch, Douglas. "Introduction." In *Small Wars: Their Principles and Practice*, by Charles Edward Callwell, 1–20. Lincoln, NE: University of Nebraska Press, 1899.

Potts, John. *Ideas in Time: The Longue Durée in Intellectual History*. Aix-en-Provence: Presses universitaires de Provence, 2019.

Press, Steven. *Rogue Empires: Contracts and Conmen in Europe's Scramble for Africa*. Cambridge, MA: Harvard University Press, 2017.

Quaglioni, Diego. "The Italian 'Readers' of Bodin, 17th–18th Centuries: The Italian 'Readers' Out of Italy – Alberico Gentili (1552–1608)." In *The Reception of Bodin*, edited by Howell A. Lloyd, 371–86. Leiden: Brill, 2013.

Quaglioni, Diego. "Il "Machiavellismo" di Jean Bodin ("République," V, 5–6)." *Il pensiero politico* 22, no. 2 (1989): 198–207.

Quaglioni, Diego. "Pour une histoire du droit de guerre au début de l'âge moderne. Bodin, Gentili, Grotius." Translated by Jean-Louis Fournel. *Laboratoire italien. Politique et société*, no. 10 (2010): 9–20.

Rasch, William. "Introduction: Carl Schmitt and the New World Order." *South Atlantic Quarterly* 104, no. 2 (2005): 177–83.

Rasilla del Moral, Ignacio de la. "Francisco de Vitoria's Unexpected Transformations and Reinterpretations for International Law." *International Community Law Review* 15, no. 3 (1, 2013): 287–318.

Rasilla del Moral, Ignacio de la. "Grotian Revivals in the Theory and History of International Law." In *The Cambridge Companion to Hugo Grotius*, edited by Randall Lesaffer and Janne E. Nijman, 578–96. Cambridge: Cambridge University Press, 2021.

Rasilla del Moral, Ignacio de la. "The Problem of Periodization in the History of International Law." *Law and History Review* 37, no. 1 (2019): 275–308.

Rasilla del Moral, Ignacio de la. "The Shifting Origins of International Law." *Leiden Journal of International Law* 28, no. 3 (2015): 419–40.

Rava, Luigi. *Ministro della istruzione pubblica, Alberico Gentili: Discorso pronunciato all'inaugurazione del monumento in San Ginesio, 26 Settembre 1908.* Roma, 1908.

Ravndal, Ellen. "Acting Like a State: Non-European Membership of International Organisations in the Nineteenth Century." In *De-Centering State Making Comparative and International Perspectives*, edited by Jens Bartelson, Martin Hall, and Jan Teorell, 175–96. Cheltenham and Camberley: Edward Elgar, 2018.

Ravndal, Ellen. "Colonies, Semi-Sovereigns, and Great Powers: IGO Membership Debates and the Transition of the International System." *Review of International Studies* 46, no. 2 (2020): 278–98.

Ravndal, Ellen. "From an Inclusive to an Exclusive International Order: Membership of International Organisations from the 19th to the 20th Century." *STANCE Working Paper Series, Lund: Department of Political Science, Lund University* 8 (2016).

Rech, Walter. *Enemies of Mankind: Vattel's Theory of Collective Security.* Leiden: Martinus Nijhoff, 2013.

Rech, Walter. "Rightless Enemies: Schmitt and Lauterpacht on Political Piracy." *Oxford Journal of Legal Studies* 32, no. 2 (2012): 235–63.

Reid, Julian. "Reappropriating Clausewitz: The Neglected Dimensions of Counter-Strategic Thought." In *Classical Theory in International Relations*, edited by Beate Jahn, 277–95. Cambridge: Cambridge University Press, 2006.

Reus-Smit, Christian, and Duncan Snidal, eds. *The Oxford Handbook of International Relations.* Oxford: Oxford University Press, 2008.

Riall, Lucy. *The Italian Risorgimento: State, Society and National Unification.* London: Routledge, 1994.

Richter, Melvin. *The History of Political and Social Concepts: A Critical Introduction.* Oxford: Oxford University Press, 1995.

Ricœur, Paul. "Appropriation." In *Hermeneutics and the Human Sciences: Essays on Language, Action, and Interpretation*, by Paul Ricœur, 182–93. Cambridge: Cambridge University Press, 1981.

Ringmar, Erik. *Identity, Interest and Action: A Cultural Explanation of Sweden's Intervention in the Thirty Years War.* Cambridge: Cambridge University Press, 1996.

Rivier, Alphonse. "Review: An Inaugural Lecture on Albericus Gentilis. Delivered at All Souls College, by Thomas Erskine Holland." *Revue de droit international et de législation comparée* 7 (1875): 321–24.

Rivier, Alphonse. "Review: The Law of Nationals Considered as Independent Political Communities. On the Rights and Duties of Nations in Times of War." *Revue de droit international et de législation comparée* 7 (1875): 699–702.

Rolin-Jaequemyns, Gustave. "Albéric Gentil. Hommages à sa mémoire." *Revue de droit international et de législation comparée* 8 (1876): 141–44.

Rolin-Jaequemyns, Gustave. "Quelques mots sur les hommages projetés à la mémoire de Grotius et d'Albéric Gentil, et sur les dernières publications y relatives." *Revue de droit international et de législation comparée* 8 (1876): 690–96.

Rösch, Felix. *Power, Knowledge, and Dissent in Morgenthau's Worldview.* New York: Palgrave Macmillan, 2015.

Rosenfeld, Sophia. *Common Sense: A Political History.* Cambridge, MA: Harvard University Press, 2011.

Roshchin, Evgeny. "(Un)Natural and Contractual International Society: A Conceptual Inquiry." *European Journal of International Relations* 19, no. 2 (2013): 257–79.

Rossi, Christopher R. *Broken Chain of Being: James Brown Scott and the Origins of Modern International Law.* Alphen aan den Rijn: Kluwer, 1998.

Rothschild, Emma. "Arcs of Ideas: International History and Intellectual History." In *Transnationale Geschichte: Themen, Tendenzen und Theorien,* edited by Gunilla Budde, Sebastian Conrad, and Oliver Janz, 217–26. Göttingen: Vandenhoeck & Ruprecht, 2006.

Rubin, Alfred P. *The Law of Piracy.* Newport, RI: Naval War College Press, 1988.

Rubin, Alfred P., and B. A. Boczek. "Private and Public History; Private and Public Law." In *Proceedings of the Annual Meeting (American Society of International Law),* 30–39, 1988.

Sarkees, Meredith Reid, Frank Whelon Wayman, and J. David Singer. "Inter-State, Intra-State, and Extra-State Wars: A Comprehensive Look at Their Distribution over Time, 1816–1997." *International Studies Quarterly* 47, no. 1 (2003): 49–70.

Sbarbaro, Pietro. *Da Socino a Mazzini.* Rome: Edoardo Perino, 1886.

Scarfi, Juan Pablo. *The Hidden History of International Law in the Americas: Empire and Legal Networks.* Oxford: Oxford University Press, 2017.

Scheipers, Sibylle. *Clausewitz on Small War.* Abingdon: Taylor & Francis, 2016.

Scheipers, Sibylle. "'The Most Beautiful of Wars': Carl von Clausewitz and Small Wars." *European Journal of International Security* 2, no. 1 (2017): 47–63.

Scheipers, Sibylle. *Unlawful Combatants: A Genealogy of the Irregular Fighter.* Oxford: Oxford University Press, 2015.

Schellhase, Kenneth C. *Tacitus in Renaissance Political Thought.* London: University of Chicago Press, 1976.

Scheuerman, William E. *Carl Schmitt: The End of Law.* Lanham, MD: Rowman & Littlefield, 1999.

Schmidt, Brian. *The Political Discourse of Anarchy: A Disciplinary History of International Relations.* Albany: State University of New York Press, 1998.

Schmitt, Carl. "The Changing Structure of International Law." *Journal for Cultural Research* 20, no. 3 (2016): 310–28.

Schmitt, Carl. "The Concept of Piracy (1937)." *Humanity: An International Journal of Human Rights, Humanitarianism, and Development* 2, no. 1 (2011): 27–29.

Schmitt, Carl. "Forms of Modern Imperialism in International Law." In *Spatiality, Sovereignty and Carl Schmitt: Geographies of the Nomos,* edited by Stephen Legg, 29–45. Abingdon: Routledge, 2011.

Schmitt, Carl. "Der Führer schützt das Recht." *Deutsche Juristen-Zeitung*, no. 39 (1934): 945–50.

Schmitt, Carl. "The Großraum in International Law with a Ban on Intervention for Spatially Foreign Powers." In *Writings on War*, edited by Timothy Nunan, 75–124. Cambridge: Polity Press, 2011.

Schmitt, Carl. "Großraum versus Universalism: The International Legal Struggle over the Monroe Doctrine," In *Spatiality, Sovereignty and Carl Schmitt: Geographies of the Nomos*, edited by Stephen Legg, 46–54. Abingdon: Routledge, 2011.

Schmitt, Carl. "The International Crime of Aggression and the Principle 'nullum crimen, nulla poena sine lege'." In *Writings on War*, edited and translated by Timothy Nunan, 125–97. Cambridge: Polity Press, 2011.

Schmitt, Carl. *The Nomos of the Earth in the International Law of the Jus Publicum Europaeum*. New York: Telos Press, 2003.

Schmitt, Carl. *Political Theology: Four Chapters on the Concept of Sovereignty*. Chicago: University of Chicago Press, 2005.

Schmitt, Carl. "Reich Staat Bund. Antrittsvorlesung, Gehalten an der Kölner Universität Am 20. Juni 1933." In *Positionen und Begriffe: Im Kampf mit Weimar – Genf – Versailles 1923–1939*, 190–98. Berlin: Duncker & Humblot, 1994.

Schmitt, Carl. *Theory of the Partisan: Intermediate Commentary on the Concept of the Political*. New York: Telos Press, 2007.

Schmitt, Carl. "The Turn to the Discriminating Concept of War." In *Writings on War*, edited by and translated Timothy Nunan, 30–74. Cambridge: Polity Press, 2011.

Schöndorf, Roy S. "Extra-State Armed Conflicts: Is There a Need for a New Legal Regime?" NYU *Journal of International Law and Politics* 37 (2004): 1–78.

Schröder, Peter. "Carl Schmitt's Appropriation of the Early Modern European Tradition of Political Thought on the State and Interstate Relations." *History of Political Thought* 33, no. 2 (2012): 348–71.

Schröder, Peter. *Trust in Early Modern International Political Thought, 1598–1713*. Cambridge: Cambridge University Press, 2017.

Schröder, Peter. "Vitoria, Gentili, Bodin: Sovereignty and the Law of Nations." In *The Roman Foundations of the Law of Nations*, edited by Benedict Kingsbury and Benjamin Straumann, 163–86. Oxford: Oxford University Press, 2010.

Schroeder, Paul W. *The Transformation of European Politics, 1763–1848*. Oxford: Oxford University Press, 1994.

Schulz, Carsten-Andreas. "Civilisation, Barbarism and the Making of Latin America's Place in 19th-Century International Society." *Millennium* 42, no. 3 (2014): 837–59.

Schwab, George. *The Challenge of the Exception: An Introduction to the Political Ideas of Carl Schmitt between 1921 and 1936*. New York: Greenwood Press, 1989.

Schwab, George. "Introduction." In *Political Theology: Four Chapters on the Concept of Sovereignty*. Edited and translated by George Schwab. Foreword by Tracy B. Strong. Chicago: University of Chicago Press, 2006, xxxvvii–lii.

Schwartz, Benjamin. "Some Polarities in Confucian Thought." In *Confucianism in Action*, edited by David S. Nivison and Arthur F. Wright, 50–62. Stanford, CA: Stanford University Press, 1959.

Seigel, Jerrold. *The Idea of the Self: Thought and Experience in Western Europe since the Seventeenth Century*. Cambridge: Cambridge University Press, 2005.

Sharman, J. C., and Andrew Phillips. *Outsourcing Empire: How Company-States Made the Modern World*. Princeton, NJ: Princeton University Press, 2020.

Sharp, Andrew. "Alberico Gentili's Obscure Resurrection as a Royalist in 1644." In *Alberico Gentili: l'ordine internazionale in un mondo a più civiltà: atti del convegno decima giornata gentiliana*. Milan: A. Giuffrè, 2002, 285–313.

Shiller, Robert J. *Narrative Economics: How Stories Go Viral and Drive Major Economic Events*. Princeton, NJ: Princeton University Press, 2020.

Simmonds, K. R. "The Gentili Manuscripts." *Zeitschrift der Savigny-Stiftung für Rechtsgeschichte/Romanistische Abteilung* 76, no. 1 (1959): 534–52.

Simmonds, K. R. "Hugo Grotius and Alberico Gentili." *German Yearbook of International Law* 8 (1959): 85–100.

Simpson, Gerry. "Enemies of Mankind." In *Ethics, Law, and Society*, Vol. 2, edited by Jennifer Gunning and Søren Holm, 85–94. Chalgrove: Ashgate, 2006.

Singh, Prabhakar. "Book Review: Lauren Benton and Lisa Ford. Rage for Order: The British Empire and the Origins of International Law, 1800–1850; Andrew Fitzmaurice. Sovereignty, Property and Empire, 1500–2000." *European Journal of International Law* 28, no. 3 (2017): 975–86.

Skinner, Quentin. *Forensic Shakespeare*. Oxford: Oxford University Press, 2014.

Skinner, Quentin. *The Foundations of Modern Political Thought*. Cambridge: Cambridge University Press, 1978.

Skinner, Quentin. "A Genealogy of the Modern State (British Academy Lecture)." *Proceedings of the British Academy* 162 (2008): 325–70.

Skinner, Quentin. *Liberty before Liberalism*. Cambridge: Cambridge University Press, 1998.

Skinner, Quentin. "Meaning and Understanding in the History of Ideas." *History and Theory* 8 (1969): 3–53.

Skinner, Quentin. "A Reply to My Critics." In *Meaning and Context: Quentin Skinner and His Critics*, edited by James Tully, 231–88. Cambridge: Polity Press, 1988.

Skinner, Quentin. "Some Problems in the Analysis of Political Thought and Action." In *Meaning and Context: Quentin Skinner and His Critics*, edited by James Tully, 97–118. Cambridge: Polity Press, 1988.

Skinner, Quentin. *Visions of Politics (3 vols)*. Cambridge: Cambridge University Press, 2002.

Skodo, Admir. "Post-Analytic Philosophy of History." *Journal of the Philosophy of History* 3, no. 3 (2009): 308–33.

Slomp, Gabriella. *Carl Schmitt and the Politics of Hostility, Violence and Terror*. Basingstoke: Palgrave Macmillan, 2009.

Smeltzer, Joshua. "On the Use and Abuse of Francisco de Vitoria: James Brown Scott and Carl Schmitt." *Journal of the History of International Law* 20, no. 2 (2018), 345–72.

Somos, Mark, and Joshua Smeltzer. "Vitoria, Suárez, and Grotius: James Brown Scott's Enduring Revival." *Grotiana* 41, no. 1 (2020): 137–62.

Specter, Matthew G. "What's 'Left' in Schmitt? From Aversion to Appropriation in Contemporary Political Theory." In *The Oxford Handbook of Carl Schmitt*, edited by Jens Meierhenrich and Oliver Simons, 426–54. New York: Oxford University Press, 2017.

Spiers, Edward M. "The Use of the Dum Dum Bullet in Colonial Warfare." *The Journal of Imperial and Commonwealth History* 4, no. 1 (1975): 3–14.

Steiger, Heinhard. "Die Träger des ius belli ac pacis 1648–1806." In *Staat und Krieg: Vom Mittelalter bis zur Moderne*, edited by Werner Rösener, 595–613. Göttingen: Vandenhoeck & Ruprecht, 2000.

Stern, Philip J. *The Company-State: Corporate Sovereignty and the Early Modern Foundations of the British Empire in India*. Oxford: Oxford University Press, 2011.

Straumann, Benjamin. "The Corpus iuris as a Source of Law Between Sovereigns in Alberico Gentili's Thought." In *The Roman Foundations of the Law of Nations: Alberico Gentili and the Justice of Empire*, edited by Benedict Kingsbury and Benjamin Straumann, 101–25. Oxford: Oxford University Press, 2010.

Straumann, Benjamin. *Crisis and Constitutionalism: Roman Political Thought from the Fall of the Republic to the Age of Revolution*. New York: Oxford University Press, 2016.

Straumann, Benjamin. "The Energy of Concepts: The Role of Concepts in Long-Term Intellectual History and Social Reality." *Journal of the Philosophy of History* 14, no. 2 (2019): 147–82.

Strong, Tracy. *Foreword to Political Theology: Four Chapters on the Concept of Sovereignty by Carl Schmitt*. London: University of Chicago Press, 2005.

Suin, Davide. "Principi supremi e societas hominum: il problema del potere nella riflessione di Alberico Gentili." *Scienza & Politica. Per una storia delle dottrine* 29, no. 56 (2017), 107–24.

Sylvest, Casper. *British Liberal Internationalism, 1880–1930: Making Progress?* Manchester: Manchester University Press, 2009.

Sylvest, Casper. "'Our Passion for Legality': International Law and Imperialism in Late Nineteenth-Century Britain." *Review of International Studies* 34, no. 3 (2008): 403–23.

Sylvester, Christine. "War Experiences/War Practices/War Theory." *Millennium Journal of International Studies* 40, no. 3 (2012): 483–503.

Tai, Emily Sohmer. "Marking Water: Piracy and Property in the Pre-Modern West." In *Seascapes, Littoral Cultures, and Trans-Oceanic Exchanges (Perspectives on the Global Past)*, edited by Jerry H. Bentley, Renate Bridenthal, and Karen Wigen, 205–20. Honolulu: University of Hawaii Press, 2007.

Teschke, Benno. "Carl Schmitt's Concepts of War: A Categorical Failure." In *The Oxford Handbook of Carl Schmitt*, edited by Jens Meierhenrich and Oliver Simons, 367–400. Oxford: Oxford University Press, 2014.

Teschke, Benno. "Decisions and Indecisions: Political and Intellectual Receptions of Carl Schmitt." *New Left Review*, no. 67 (2011): 61–95.

Teschke, Benno. "Fatal Attraction: A Critique of Carl Schmitt's International Political and Legal Theory." *International Theory* 3, no. 2 (2011): 179–227.

Teschke, Benno. *The Myth of 1648: Class, Geopolitics, and the Making of Modern International Relations*. London: Verso, 2003.

Thompson, Martyn. "Reception Theory and the Interpretation of Historical Meaning." *History and Theory* 32, no. 3 (1993): 248–72.

Thomson, Janice. *Mercenaries, Pirates, and Sovereigns: State-Building and Extraterritorial Violence in Early Modern Europe*. Princeton, NJ: Princeton University Press, 1996.

Thorup, Mikkel. "Enemy of Humanity: The Anti-Piracy Discourse in Present-Day Anti-Terrorism." *Terrorism and Political Violence* 21, no. 3 (2009): 401–11.

Tilly, Charles. *Coercion, Capital, and European States, AD 990–1992.* Malden, MA: Blackwell, 1992.

Tilly, Charles. "War Making and State Making as Organized Crime." In *Bringing the State Back In,* edited by Charles Tilly, Peter B. Evans, Dietrich Rueschemeyer, and Theda Skocpol, 169–91. Cambridge: Cambridge University Press, 1985.

Tischer, Anuschka. "Princes' Justifications of War in Early Modern Europe: The Constitution of an International Community by Communication." In *The Justification of War and International Order: From Past to Present,* edited by Lothar Brock and Hendrik Simon, 65–80. Oxford: Oxford University Press, 2021.

Toffanin, Giuseppe. *Machiavelli e il "tacitismo": la "politica storica" al tempo della controriforma.* Padova: A. Draghi, 1921.

Tribe, Keith. *The Economy of the Word: Language, History, and Economics.* Oxford: Oxford University Press, 2015.

Tuck, Richard. *Philosophy and Government, 1572–1651.* Cambridge: Cambridge University Press, 1993.

Tuck, Richard. *The Rights of War and Peace.* Oxford: Oxford University Press, 2001.

Tuck, Richard. *The Sleeping Sovereign: The Invention of Modern Democracy.* Cambridge: Cambridge University Press, 2016.

Turner, Henry S. *The Corporate Commonwealth: Pluralism and Political Fictions in England, 1516–1651.* Chicago, IL: University of Chicago Press, 2016.

Twiss, Travers. "Albericus Gentilis on the Right of War." *The Law Magazine and Review* 3, no. 5 (1878): 137–61.

Twiss, Travers. *The Law of Nations Considered as Independent Political Communities: On the Rights and Duties of Nations in Time of Peace.* Oxford: Clarendon Press, 1884.

Twiss, Travers. "Les travaux de l'association pour la réforme et la codification du droit des gens pendant sa session du mois d'août 1879." *Revue de droit international et de législation comparée* 11 (1879): 440–42.

Vadi, Valentina. "Alberico Gentili on Roman Imperialism: Dialectic Antinomies." *Journal of the History of International Law* 16, no. 2 (2014): 157–77.

Vadi, Valentina. *War and Peace: Alberico Gentili and the Early Modern Law of Nations.* War and Peace. Leiden: Brill Nijhoff, 2020.

Valdarnini, Angelo. *Alberico Gentili fondatore del diritto internazionale [con una lettera di E. Laboulaye].* Florence: Tipografia e Litografia di G. Carnesecchi E Figli, 1875.

Van Creveld, Martin. *Nuclear Proliferation and the Future of Conflict.* New York: Free Press, 1993.

Van Creveld, Martin. *The Transformation of War.* London: Free Press, 1991.

Van der Molen, Gesina H. J. *Alberico Gentili and the Development of International Law: His Life, Work and Times.* Leiden: Albertus Willem Sijthoff, 1968.

Van Ittersum, Martine. "Confronting Grotius' Legacy in an Age of Revolution: The Cornets de Groot Family in Rotterdam, 1748–98." *The English Historical Review* 127, no. 529 (2012): 1367–1403.

Van Ittersum, Martine. "Hugo Grotius: The Making of a Founding Father of International Law." In *The Oxford Handbook of the Theory of International Law*, edited by Anne Orford, Florian Hoffmann, and Martin Clark, 82–100. Oxford: Oxford University Press, 2016.

Vattel, Emer de. *Le droit des gens, ou principes de la loi naturelle, appliqués à la conduite et aux affaires des nations et des souverains*. Washington, DC: Carnegie Institution of Washington, 1916.

Vaughan, Geoffrey M. "The Decline of Sovereignty in the Liberal Tradition: The Case of John Rawls." In *Souveränitätskonzeptionen: Beiträge zur Analyse politischer Ordnungsvorstellungen im 17. bis zum 20. jahrhundert*, edited by Peter Schröder and Martin Peters, 157–85. Berlin: Duncker & Humblot, 2000.

Vecchio, Giorgio del. "The Posthumous Fate of Alberico Gentili." *American Journal of International Law* 50, no. 3 (1956): 664–67.

Veith, Jerome. *Gadamer and the Transmission of History*. Bloomington: Indiana University Press, 2015.

Vergerio, Claire. "Alberico Gentili's De iure belli: An Absolutist's Attempt to Reconcile the Jus Gentium and the Reason of State Tradition." *Journal of the History of International Law* 19, no. 4 (2017): 1–38.

Vergerio, Claire. "Beyond the Nation-State." *Boston Review* (blog), May 27, 2021. https://bostonreview.net/politics/claire-vergerio-beyond-nation-state.

Vergerio, Claire. "Context, Reception, and the Study of Great Thinkers in International Relations." *International Theory* 11, no. 1 (2019): 110–37.

Vergerio, Claire. "International Law and the Laws of War." In *The Routledge Handbook of Historical International Relations*, edited by Julia Costa Lopez, Halvard Leira, and Benjamin de Carvalho, 321–29. Abingdon: Routledge, 2021.

Viano, Francesca Lidia. *Sentinel: The Unlikely Origins of the Statue of Liberty*. Cambridge, MA: Harvard University Press, 2018.

Vick, Brian E. *The Congress of Vienna: Power and Politics after Napoleon*. Cambridge, MA: Harvard University Press, 2014.

Vigneswaran, Darshan, and Joel Quirk. "Past Masters and Modern Inventions: Intellectual History as Critical Theory." *International Relations* 24, no. 2 (2010): 107–31.

Viroli, Maurizio. *From Politics to Reason of State: The Acquisition and Transformation of the Language of Politics, 1250–1600*. Cambridge: Cambridge University Press, 1992.

Vitalis, Robert. *White World Order, Black Power Politics: The Birth of American International Relations*. Ithaca, NY: Cornell University Press, 2015.

Vitoria, Francisco de. *Political Writings*. Edited by Anthony Pagden and Jeremy Lawrance. Cambridge: Cambridge University Press, 1991.

Vollerthun, Ursula, and James L. Richardson. *The Idea of International Society: Erasmus, Vitoria, Gentili and Grotius*. Cambridge: Cambridge University Press, 2017.

Walker, Lydia. "Decolonization in the 1960s: On Legitimate and Illegitimate Nationalist Claims-Making." *Past & Present* 242, no. 1 (2019): 227–64.

Walker, Rob. "History and Structure in the Theory of International Relations." *Millennium* 18, no. 2 (1989): 163–83.

Walker, Thomas Alfred. *A History of the Law of Nations*. Cambridge: Cambridge University Press, 1899.

Wallenius, Tomas. "The Case for a History of Global Legal Practices." *European Journal of International Relations* 25, no. 1 (2017): 108–30.

Waltz, Kenneth Neal. *Man, the State, and War: A Theoretical Analysis*. New York: Columbia University Press, 2001.

Walzer, Michael. *Just and Unjust Wars: A Moral Argument with Historical Illustrations*. New York: Basic Books, 2006.

Ward, Robert Plumer. *An Enquiry into the Foundation and History of the Law of Nations in Europe: From the Time of the Greeks and Romans, to the Age of Grotius*. London: J. Butterworth Fleet-Street, 1795.

Warren, Christopher. "Gentili, the Poets, and the Laws of War." In *The Roman Foundations of the Law of Nations: Alberico Gentili and the Justice of Empire*, edited by Benedict Kingsbury and Benjamin Straumann, 146–62. Oxford: Oxford University Press, 2010.

Warren, Christopher. "Hobbes's Thucydides and the Colonial Law of Nations." *The Seventeenth Century* 24, no. 2 (2013): 260–86.

Weigley, Russell F. *The Age of Battles: The Quest for Decisive Warfare from Breitenfeld to Waterloo*. Bloomington: Indiana University Press, 1991.

Welch, David A. "Why International Relations Theorists Should Stop Reading Thucydides." *Review of International Studies* 29, no. 3 (2003): 301–19.

Wells, Nathan. "Westlake, John (1828–1913)." In *Oxford Dictionary of National Biography* (online ed.). Oxford: Oxford University Press. https://doi .org/10.1093/ref:odnb/33944

Wendt, Alexander. *Social Theory of International Politics*. Cambridge: Cambridge University Press, 1999.

Westlake, John. "Review: De iure belli libri tres." *The Academy*, January 5, 1878.

Weststeijn, Arthur. "The VOC as a Company-State: Debating Seventeenth-Century Dutch Colonial Expansion." *Itinerario* 38, no. 1 (2014): 13–34.

"What Makes It a War?" *The Economist*, November 9, 2013. www.economist .com/news/briefing/21589432-some-say-killing-25-people-year-enough-others-suggest-1000-what-makes-it-war.

Wheaton, Henry. *Histoire des progrès du droit des gens en Europe et en Amérique: depuis la paix de Westphalie jusqu'à nos jours*. Leipzig: F.A. Brockhaus, 1853.

Whelan, F.G. "Vattel's Doctrine of the State." *History of Political Thought* 9, no. 1 (1988): 59.

White, Hayden, and Erlend Rogne. "The Aim of Interpretation Is to Create Perplexity in the Face of the Real: Hayden White in Conversation with Erlend Rogne." *History and Theory* 48, no. 1 (2009): 63–75.

Whitman, James Q. *The Verdict of Battle: The Law of Victory and the Making of Modern War*. Cambridge, MA: Harvard University Press, 2012.

Whittingham, Daniel. "'Savage Warfare': CE Callwell, the Roots of Counter-Insurgency, and the Nineteenth Century Context." *Small Wars & Insurgencies* 23, no. 4–5 (2012): 591–607.

Whyte, Jessica. "The 'Dangerous Concept of the Just War': Decolonization, Wars of National Liberation, and the Additional Protocols to the Geneva Conventions." *Humanity: An International Journal of Human Rights, Humanitarianism, and Development* 9, no. 3 (2018): 313–41.

Wigen, Einar. "Two-Level Language Games: International Relations as Inter-Lingual Relations." *European Journal of International Relations* 21, no. 2 (2015): 427–50.

Wight, Gabriele, and Brian Porter, eds. *International Theory: The Three Traditions: Martin Wight*. Leicester: Leicester University Press for the Royal Institute of International Affairs, 1991.

Wight, Martin. "Why Is There No International Theory?" *International Relations* 2, no. 1 (April 1, 1960): 35–48.

Wijffels, Alain. "Alberico Gentili and the Hanse: The Early Reception of De Iure Belli (1598)." In *The Roots of International Law/Les fondements du droit international: Liber amicorum Peter Haggenmacher*, edited by Pierre-Marie Dupuy, Vincent Chetail, and Peter Haggenmacher, 181–209. Leiden: Martinus Nijhoff, 2013.

Wijffels, Alain. "Antiqui et recentiores: Alberico Gentili – Beyond mos italicus and Legal Humanism." In *Reassessing Legal Humanism and Its Claims*, edited by Paul J. du Plessis and John W. Cairns, 11–40. Edinburgh: Edinburgh University Press, 2016.

Wijffels, Alain. "Assolutismo politico e diritto di resistenza: la disputatio gentiliana 'De vi civium in regem semper iniusta'." Appendice. In *Alberico Gentili, L'uso della forza nel diritto internazionale. Atti del Convegno Undicesima Giornata Gentiliana, San Ginesio, 2004*. Milano: Dott. A Giuffrè Editore, 459–96.

Wijffels, Alain. "From Perugia to Oxford: Past and Present of Political Paradigms." In *Alberico Gentili: la traduzione giuridica perugina e la fondazione del diritto internazionale*, edited by Ferdinando Treggiari, 57–78. Perugia: Università degli Studi di Perugia, 2008.

Williams, Michael C. "The Hobbesian Theory of International Relations: Three Traditions." In *Classical Theory in International Relations*, edited by Beate Jahn, 253–76. Cambridge: Cambridge University Press, 2006.

Wilson, Peter H. *Heart of Europe: A History of the Holy Roman Empire*. Cambridge, MA: Harvard University Press, 2016.

Wimmer, Andreas, and Brian Min. "From Empire to Nation-State: Explaining Wars in the Modern World, 1816–2001." *American Sociological Review* 71, no. 6 (2006): 867–97.

Withington, Phil. *The Politics of Commonwealth: Citizens and Freemen in Early Modern England*. Cambridge: Cambridge University Press, 2005.

Witt, John Fabian. *Lincoln's Code: The Laws of War in American History*. New York: Free Press, 2012.

Zolo, Danilo. *Invoking Humanity: War, Law and Global Order*. London: Bloomsbury, 2002.

Index

Abd el-Kader, 207
Absolutism
  and 19th century lawyers, 179, 185
  and Carl Schmitt. *See* Schmitt, Carl
    and absolutism
  and Gentili. *See* Gentili, Alberico and
    absolutism
Alciatus, 60, 64, 65, 89, 101–5, 119, 222
Algeria, war of, 174, 207, 239, 249
American Civil War, 14, 165, 166, 187,
  188
American War of Independence,
  205–6
Anglo-Spanish War, 1, 57, 107–8
Aquinas, Thomas, 38, 96, 99
Aristotle, 26, 34, 37, 64, 65
Asser, Tobias, 146
Association for the Reform and
  Codification of the Law of Nations.
  See International Law Association
Augustine, 65, 99, 119
Ayala, Balthazar de, 94, 105–8, 110–14,
  121, 130, 175, 182–84, 216, 221–25,
  227, 228, 234, 235

Balch, Thomas Willing, 152
Baldus (de Ubaldis), 59, 60, 62, 65, 69,
  89, 96
Bartolism. *See mos italicus*
Bartolus (de Saxoferrato), 59, 69, 85, 86,
  109
Bayle, Pierre, 8, 126, 127
Begnigni, Telesforo, 129
Belli, Pierino, 6, 94, 105, 111, 177, 183
Bernard, Mountague, 159, 161
Bluntschli, Johann Kaspar, 164, 198
Bodin, Jean, 15, 46–60, 62, 65, 71–78,
  80, 82, 85–90, 95, 105, 112, 124,
  131, 211, 216, 222, 225, 228,
  233–34, 247, 249
  and absolute sovereignty, 54–55,
    68–70, 72–73, 75, 77, 105, 124

  and just war, 72
  and limits to sovereignty, 75
  and the *Methodus*, 69, 85
  and the *République*, 59, 72, 75–76, 111,
    211
  and the use of history, 59–60, 72, 86
Bonfils, Henri, 181
Bossuet, Jacques-Bénigne, 233
Botero, Giovanni, 77, 80, 82, 102
Brownlie, Ian, 217, 237
Budaeus, Guilielmus, 60, 101, 222
Bugeaud, Thomas, 207
Bull, Hedley, 4, 217, 241–42, 246
Bynkershoek, Cornelis van, 6, 126, 182

Callwell, Charles Edward, 207
Cambridge School, 8, 12, 22, 25–27,
  30–36, 40, 47, 128
  and contextualism, 8, 22, 29–35, 43,
    47
  and interpretivism, 25, 31–32
  and the mythology of prolepsis
    (precursorism), 12, 128
Carlyle, Thomas, 10
Cassius, 64, 65
Castelar, Emilio, 152
Castiglione, Giovanni Battista, 56
Central Committee of the International
  League for Peace and Freedom,
  152
Cephalus, 65, 124
Cicero, 26, 34, 60, 64, 65, 80–82, 113,
  115–16, 119
Cobden, Richard, 150
Colonialism 204–8
  and high imperialism, 5, 203,
    211
  and insurgencies, 205
  and international law, 19, 167, 196,
    200–4, 261
  and small war manuals, 175, 204–5,
    207, 209, 249

Made in the USA
Middletown, DE
24 March 2024

51982622R00179